FOLKLORE IN THE

WRITINGS OF

ROWLAND E. ROBINSON

FOLKLORE IN THE

WRITINGS OF

ROWLAND E. ROBINSON

By

Ronald L. Baker

Bowling Green University Popular Press
Bowling Green, Ohio 43403

Library of Congress Card Catalog Number 74-186630

ISBN: 0-87972-038-7 Clothbound
       0-87972-039-5 Paperback

FOREWORD
by
Richard M. Dorson

Literary scholars have begun to learn from folklorists how pervasive is the debt of fiction to oral traditions. Whether or not he knows such a thing as folklore exists, the writer often displays a special sensitivity to the folk culture around him. Because he is by profession a listener and observer, he takes on the role of the amateur ethnographer and fieldworker in noting cultural behavior and expression, for incorporation into his literary product. Sometimes the debt is fairly obvious, as in the case of Chaucer, whose *Canterbury Tales* are threaded together in a sequence of recited tales that we now know traveled independently by word of mouth. Nathaniel Hawthorne set down in his notebooks legends of buried treasure and local eccentrics he heard from talkative villagers, and in such a story as "The Village Uncle" he reveals his close familiarity with oral narrative style and milieu. In other cases the debt is disclosed only after considerable research. The investigations of a number of scholars have established the influence of frontier yarn-spinning upon Mark Twain. Subsequent studies made clear the reliance by Herman Melville upon sailors' folklore of the sea and of the Mississippi River. In every literature, whether the Russian, the Chinese, or the African, we can see the same intimate bonds between the literature of the folk and the literature of the intellectuals.

Modern African writing is an excellent case in point. Since the 1950's, a number of gifted African authors have composed novels, short stories, plays, and poems in English and French that frequently draw upon their own tribal traditions. This literature was ushered in by Amos Tutuola, the self-taught Nigerian who in *The Palm-Wine Drinkard* and *My Life in the Bush of Ghosts* elaborated folktales into a new kind of fiction. He was followed by such expert novelists as Chinua Acebe, whose *Things Fall Apart* views the tribal culture of the Niger delta from the inside, and Camara Laye, whose autobiographical novel *L'Enfant Noir* has been translated into twenty-seven languages. Laye takes a tape recorder into the bush to collect narratives of *griots*, the tribal Senegalese storytellers, saying "Une legende, un roman." So too has Birago Diop listened to a *griot* and adapted the *Tales of Amanda Koumba* (originally published in French) into his own idiom. The talented young Nigerian J. P. Clark based an heroic drama, *Ozidi*, upon his own Ijaw epic, which he recorded in three variants, and he is now publishing the original texts in Ijaw and English, as well as releasing a documentary film presenting high points of the week-long ritual performance.

Writers make use of folklore in many different ways. They may employ the structure of a tale or epic bodily and polish the rough edges into a literary gloss. Or they may incorporate proverbs, local customs, ballads, and folk beliefs into the skein of their narration. Or again they may emulate the folk form but manufacture the content, as did Coleridge in *The Rime of the Ancient Mariner*, which employs ballad stanza and meter. Or still again they may adapt, to greater or lesser degree, bodies of oral narrative, as did Joel Chandler Harris and Henry Wadsworth Longfellow with American Negro and American Indian sources. There is also the possibility that writers may learn about folklore from books. While Hawthorne and Whittier did directly hear New England supernatural legends, they made use too of those legends recorded a century and a half earlier in Cotton Mather's compendium of colonial wonders, *Magnalia Christi Americana.*

No writer better illustrates the literary use of folklore than Rowland Robinson. Relegated to a minor role in the conventional literary histories, if he is mentioned at all, Robinson always maintained his own audience, during his lifetime and from his death in 1900 until the present. His readers were mainly lovers of the outdoors and of country scenes who read his pieces in *Forest and Stream*, but they also came to include well-known publishers and authors and critics who summered in Vermont and learned about the local writer who dealt only with the Green Mountain State. In 1938, just after graduating from college, I took a job with the Tuttle Publishing Company in Rutland, Vermont, obtained through my classmate Charles E. Tuttle, now an eminent publisher in Tokyo. Charles's father, who conducted a rare-book business, told me about the continued demand for out-of-print editions of Robinson's volumes which had led the Tuttle Company to bring out a centennial edition of Robinson's works a few years earlier.

By a curious coincidence, Robinson's writings fitted into the doctoral dissertation on "New England Popular Tales and Legends" on which I shortly embarked at Harvard. In such books as *Uncle Lisha's Shop* and *Danvis Folks* Robinson transcribed yarning sessions he had heard in Ferrisburgh, Vermont into skilfully wrought vignettes, loosely held together by the stable cast of raconteurs. For my dissertation, he provided a shining example of how a long groundswell of oral folk narrative eventually is raised by some craftsman into literary art.

About Robinson's literary artistry there was consensus and appreciation in the fourteen introductions and prefaces written for the Centennial Edition by such notables as Sinclair Lewis, Dorothy Canfield Fisher, Fred Lewis Pattee, and John Farrar. All had good things, and different things, to say about Robinson's eye for the seasons, ear for prose rhythms, adroit sense of Yankee characterization, and limpid style. Yet not one understood the chief source of his fiction, the tall tales, hunting yarns, village anecdotes, and place legends that swirled through Ferrisburgh. Nor was there any reason why they should have, since none of these writers and critics had been trained in folklore. It is a tribute to Robinson that his work should have received this recognition on its own literary merits, without consideration of its intimate relationship to folk materials. For literature is neither better nor worse for using folklore. What we do now recognize is that many celebrated writers have found stimulus and nourishment in folk traditions.

The present study is noteworthy as the first sophisticated full-length analysis of how an author uses folklore. A great many studies, usually of article length, have in recent years fastened on this kind of source-hunting, and most are poor. They are often undertaken by literary scholars unacquainted with the techniques of identifying folklore, and sometimes they are produced by folklorists insensitive to the literary matrix who simply count proverbs or beliefs. Ronald Baker holds a doctor's degree in folklore and teaches in an English department, and he is at home in both fields. In the course of his research he visited Robinson's home in

Ferrisburgh, surveyed the scenes about which Robinson wrote, and discovered some of Robinson's papers still lying in his desk. But his major achievement is a thorough and exhaustive treatment of the genres of folklore and folklife that so liberally strew Robinson's writings. His study is a model in the method of folk-literary analysis. He acts both as the detective ferreting out the items of folk matter and the critic explaining their place in the literary fabric. Further, his book elevates the stature of Rowland Robinson in American literary history. Because his particular artistic form was little understood, Robinson was usually dismissed in a line or two as a turn of the century local colorist. Now through Ronald Baker's deft explication we can see Robinson's special genius, and understand better the relation of the writer to the teller of stories.

PREFACE

This book attempts to show that sometimes literature can serve as ethnography. Although Rowland E. Robinson was a creative writer and not a folklore technician, his writings offer a kind of encyclopedia of nineteenth-century Vermont folklife. In his fiction he uses many traditional texts, reports setting and function of oral literature, and describes traditional material culture.

Robinson's writings are of value to Americans generally as well as to folklorists. Although he wrote nearly a century ago, his works are timely, for he foresaw the plight of contemporary America with her polluted environment. He observed that of all things on earth only man upsets nature's balance, and he preached and practiced living in harmony with nature.

To Richard M. Dorson I am indebted for both the thesis and method of this book. Although some folklorists dealing with literary and folklore relations are now interested in the process of creativity and not with texts, in structural analysis and not with motifs—I am convinced that Dorson's method of identifying folklore in literature is a good one when examining folklore in any author and the best one when analyzing folklore in a regional realist like Robinson.

The sections of this book dealing with setting and function of oral storytelling owe a great deal to Linda Degh, while the sections on folktales and material culture owe much to Warren E. Roberts. Moreover, I thank John W. Ashton and Terence Martin for reading the manuscript, Ray B. Browne for editing the manuscript, Leon W. Dean and the Rowland E. Robinson Memorial Association for providing access to manuscript material, and John T. Flanagan for convincing me that identifying folklore in American literature is rewarding. Some of the material dealing with folk medicine in Chapter 13 was printed in another form in *Vermont History* (Summer 1969) and appears here with the permission of Charles T. Morrissey, Director of the Vermont Historical Society, who also provided me with bibliographical material about Robinson.

Terre Haute, Indiana   R.L.B.

CONTENTS

FOREWORD   v

PREFACE   ix

CHAPTER 1   Identifying Folklore in American Literature   1

CHAPTER 2   Robinson's Contact With Oral Traditions   5

CHAPTER 3   Robinson as Writer   17

CHAPTER 4   The Function and Milieu of the Folklore   26

CHAPTER 5   Village Shops and Stores as Centers for the Performance
             of Folklore   32

CHAPTER 6   Collectively Performed Tasks and the Performance of
             Folklore   42

CHAPTER 7   Calendar Customs and the Performance of Folklore . . .   55

CHAPTER 8   The Rites of Passage and the Performance of Folklore . .   62

CHAPTER 9   Hunting, Fishing, and Camping Trips and the Performance
             of Folklore Away From the Village . .   70

CHAPTER 10   Sugaring and Bee Hunting   79

CHAPTER 11   Household Crafts   88

CHAPTER 12   Folk Architecture   98

CHAPTER 13   Folk Beliefs and Folk Medicine 109

CHAPTER 14   Traditional Nonsinging Games, Rhymes, and Riddles . . . 130

CHAPTER 15   Proverbs and Proverbial Phrases 135

CHAPTER 16   Folksongs 159

CHAPTER 17   Tall Tales 177

CHAPTER 18   Other Folktales 197

CHAPTER 19   The Contribution of Folklore to Robinson's Fiction . . . 216

BIBLIOGRAPHY 233

CHAPTER 1

IDENTIFYING FOLKLORE IN AMERICAN LITERATURE

The analysis of folklore in written literature is of value to both the student of folklore and the student of literature. Speaking for the folklorist, Warren E. Roberts says that "much can be learned about the folklore of a past era by a close study of the works of an author of that era, especially if that author be one who wrote for a popular audience and one who was in close contact with the common people."[1] Of course, the professional folklorist realizes that no literary text can quite approach the fidelity of a text scientifically collected from the oral tradition. Unfortunately, however, although some collecting from the oral tradition was done in the nineteenth century, mainly in Europe, virtually all of the scientific field collections of folklore in the United States were not made until the twentieth century. Moreover, even in the twentieth century there are a number of geographical areas in the United States where no complete field collections have been made. Consequently, the identification of folklore in literature is one of the important techniques of the professional folklorist. The folklorist must necessarily work with literary texts in order to find analogues of folk materials from times and places in which no field collections have been made. Culling folklore from written literature gives the comparative folklorist more examples of traditional materials with which to work.

In addition, the identification of folklore in literature is important to the student of literature. Speaking for the student of literature, Daniel Hoffman says that such major American authors as Hawthorne, Melville, and Twain "do not merely record local foibles. . .Folk traditions contribute to their major writings at a pitch of first intensity concepts of character, of theme, of action, of language."[2] Accordingly, the analysis of folklore in a literary work can tell the student of literature much about an author's sources and techniques. In a word, if the critic can clearly demonstrate that an author has used folklore in his writings, then the critic can proceed to show that the use of folk materi-

1

als affords new insights into the understanding of the works of that author.

Consequently, as Richard M. Dorson points out, "Folklore can no longer be gainsaid as an instrument of literary analysis."[3] And to support his statement Dorson cites an impressive number of studies dealing with the relationship of folklore to creative writing. But Dorson stresses that the problem with most of the studies concerning the debt of literature to folklore is that they either employ a fuzzy concept of folklore or fail to demonstrate the presence of folklore in literary works. Dorson aptly sees three flaws in the scholarship of most critics who have attempted to identify folklore in American literature: 1) some critics have confused "folk" with "folklore" and believe any literary work about the common man is indebted to folklore; 2) other critics have simply isolated alleged folk items without actually proving their folk quality by providing the proper comparative annotations; 3) still other critics, following the example of Constance Rourke's *American Humor*,[4] have confused popular, nonbelletristic writings with folklore and have concentrated almost entirely on humorous exaggeration, ignoring other items of early printed folklore, such as supernatural legends and folk custom.[5]

Dorson maintains that in order to satisfactorily establish the relationship of literature to folklore the critic must provide three principal kinds of evidence: 1) biographical evidence—the critic must show that an author was in direct contact with the oral tradition; 2) internal evidence—the critic must show that an author plausibly describes the folk milieu and therefore must have observed folklore firsthand; 3) corroborative evidence—the critic must cite the folklore indexes and refer to analogues from field collections to show that the author has used an item with an independent traditional life.[6] Naturally Dorson's method, like most methods, has had its critics. For example, Daniel Hoffman thinks the method limits the critic to studying minor regional and provincial authors and precludes the critic from studying major urban authors.[7] But as Dorson has emphasized, folk traditions flourish in urban areas as well as in rural areas, and furthermore it can be documented by using his method that major American authors like Hawthorne, Melville, and Twain had direct contact with oral traditions and used them in their works.[8] Consequently, the method certainly does not limit the critic to the study of minor regional authors. Moreover, since most critics who have studied folklore in literature have failed to document the contact of authors with oral traditions, they apparently feel that it makes little difference whether an author gets his folklore material from the oral tradition or from written sources. But anyone who has done field work realizes that the influence of a literary text on an author is not at all the same thing as the impact of an oral performance on a creative writer. The author who incorporates in his work a folktale whose text he has read in a book can only imagine his reaction to the dramatic performance of a living narrative functioning in its own milieu.

Accordingly, presenting all three kinds of evidence—biographical, internal, corroborative—is an excellent method for analyzing folklore in literature, since documenting an author's contact with oral tradition eliminates guesswork. Clearly only someone trained in folklore can adequately identify folklore in literature by using Dorson's method, for only the student trained in field work can hope to appreciate the vast difference between literature based on oral traditions and literature based on other written sources. Likewise, only the student trained in using the folklore indexes can hope to provide the corroborative evidence that Dorson's method demands.

Furthermore, most critics while failing to distinguish invention and literary influences from tradition, also have failed to recognize any aesthetic merit in literary renderings of traditional material. So it is in the writings of the nineteenth century Vermont author, Rowland Evans Robinson, who in contemporary circles is all but forgotten. Only rarely is he the subject of critical studies. He has never been the subject of a major biography. He has been the subject of only two graduate theses.[9] He is seldom mentioned in college anthologies of American literature.[10] In short, Rowland Robinson has been almost totally ignored by literary historians. Consequently, since major critics have not discussed Robinson's works, many students of American literature and culture have never heard of Rowland Robinson. As Dorson has pointed out, however, "The many superb yarns that flavor Robinson's writing of Vermont backmountain folk entitle their author to a special place in American literary history, for bringing into literature a wide range of living native folktale."[11] The present work borrows both its method and thesis from Richard M. Dorson. It is an attempt to demonstrate through biographical, internal, and corroborative evidence that Rowland Robinson's use of folklore—including folk custom and material culture as well as oral literature—contributes to the materials, techniques, and art of his fiction. In short, Rowland Robinson's works deserve to be read because they preserve an artistically wrought picture of nineteenth century Vermont folklife.

NOTES

[1] Warren E. Roberts, "Folklore in the Novels of Thomas Deloney," *Studies in Folklore*, ed. W. Edson Richmond (Bloomington, 1957), p. 119.

[2] Daniel Hoffman, *Form and Fable in American Fiction* (New York, 1965), p. x.

[3] Richard M. Dorson, "The Identification of Folklore in American Literature," *Journal of American Folklore*, LXX (1957), 1.

[4] Constance Rourke, *American Humor* (New York, 1931).

[5] Dorson, "The Identification of Folklore in American Literature," pp. 2-4.

[6] Dorson, "The Identification of Folklore in American Literature," pp. 5-8.

[7] Daniel Hoffman, "Folklore in Literature: Notes Toward a Theory of Interpretation," *Journal of American Folklore*, LXX (1957), 15.

[8] Richard M. Dorson, "Folklore in American Literature: A Postscript," *Journal of American Folklore*, LXXI (1958), 158. For a good example of folklore in an urban area, see Roger D. Abrahams' analysis of urban Negro folklore in *Deep Down in the Jungle* (Hatboro, Pa., 1964).

[9] Genevra M. Cook, "Rowland Evans Robinson (1833-1900): Portrayer of Vermont Background and Character" (unpublished M. A. Thesis, University of Vermont, Burlington, 1931). The latest is my own Ph.D. dissertation, "Folklore in the Writings of Rowland E. Robinson" (Indiana University, 1968).

[10] One exception is John T. Flanagan and Arthur Palmer Hudson, *Folklore in American Literature* (Evanston, Ill., 1958).

[11] Richard M. Dorson, *Jonathan Draws the Long Bow* (Cambridge, Mass., 1946), p. 230.

CHAPTER 2

ROBINSON'S CONTACT WITH ORAL TRADITIONS

Rowland Evans Robinson, the youngest of four children of Rowland Thomas Robinson and Rachel Gilpin Robinson, was born May 14, 1833, at the Robinson homestead, Rokeby, in Ferrisburg, Vermont, where he spent all but a few of his sixty-seven years. In a concise autobiographical sketch written in 1896 for Gilman's *Bibliography of Vermont*, Robinson summarizes the main points of his life and suggests its importance to students of folklife:

. . . I am a farmer, and with the exception of a few years spent in New York as a designer on wood, have lived on the farm to which my grandfather came in 1797, from Vergennes, where he came with his wife from Newport, R. I. in 1792. He was the great-grandson of Rowland Robinson, who came from England to Newport in 1675. For many generations my ancestors, on both sides, were Quakers, with the exception of my mother's grandfather, George Gilpin, who was a Colonel in the Revolutionary Army, a member of Washington's staff, and a pallbearer at his funeral. My life has been uneventful. In 1870 I was married to Anna Stevens of East Montpelier, and we have three children. For more than two years I have been entirely blind, and for a longer time quite dependent on my wife for the revision and copying of my manuscripts.[1]

Because Robinson was a quiet, unassuming man, his statement that his life "has been very uneventful" is somewhat modest. Nevertheless Robinson's life was significant, if simple, especially to the student of traditional American culture. He lived nearly all his life on the same Ferrisburg farm and was intimately acquainted with village folk. His writings have preserved a relatively authentic picture of folklife in a small Vermont village in the first half of the nineteenth century.

Robinson's earliest interest in oral traditions was a part of his family's tradition. While still a boy he kept a journal of some of the tales that his grandfather told him about the Robinson family's migration from Rhode Island in 1791, the year that Vermont joined the Union. Some of these stories—written when Robinson was eighteen, al-

5

though not published until 1934—not only attest to Robinson's early interest in oral traditions but also provide examples of his first, unpolished prose. Robinson was originally interested in his own ancestors, for his family was rich in tradition. As Robinson suggests in the autobiographical sketch cited above, his Christian name, "Rowland," was an old one in the Robinson family, for the first of the family to come to America was Rowland Robinson (1654-1716), who was born in Long Bluff, Cumberland County, England, and came to America in 1675.[2]

Another Rowland Robinson was Rowland E. Robinson's father, Rowland Thomas Robinson (1796-1879), the first of the Robinson family to be born in the Robinson homestead in Ferrisburg, Vermont. Like his grandfather, Thomas Robinson (1731-1817), a whaling merchant of Newport, Rhode Island, who freed all the slaves he inherited, Rowland Thomas Robinson was an ardent abolitionist. In fact, his home served as a station on the Underground Railroad, and a number of the leaders of the anti-slavery movement, including William Lloyd Garrison, were frequent visitors.[3] Rowland E. Robinson's daughter, Mary Robinson Perkins, says that one of the rooms in the Robinson homestead was even called "the slave room":

. . . the "east chamber" [of the Robinson home] . . . was often called the "slave room." It is not a hidden room, but the doorway is inconspicuous and at the far end of another bedroom. There the runaway slaves found a comfortable harbor. My father and his sister and brothers were never allowed to ask any questions about meals that were taken by Aunt Anne King up the back-stairs to this room, but they understood from the act that a dusky fugitive was stopping there for a little while. The travellers were always taken by team at night to the next "station" nearer Canada. While they were not often followed so far north by the slaveholders, the tradition in our home was that at one time a Southerner came to Vergennes, four miles away, looking for a slave who had just been taken north from our place. . . .[4]

Naturally then some of Rowland Robinson's stories, such as "Out of Bondage," are about runaway slaves.

Since his parents were devout Quakers, Robinson's earliest memories were associated with the customs of the Friends. In "Recollections of a Quaker Boy," an autobiographical essay, Robinson writes:

My earliest recollections are associated with the dress, speech, and manners of a sect that has become almost obsolete but in name. They are not as of things at all peculiar or unusual, but as the most familiar objects in my daily life. The broad-brimmed hat, the "shad-bellied" coat with its narrow standing collar, the pale drab sugar-scoop bonnet, the scant sleeved and skirted gown with the white kerchief folded across the bosom, the addressing of every person by the singular pronouns, the naming of the months and days of the week by their numbers, seemed not so strange to my childish eyes and ears as did the dress and speech of the "world's people." From my point of view, it was these people, not my own, who had departed, unwisely if not sinfully, from the ordinary and proper way of life.[5]

Robinson recalls that as a boy on each First Day and Fifth Day he put on a clean "shirtee"—a wide, stiff collar attached to a gathered front piece—and with his family attended Quaker meeting in a large, square, unpainted building. Sitting on the hard, plain, unpainted seats in the meeting house, he sometimes found it difficult to control his drowsiness and occasionally fell asleep. He says whenever he fell asleep "my father would set me on my feet, to my extreme mortification; for I imagined Friends would think the Spirit had moved me to speak, when I had no message to deliver."[6] Each time the clerk opened the meeting by reading the list of nine queries, young Robinson always felt guilty and thought all the Friends were looking at him when the clerk asked, "Are Friends clear of sleeping in meeting and other unbecoming behavior?"[7]

Robinson confesses, however, that even as a small boy he was far more interested in the oral tales of pioneers and wild beasts than he was in the sermons at Quaker meetings:

I am afraid that I was not religiously inclined or as Friends would say, not a "tender youth"; for what was said and done at meeting is not so strongly impressed upon my memory as the home events incidental to Quarterly Meeting. How distinctly through the mists of near threescore years I see the circle of worthies gathered around the Franklin stove, all arrayed in their best sober-hued attire; the men eating apples, if doing any thing, the women almost always knitting, and all busily chatting. No one was addressed as Mrs., Miss, or Mr., but by the first or full name, or as Friend So-and-So, whether man or woman. From another room came the subdued sound of the young people's decorous merriment, in which I was too young to be permitted to take part, but was assigned to the humblest place in the circle of the elders, a footstool or little chair by my father's knee. Much of the conversation was of so grave a nature that it did not interest me; but it never failed to do so when it drifted into reminiscences of the past, the trails of early Friends, the hardships of the pioneers in the northern wilderness, and stories of the wild beasts that had not then long been rare. Even now I feel the pain of the bitter disappointment I suffered when, as the most thrilling point of some story was approached and the name of an actor was mentioned, some worthy woman Friend would interrupt with the incongruous inquiry, "Now thee speaks of Ichabod Frost, John Holmes. I want to ask thee if his wife wasn't Zebulon Thorne's daughter?"

Then they would go off on the genealogical trail of the Frosts and Thornes, till the subject in which I was so deeply interested was lost sight of; and remembering the oft-repeated maxim that children were to be seen, not heard, I never dared to lead them back to it.[8]

The early years of Robinson's youth were spent almost entirely in a Quaker environment. When he first attended the district school he was "as much surprised as grieved" when the other children scoffed at him for being a Quaker and derided his Quaker dress and speech. Under such ridicule by his worldly schoolmates, young Robinson soon gave up his "thees" and "thous" and, as he says, "fell into the worldly custom of addressing a playmate as 'you,' and calling his belongings 'yours,' but it was very difficult for me to learn the heathenish titles of the days of the week in their proper order."[9]

Robinson's early years at the small, shingled, district schoolhouse were not pleasant, and it would be easy to deduce why he did not like school. But this would be oversimplifying things, for later when he attended the two-storied, brick Ferrisburg Academy, which stood just north of Rokeby on the Robinson farm, he was still not a willing student.[10] At the age of thirteen Robinson terminated his formal education.[11] Although he hated school, he liked to read. Fortunately, his father had a fairly good library at Rokeby, so Robinson was able to continue his education at home. He especially liked histories, historical novels, travel books, and adventure stories. His favorite books were the novels of another literary folklorist, Sir Walter Scott, which Robinson read again and again.[12] Robinson's writings show that he was acquainted with histories and almanacs, Greek mythology and the Bible. Among the authors Robinson mentions or alludes to are Shakespeare, Swift, Defoe, Bunyan, White, Cooper, Longfellow, Whittier, Thoreau, and Francis Parkman.

Although Robinson loved books, he loved the woods and field sports even more. After rhetorically questioning if a camper should spend a wet day in camp with books and papers, Robinson replies:

Nay, if they were not left behind in the busy, plodding world that he came here to escape from, they should have been. He wants nothing here that reminds him of traffic or politics; nothing of history, for now he has only to do with the present; nothing of travel, for his concern now is only with the exploration of this wild domain. He does not wish to be bothered with fiction, idealized reality is what he desires. Neither does he care for what other men have written of nature. Her book is before him and he may read it from first hands.[13]

Although written literature is out of place on a camping trip, oral literature, on the other hand, is not; for Robinson suggests that a rainy day in camp might be well spent listening to stories of hunting, fishing, or adventure.[14] Robinson apparently thought tales of pioneer adventures to be on a par with the exploits of the ancient Greeks, only far more interesting. In *Sam Lovel's Boy*, when schoolmaster Mumpson boards with the Hill family and Captain Hill settles in his armchair one evening and begins to relate the adventures of the pioneers, Mr. Mumpson's "finger slipped from its place in the shut volume of the Iliad, and he forgot the battles of the Greeks and Trojans as he listened, with pride swelling his heart, to the unsung heroic deeds of his own humble ancestors."[15]

The Robinson farm consisted of over three hundred acres of forest and fields with several small streams winding through them, and like most country boys Robinson went hunting in the woods and fields and fishing in the streams and lakes near his home. But in his essay "The Farmer's Boy" he makes it quite clear that he was not like many country boys "who spend their lives on a farm, who never see the beauty that is all around them." Robinson says that to those farm boys:

. . . a tree is so much lumber, so many cords of wood, and nothing more; a moss-grown rock is rubbish or available material, as the case may be; the brook, a convenience for watering stock. He would not spare for the woodcock's sake a rod of alder copse that the brook crawls through, any more than for beauty's sake he would save the willow that ripples the current with its trailing branches. His mission seems to be to destroy, not to preserve, the beauty of that portion of the world which has been committed to his care. He is above the weakness of indulgence in field sports which he considers a mere pretext for useless idleness. Therefore, he is quite indifferent to the protection of fish and game, for since he is virtuous there shall be no cakes and ale. He may be a better and more successful farmer, but not a wiser nor a happier man, than his brother, who finds a wholesome, harmless recreation with rod and gun in his own woods and stream, and though confessing to no sentimentalism, gets genuine pleasure from communion with nature.[16]

Since Robinson felt a communion, an intimate spiritual relationship, with nature, he was more than a casual observer of the flora and fauna of Addison County, Vermont; he was a most sympathetic student. "Sad indeed must it be," says Robinson in his essay "June Days," "to have a soul so poor that it responds to no caress of nature, sadder than any imposition of servitude or exile which yet hinders not one's soul from arising with intense longing for the wild world of woods and waters when Kukushna sounds his soft trumpet call."[17]

Although Robinson was fond of hunting and fishing, he did not hunt and fish merely for the sport of the kill. He was opposed to killing merely for sport. Hunting, he points out, is "the survival of barbarism."[18] He even suggests that the hunter try hunting with a camera instead of with a gun.[19] In an effort to spare game, he appeals to Yankee practicality. He thinks that just as farmers find it improvident to kill breeding ewes, sportsmen should find it improvident to slaughter game, for neither pays in the long run.[20] "Of all living things," Robinson asserts, "only man disturbs the nicely adjusted balance of nature. The more civilized he becomes the more mischievous he is. The better he calls himself, the worse he is. For uncounted-centuries the bison and the Indian shared a continent, but in two hundred years or so the white man has destroyed the one and spoiled the other."[21] Fishing the streams and roaming the fields and woods on and around the Robinson farm, Robinson, like Thoreau and other nineteenth century writers, came to love nature and those living close to her. He carefully observed his surroundings, and his photographic memory stored a wealth of images and impressions that he later incorporated into his descriptive nature essays.

Although much of Robinson's knowledge of outdoor life came through his own careful observation, the young naturalist had able teachers, too. For instance, from Mingo Niles, their Negro hired man, young Robinson learned the "gentle art" of fishing and the "simple art" of trapping. In one of his local histories, *Along Three Rivers,* Robinson reports that Mingo was brought to Vermont.[22] After gaining his freedom, Mingo worked intermittently for the Robinson family, and on occasion he even claimed kinship with the Robinsons. Robinson says that one time when Mingo had drunk too much and "lay in the ditch and a passing samaritan offered a helping hand, he resented it as an unwarranted interference with his rights and cried out, 'G'way an' le' me 'lone; I'm some o' Rowl'n Rob'son's relation.' "[23] According to Robinson, Mingo served a second term of a kind of servitude, though, when he married a shrewish Negress. But Mingo gained his freedom once again when his wife was sentenced to prison for burning a neighbor's barn in a fit of revenge.[24]

Mingo Niles cut young Robinson's first pole and gave Robinson his first instruction in trapping the woodchuck and skunk. Skunk oil he considered a sovereign remedy for croup and rheumatism.[25] Mingo was full of oral folklore, too. Speaking of Mingo, Robinson says that no one could be "so wise nor so funny with proverbs and saws for every occasion," or have such a fund of unguessable riddles. Mingo not only knew where the earliest "cowslops" grew for the first dish of greens each spring, he also "had profound knowledge of medicinal and edible roots and herbs, especially such as . . . 'sarsaparil pigmit,' 'jingshang,' princess pine and wintergreen, and a delectable bulb that he called 'a taller ball' . . ."[26] Mingo was indeed what Swedish folklorist C. W. von Sydow has called an active bearer of tradition, one of the few individuals in any given community who maintain and disseminate traditions.

The Indians also instructed Robinson in woodcraft. For years a small band of St. Francis Indians, descendants of the Abnaki who once occupied much of northern New England, came from Canada each spring to camp on the East Slang River near Robinson's home. Throughout the summer they made baskets and birchbark canoes to sell to the white people. Robinson enjoyed spending much of his time visiting these Indians. In fact, he learned their language and a great deal of their folklore. He even consciously collected their oral traditions. In "On a Glass Roof" Robinson tells of meeting an Abnaki who was ice fishing and relates a legend he collected:

The ice was now whooping like a legion of Indians. Its wild, mysterious voice would first be heard faint and far way, then come rushing toward us swifter than the wind, with increasing volume of groans and yells, till it seemed as if the ice was about to yawn beneath us and devour us. The fish quit biting—as well they might, with a pother overhead enough to frighten a hungry saint from his meals. If I had been alone I should have fled to the shore, but, seeing my companion undisturbed by the uproar, I tried to feel at ease. When I asked him what made this noise, he simply answered, "The ice." That was reason enough for him, and he evidently thought it should satisfy me. I asked him if his people had any legend connected with it, and he answered, with a quiet laugh, "I've heard some stories 'bout it, but I guess they wa'n't very true." After some coaxing, he told me this: "You know that big rock in the lake off north—Rock Dunder, you call it? Wal, our people use to call that Wojahose—that means 'the forbidder'—'cause every time our people pass by it in their canoes, if they didn't throw some tobacco or corn or something to it, the big devil that live in it wouldn't let 'em go far without a big storm come, and maybe drowned 'em. He forbid 'em. Wal, bimeby they got sick of it—s'pose maybe they didn't always have much corn an' tobacco to throw 'way so—and the priests all pray their god to make Wojahose keep still an' not trouble 'em. After they prayed a long time, he promised 'em he'd keep Wojahose from hurtin' on 'em for a spell every year. So he froze the lake all over tight every winter for two or three months, and then our people could go off huntin' and fightin' all over the lake without payin' Wojahose. That made him mad, an' every little while he'd go roarin' round under the ice, tryin' to git out. But he couldn't do much hurt, only once in awhile git a man through a hole in the ice. That's the way I've heard some of our old men tell it; but I guess it's a story."[27]

Robinson, unlike some early field workers, gives the informant's attitude toward the stories and suggests the degree of acculturation of the Indians of the eastern part of the United States in the nineteenth century. Robinson uses part of this same legend in "McIntosh of Vergennes," when he tells of an Indian friend of Donald McIntosh who "had thrown his last handful of tobacco to dread Wajahose, the Forbidder, and so made safe his journey thence to the end of the lake . . ."[28] Several other stories are based on visits with the St. Francis Indians, including "A Sportsman" in *Uncle Lisha's Outing*, "New Comrades" in *Sam Lovel's Boy*, and "Indians in Danvis" in *Uncle Lisha's Shop*.

Robinson also acquired direct knowledge of these Indians' material culture. In *Sam Lovel's Boy* he recreates a bit when young Sammy Lovel, Sam Lovel's son, and Uncle Lisha visit a camp of Indians. Robinson's daughter verifies that several of the incidents in *Sam Lovel's Boy* are from her father's own boyhood.[29]

Robinson also frequently visited the French Canadians who traveled from farm to farm during the haying season. As they mowed and cradled hay by hand in the fields or fished and trapped in the streams, Robinson talked with the men and listened to their tales, becoming so proficient in the Canuck dialect that he was able to pass himself off as a French Canadian. Several of Robinson's French Canadian boyhood companions told him numerous tales. One of these boyhood Canadian friends even in later years continued to visit Rokeby in evenings, and the Canuck still told tales that were set in Canada, as Antoine Bassette does in Robinson's Danvis Stories. When Robinson was living at Rokeby with his wife and children, a French Canadian, Joe Le Clair, stayed at the Robinson home during one of the haying seasons. In the evenings Robinson and his children sat around the fireplace with Le Clair and told tales. On one occasion Le Clair told a story about a *loup garou* and the next day Robinson wrote the chapter "Le Loup Garou" of *Danvis Folks*, in which Antoine Bassette tells the same story.

Fortunately for the folklorist, Robinson did not confine his attention to wildlife alone; he was equally interested in observing human life. He appreciated the culture of the people around him who lived close to nature as much as he loved the New England fields and woods, for to Robinson, as to romantic folklorists and writers, living close to nature puts one in a privileged position to respond to the objects of the natural world. Robinson saw a close relationship between external nature and the folk and therefore between the outdoorsman and folklore. In his sketch of one outdoorsman, "The Trapper," he even uses the term "folk lore," which suggests that Robinson, like other late nineteenth century American writers, understood the still young concept of folklore.

Robinson, however, was more than a passive bearer of tradition. He did not merely listen to the performances of other storytellers. He, like Mingo Niles, was an active bearer of tradition, a good storyteller. When Robinson was sixty-five, J. B. Burnham said of him, "He is a natural story-teller, as any one who listens to him five minutes finds out."[30] Also he had a "sweet though untrained voice, and knew many old songs,"[31] and of her father's oral tales, his daughter Mary wrote:

. . . His stories were original and interesting. I can hear him yet, in some tale of frontier days, making the wild howl of the wolf now faint, now growing louder until the beast seemed following me instead of the pioneer family in the story, and the shivers can go up and down my back now at the memory, as they did then when the stories were told . . . his stories of Canucks, old Vermonters, and even negroes were inimitable. Most of the anecdotes in his written works he had actually heard. . . .[32]

The probable reason for Robinson's long retention of his material was that he was, himself, an active bearer of tradition, which was fortunate since his first love was drawing, not writing, though he received very little instruction in art. His mother was an artist, but Robinson received no formal training until his early twenties when he left the farm for a short time and found employment in New York City with a draftsman, who taught Robinson little besides wood engraving. While employed with the draftsman, Robinson found time to do some drawing on his own, and in 1858 and 1859 several of his comic drawings were printed in such magazines as *Harper's Weekly*, *Yankee Notions*, and the publications of Frank Leslie, the pioneer publisher of illustrated journals. For the most part, however, Robinson's first attempt as an illustrator was not successful; consequently, he returned to his Ferrisburg home.[33]

Back at the homestead, Robinson found that he was more interested in illustrating than in farm work. In 1866 he returned to New York and became a draftsman for Orange Judd's agricultural publications. This time, he was more successful, for he sold a number of humorous drawings and rural scenes to periodicals and somehow found time to illustrate seed catalogs and fashion magazines.

While in New York, Robinson was married on July 24, 1870, to Anna Stevens, daughter of Stephen F. and Rachel Stevens of East Montpelier, Vermont. Anna, a graduate of Glenwood Seminary in Brattleboro, Vermont, was an artist, too, and shared her husband's interest in illustrating. Despite Robinson's career in illustrating and his disinterest in farm work, he preferred life in Vermont to that in New York City. Consequently, in 1873 Robinson returned to his Ferrisburg home with the promise of a position on the art staff on the *American Agriculturist*. The promise was not kept, but as long as he could see, Robinson continued to depict farm scenes in woodcuts, oils, and watercolors. A number of Robinson's scenes of rural life, such as his drawings of nine traditional fences,[34] are of interest to the student of traditional material culture.

Although Robinson disliked most farm work, he enjoyed caring for his orchard and making butter. He often added his skill as an artist to his packaging, for he sent his butter to market in Boston and New York in tubs on which he drew sketches and cartoons. Robinson also liked tending his garden and sheep. On the whole, however, he never found farm work especially satisfying, and each evening after farm chores were finished, he continued to do illustrations for magazines by the light of kerosene lamps. Robinson always had weak vision, for when he was a child, an older person accidentally stuck a comb in his eye while combing his hair. No doubt the close work illustrating by poor lighting aggravated the condition, and in 1887 Robinson's eyesight began to fail. After losing the sight of one eye, he went to New York where specialists attempted to save the sight of the other surgically. But the operations were unsuccessful, and Robinson was forced to give up illustrating. In 1893 he became totally blind.

For Robinson, an artist who loved to observe village life and nature, the loss of sight must have been especially difficult. In a letter to two fellow contributors to *Forest and Stream* written in October 1893, just after he became totally blind, Robinson says, " 'I'm dead, I'm dead,' as my schoolfellow, Charley R., shouted when he got a licking; and I know something how it seems to a man to hear the world going on around him, and he lying quiet under the grave."[35] Robinson also comments on his misfortune in "A Voyage in the Dark," a short narrative about a fishing trip down Little Otter that he took with his twelve-year old son and a friend just after his blindness. Robinson says, "It was with a fresh realization of my deprivation that I passed along the watery way once as familiar as the dooryard path, but now shrouded for me in a gloom more impenetrable than the blackness of the darkest night."[36] In another revealing passage Robinson has Uncle Lisha saying, "Deaf folks an' blin' folks lives in worlds by theirselves, still worlds an' dark worlds, an' I cal'late it makes a man sort' o' crabbed tu live by hisself."[37]

Blindness helps to explain why after middle age Robinson turned to writing about bygone days. In "Trapping up Little Otter," after telling about a trapping experience with two other young friends, Robinson concludes, "Well, there are no more of the happy, care-free days of camping out for us three comrades—one sleeping his long sleep under the sumacs in the old burying grounds; one other is a man of affairs, too busy to go camping; and the other bed-ridden, shut in from the bright and beautiful world by a wall of perpetual night. What wonder that he loves to babble of the days when the joy of beholding the beauty of the world was his. For him is only the inward sight to read the pages of memory whereon the record of things seen long ago is written in the story of youth."[38] Van Wyck Brooks suggests and Walter Prichard Eaton conjectures that Robinson's loss of sight might have sharpened his memory and ear.[39]

NOTES

[1]M. D. Gilman, *Bibliography of Vermont* (Burlington, Vermont, 1897), p. 234.

[2]For the genealogy of Rowland Evans Robinson see Hiram Carleton, *Genealogical and Family History of the State of Vermont* (New York, 1903), pp. 102-105.

[3]Mary Robinson Perkins, "Rowland Evans Robinson," in *Out of Bondage and Other Stories*, ed. Llewellyn R. Perkins (Rutland, Vermont, 1936), p. 12.

[4]Mary Robinson Perkins, pp.11-12.

[5]Rowland E. Robinson, "Recollections of a Quaker Boy," *Atlantic Monthly*, LXXXVIII (July 1901), 100.

[6]"Recollections," p. 101.   [7]"Recollections," p. 102.

[8]"Recollections." pp. 103-104.   [9]"Recollections," p. 100.

[10]Mary Robinson Perkins, p. 12.

[11]Lewis E. Stoyle, "A New England Exponent of Woods and Fields," *The Boston Evening Transcript* (April 22, 1933), Book Section, p. 1.

[12]Mary Robinson Perkins, p. 12.

[13]Rowland E. Robinson, *In New England Fields and Woods*, ed. Llewellyn R. Perkins (Rutland, Vermont, 1937), pp. 66-67.

[14]Robinson, *In New England Fields and Woods*, p. 68.

[15]Rowland E. Robinson, *Sam Lovel's Boy with Forest and Stream Fables*, ed. Llewellyn R. Perkins (Rutland, Vermont, 1936), p. 131.

[16]*In New England Fields and Woods*, pp. 218-219.

[17]*In New England Fields and Woods*, p. 49.

[18]*In New England Fields and Woods*, p. 113.

[19]*In New England Fields and Woods*, pp. 58-59.

[20]*In New England Fields and Woods*, p. 39.

[21]*In New England Fields and Woods*, p. 41.

[22]Rowland E. Robinson, *Uncle Lisha's Outing and Along Three Rivers*, ed. Llewellyn R. Perkins (Rutland, Vermont, 1934), p. 237.

[23]Robinson, "Mingo—A Silhouette," *Out of Bondage and Other Stories*, p. 69.

[24]Robinson, *Uncle Lisha's Outing and Along Three Rivers*, pp. 238-239.

[25]Robinson, "Reminiscences," *Forest and Stream* (Oct. 13, 1900), p. 285.

[26]Robinson, "Mingo—A Silhouette," pp. 66, 67.

[27]Robinson, "On A Glass Roof," *Silver Fields and Other Sketches of a Farmer-Sportsman* (Boston and New York, 1921), pp. 137-138. For further discussion of this legend by Rowland E. Robinson see *Vermont: A Study of Independence* (Boston and New York, 1892), p. 6.

[28]*Out of Bondage and Other Stories*, p. 117.   [29]Mary R. Perkins, p. 12.

[30]J. B. Burnham, "A Visit to Rowland Robinson's," *Forest and Stream* (Oct. 20, 1900), p. 302.

[31]Mary Robinson Perkins, pp. 14-15.   [32]Mary R. Perkins, pp. 14-15.

[33]Stoyle, p. 1; Mary Robinson Perkins, pp. 12-13.

[34]Rowland E. Robinson, "New England Fences," *Scribner's Monthly*, XIX (February 1880), 502-511.

[35]Mary Robinson Perkins, p. 16.

[36]Robinson, *In New England Fields and Woods,* pp. 70-71.

[37]Robinson, *Uncle Lisha's Outing and Along Three Rivers,* p. 153.

[38]Robinson, *Silver Fields and Other Stories of a Farmer-Sportsman,* p. 181.

[39]Van Wyck Brooks, *New England Indian Summer, 1865-1915* (New York, 1940), p. 458; Walter Prichard Eaton, Foreword to *Danvis Folks and A Hero of Ticonderoga,* p. 7.

CHAPTER 3

ROBINSON AS WRITER

Robinson would likely have spent most of his creative energy on illustrating rather than on writing if he had not become blind, but even before he became totally blind, his wife encouraged him to try writing. He already had written "A Sketch of the Early History of Ferrisburgh," which was to be included in Miss Abby Maria Hemenway's projected *Vermont Historical Magazine.*

Robinson's job of recording the early history of Ferrisburg was hampered by the loss of early records, destroyed by fire in 1785. Robinson lacked documentary evidence of deeds and other records with the dates, locations, and names of the first settlers, but unlike many modern historians who disparage the oral traditions of the people as unreliable, Robinson went to the people and collected their oral stories about the early town history. He interviewed the descendants of the first settlers and those of the Indians who camped on the East Slang. He examined traces of early houses, mills, roads, and bridges. In fact, he reconstructed nearly all of his early history of Ferrisburg from oral sources. While doing this research he visited a number of homes in his region and interviewed many people, consequently uncovering a lot of folklore, too.[1] In some cases he collected variants of local legends. Thus, in *Along Three Rivers*, a history of Robinson's region of Vermont based on the author's research for his "Sketch of the Early History of Ferrisburgh," Robinson reports:

The "Dugway" is a narrow canal of unknown origin, which makes a short cut from the Creek to Kellogg's Bay. There is no record nor authentic tradition concerning it. One tradition is that it was made by smugglers at the time of the Embargo, to avoid revenue officers at the mouth of the Creek. Another more probable conjecture is that it was made by Commodore McDonough to afford a passage for his gunboats to the lake in case the British should blockade his fleet where it lay in the river, with some of its vessels not yet ready for service.[2]

A few paragraphs later in the same local history Robinson adds another variant:

Since that concerning the Dugway was written, I have heard another tradition of its origin from Allen P. Beach, an old and respected resident of the south-western part of the town. According to accounts received by him in his youth from his father and others, this canal was made by Platt Rogers to shorten the route of the inhabitants south of the mouth of the river to Vergennes whither, from as far as Chimney Point, they came for the grinding of their grain, transporting it in small boats and batteaux. Platt Rogers was an early settler, an enterprising and public spirited man and an extensive land owner, the land through which the canal runs from the bay to the river being at one time a part of his possessions. So goes the story, which seemed quite as probable as any that have come down to us concerning the origin of this mysterious passage. The name of Platt Rogers first appears on the town records in 1790, when he purchased land of David Callender.[3]

Although Robinson would have agreed with Richard M. Dorson that "the historian can find history alive in the field as well as entombed in the library," he would have agreed also with Dorson that "The history of town, country, and region abound in legendary traditions, which often parade as real occurrences."[4] Accordingly, Robinson used discrimination to separate fact from fancy in the oral traditions that he uncovered. For instance, Robinson writes:

The defense of Fort Cassin has been passed over very lightly by historians of that war, yet it saved McDonough's fleet and made possible the decisive victory of Plattsburgh bay. The British were much chagrined by the failure of the attack and Captain Pring, who directed it, was severely censured by his superiors.

The uproar of the Plattsburgh fight was distinctly heard in the western part of our town. My grandfather told me that it was like a continuous peal of distant thunder. Ransom Beers, whose home was in the southeastern part, tells me that he remembers as a child putting his ear to the ground in imitation of his elders and so hearing the dull thunder of the battle.

With what anxious hearts they must have awaited the slow news brought first by express riders from Burlington and confirmed a little later by returning militiamen. John Hough, who was a lad at the time, told me that Amos Barnum and others rode out from Vergennes to the top of Mt. Philo where through spy glasses they watched the fight, till with loud rejoicing, they beheld the stars and stripes alone floating above hostile fleets. It was an absurd story, but it was none the less pleasant for a boy to believe.[5]

Robinson's literary career began fifteen years after he wrote "A Sketch of the Early History of Ferrisburgh." In 1875 his first articles appeared in Forest and Stream, a weekly "of the Rod and Gun," which merged into Field and Stream in 1930. Robinson's first contributions to Forest and Stream, such as "Reminiscences of an Old Trapper" in 1875, were signed with his pen name, "Awahoose," an Indian word for bear. The following year, 1876, Robinson contributed similar articles on trapping to Forest and Stream and published others in the American

Agriculturist and the *Daily Graphic*. A verse "In Memory of a Good Dog," was printed in *Forest and Stream*, November 8, 1877.[6]

Robinson, however, did not take seriously his early attempts at writing. He considered himself an illustrator and thought his magazine articles only supplementary to his magazine illustrations. But when his sight continued to fail, he realized that his career as illustrator was finished. His wife, in order to take his mind off his encroaching blindness, urged Robinson to write about the traditional way of life in which he had always been so interested.[7] Encouraged, Robinson wrote "Fox Hunting in New England" and sent it with seventeen illustrations to *Scribner's Monthly*. When the article was rejected, he sent it to other periodicals. Finally, Robinson sent it to *Scribner's Monthly* again; this time it was accepted and appeared in the January 1878 issue. With "Fox Hunting in New England" at last published, Robinson began to devote more of his time to writing. These early articles show his interest in folklife. *Scribner's Monthly* accepted his "Glimpses of New England Farm Life" for their August 1878 number, and his subsequent contributions were soon published: "New England Fences," including nine illustrations of various types of fences, in the issue of February 1880, and "Hunting the Honey-Bee" in that of December 1880. Also in 1880, Robinson's "The Rhyme of the Bass" appeared in the *American Agriculturist* and was reprinted in *Forest and Stream* in 1884. "On a Glass Roof," an article about ice fishing on Lake Champlain, appeared in *Lippincott's* in February 1884. Between 1882 and 1884 Robinson's adventures of his Munchausen character appeared serially in *Forest and Stream* under the title of "Major Joseph Verity: Some Of His Sporting Adventures as Modestly Set Forth by His Own Hand." Between 1882 and 1883 a series of fables appeared in *Forest and Stream*, and in 1886 seven were collected and published in the 24-page pamphlet *Forest and Stream Fables*. This was Robinson's first book; his wife maintained that Robinson was prouder of this slight collection of fables about hunting and fishing than of any of his later and more substantial books.[8]

Although Robinson became familiar to the readers of *Scribner's Monthly*, the *Century*, *Harper's*, *Lippincott's*, and the *Atlantic Monthly*, his works were published most frequently in *Forest and Stream*, whose editors liked his work enough to make him a member of their editorial staff and asked him to write a weekly column for the journal. However, since Robinson was a farmer he did not have to depend upon writing for his means of support and chose not to write a weekly column, although he nevertheless contributed regularly to *Forest and Stream*.[9]

Robinson's first story set in the small fictitious village of Danvis, Vermont, was "Uncle Lisha's Spring Gun," which appeared in the issue of March 17, 1881, of *Forest and Stream*. From June 5, 1884, to March 12, 1885, under the title of "Uncle Lisha's Shop," a series of similar stories set in Danvis and centered around storytelling sessions in the shop of shoemaker Uncle Lisha Peggs appeared in the same magazine. In 1887 twenty-two of these Danvis stories were collected and published by the Forest and Stream Publishing Company as *Uncle Lisha's Shop: Life in a Corner of Yankeeland*, Robinson's first hardcover book. The structure of *Uncle Lisha's Shop*, like that of the other Danvis stories, is simple. Several Danvis males—including Sam Lovel, Antoine Bassette, Joseph Hill, Solon Briggs, and Pelatiah Gove—meet each evening in Uncle Lisha Peggs' shop to swap tales and talk of hunting and fishing. Only at the end of the book is the routine interrupted when Uncle Lisha moves from Danvis to Wisconsin.

Other Danvis stories followed, although the central figure changed from the Danvis shoemaker, Uncle Lisha Peggs, to the Danvis Nimrod, Sam Lovel. The series of stories about Sam Lovel's spring camp on the Slang appeared in *Forest and Stream* in 1885 and 1886, and the stories about Sam Lovel's fall camp on Little Otter appeared in the same publication in 1887 and 1888. In 1889 these two sets of stories were combined to form *Sam Lovel's Camps*, which was published by the Forest and Stream Publishing Company. *Sam Lovel's Camps* consists mainly of daily hunting and fishing exploits, although tales are constantly swapped around the evening campfire and on rainy days.

By the time *Sam Lovel's Camps* reached Robinson from the publisher, the author could see only the silhouette of his book; in fact, of the fourteen books that he wrote, he was able to read only the first two: *Forest and Stream Fables* and *Uncle Lisha's Shop*.

Robinson remained fond of history and historical novels all his life.[10] His interest in history generally, his fondness for the tales of the American pioneers, his research into the early history of Ferrisburg, and his contribution to the chapter on Ferrisburg in H. P. Smith's *History of Addison County, Vermont* (Syracuse, 1886), gave him a modest reputation as authority on state and local history.[11] He was chosen by the Houghton, Mifflin Company to write a volume on Vermont for the American Commonwealth Series. By this time, however, Robinson was nearly blind, and only with the aid of a grooved writing board procured from the Perkins Institution for the Blind and with the assistance of his wife was he able to continue writing. The writing board was a heavy piece of cardboard with one-eighth inch grooves spaced about a half inch apart. As Robinson wrote each word with a lead pencil, he would move his left forefinger over the word to avoid writing another word over it.[12]

After each chapter, story, or essay, his wife copied the material and read it to him for corrections. Then Mrs. Robinson prepared the final draft. In fact, Robinson's books were truly family affairs, for his daughters illustrated the texts and drew the cover designs for all but the first two books.[13]

In addition, Anna Stevens Robinson had to collect the material for the history of Vermont. Then Robinson organized the material and wrote on his grooved writing board. Naturally the writing of a history can be difficult without eyes to glean countless written documents, and one reviewer of *Vermont* calls the history a "superficial investigation" and "a work of no great research."[14] As Edward D. Collins has pointed out, however, the history "is not chronology, is not a chronicle of events, but is a well-rounded interesting story. No historian was less a slave than he to facts and dates; and no previous author of a single volume on Vermont has revealed such masterly organization of the historical material he chose to use."[15] Regardless of the book's value to the historian, the folklorist will be especially interested in one chapter, "Old-Time Customs and Industries." But throughout the book Robinson vividly pictures the emigration, battles, customs, material culture, religion, education, and people of Vermont, as the generally unfavorable review in *The Nation* recognized.

Although *Vermont* occupied much of Robinson's time, he continued writing stories set in the small village of Danvis for *Forest and Stream,* and in 1894 twenty-five of these Danvis stories and "Gran'ther Hill's Pa'tridge," Robinson's first contribution to the *Atlantic Monthly,* were collected for his fourth book, *Danvis Folks.* In this work Uncle Lisha Peggs returns to Danvis from Wisconsin to live with Sam and Huldah Lovel, and the evening storytelling sessions in Uncle Lisha's shop, now a lean-to on the Lovels' home, begin once again. In 1895 he made several more contributions to the *Atlantic Monthly*: "A Voyage in the Dark" (February 1895), "The Apparition of Gran'ther Hill" (November 1895), and "A New England Woodpile" (December 1895).

In 1896 Robinson published his first book of nature essays, *In New England Fields and Woods.* Most of the fifty-seven essays were written after Robinson had become completely blind, and most of them had previously appeared in *Forest and Stream.* Since folklore is a social phenomenon, one finds very little mention of traditional culture in these personal observations of outdoor life.

Also in 1896 "Old Time Sugar Making" appeared in the April issue of the *Atlantic Monthly,* and another series of Danvis stories, later collected as *Sam Lovel's Boy* (1901), was begun in *Forest and Stream. Sam Lovel's Boy,* the final story in the Danvis series, is an account of Timothy Samuel ("Sammy" in the stories), Sam Lovel's son, from his infancy to the end of his enlistment in the Civil War.

In the following year, 1897, *Uncle Lisha's Outing,* a series of stories about another camping trip on Little Otter, was published by Houghton, Mifflin. And in the same year, "Out of Bondage" was first published in the *Atlantic Monthly* (August). Like a number of Robinson's stories

"Out of Bondage" deals with a Negro's escape on the Underground Railroad from enslavement and tells how a Vermont Quaker family saves him from his pursuers. This and sixteen other stories were collected in 1905 to form *Out of Bondage and Other Stories*, published by Houghton, Mifflin.

From 1898 to 1900, Robinson published three books based on historical events, including another Danvis story. *A Hero of Ticonderoga* (1898), relates how a young boy, Nathan Beeman, helped Ethan Allen and the Green Mountain Boys capture Fort Ticonderoga in 1775. The second book based on an historical event, *In the Green Wood* (1899), tells of one of the many disputes between holders of New Hampshire and New York grants.

In *A Danvis Pioneer* (1900), based in part on historical events, Robinson takes the reader back to the youth of Josiah Hill, known as Gran'ther Hill in the other Danvis stories. Just before the American Revolution Josiah Hill of Connecticut buys some land on Little Otter Creek in Vermont and with a partner builds a cabin there. But Josiah soon learns that the seller of the land did not have title to it, so he leaves his pitch, becomes a ranger, and has a series of adventures, which include taking part in the battles of Ticonderoga, Hubbardton, and Bennington. When the war ends, Josiah, now a captain, settles in Danvis Township under a Vermont charter and begins a pioneer life once again, but this time with a wife, Ruby, whom he found parentless on one of his adventures and married after an unconventional proposal. Josiah's offer of marriage goes:

"I want tu talk tu you a minute. . . ," he said, speaking low; and she arose and sat down near the freshly kindled fire. "I gin your father my word, an' him a-dyin', 'at I'd keer on ye faithful," he began abruptly, looking straight into her sad dark eyes; "an' I'm a-goin' tu, fur as I can. It hain't alone keepin' your body from bein' hurt, but your good name, an' a gal can't go traipsin' raound the country wi' a man 'at nothin' tu her by blood nor noways wi'-aout bein' hurt; so I've got tu marry you, the fust square or minister we light on."

"Oh, I can't! I-I don't want tu," she gasped, all in a tremble, and pale and red by turns.

"I do' want tu nuther," he said in blunt honesty. "I never thought tu come to 't, but I got tu, an' so we got tu make the best on 't. Naow we'll eat what we've got an' be off."[16]

At the end of *A Danvis Pioneer*, Josiah Hill is already the familiar Gran'ther Hill of the other Danvis stories, "the patriarch of a populous town whereof he was once almost the sole human inhabitant. The contemporaries of his early manhood were all gone, and to him alone were left memories of the old pioneer days, their hardships and the unsung deeds of humble heroes and heroines."[17]

In May 1899 Robinson was stricken with cancer, and for the remaining eighteen months of his life was confined to the bed in the room where he was born. Bedridden and blind, Robinson often listened to his wife or one of his three children—Rachel, Rowland T., or Mary—read to him. During this time, however, writing was his main comfort, and he was nearly always at work, although at times the intense pain caused him to cry out. Nevertheless, flat on his back in bed with his grooved writing board placed on his bent knees, Robinson wrote until almost the day he died, October 15, 1900.[18] Just three days before his death he wrote his last sentence, which runs, "The lifting veil disclosed the last flash of blue plumage disappearing in the mist of budding leaves from behind the cloud of smoke that now hid my mark."[19]

Several of Robinson's stories and essays and four of his books were published posthumously, attesting to his popularity. In the *Atlantic Monthly* "Recollections of a Quaker Boy" appeared in July 1901, "The Goodwin Spring" and "The Purification of Cornbury" in January 1902, and "An Old Time March Meeting" in March 1902. In addition to *Sam Lovel's Boy* (1901) and *Out of Bondage and Other Stories* (1905), two books of essays and stories, *Hunting Without a Gun and Other Papers* (1905) and *Silver Field's and Other Sketches of a Farmer-Sportsman* (1921), were published after Robinson's death. Between the years 1933 and 1937 the Tuttle Company of Rutland, Vermont, reprinted most of Robinson's writings in a seven-volume Centennial Edition, edited by Middlebury College professor Llewellyn R. Perkins, whose wife was Robinson's youngest daughter, Mary.

Robinson's total writing production includes nature essays, historical sketches, hunting and fishing articles, short stories, and the Danvis stories. But the Danvis stories constitute the bulk, and one finds most of the folklore in the Danvis chronicles and in the other stories with the same Vermont setting.

When Robinson died, the Vermont legislature was in session, and on October 18, 1900, it passed an appreciative resolution:

Resolved by the Senate and House of Representatives, That in the decease of Rowland E. Robinson, of Ferrisburg, we feel that Vermont hath lost an eminent citizen whose literary work has added to its wealth and renown, and whose genial disposition, high character and genuine worth, and whose earnest devotion to his family, his State, his country, to nature, and to the bountiful Creator of every good and perfect gift made his life an illustrious example of Christian patriotism, which will forever preserve his memory in the hearts of the sons and daughters of the Green Mountain State.[20]

Robinson's wife, who by a very strange coincidence also lost her sight near the end of her life,[21] asserted that "if Rowland had been told that the legislature of Vermont would take any notice of his death, he would not have believed it. He did not think people cared much for him."[22] Robinson's modesty was due in part to his unassuming nature and in part to his literary isolation. For he, a Vermont farmer-sportsman with little formal education, belonged to no literary circle. New York City was the farthest he ever traveled from his Ferrisburg home, and except for the few years spent in New York as an illustrator and for a part of a year spent in Nantucket with his sister, Robinson never left his area of Vermont.[23] He had a lifelong interest in the folklore and history of Vermont, and hiking, hunting, trapping, and sketching around his Ferrisburg home enabled him to come in direct contact with the oral traditions and to become thoroughly acquainted with the folk-life of his region. Consequently, as A. W. Peach has pointed out, Robinson's writings represent intimate experiences and not merely studied efforts of the author.[24]

Robinson had an intimate contact with the village folk. He drew his folk material from his own experiences.

NOTES

[1]Collins, p. 9.

[2]Robinson, *Uncle Lisha's Outing and Along Three Rivers,* p. 249.

[3]Robinson, *Uncle Lisha's Outing and Along Three Rivers,* p. 250.

[4]Richard M. Dorson, "Oral Tradition and Written History: the Case for the United States," *Journal of the Folklore Institute,* I (December 1964), pp. 234, 228.

[5]Robinson, *Uncle Lisha's Outing and Along Three Rivers,* p. 252.

[6]Cook, p. 24. One value of Miss Cook's thesis is that she cites a number of Robinson's writings that first appeared in periodicals. Since 1931 when her thesis was written, however, most of the essays and stories she cites have been collected in the seven-volume Centennial Edition of Robinson's works (Rutland, Vermont, 1933-1937). But as Harold Goddard Rugg points out in his partial bibliography of Robinson's writings in *In New England Fields and Woods,* pp. 5-11, it would be nearly impossible to locate every magazine article by Robinson since some of Robinson's articles in *Forest and Stream* are unsigned.

[7]Mary Robinson Perkins, p. 15.   [8]Mary Robinson Perkins, p. 16.

[9]Henry Lincoln Bailey, "The Chronicler of 'Danvis Folk,' " *New England Magazine,* XXIII (December 1900), 433.

[10]Mary Robinson Perkins, p. 12.   [11]Collins, p. 10.

[12]Stoyle, p. 2.   [13]Stoyle, p. 2.

[14]Anonymous review of *Vermont, The Nation,* LIV (June 2, 1892), 418-419.

[15]Collins, p. 5.

[16]Robinson, *Uncle Lisha's Shop and A Danvis Pioneer,* p. 83.

[17]Robinson, *Uncle Lisha's Shop and A Danvis Pioneer,* p. 117.

[18]Mary Robinson Perkins, p. 17.

[19]Julia C. R. Dorr, "Rowland Robinson," *Atlantic Monthly,* LXXXVII (January 1901), 122.

[20]Quoted in Cook, p. 40.   [21]Mary Robinson Perkins, p. 18.

[22]Dorr, p. 120.   [23]Mary Robinson Perkins, p. 13.

[24]Arthur Wallace Peach, Introduction to Rowland E. Robinson, *Sam Lovel's Camps and In the Green Wood,* ed. Llewellyn R. Perkins (Rutland, Vermont, 1923), p. 14.

CHAPTER 4

THE FUNCTION AND MILIEU OF THE FOLKLORE

Until recently most American folklorists, like their British counterparts of former years, have been interested primarily in oral folklore and have almost totally neglected the material aspects of traditional life. Folklife research, which is engaged in studying all aspects of life in a traditional society, although firmly established in some European countries, is a relatively new discipline for Anglo-Americans. Accordingly, since Robinson was a nineteenth century writer during the heyday of the great team of British survivalists,[1] one might conclude that he, too, was interested only in verbal folklore. But Robinson, in fact, was interested in both oral and material folklore and was, in a sense, one of the first real students of folklife studies in the United States. In both fiction and essay he offers a fairly full picture of Vermont folklife, including settlement, historical traditions, arts, crafts, architecture, subsistence, transportation, community life, folk medicine, customs, beliefs, oral literature, amusements and games.

Literary folklorists in the United States have been little concerned with the function and social milieu of the texts of folk literature they have given us. As Alan Dundes has pointed out, too many folklorists have studied the texts of folklore without studying the context of folklore, have studied the lore but not the folk.[2] Even today, the presentation of collected folklore remains a problem for folklorists, for once the text is removed from the oral tradition and written down it becomes lifeless. Although Bronislaw Malinowski's brand of functionalism has not weathered well and his failure to use the comparative method has not pleased folklorists, modern folklorists must remember Malinowski's advice in "Myth in Primitive Psychology" that to understand the folk literature of any society one must have a good knowledge of the people's social organization and material culture; for the functional, cultural, and pragmatic aspects of traditional narratives are manifested as much in the enactment, embodiment, and contextual relations of the texts as in the texts themselves. Malinowski maintains that a traditional tale loses almost all of its meaning when it is extracted from the people who live with it and who carry it. Thus the folk story in itself is trivial and unimportant. What really matters about a tale is not simply its text but also its social function. "Folk tales, legends, and myths," he says, "must be lifted from their flat existence on paper, and placed in the three-dimensional reality of full life."[3]

Contemporary folklorists have learned through experience that a folk narrative loses much of its meaning when it is extracted from the people who live with it and who carry it. William R. Bascom has maintained that the scientific folklorist must consider the people who tell folklore and the local conditions in which folklore lives. Specifically, the folklorist must consider when, where, and by whom the various forms of folklore are performed. He must record the dramatic devices used by the narrator and must note the audience's participation. Moreover, the folklorist must concern himself with the attitude of the folk toward the categories of folklore that the people themselves recognize.[4] Thanks, in part, to Malinowski, folklorists are becoming more and more interested in the whole social context and functions of the folklore texts that they collect.

It is to Robinson's credit that he did not wish to extract folklore from its social context, choosing instead to present it as an important element in a cultural matrix. While early field collectors were content to furnish merely the folklore texts, Robinson, with his artistic ability, was able to depict accurately in his fiction the folklife of his region of Vermont, and nearly a half century before Malinowski's dictum, he was placing collected folklore "in the three-dimensional reality of full life." Today the best way of showing folklore in its cultural setting is to collect it with the sound camera, but with his artistic talent, Robinson perhaps gave us the next best thing by weaving authentic folklore into realistic stories. By doing so, he did not give the reader dead texts, but rather illustrated folklore in action. In Robinson's stories we see how the traditional material culture and the oral folklore intermingle. He tells us, as well, something of the attitudes toward the various genres of folklore, and informs us when, where, and by whom oral folklore is told.

Since the microcosm of Danvis is a fictional communtiy, the folk milieu is idealized, and the actual functions and settings of folklore are somewhat obliterated. Since Robinson uses a literary rather than a scientific form to present folklore the precise controlling data about informant, time, place, and audience that the modern scientific folklorist likes is missing. Nevertheless, Robinson has given us more information about the function and setting of folklore in early nineteenth century New England than any field collector has. Indeed, the perceptual model of folklife of the artist Robinson strays no farther from the actual folk society than does the conceptual model of folklife of the social scientist Robert Redfield. Both models are based on the close study of folklife, but Robinson's is an idealization and Redfield's an abstraction, as Redfield himself points out.[5] Accordingly, Robinson's works differ considerably from the modern presentation of folklore in that his stories are artistic and synthetical, not expository and analytical. Robinson retells folktales, for example, by putting them in a recreated general setting or a frame device. But as MacEdward Leach points out, "This device by which the reader is allowed to hear folktales told in a natural context is the best possible way a folktale can be socialized for a reading audience."[6] On the whole, then, Robinson presents a carefully wrought picture of nineteenth century Vermont folklife. He interweaves his oral folklore naturally into authentically reproduced scenes of the social situations and material culture of village life. By using a frame device of telling folktales, among other genres of folklore, within created stories, Robinson is able to give us an excellent picture of Vermont storytelling sessions, including time, place, and audience.

To most of Robinson's Danvis folk, agriculture is both a livelihood and a way of life. Robinson, a farmer, was fully aware of the demands of subsistence farming and the regularity of the agricultural year. Since farm chores demand so much of the time of the Danvis folk, any form of diversion, including storytelling, must be worked into the rhythm of the agricultural cycle when there is a lull in the vital farming duties. The important days of the agricultural years, special events concerned with the rites of passage, and holidays are all festive occasions and afford the Danvis people the opportunities for relaxation, social intercourse, and storytelling. At collectively performed jobs, too, the village folk amuse themselves with both stories and songs to make the work go easier. Moreover, throughout the agricultural year, after a day's hard work, storytelling is virtually the sole entertainment available in the remote hill town of Vermont. He makes quite clear the function of the stories: they "sarve to while away the time."[7] Each winter evening, for instance, after supper and chores, "the brotherhood of hunters and fishers, story tellers and listeners came stumbling along the rough frozen roads and across the frosty fields to Lisha's shop" to swap yarns.[8] Thus, the oral folklore in Robinson's stories serves to make tedious work easier and to offer entertainment after working hours and on special occasions.

Since Robinson concentrates mainly on the activities of the village males, it is generally the men who spin the tales and sing the songs. Gran'ther Hill, for instance, "knows more stories 'n the' 'Rabian Nights' tells on."[9] When his Danvis cronies are not available to listen to his yarns, he always finds a willing audience in his grandson, young Josiah. For example, in "Raspberrying in Danvis," when a number of the Danvis folk set out to pick wild raspberries, young Josiah keeps close to his grandfather in hopes that the wilderness might suggest a tale. For listening to stories, says Josiah, is "lots more fun 'an the plaguey baries."[10] Similarly, in *A Danvis Pioneer,* while Gran'ther Hill lies ill in bed, young Josiah sits beside him brushing the flies away with an asparagus stalk and "wishing his grandfather would awake and tell a story."[11]

In Robinson's stories it is the old men living in the house who tell tales to children; the parents do not seem to have time for telling stories. As we have seen, Gran'ther Hill is the main source of tales for his grandson; also Uncle Lisha, who lives with the Lovels after he returns from Wisconsin, is the main source of stories for Sam Lovel's children, and he must do "his best to satisfy their insatiable appetite for stories of old times."[12] On rainy days when the children cannot play outside, Uncle Lisha tells stories to Sammy.[13] Although the men generally tell the tales and sing the songs in Robinson's writings, the women enjoy listening. For example, while the men swap stories in Uncle Lisha's shop, Aunt Jerusha frequently listens through the crack of the door.[14] Likewise, in *Danvis Folks* when Lisha, Solon, Joseph, Pelatiah, Antoine, and Antoine's father sing songs in Uncle Lisha's shop, Huldah and Aunt Jerusha stop working and listen.[15]

Since the primary function of the folktales told in Robinson's frame stories is to entertain, most are not believed by the Danvis folk. Nevertheless, the tall tales are recounted as if they are true stories anyway. In *Uncle Lisha's Shop,* for example, Uncle Lisha tells a whopper about a shoemaker who was so skillful with his shoeknife that he was hired to cut bread at "all gret duins" until at one shearing party he began cutting bread so fast that with a single lick he cut himself and a man behind him in two and wounded another man. The truncated men were stuck back together, but the incident ruined the shoemaker's breadcutting business.[16] Before telling this tale, Uncle Lisha says that it is "a true story, Ann Twine, an' 'f I tell it ye got t' b'lieve it." The tale begins, "Wal, the' was a shoemaker 't lived in Connecticut, an' my father knowed him . . ." But in spite of Uncle Lisha's preliminary remarks about the veracity of the tale and in spite of its realistic setting, this tale, like all the tall tales in Robinson's works, is not believed by the audience.

In the short story "Antoine on the Rail," when Antoine tells Uncle Lisha and the other frequenters of the cobbler's shop about his first ride on a train, a story that involves the motif in which a man does not recognize his own reflection in water or in a mirror,[17] Antoine tells the embellished experience as the truth; however, when the tale is finished and Antoine leaves the shop for the kitchen to tell the "women folk" about his train ride, Lisha says, "I'll go 'long in an' see if he tells his story twice alike."[18] On the other hand, legends and supernatural tales are generally believed by most of the Danvis folk in Robinson's stories. When Uncle Lisha tells a legend about buried treasure, Solon Briggs and Antoine Bassette try to find the spot where the treasure is supposedly buried. They even dig unsuccessfully for it. Moreover, after Antoine tells supernatural tales of the *loup-garou* in an awed voice, Robinson writes that "Antoine's scared face gave evidence of his implicit faith in the story of the *loup-garou* . . ."[19]

NOTES

[1]For a survey of these British folklorists see Richard M. Dorson, "The Great Team of English Folklorists," *Journal of American Folklore,* LXIV (January-March 1951), 1-10.

[2]Alan Dundes, "The American Concept of Folklore," *Journal of the Folklore Institute,* III (December 1966), 242-244.

[3]Malinowski, p. 146.

[4]William R. Bascom, "Four Functions of Folklore," *Journal of American Folklore,* LXVII (1954), 334.

[5]Robert Redfield, "Peasant Society and Culture," in *The Little Community and Peasant Society and Culture* (Chicago, 1965), p. 11. Also see Robert Redfield, "The Folk Society," *American Journal of Sociology,* LII (January 1947), 293-308.

[6]MacEdward Leach, "Folklore in American Regional Literature," *Journal of the Folklore Institute,* III (December 1966), 388.

[7]Robinson, *Out of Bondage and Other Stories,* p. 114.

[8]Robinson, *Uncle Lisha's Shop and A Danvis Pioneer,* p. 140.

[9]Robinson, *Sam Lovel's Boy with Forest and Stream Fables,* p. 36.

[10]Robinson, *Sam Lovel's Boy with Forest and Stream Fables,* p. 177.

[11]Robinson, *Uncle Lisha's Shop and A Danvis Pioneer,* p. 107.

[12]Robinson, *Sam Lovel's Boy with Forest and Stream Fables,* p. 76.

[13]Robinson, *Sam Lovel's Boy with Forest and Stream Fables,* p. 33.

[14]Robinson, *Uncle Lisha's Shop and A Danvis Pioneer,* p. 146.

[15]Robinson, *Danvis Folks and A Hero of Ticonderoga,* p. 134.

[16]Robinson, *Uncle Lisha's Shop and A Danvis Pioneer,* p. 139. The tales mentioned in this chapter are discussed and annotated in Chapter 17.

[17]The motif is J1791.7 in Stith Thompson, *Motif-Index of Folk-Literature,* 6 vols. (Bloomington and London, 1966). Unless otherwise indicated, all references to motifs are to this index.

[18]Robinson, *In New England Fields and Woods,* p. 242.

[19]Robinson, *Danvis Folks and A Hero of Ticonderoga,* p. 124.

CHAPTER 5

VILLAGE SHOPS AND STORES AS CENTERS
FOR THE PERFORMANCE OF FOLKLORE

Since most of the Danvis men are farmers, the majority of the performances of oral folklore in the Danvis stories take place in or near the village in evenings after supper and chores or on rainy or snowy days when farming activities are interrupted. Robinson says that in bad weather, for instance, "No one but a shoemaker could work, and the rest of the world could only go a-visiting."[1] Therefore in inclement weather and on most evenings after supper, a genial group of Danvis men gather in the small shop of Uncle Lisha Peggs, the village shoemaker, to tell stories, to swap jokes, and to sing songs. Uncle Lisha's shop is "a sort of sportsman's exchange, where, as one of the fraternity expressed it, the hunters and fishermen of the widely scattered neighborhood met of evenings and dull out-door days 'to swap lies.' Almost every one had a story to tell, but a few only listened and laughed, grunted, or commented as the tale told was good, bad or of doubtful authenticity."[2]

The model for Uncle Lisha's shop was Uncle Lisha Green's cobbler shop, at one time located in Vergennes, only two miles from Robinson's home. A photograph of this shop is accompanied by a card that reads: "An actual photograph of Uncle Lisha Green's shop, verified by Mr. Moses Lee who had his boots tapped there when he was 18. This shop, the scene of many of Mr. Robinson's books, was a woodshed chamber of the second house north of the bridge which has taken the place of the old covered bridge. Uncle Lisha's shop was a popular gathering place for the men and boys of the community."[3] No doubt Robinson had this shop in mind when he chose a shoemaker's shop as the popular gathering place for his convivial group of Danvis males. Likewise, there can be little doubt that Uncle Lisha Peggs, the shoemaker who dominates most of Robinson's storytelling scenes, was based on the real shoemaker Uncle Lisha Green.

Robinson was familiar with another Ferrisburg cobbler, too. Uncle Nat Martin, who had a shoemaker's shop and tannery near Ferrisburg. As he does so often with other aspects of folklife, Robinson incorporates into his fiction his firsthand knowledge of the traditional craft of shoemaking. In *Danvis Folks* when Uncle Lisha measures the feet of Antoine's father for a pair of straight boots, Robinson writes:

With Antoine's help, the old man was backed up to the wall with his heel against the mopboard and Uncle Lisha stooped over his foot with a sharp-pointed jack-knife poised threateningly above his toes which were instinctively curved.

"Quit a-wigglin' yer dumbd ol' toes. I hain't a-goin' tu jab 'em. No wiggly paw de toe. There, I thought I could make you ondestan'," and he succeeded in driving his knife in the floor at the end of old Pierre's big toe. He transferred the measurement to the pine stock and marked it by a notch as he did several circumferences obtained with a string, and pronounced the preliminary labor accomplished, and the old Canadian drew on his boot with an air of great relief.[4]

Robinson was thoroughly familiar with other leather-working crafts, although he has more to say about shoemaking than he does about tanning and harnessmaking. There is no description in Robinson's writings of a tannery, but in *Along Three Rivers* he points out that there was once a tannery on Little Otter Creek at a spot called Dover or Walker's Falls.[5] In both essay and story, he briefly describes the process of tanning a hide. In the essay "Reminiscences" he tells how the hired man of his family, Mingo Niles, trapped woodchucks and tanned their hides:

Sometimes a woodchuck was found taking refuge in an old stone wall, and if his head was in sight a slip knot was tied in a stout cord, which was fastened to the end of a stick and so presented to the animal. He seized it at once, the noose was drawn tightly around the hooked incisors, and the poor woodchuck was hauled steadily forth in spite of his protesting whistle and growls. Next day his skin was immersed in the soap barrel, or buried first in wet ashes to remove the hair. After the grease was quite removed from the skin, it went through a long process of rubbing and stretching until it was the perfection of toughness and pliability, and ready to be manufactured into whiplashes, shoestrings, ball covers and mittens.[6]

Similarly, in *Sam Lovel's Boy* Robinson tells how the shoemaker Uncle Lisha Peggs tans a woodchuck hide: "Uncle Lisha consigned the skin to the soap barrel without knowledge of the too fastidious womenkind, whence it was taken after a couple of days, ready to yield the bedraggled hair to persuasive scraping, and then was pulled, rubbed, and kneaded until it became as pliable as a glove, and as yellow as a lemon."[7] Uncle Lisha makes the tanned hide into a ball cover for Sam Lovel's son, although Lisha, too, sometimes braids woodchuck hide into whiplashes, as Mingo did.[8]

Although harnessmaking was an indispensable craft in the nineteenth century, as Van Wagenen points out, it was not usually as big a business as shoemaking; consequently, either the tanner or the village shoemaker also might have been a harnessmaker incidentally.[9] In *Along Three Rivers* Robinson mentions a craftsman who had a harness shop in Ferrisburg,[10] but in the Danvis stories the shoemaker Lisha Peggs mends harness as well as shoes.[11] Thus, Robinson, like Van Wagenen, recognizes that tanning, harnessmaking, and shoemaking are intimately related traditional crafts.

Since one of his main characters is a shoemaker, Robinson naturally has much to say about this craft. Like many early craftsmen in small American villages, Uncle Lisha was only a part-time cobbler. He became a shoemaker in order to supplement his farm income during the winter months. As Robinson maintains in *Vermont,* the traveling cobbler was received gladly in every home yearly as a bearer of news, gossip, and tales. He was:

. . . a welcome visitor of every homestead in his beat, bringing to it all the gossip for the womenfolk, all the weighty news for the men, and all the bear stories for the children which he had gathered in a twelve months' "whipping of the cat," as his itinerant craft was termed. These he dispensed while, by the light of the wide fireplace, he mended old foot-gear or fashioned new, that tortured alike either foot whereon it was drawn on alternate days.[12]

After Uncle Lisha married Jerusha Chase and after he bought a small farm near the Green Mountains in Danvis, he quit "whipping the cat" and established a small shop in a lean-to attached to his house, where "in slack times, as well as in evenings and rainy days, he mended the boots and shoes of his neighbors, and was sometimes persuaded, as a special favor, to exercise the craft to the extent of building a pair of leathern conveniences."[13] In his description of Lisha's shop Robinson speaks of "the odors of tannin', wax and mouldy boots that always hold their own in the atmosphere of the cobbler's shop."[14] And in another place, Robinson writes:

. . . Uncle Lisha led the way into his little shop and lighted the candle which, stuck in the end of a jointed wooden sconce, illumined his nightly labors. Then he deliberately donned his leather apron, lowered himself into the polished leathern seat of his shoebench, set his iron-rimmed, owl-eyed spectacles astride his nose, fished out the boots from a clutter of clumsy lasts, broad slabs of sole leather, rolls of cowhide and sheepskin, gave his long shoe-knife a rasping on the peculiar, course, gritty stone used only by shoemakers, and was ready for work. . . .[15]

In addition to the cobbler's bench, lasts, shoeknives, and lapstone, Robinson mentions most of the other tools and supplies of the village cobbler, including hammer, awls, tug, shoemaker's wax, tub for soaking leather, and stiff hog bristles waxed to thread that serve as the rural shoemaker's needles.[16] Some techniques of the cobbler that Robinson must have learned by close observation are "scraping the sole of a boot with a bit of broken glass," "punching a hole in a patch with a crooked awl and inserting the bristle of a waxed end," daubing "the edges of the tap with lampblack and oil," and "closing up the seam of a boot leg with long, strong pulls of two waxed ends, the crooked awl going out on one side and jabbing the air, then coming back and stabbing the leather, the threads following with a squeaking swish and a tightdrawn tug."[17]

In Robinson's writings other centers of village life where the folk gather to swap stories and gossip include the village store, the tavern, the blacksmith shop, and the mills. In *Along Three Rivers*, for example, Robinson mentions that the "old-time stores were centers of social intercourse with hospitable if hard seats for loungers, and wine and liquors on tap, free, with proper limitations, to all comers."[18] Although the drinks were not free, barrooms, too, according to Robinson, were centers of village social life and therefore centers of folklore dissemination.[19] In *Along Three Rivers* Robinson reports of hearing a wandering veteran of the Revolution singing old songs in a tavern, and he regrets that in his youth he failed to consciously collect folklore from not only the old veteran but from all old people. Speaking of the veteran of the Revolution, Robinson says:

. . . When his heart was warmed with a mug of hard cider by the barroom fire, he would lift up his cracked, whistling, toothless voice in songs of the Revolution, whereof I remembered but the first line of one.

" 'Twas the seventeenth of June that they landed on our shores!" Why did we not exercise our Yankee prerogative and ask the veterans and all the old people of our youth, more questions? What tales they might have told us that now, alas, can never be told![20]

Another favorite gathering and gossiping place of men was the village blacksmith shop. About the important traditional craft of blacksmithing, Robinson reports:

. . . for many years later there was a considerable demand for charcoal by blacksmiths. Of these there were many more then than now, for the scope of the smith's craft was far broader in the days when he forged many of the household utensils and farming tools that, except such as have gone out of use, are now wholly supplied by the hardware dealer. A common appurtenance of the smithy, when every farmer used oxen, was the "ox-frame," wherein those animals, who in the endurance of shoeing belie their proverbial patience, were hoisted clear of the ground, and their feet made fast while the operation was performed. The blacksmith's shop was also next in importance, as a gossiping place, to the tavern barroom and the store . . .[21]

Generally speaking Robinson has little to say about the important craft of the blacksmith. In *Along Three Rivers*, however, he refers to a blacksmith's shop that was once located on Little Otter Creek,[22] and in "How Elijah was Fed at Christmas," he mentions that the village blacksmith was also "the repairer of all the guns of the township."[23] The gunsmith, however, in both peace and war an important craftsman in his own right in early America, especially when both subsistence and safety depended to a large extent on the gun, is usually depicted by Robinson as a specialist, not as a half-time blacksmith. The Danvis Nimrods are proud of having their guns built by a famous craftsman. For example, in *A Danvis Pioneer*, Josiah Hill bends the barrel, breaks the lock, and splinters the stock of his rifle, "Sartin Death," when he uses the gun to club a charging bear, and he barters a two-year-old heifer, "trade being then chiefly conducted by barter," for the building of "a sixteen-gauge smooth-bore, with four-foot barrel, brass mountings, curled maple stock of rifle pattern, with patch box." The gunsmith in this story is Thomas Hill of Charlotta, "the most famous gunsmith of the region," and Josiah is very "proud to have so skillful and honest a workman as its maker for namesake."[24] Again, Robinson had first-hand knowledge of the gunsmith's craft. In an essay, "Cleaning the Old Gun," for instance, he writes:

I take down the old gun from the hooks whereon in these idle hours she has hung since the days I first knew there were guns and began to covet their use and possession. Many changes and much rough usage she has undergone since then when her igniting force slept in the cool flint of her comely lock, and its flash awakened fire and thunder that burst from her three feet and six inches of octagonal and round barrel of seventeen-gauge. Longer ago than I can remember, her lock was clumsily changed to the incoming percussion fashion by Seaver, of Vergennes, a gunsmith who scoffed at the idea of barrels ever being twisted or made in any way but by longitudinal welding of the tube. How distinctly I remember the old man and his low-roofed shop. Spectacled and so bent with years, he need not stoop to his work of filing a stiff sear spring while he gossiped of his townsmen, one of whom was "jest a-dyin' of reg'lar ol' fashioned rum consumption, poor ol' creetur." The grimy walls of his den were arrayed with guns of all sorts, repaired and awaiting repairs, and bunches of new steel traps, of which he was a famous maker in those days when the Newhouse trap was unknown. Nine dollars a dozen was the regular price of good hand-made traps. I doubt not he was tinkering the militiamen's muskets, perhaps in this same shop, in the martial days of the last war with England, when all the Champlain Valley was alert for British invasion, and McDonough's fleet was threatened with blockade or destruction where it lay at the Buttonwoods in Otter Creek.[25]

Seaver, the gunsmith of Vergennes whom Robinson knew, is found in Robinson's fiction. In *Sam Lovel's Boy* when his son is old enough to handle a gun, Sam Lovel returns one day from Vergennes and brings with him "from the old gunsmith Seavers a brand-new fowling piece with a percussion lock and a walnut stock and a silver sight,—a beauty of a gun in those days."[26] Still, Sammy's gun has a walnut stock, and the most esteemed wood for the stock of a gun seems to be curly maple. The stock of Josiah Hill's new gun is curly maple; and in the story "How Elijah was Fed at Christmas" the stock of Elijah's gun, also from Hill's shop, is the same wood.[27] Furthermore, the most famous gun in Danvis, Sam Lovel's "Old Ore Bed," has a "long octagonal barrel cased to the muzzle in the 'curly maple' stock, its trimmings, hooked heel plate, and patchbox of brass that glistened like gold where hand or shoulder had brightened them with wear."[28]

Curly maple is of course a particularly attractive wood and was therefore often used by early country cabinetmakers, too. Robinson refers to a curly maple bureau, for example, in "A September Election."[29]   A more highly esteemed wood for cabinetmaking, however, was wild cherry since its natural reddish-brown color takes a beautiful finish.   In "A New England Woodpile" Robinson mentions a "great wild-cherry tree that somehow escaped the cabinet maker when there was one in every town and cherry wood was in fashion."[30]   But the only piece of furniture made of cherry that he mentions is a chest of drawers in *A Danvis Pioneer*.[31]   Nevertheless, Robinson is probably accurately reporting folklife, for pine was a wood with which many early cabinetmakers frequently worked because it was light, durable, available, and easy to shape.   In "Silver Fields," among other places, Robinson refers to pine furniture in rooms with low whitewashed ceilings and rag carpets.[32]   Moreover, in a number of places Robinson also mentions the products of the early cabinetmakers, especially chairs. Especially popular in the nineteenth century were ladderback chairs with splint-bottom seats,[33] and these are the items of country furniture that Robinson mentions most frequently.[34]   In addition, Robinson refers to wooden-bottom chairs, a windsor chair, and the popular three-legged stool.[35] Like modern students of folk crafts, Robinson generally distinguishes between the cabinetmaker and the carpenter, although as Van Wagenen suggests there was probably no clear-cut distinction between the two crafts, especially in small villages;[36] and in "Uncle Gid's Christmas Tree," Robinson portrays one craftsman, Nathan Sherman, as both joiner and carpenter.[37]

Other than cordwainer Uncle Lisha Peggs the craftsmen mentioned in Robinson's works are minor characters, so their shops do not generally serve as centers for the performance of folklore. Nevertheless, these craftsmen have a significant function in Robinson's writings in rounding out his picture of village life and adding verisimilitude.

Although Robinson says little about such pioneer industries as cabinetmaking and blacksmithing, he says more about early American mills. The gristmill and sawmill, of course, were indispensable industries in early America and were built almost everywhere where water power was available.   In Vermont there was a stream with a good fall almost everywhere.[38]   The mills served as centers for social intercourse, and the sites provided a center around which other industries grew. As soon as the mills were built, other craftsmen established their shops nearby to form a small community of diverse crafts. Such a situation Robinson reports in *Along Three Rivers* where a gristmill was built and other craft shops were later established. This mill, in fact, was at one time owned by Robinson's father, who was prosecuted when he refused to grind corn for a nearby distillery.

It was not until the last years of the eighteenth century that almost every Vermonter had a gristmill conveniently nearby. The pioneer either built his own plumping mill—a rude device consisting of a large wooden mortar with a pestle hung from a spring pole that was generally mortised into one side of the house—or journeyed up to forty miles on horseback or on foot to the nearest gristmill.[39] In *A Hero of Ticonderoga* the Beemans must either slowly and laboriously pound their corn into meal on their own crude plumping mill or travel two days to the nearest gristmill.[40] The earliest settlers, of course, had only their own plumping mills. Thus, in *A Danvis Pioneer* almost as soon as Josiah Hill arrives at his pitch in Vermont he makes a plumping mill, of which Robinson briefly describes both the construction and appearance:

Not many days later Josiah was fashioning a huge mortar out of an oak stump close by the end of the house by alternate burning and gouging. This was for a plumping mill, that, when complete, consisted of the mortar, a heavy pestle slung at the end of a spring pole, the butt of which was fastened in the logs of the house, and all with a view to the coming corn crop. As he chipped away the wood or rekindled the fire and wet the edge of the slowly shaping mortar to keep it from burning, he caught the sound of footsteps . . .[41]

The pioneer needed mills to saw his timber as much as he needed mills to grind his grain, for sawing planks and boards by hand, like grinding corn on the plumping mill, cost too much time and labor.[42] Consequently, near the water that powered the gristmills, sawmills were soon constructed. Building a sawmill on the frontier was no easy matter, as Robinson indicates in *In the Green Wood*. Robinson writes that "all the iron-work of the mill had to be transported a long distance through the almost pathless wilderness. The shaft and crank were drawn for miles through the woods on a hand-sled, while the saw and some other parts had come less laboriously by oxteam down the frozen current of the river."[43] Robinson's description of Pangborn's sawmill suggests that he almost certainly had firsthand knowledge:

A great pine log was rolled upon the carriage and dogged in its place; the lever of the gate was pressed down; the water rushed from the flume, adding its small volume to the roar of the falls; the water-wheel began to revolve; the sawgate slowly arose and descended, and then, with quicker strokes, the flashing saw menaced the advancing log; then with sharp, quick bites began to gnaw it through from end to end. The rapid swish of the saw, the throbbing creak of the gate, and clank of the ratchet on the rag-wheel were sweet music to the little audience, whose keen ears heard it all, piercing the deep thunder of the cataract.

The father watched intently every movement of the machinery, and the strained anxiety of his face gradually gave way to triumphant satisfaction as each part performed its work, and the regular jets of sawdust spurted up and fell to the roaring nether depths, to mingle with the beaver-chips drifting down from the wild mountain torrents. The carriage tripped the gate-lever, and all the swish and clatter ceased as the saw slowly rose and fell and stopped midway in its next ascent. This moment of success rewarded months of labor and deprivation.[44]

Additional evidence that Robinson was acquainted with the village mills appears in "Glimpses of New England Farm Life," in which he not only suggests that the mills served as centers where village males might lounge and gossip while awaiting their milling but also indicates that the mills were subjects of folklore, too:

Loads of logs are drawn to the saw-mill, a quaint old structure, whose mossy beams have spanned its swift race-way for half a century or more. The green ooze of the leaky flume turns the icicles to spikes of emerald, and the caves beneath the log dam have crystal portals of fantastic shapes. Heaps of logs and piles of boards and slabs environ it on the landward side, and a pleasant odor of freshly cut pine pervades the neighborhood. Its interior is as comfortless in winter as a hill-top, "Cold as a saw-mill" being a New England proverb; and it is often said of one who leaves outer doors open in cold weather, "Guess he was brought up in a saw-mill, where there wa'n't no doors." It is a poor lounging place now for our farmer, but the dusty gristmill, hard by, offers greater attractions. May be he has brought a grist a-top his logs, and has good excuse to toast his shins by the miller's glowing stove, while he waits the grinding.[45]

Robinson's casual remark that the warm gristmill was a more pleasant place to lounge during the cold winter months than was the drafty sawmill also suggests that the village centers for social intercourse, and therefore the centers of folklore dissemination, varied according to the season. Internal evidence suggests that Robinson must have observed firsthand the workings of the mills and participated in the gossip sessions in them.

NOTES

[1] Robinson, *Danvis Folks and A Hero of Ticonderoga*, p. 131.

[2] Robinson, *Uncle Lisha's Shop and A Danvis Pioneer*, p. 137.

[3] The picture of Uncle Lisha Green's shop and the information accompanying it have been reproduced on the frontispiece of *Uncle Lisha's Shop and A Danvis Pioneer*.

[4] Robinson, *Danvis Folks and A Hero of Ticonderoga*, pp. 137-138.

[5] Robinson, *Uncle Lisha's Outing and Along Three Rivers*, p. 242.

[6] Robinson, "Reminiscences," p. 285.

[7] Robinson, *Sam Lovel's Boy with Forest and Stream Fables*, pp. 45-46.

[8] Robinson, *Sam Lovel's Boy with Forest and Stream Fables*, p. 133. For a similar account of tanning woodchuck hides in Vermont, see Walter Needham and Barrows Mussey, *A Book of Country Things* (Brattleboro, Vermont, 1965), pp. 70-71.

[9] Jared Van Wagenen, Jr., *The Golden Age of Homespun* (Ithaca, New York, 1953), p. 201.

[10] Robinson, *Uncle Lisha's Outing and Along Three Rivers*, p. 231.

[11] Robinson, *Uncle Lisha's Shop and A Danvis Pioneer*, p. 185.

[12] Robinson, *Vermont*, pp. 293-294.

[13] Robinson, *Uncle Lisha's Shop and A Danvis Pioneer*, p. 128.

[14] Robinson, *Uncle Lisha's Shop and A Danvis Pioneer*, p. 40.

[15] Robinson, *Uncle Lisha's Shop and A Danvis Pioneer*, p. 132.

[16] Robinson, *Sam Lovel's Boy with Forest and Stream Fables*, pp. 29, 33; *Uncle Lisha's Shop and A Danvis Pioneer*, pp. 124, 137, 139, 154, 185, 201, 221; *Uncle Lisha's Outing and Along Three Rivers*, p. 24.

[17] Robinson, *Uncle Lisha's Shop and A Danvis Pioneer*, pp. 145, 158; *Uncle Lisha's Outing and Along Three Rivers*, p. 24.

[18] Robinson, *Uncle Lisha's Outing and Along Three Rivers*, p. 257.

[19] Robinson, *Uncle Lisha's Shop and A Danvis Pioneer*, p. 19.

[20] Robinson, *Uncle Lisha's Outing and Along Three Rivers*, p. 241.

[21] Robinson, *Vermont*, p. 304.

[22] Robinson, *Uncle Lisha's Outing and Along Three Rivers*, p. 241.

[23] Robinson, *Out of Bondage and Other Stories*, p. 190.

[24] Robinson, *Uncle Lisha's Shop and A Danvis Pioneer*, pp. 92-93.

[25] Robinson, *In New England Fields and Woods*, pp. 173-174.

[26] Robinson, *Sam Lovel's Boy with Forest and Stream Fables*, p. 90.

[27] Robinson, *Out of Bondage and Other Stories*, p. 187.

[28] Robinson, *Sam Lovel's Camps and In the Green Wood*, p. 33.

[29] Robinson, *Sam Lovel's Boy with Forest and Stream Fables*, p. 163.

[30] Robinson, *In New England Fields and Woods*, p. 122.

[31] Robinson, *Uncle Lisha's Shop and A Danvis Pioneer*, p. 109.

[32] Robinson, *Silver Fields and Other Sketches of a Farmer-Sporstman*, p. 15.

[33] Ralph and Terry Kovel, *American Country Furniture 1780-1875* (New York, 1965), p. 85.

34Robinson, *Out of Bondage and Other Stories,* pp. 73, 148; *Uncle Lisha's Shop and A Danvis Pioneer,* pp. 106, 179; *Uncle Lisha's Outing and Along Three Rivers,* p. 42.

35Robinson, *Sam Lovel's Boy with Forest and Stream Fables,* p. 79; *Out of Bondage and Other Stories,* p. 137; *Uncle Lisha's Shop and A Danvis Pioneer,* pp. 37, 129.

36Van Wagenen, p. 112.

37Robinson, *Out of Bondage and Other Stories,* p. 203.

38Earle Newton, *The Vermont Story* (Montpelier, 1949), p. 92.

39Robinson, *Vermont,* p. 250.

40Robinson, *Danvis Folks and A Hero of Ticonderoga,* p. 236.

41Robinson, *Uncle Lisha's Shop and A Danvis Pioneer,* p. 44.

42Harold R. Shurtleff, *The Log Cabin Myth* (Cambridge, Mass., 1939), pp. 46-47.

43Robinson, *Sam Lovel's Camps and In the Green Wood,* pp. 211-212.

44Robinson, *Sam Lovel's Camps and In the Green Wood,* p. 212.

45Robinson, "Glimpses of New England Farm Life," pp. 514-515.

CHAPTER 6

COLLECTIVELY PERFORMED TASKS
AND THE PERFORMANCE OF FOLKLORE

The rural life that Robinson describes is homogeneous, character-ized by interdependence and cooperation. The close-knit people of Danvis are so self-sufficient that they seldom get away from their own little village. For instance, when Uncle Lisha and Aunt Jerusha leave Danvis for Wisconsin, "After the kindly fashion of those days, some of their neighbors accompanied them to the place where they were to embark in the canal-boat"; and Pelatiah Gove, who drives the lumber wagon with the Peggs' "housel stuff," is astonished by the sights less than a day's drive by team from Danvis.

In *Sam Lovel's Camps* when Sam Lovel, Antoine Bassette, Solon Briggs, and Joseph Hill leave their mountains to go fishing in the low-lands near Lake Champlain, the lowlanders, who live less than fifteen miles from Danvis, do not share the enthusiasm of the Danvis hill folk for catching pickeral. In *Uncle Lisha's Outing* when some of the Danvis people visit Vergennes to see a caravan, Uncle Lisha overhears two boys exchanging retorts, and the Danvis shoemaker "was impressed by the depravity of town boys in calling each other by their last names."[1] In fact, the provincialism of the Danvis folk occasionally quite naturally reveals naivete. At the caravan show, for instance, Aunt Jerusha, failing to understand a clown's antics when as part of his act he runs into a pole, doctors the clown's painted nose with camphor.[2]

References to the interdependence and cooperation of the homo-geneous Danvis folk can be found throughout Robinson's writings. In *Along Three Rivers* he points out that the concept of neighbor was not so restricted in pioneer days as it is now.[3] Then people living a mile or two away were neighbors, always ready to help if illness or accident be-fell another. In *Uncle Lisha's Shop* when it is thought that Uncle Lisha has been mangled by a bear, "Some neighbors . . . came dropping in to offer their help with the ready kindness of our primitive communities."[4] Visiting neighbors in time of illness or injury also provides the Danvis folk opportunity to gossip and tell stories. When Uncle Lisha is supposedly dying from injuries inflicted by a bear, the women sit in the square room "magnifying in whispers the latest neighborhood gossip" and the men "lounged in the doorways or against the side of the house and dooryard fence, and told in low voices their experience with bears."[5] Furthermore, when fires went out in pioneer homes, it was customary to visit a neighbor to borrow coals, providing opportunities for telling tales. In *Along Three Rivers*, Robinson reports:

It was easier to go half a mile to borrow fire than to kindle it with flint and steel and tinder and brimstone matches, when it had been lost, and this gave a frequent pretext for a neighborly call. It was a common custom for a family to embark in the lumber sled, and nestled in straw and quilts, fare over miles of rough forest-hedged roads to spend the long winter evening at a neighbor's, to be received without ceremony or show of ostentation, but always with a hearty welcome. The spinning wheel was set aside, the fireside circle widened and while the johnny cakes baked on boards before the coals, and potatoes roasted in the ashes, the elders told tales of revolutionary days or the hardships of pioneering times with which they contrasted their own happy lot, the children listening agape, and the older young folks chatting apart of lighter present affairs.[6]

Visitors in the pioneer home, especially when they had stories to tell, were always welcome. In his short history, *Along Three Rivers*, Robinson writes, for example, that Thomas Champlin often mounted his gray mare of an evening to ride over to the home of his friend Robert Hazard "to sit the livelong night by the great open fire of the log house and talk of good old Narragansett days, while upon occasion the cronies regaled themselves with potatoes roasted in the ashes, and I never heard that the host tired of his long-winded guest, for it was the frequent fashion of old time visiting."[7] Visitors are always received gladly. For instance, in *A Danvis Pioneer*, after Josiah Hill and Kenelm Dalrymple build their log house in Vermont, visitors bearing news and tales are greeted hospitably, and food and liquor are readily shared with the guests. "In those days, not to have liquor in the house for the entertainment of a guest was thought to be more disgraceful than to be without bread."[8] An especially welcome guest to the pitch of Josiah and Kenelm was Ethan Allen, who spent the day with them "and helped make the night jovial, at which he was an exceedingly good hand, having no end of stories to tell and a great capacity for strong drink."[9]

Indeed, the Danvis neighbors are so friendly that when Joseph Hill visits the Lovel homestead, he enters the house "without knocking, after the neighborly fashion of Danvis."[10] The friendliness of the Danvis folk results, in part, from their interdependence, which Robinson pictures as an important characteristic. In *Along Three Rivers*, speaking of his own area of Vermont, he says, "Our three rivers, shrunken though they be from their old estate, flow on over their ancient beds, but the homes the pioneers built beside them have vanished like their founders, and with them manners and customs that were a part of their daily life, industires that were their daily toil, the simplicity of their enjoyments, and the friendliness begot of their interdependence."[11] Similarly, in *Danvis Folks*, he writes, "Because of the greater interdependence of the people, 'bees' had been much more common in the days of Uncle Lisha's youth than in these of his old age, but he had not lost his fondness for attending them."[12]

Robinson saw the importance of cooperative labor. He recognized, too, that the collective jobs were continued for social reasons long after the need for collectively performed tasks had disappeared. In *Along Three Rivers* he reports, "There were frequent helpful gatherings, 'bees' for raising buildings, hauling and piling logs for burning, and for harvesting belated crops, with less of work than of merry-making, the huskings, apple-bees and quiltings, participated in by both sexes."[13] About the logging, raising, drawing, harvesting, husking, paring, and quilting bees Robinson has more to say throughout his writings.

Logging bees were held when the felled logs were ready for piling and burning. In "Glimpses of New England Farm Life," however, he reports that logging bees, among others, had fallen into disuse.[14] But since Robinson's stories are set in times earlier than 1878, the logging bees have a place, especially in his historically earliest stories in which they serve as occasions for swapping jokes. In *A Danvis Pioneer,* Robinson says, "Every one had a logging-bee when the felled trees were ready for piling, but Josiah was first at all, organizing the work and keeping all hands at it till it was finished, before the inevitable black bottle went its rounds oftener than necessary, and skylarking and practical joking began too soon."[15]

When the logs were finally piled and burned, the ashes generally were not wasted. In *A Danvis Pioneer*, they are stored for future potash making.[16] In *A Hero of Ticonderoga*, ash gathering is "hard, unpleasant work, irritating to skin, eyes, and temper."[17] Robinson does not overestimate the importance of saving the ashes of the burned logs. As Van Wagenen points out, the making of potash was of major importance during the pioneer period, for potash was used in making soap, glass, and for cleaning from wool the gummy secretions in the fleece. In *Along Three Rivers,* Robinson mentions a potashery that was at one time located on Little Otter Creek not far from his home,[18] and in "A Story of the Old Frontier," set in the last part of the eighteenth century, he describes that of Simeon Draper:

Near the southern border of Vermont a little brook leaps and races down the hills to an intervale, through which it creeps in devious windings to a tributary of the

Connecticut. One unacquainted with the industries of the pioneer settlers might be puzzled to account for the origin of its name, Potash Brook, which it has borne since the first settler here gathered the ashes of the fallow burnings and turned them to account in the manufacture of a marketable commodity.

One hundred and fifty years have passed since Simeon Draper made a clearing and built a rude potashery on the bank of the brook, half a mile up the larger stream from his home. It consisted of a rough stone chimney and fireplace, in which a great potash kettle was set sheltered by a bark-roofed shed that was inclosed with logs on three sides. Near this and close by the brook, for the sake of the necessary water, three leach tubs, sawn from large hallow elms, stood on a slanting platform of hewn plank or puncheons, from which the lye dripped into a great log trough, and near by was the important ash bin, carefully roofed.[19]

Another gathering where work was done, games played, stories exchanged, and refreshments served was the raising bee. In "Glimpses of New England Farm Life" Robinson says when building a barn as soon as the carpenter gets the frame ready for setting up, the farmer invites all of his neighbors to a raising bee, which, writing in 1878, Robinson points out is "one of the few 'bees' remaining of those so common and frequent in the earlier days of interdependence." Robinson's intimate knowledge of this folk gathering was put to good use in a chapter in *Danvis Folks.* In this chapter Sam Lovel, Sam's father, and Uncle Lisha attend the raising of Jonathan Young's new barn, and Robinson mentions the tools, techniques, and atmosphere of the raising bee. Here, as in his essay "Glimpses of New England Farm Life," he tells how the men too old to participate in the actual raising sit around gossiping and criticizing, while the boys too young to participate in the actual raising romp around playing ball and wrestling. Robinson shows how those actively participating in the raising of the barn lift the heavy frame and swap jokes:

"Naow then, men," the carpenter shouted in an authoritative voice, "come right this way," and there was a general movement toward the place indicated.

"Take a holt o' this 'ere bent."

The men swarmed upon the sills and sleepers and laid hold of the section of frame.

"Be ye ready? Then up with it. All together. Hang tu the foot o' them pos's, you men wi' the crowbars. Up she goes."

The parallelogram of heavy timbers rose at first almost with a jerk, then more slowly, as it was reared beyond the reach of some.

"Put in your pike-poles there," cried the carpenter, and those being set and manned, it started upward again more rapidly, then more slowly as it reached the perpendicular. The carpenter was off one side squinting at it.

"Up with her, more! Don't be afeared. Put in some pike-poles t' other side. Up a leetle more. There, whoa up. All right. She's up an' daown as a clever cat's tail. Naow, stay lath it."

The bent was temporarily fastened in place with boards nailed diagonally upon it and the sills, and so in turn the others were raised and the girts entered and pinned. Then the long plates were uplifted by strong hands and pike-poles and shoved along the beams, to which the surest-footed of the company mounted and raised them to their place on top of the posts and fastened them.

All the while a running fire of jokes was kept up, not a few of which were directed against the carpenter, whose orders nevertheless were implicitly obeyed.[20]

Another collectively performed task at which the Danvis folk amuse themselves with jokes and refreshments while performing an otherwise tedious job is the drawing bee, which Robinson describes in "Glimpses of New England Farm Life":

One kind of "bee," as these gatherings for mutual help are called, which has only lately gone out with the oxen who were the chief actors in it, was the "drawing bee." A farmer, having cause to change the site of a barn or other structure, would, with the carpenter's help, usually in early spring but sometimes in the fall, get runners under his building. These were long timbers of something more than the building's length, cut with an upward slope at the forward end. Having properly braced the inside of his barn, to withstand the rack of transportation, all his oxen-owing [sic] neighbors were bidden to his aid. The yokes of oxen were hitched in two "strings," one to each runner, and, all being ready, were started off at the word of command, amid a clamor of "whoahush!" "whoahaw!" and "gee!" addressed to the Bucks, Broads, Stars, Brindles and Brights, who were the motive power, the creaking of the racked frame and the shrill shouts of the boys, without whose presence nothing of such moment ever is, if it ever could be, done.

The barn being safely set in its new place, the bee ended in feasting and jollification. Now that oxen have become so scarce, it would need the mustering of a whole county to provide the necessary force . . .[21]

In a chapter of *Danvis Folks* entitled "The Drawing Bee," Robinson tells of Uncle Lisha's participation in a drawing bee that was held on a spring day. After the barn is moved, the oxen are first unyoked from each of the two lines attached to the large wooden runners under the sills of the barn, and then they are given rations of hay. Once the animals are fed, the participants are served yellow gingerbread, twisted doughnuts, cheese, and a large pail of cider. Finally, as the company begins to disperse, the workers are told, "Ef any one hes bruck his chains, he c'n leave 'em at Dan'l Ackley's blacksmith's shop an' I'll foot the bill."[22]

Although Robinson's account of haying in Vermont is not as detailed as the modern student of folklife would like it to be, considerable information about haymaking can be found in "Glimpses of New England Farm Life" and in the last chapter of *A Danvis Pioneer*. Robinson mentions the season for cutting hay, the pattern of cutting the field, the tools and machines used, some of the terms used in haying, some of the associated customs, the food and drink of the mowers, the making of cocks and ricks, the places where meals were taken, storms during haymaking, hayfield pests, methods of drawing the hay from the meadow, the use of carts by earlier farmers, shaking out the hay, and the discovery of honey in the meadow.[23] Robinson's account of haying in "Glimpses of New England Farm Life" is worth quoting at length, for he tells the occasions on which folksongs were sung and folktales told. The itinerant Canucks who helped with the haying swung "their scythes in unison to some old song sung centuries ago in France"[24] to make their work easier; when the rain interrupted haying the men lounged in the village store or in the barn and swapped jokes:

About the Fourth of July haying begins. The rank growth about the barns is hand-mowed, and the mowing-machine is trundled out from its rusting idleness, and, being tinkered into readiness, goes jingling and clattering afield, where, having fairly got at its work, it gnaws down with untiring tooth its eight or ten acres a day. The incessant unmodulated "chirr" of this modern innovator has almost banished the ancient music of the whetted scythe, a sound that for centuries had been as much a part of hay-making as the fragrance of the new-mown hay. But its musical voice cannot save it. The old scythe must go, and we cannot deny that the noisy usurper is a blessing to us all in lightening labor, and, not least among us, to the boy, for whom I cherish a kindly feeling, and for any softening of whose lot I am thankful.

In the days before mowing-machines, hordes of Canadian French swarmed over the borders to work in haying, in crews of two or three, jiggling southward in their rude carts, drawn by tough, shaggy little ponies. They were doughty workmen in the field and at the table; merry-hearted and honest fellows, too; for, when they departed, they seldom took, beside their wages, more than a farming tool or two, or the sheets from their beds, doubtless as mementos of their sojourn in the States. But the Batistes, and Antoines, and innumerable Joes and Pierres bide on their own arpents now all the summer through and come to us no more. If we miss them, with their baggy trowsers and gay sashes, the shuffle of their moccasined feet and their sonorous songs that had always a touch of pathos in them, we do not mourn for them.

As the cut grass dries under the downright beams of the summer sun and becomes ready for the raking, the windrows (always "winrows," here) lengthen along the shaven sward as the horse-rake goes back and forth across the meadow, and the workmen following with forks soon dot the fields with cocks, if the hay is to wait to-morrow's drawing, or with less careful tumbles if it goes to barn or stack today.

Now the wagon comes surmounted by its rattling "hay-riggin'," with the legs of the pitcher and the unfortunate who "mows away" and "rakes after," dangling over its side, and the man who loads, the captain, pilot and stevedore of this craft, standing forward driving his horses, for the oxen and cart, too slow for these hurrying times, have lumbered into the past. The stalwart pitcher upheaves the great forkfuls, skillfully bestowed by the loader, till they have grown into a load which moves off with ponderous statelines across the meadow to the stack or barn. Seen from astern as it sways and heaves along its way, one might fancy it an enormous elephant with a Yankee mahout on its back.

In the middle of the long afternoon is luncheon-time, when all hands gather in the shade of tree or barn and fortify themselves with gingerbread and cheese. Showers interrupt, foreshadowed by pearly mountains of "thunder-heads" that uplift themselves above the more material mountains of earth which are soon veiled with the blue-black film of the coming rain, when there is bustle in the hay-field, rapid making of cocks that are no sooner made than blown over by the rain-gust, and drivers shouting to their teams hurrying to shelter with loads. And days arrive when morning till night the rain comes steadily down, stopping all out-door work. Then some go a-fishing or to lounge in the village store, or perhaps all gather in the barn to chat and joke and doze away the dull hours on the fragrant hay. Some harvesting intervenes and the cradles swing in the fields of rye and wheat with graceful sweep and musical ring. The binders follow and soon the yellow shocks are ranked along the field whence they go duly to the barn.[25]

Robinson incorporates more of his intimate knowledge of haying in *A Danvis Pioneer*. During the middle of July haymaking in Danvis is well under way, and Joseph Hill has hired a boy, Pelatiah Gove, and a Canuck, Antoine Bassette, to help him with the mowing. While Pelatiah and Antoine cut the hay in a "lessening parallelogram," however, Joseph "preferred to 'carry his swaths,' which gave his back long intervals of rest from bending, and afforded opportunities of sweetening toil with scraps of conversation when a neighbor passed along the highway."[26] Such a neighbor who stops to chat with Joseph Hill is Mrs. Purington, who, although characteristically negative, no doubt expresses something of the woman's attitude toward haying in telling Joseph, "So you're a a-hayin' of it, be ye? . . . Wal, he is tew. Ho, hum, sussy day! I allers du dread hayin' dretf'l, it does make sech a lot o' work for the women folks; men folks does eat so, an' so many on 'em!"[27] In addition, Joseph occasionally refreshes himself with a draught of switchel from his wooden canteen. "This once popular but now obsolete summer drink of temperate haymakers was compounded of molasses and water, with a dash of vinegar and a spice of ginger, and was supposed to be less hurtful than water to heated men."[28] Finally, in Robinson's treatment of haying one sees the attitude of the village folk toward change. For although the mowing in *A Danvis Pioneer* is done by hand with scythes, Joseph does have a "new-fangled, half-distrusted revolving horse rake, just from Morrison's shop . . . with its double rows of wooden teeth." The sight of the rake, however, "brought no thrill of proud possession" to Joseph, "but rather a twinge of remorse for having bought it against the will of his father, who spurned it as a 'consarned flipperty-flop, rattle-trap, Tory thingum-a-jig, with teeth a-p'intin' both ways.' "[29] Another popular gathering where communal labor was performed and folklore propagated was the husking bee, held as soon as the corn was ripe. Robinson says that every Danvis farm had its husking bee in the October evenings. Although the young and old of both sexes attended the huskings, these gatherings of "industrial merrymaking" were especially favored by young people and matchmaking mothers.[30] When Robinson writes of the husking bee in "Glimpses of New England Farm Life," he refers to a widespread folk belief that finding a red ear of corn is lucky, the usual reward being a kiss.

If the husking bee were held in the open field and lighted by a great bonfire, the shocks were arranged around the fire like a circle of wigwams. If the bee were held in a barn, the uncertain rays of the lanterns of punched tin, the deep shadows, and the constant rustle of corn husks and leaves "were great aids to the bashful wooers."[31] After the husking was completed the participants were fed the traditional feast of pumpkin pie, doughnuts, and cider. Then, if the husking were held in a barn, the floor was cleared and "the fiddler mounted the scaffold and made the gloom of the roof-peak ring with merry strains, to which twoscore solidly clad feet threshed out time in 'country dance' and 'French four'."[32]

Another popular gathering was the paring bee held in the long evenings of late autumn and early winter. In "The Path of Boatless Generations"[33] and "Glimpses of New England Farm Life," Robinson provides information about the paring bee:

About apple-picking time, and for a month after, "apple cuts," or "paring bees" used to be frequent, when all the young folks of a neighborhood were invited, never slighting the skilled parer with his machine. After some bushels of apples were peeled, quartered, cored and strung for drying, the kitchen was cleared of its rubbish of cores and skins, and after a feast of "nut-cakes," pumpkin pies and cider, the plays began to the tunes of "Come, Philander, le's be marchin'," "The needles's eye that doth supply the thread that runs so true," and "We're marchin' onwards toward Quebec where the drums are loudly beatin'," or the fiddle or "Lisha's" song of "Tol-liddle, tol-liddle, tol-loday, do-day-hum, tolli-day" set all feet to jigging "Twin Sisters," or "French four." These jolly gatherings, though by many years outliving the old-fashioned husking bee, have at last fallen into disuse and their hearty New England flavor is poorly supplied by the insipid sociables and abominable parties that are now in vogue.[34]

In *A Danvis Pioneer*, Robinson writes that "When the young orchards came into bearing, paring-bees became as common and as popular entertainments,—a way of making work light with many hands."[35] In *Danvis Folks*, he devotes an entire chapter to these bees. Here Huldah Lovel's apples get "turrible meller" and "wa'n't a-goin' tu keep no gret spell," so she decides to have a paring bee in order to "get the apples worked off an' the young folks 'd have a good time." Huldah and Aunt Jerusha spend a whole day frying doughnuts, baking pumpkin pies, and cleaning the house. Meanwhile, the invitations are sent, "not on perfumed paper, but by hearty word of mouth."[36] On the evening of the bee, after the guests arrive, pans and knives are supplied, bushels of apples are carried in, chairs are pulled up into groups, and the actual paring begins.

The gossiping, the chat, and the paring continued until six bushels of apples "were on the strings and ready to festoon the kitchen walls and poles that hung from hooks in the ceiling, and the welcome announcement was made that the labor of the evening was over."[37] Before the floor is cleared of the scattered apple skins and cores, though, a dozen girls try "for their lover's initials with apple parings whirled thrice above their heads and cast over the right shoulder to the floor behind them."[38] After the girls' lovers have been portended by the performance of this widespread folk practice, the floor is cleaned of "the thickest o' this mess," and doughnuts, pies, cheeses, and cider are served:

Then the young people engaged in romping games, the Needle's Eye, wherein every one who could or could not sing, sang, or tried to, at the top of their voices:

> "The needle's eye, that doth soffy
> The thread that runs so treue,
> It has caught many a smiling lass
> And naow it has caught yeou!"

or with a volume and zest that would have pleased Gran'ther Hill more than the melody, "We're marching onward tow-ard Quebec." In every game the forfeits were invariably kisses, given and paid in the simplest and most direct manner, or when so decreed, in the contortions of a "double and twisted Loddy massy." The movements of another popular game were timed to the words of "Come, Philander, le' 's be a-marchin'." The elders looked on in amused toleration, while a few joined the young folks' games only to be reminded, by grudgingly paid forfeits, that the freshness of youth had departed from their wrinkled cheeks.[39]

Finally, Uncle Lisha announces that "you young folks orter be abaout cl'yed wi' bussin' an' we ol' folks has eat saour grapes long 'nough, so le' 's all turn tu an' hev a leetle sensible enj'yment a dancin'. Where's that aire leetle fiddler?" The fiddler not being present, Uncle Lisha is obligated to sing the following song (for which Robinson also gives the music):

> "Turn yer pardener half way raound.
> Lum tiddle, lum tiddle, t'l law day,
> Half way raound, half way raound, do day hum,
> t'l law day."

While Uncle Lisha sings in "stentorian tones," Antoine plays an imaginary fiddle and chimes in with, "Turn yo' pahdny wrong side aout." During a lull in Lisha's singing, though, "the company became aware of the notes of a fiddle, whence coming no one could conjecture, faintly yet distinctly playing the familiar air of 'Money Musk'." Suggesting that at least some of the Danvis folk believe in revenants, Robinson writes that everyone at the paring bee listens to the music, "some puzzled and some breathless, and some superstitiously alarmed." One of those inclined to be superstitious is Solon Briggs, who "oracularly voiced the prevailing feeling, in a solemn, awe-stricken tone." Solon asserts, "That fiddle hain't performed by no livin' han's. Watson Parmer has pairished, mis'rable, in the element of the snow, and his speerit has come to fulfill his 'pintment made to Samule. It's Watson Parmer's indivisible apperagotion."[40] Thus, Robinson's account of the paring bee in *Danvis Folks* is not only a good account of a folk custom, but it is also a good illustration of the milieu of traditional songs, games, beliefs, dance, and proverbs.

Another important function in early American folklife was the quilting bee, where pieces of cloth from the participants' scrapbags were interchanged and gossip was exchanged; thus, both economic and social needs were served. In America quiltmaking has been practiced for the longest continuous period of any of the decorative domestic folk crafts, and in some parts of the United States, including Vermont, quiltmaking is still the most widely practiced of the home handicrafts. Since quilting and the quilting bee have been and still are such important parts of folklife, no account of village folklore would be complete without mention of them. In his nearly complete account of Vermont folklife, Robinson discusses quiltmaking. In *Vermont*, he reports that the quilting party in its first laborious stage was attended only by women; however, in the final stages it became a merry gathering when the men joined the party "to assist in the ceremony of 'shaking the quilt,' and in the performance of this the fiddler was as necessary as in the closing rites of the husking-bee."[41] Robinson incorporates this material in his fiction, too, when in *Danvis Folks* he reports, "Quiltings were more the affairs of matrons and maids, but the men were in demand when the 'quilt was shaken,' and dancing was in order."[42]

In a few places Robinson refers to the products of the quiltings, the quilts themselves. In "A September Election," he writes that the Pipers have a "gay patchwork quilt" on the bed in their spare bedroom,[43] and in Uncle Lisha's Shop he mentions that Aunt Jerusha Peggs has a "decorous patchwork couch," quilting often being used for upholstering, too.[45] More specific, however, is Mrs. Purington's remark in *Uncle Lisha's Shop* that Mrs. Solon Briggs has "got a new quilt in the frames . . . sunflower patch-work it is."[46] This information about the quilt pattern suggests that although Robinson writes but briefly about the feminine activities of Danvis, when he does write about the household crafts he reports accurately. For as Ruth E. Finley points out in *Old Patchwork Quilts*, "Until the Pioneer period, when New Englander, Pennslyvanian and Southerner met in the settling of the West, quilts had characteristics so local that they could be classified geographically almost as easily as the Yankee twang, the Southern drawl, or the inverted sentence formations of Berks and Lancaster Counties in Pennsylvania."[47] According to Finley, the "Sunflower" patchwork quilt that Robinson refers to was one of several New England traditional quilt patterns noted for originality in pictorial design, although the "Sunflower" pattern also has been reported in North Carolina.[48]

Another important occasion for the performance of folklore in early Vermont was the shearing. In his essay "Merinos in America," Robinson reports that in June of each year the sheep were herded by farm hands, women, and children from pastures to pens beside pools, in which the sheep were washed. About two weeks later, one of the biggest events in the farmer's year came: the shearing.[49] "Shearing-time," Robinson writes in *Vermont*, "was the great festival of the year. . . . The great barn's empty bays and scaffolds resounded with the busy click of incessant shears, the jokes, songs, and laughter of the merry shearers . . ."[50] In both barn and house great preparation was made. In the house the table was furnished with the best food the farmer could afford, for the shearers were not ordinary farm laborers; they were generally farmers who were every bit as prosperous as their employer, who was most likely to take his turn shearing for other village farmers. In fact, almost every farmer who could shear did so at the village shearings. Consequently, the fatted calf was butchered, and the strawberries and green peas picked. The barn door and overhanging scaffolds were carefully swept, and the stables were littered with clean straw. The woolbench was set up, and the reel of twine was put in its place. Of the shearing as an occasion for telling stories and playing games, Robinson states in "Merinos in America":

. . . Those were merry days in the old gray barns that were not too fine to have swallows' holes in their gables, moss on their shingles, and a fringe of hemp, may-weed, and smartweed about their jagged underpinning. There was jesting and the telling of merry tales from morning till night, and bursts of laughter that scared the swallows out of the cobwebbed roofpeak and the sitting hen from her nest in the left-over hay-mow. Neighbors called to get a taste of the fun and the cider, to see how the flock "evridged," and to engage hands for their own shearing. At nooning, after the grand dinner, while the older men napped on the floor, woolbench, or scaffold, with their heads pillowed on soft places, the young fellows had trials of strength at "pulling stick" or lifting "stiff legs." The skillful wool-tyer was rarer than the skillful shearer, and in much demand in his own and neighboring townships. . . .[51]

NOTES

[1] Robinson, *Uncle Lisha's Outing and Along Three Rivers*, p. 197.

[2] Robinson, *Uncle Lisha's Outing and Along Three Rivers*, pp. 205-206.

[3] Robinson, *Uncle Lisha's Outing and Along Three Rivers*, p. 257.

[4] Robinson, *Uncle Lisha's Shop and A Danvis Pioneer*, p. 135.

[5] Robinson, *Uncle Lisha's Shop and A Danvis Pioneer*, p. 135.

[6] Robinson, *Uncle Lisha's Outing and Along Three Rivers*, p. 257.

[7] Robinson, *Uncle Lisha's Outing and Along Three Rivers*, p. 225.

[8] Robinson, *Uncle Lisha's Shop and A Danvis Pioneer*, p. 45.

[9] Robinson, *Uncle Lisha's Shop and A Danvis Pioneer*, p. 46.

[10] Robinson, *Danvis Folks and A Hero of Ticonderoga*, p. 54.

[11] Robinson, *Uncle Lisha's Outing and Along Three Rivers*, pp. 257-258.

[12] Robinson, *Danvis Folks and A Hero of Ticonderoga*, p. 157.

[13] Robinson, *Uncle Lisha's Outing and Along Three Rivers*, p. 257.

[14] "Glimpses of New England Farm Life," p. 524.

[15] Robinson, *Uncle Lisha's Shop and A Danvis Pioneer*, p. 96.

[16] Robinson, *Uncle Lisha's Shop and A Danvis Pioneer*, p. 36.

[17] Robinson, *Danvis Folks and A Hero of Ticonderoga*, p. 261.

[18] Robinson, *Uncle Lisha's Outing and Along Three Rivers*, p. 239.

[19] Robinson, *Out of Bondage and Other Stories*, pp. 96-97.

[20] Robinson, *Danvis Folks and A Hero of Ticonderoga*, pp. 159-160.

[21] Robinson, "Glimpses of New England Farm Life," p. 524.

[22] Robinson, *Danvis Folks and A Hero of Ticonderoga*, p. 152.

[23] O'Sullivan, pp. 56-57.   [24] Robinson, *Vermont*, p. 329.

[25] Robinson, "Glimpses of New England Farm Life," pp. 525-526.

[26] Robinson, *Uncle Lisha's Shop and A Danvis Pioneer*, p. 99.

[27] Robinson, *Uncle Lisha's Shop and A Danvis Pioneer*, p. 102.

[28] Robinson, *Uncle Lisha's Shop and A Danvis Pioneer*, p. 101. See Muriel Joy Hughes, "A Word-List from Vermont," *Vermont History*, XXVII (April, 1959), 162.

[29] Robinson, *Uncle Lisha's Shop and A Danvis Pioneer*, p. 105.

[30] Robinson, *Uncle Lisha's Shop and A Danvis Pioneer*, p. 97.

[31] Robinson, *Uncle Lisha's Shop and A Danvis Pioneer*, p. 97.

[32] Robinson, *Vermont*, p. 294.

[33] Robinson, *In New England Fields and Woods*, p. 165.

[34] Robinson, "Glimpses of New England Farm Life," p. 527. The songs mentioned by Robinson are discussed in Chapter 16 of the present work.

[35] Robinson, *Uncle Lisha's Shop and A Danvis Pioneer*, p. 97.

[36] Robinson, *Danvis Folks and A Hero of Ticonderoga*, pp. 85, 86.

[37] Robinson, *Danvis Folks and A Hero of Ticonderoga*, p. 89.

[38] Robinson, *Danvis Folks and A Hero of Ticonderoga*, p. 90. For an annotated variant of this traditional belief see *The Frank C. Brown Collection*, VI, 627, No. 4597.

[39] Robinson, *Danvis Folks and A Hero of Ticonderoga,* pp. 90-91. See Chapter 16 of the present work for a discussion of the singing games in Robinson's writings.

[40] This is Motif E342, "Dead return to fulfill bargain."

[41] Robinson, *Vermont,* pp. 294-295.

[42] Robinson, *Uncle Lisha's Shop and A Danvis Pioneer,* p. 97.

[43] Robinson, *Sam Lovel's Boy with Forest and Stream Fables,* p. 163.

[44] Robinson, *Uncle Lisha's Shop and A Danvis Pioneer,* p. 163.

[45] Eaton, p. 201.   [46] *Uncle Lisha's Shop and A Danvis Pioneer,* p. 180.

[47] Ruth E. Finley, *Old Patchwork Quilts* (Philadelphia, 1929), p. 39.

[48] *The Frank C. Brown Collection,* I, 266.

[49] Rowland E. Robinson, "Merinos in America," *The Century Magazine,* XXVII (February, 1884), 517.

[50] Robinson, *Vermont,* p. 298.   [51] "Merinos in America," pp. 518-519.

CHAPTER 7

CALENDAR CUSTOMS AND THE PERFORMANCE OF FOLKLORE

In addition to the bees, Robinson describes a number of calendar customs when farm chores are interrupted and celebrating and storytelling are in order. Some of these customs, such as road mending, must be worked into the busy agricultural cycle and, like the bees, combine work with pleasure. Of road mending Robinson writes in "Glimpses of New England Farm Life":

During the "breathing spell" which comes between the finishing of spring's and the beginning of summer's work on the farm, the path-master warns out the farmers to the performance of the farce termed by stretch of courtesy, road mending, which is played regularly twice a year, when all hands turn out with teams, plows, scrapers and wagons, spades, shovels and hoes and make good roads bad and bad roads worse. It is fortunate for those who travel much upon the highways that these road menders do so little, playing at work for a short time, then stopping, leaning on plow handle or spade to hold grave consultation concerning the ways of doing some part of their task, or gathering about the water-jug in the shade of a way-side tree, and spending an unconscionable time in quenching their thirst and lighting their pipes and joking or discussing some matter of neighborhood gossip.[1]

Another festive day was the second Tuesday in March, when the annual town meeting, or March meeting, was held. Such a town meeting Robinson depicts in a short story, "An Old-Time March Meeting." Typical of his interest in accurately recording actual details of village life, for the notice of the approaching town meeting in Danvis, Robinson copies an actual notice of an early Ferrisburg town meeting.[2] Although the Danvis warning was posted on the town house about two weeks in advance of the March meeting, long before, the Danvis folk had been anxiously awaiting the meeting and were discussing the proposed measures. At last the day came, and the majority of the males arrived at the town house on foot or in wagons. Anticipation of and attendance at the town meeting, as Robinson depicts it, were not simply due to the election of town officials and transaction of town business, but because it was a day of diversion. While the boys played ball and the women visited, the men during interludes of town business refreshed themselves and told stories, jokes, and beliefs. For example, Robinson writes:

. . . Old acquaintances from the farthest opposite corners of the township, who rarely met but on such occasions, exchanged greetings and neighborhood gossip. Hunters and trappers recounted their exploits to one another and an interested audience of boys. Invalids enjoyed their poor health to the utmost in the relation of its minutest details. Pairs of rough jokers were the centres of applauding groups, while other pairs exchanged experiences in the wintering of stock or discussed weather probabilities. From all arose a babble of voices, the silentest persons present being two or three of the town's poor, who had come to get the earliest intelligence of their disposal.[3]

Another annual occasion was June training, or militia training, held on the first Tuesday in June. Although the day was supposedly set aside for military drill for all the male villagers but those exempt by age, religion, or occupation, June training was, in fact, more of a holiday than a serious military training. As Sam Lovel asserts, "I'll stay tu hum an' pay my fine afore I'll jine sech foolin' ag'in. It gits wus an' wus every year, a pomponadin' back an' tu like a passel o' sheep, every man duin' jest as he's a mind tu, an' larnin' nothin'. I'd ruther stay tu hum an' du nothin' er work in Huldy's posy bed."[4] At any rate, some of the men, some of the women, and most of the boys in Danvis found June training a welcome relief from the routine of farm chores.

The day of militia training was started "according to established usage, by the ceremony of 'wakin' up officers'." At this ceremony a party of younger men went from the home of one officer to another firing volleys of musketry, first awakening the captain, who greeted his men with a brown jug of liquor to be passed around, and next awakening the lieutenants. Then the militiamen arrived in the village and met on the steps of the local tavern or store. Attempts were made to march and practice the manual of arms with weapons, clubs, and broomsticks, but occasionally some of the militiamen "dashed out of the ranks and into the barroom and presently reappeared wiping their lips, to leisurely resume their places without reprimand." Throughout the day the militiamen spent as much time in the tavern drinking or at the peddler's wagon drinking spruce beer and eating gingerbread as they did at drilling. Stories and jokes were, of course, exchanged at these gatherings. At lunch, for example, the old veterans, such as Gran'ther Hill and Uncle Lisha, told stories of the days when they were soldiers. Moreover, "The larger number of the militiamen having providently brought their rations in pockets, tin pails, and baskets, gathered in picnicking groups at centres most convenient for the irrigation of their dry fare, some squatting on the platforms of pumps and well-curbs, where the gulping crescendo of the one and the splash and bump of the other's bucket often interrupted or overbore the flow of joke and repartee."[5] Since the June trainings were still being held during Robinson's life and since he remembered observing them as a boy, the material in the chapter "June Training" in *Danvis Folks* came from firsthand knowledge. He reports in *Along Three Rivers*:

. . . Where this road strikes the stage road was George Pease's tavern, a house of excellent repute, where the stagecoach halted for a relay of horses. Here militia trainings were sometimes held. . . .

For some years after Pease, Calvin Martin was landlord, who sustained the reputation of the house. My memory goes no further back than this time, when I remember June training there and dancing that a Quaker boy was not permitted to see, and the arrival of the stagecoach and its departure with fresh horses, with the driver and Dan Field, on the box, whistling loud and clear as a fife.[6]

Again farm chores were gladly interrupted on the first Tuesday of September, the day of the annual election of justices and judges, state officers and members of Congress. In "A September Election," Robinson writes that on election day in Danvis, "Farm houses that were astir with their own busy life every other day of the year were tenantless to-day, and the henhawk wheeled low above them, making leisurely selection of the fattest pullets. Fields were so free of human presence that at midday the fox ventured boldly beyond where the wild sunflower shone in the dusky woodside."[7] Robinson points out that election day in Vermont in the early part of the nineteenth century "had then other than political excitement to enliven the day."[8] During the balloting there were feats of strength, such as stick pulling and wrestling matches; there was the swapping of tales, jokes, and gossip; and, there was the inevitable dispensing of refreshments—pies, cakes, crackers, cheese, spruce beer—from stands or booths. The atmosphere of such an election Robinson depicts in "A September Election":

Two hours before noon the dreary old townhouse and its precincts swarmed with the male inhabitants of Danvis. For the most part, the elderly, middle-aged, and staid men, and the town officers, were gathered inside the bare walls, while the younger men and boys chose the more cheerful outdoor atmosphere, some lounging upon the grass in shade and sunshine, some in groups discussing the chances of the candidates, or watching the contest of a pair of wrestlers or stick-pullers. One great centre of attraction was a booth of boards built against the side of the townhouse, where, for sale, were home-made cakes and pies, and cookies, crackers and cheese, highly colored with annatto, popularly known as "otter." There, too, were some jars of candy, in sticks striped like a barber pole, and balls similarly decorated, and cigars, at a cent apiece. The purchaser of one was fortunate if it would draw—or, considering the flavor, quite as much so if it did not. There was a box of dry, sugary raisins, a drum of ancient figs, and a basket of puckery pears, and for those who thirsted for milder potations than Hamner's bar offered, there were bottles of mead and a cask of home-brewed spruce beer. The proprietor was kept busy with a brisk trade, which increased as noon approached and the far-comers grew hungry.

"Hain't got no drawin' plasters ter sell, hev ye, Joshaway?" John Dart asked when struggling with a warped cigar. "No? Wal, you'd ort tu; I want one tu put ont' the back o' my neck to draw the smoke through this 'ere seegar."

The ancient joke was honored with a salute of laughter not at all relished by Joshua, who declared, "That's baout as good a box o' cigars as ever I hed—'most every one on 'em ill go."

"Wal, this one hain't no exception," said John Dart; "it goes aout every time. Lord, it'll ruin me a-buyin' matches for it. Gi' me a hunk o' that 'ere pink-eye cheese an' a han'ful o' crackers, an' I'll save this seegar till I git where the's a stiddy fire."[9]

Balloting over and the votes counted, the diversions of election day, including storytelling, were interrupted when the constable announced the results. Upon hearing the constable's voice, "The whittlers hastily shut and pocketed their knives, the loungers in the grass scrambled to their feet, the story-teller left his tale unfinished, and all made haste to get within closer range of the speaker's voice."[10] When the results were heard, Robinson reports in *Vermont,* the winning candidate for representative purchased what remained of the huckster's stock in order to treat his friends.[11] Accordingly, Levi Piper, the successful candidate for representative in "A September Election," "managed to thank his friends in a few stammering words, and then to deliver to their free raiding all things eatable and drinkable that the huckster's booth still held, for such was the custom of those times, and one which gave quite as much satisfaction to all concerned, especially to the successful candidate, as does the modern reception."[12]

A seasonal gathering of village sharpshooters where tales were told and songs were sung was the turkey shoot. In "The Turkey Shoot at Hamner's," a chapter in *Uncle Lisha's Shop,* the event is sponsored by the local taverner, Hamner, just before Thanksgiving. In a short story, "How Elijah was Fed at Christmas," the turkey shoot is sponsored by another taverner, Fay, just before Christmas. At these contests, for "ninepence" a shot, the Nimrod who could hit a turkey placed on a box at forty yards could take the bird home for his holiday dinner. At the turkey shoots at Hamner's hostelry almost every man in Danvis attended, some to shoot turkeys, others to talk. Among the Danvis folk who did not attend Hamner's turkey shoot were those who found more pleasure in hunting game than in merely shooting turkeys on a box, such as Sam Lovel, who called the turkey shooters "a pack o' dum'd fools," and those who were Quakers, such as Joel Bartlett, who said that the turkey shoot was "a snare of the evil one, an' a-nother pitfall digged for the feet of the onwary! These men a-shootin' at innocent faowls of the air, is a-follerin' of a custom, an' a practyse, an' a observance o' them 'at hung Mary Dyer, an' grievously pussecuted many formerly."[13] But almost all of the other Danvis males with ideals not so lofty as Sam Lovel's and Joel Bartlett's attended Hamner's turkey shoot to drink Hamner's liquor, to shoot his turkeys, and to devour his refreshments. Throughout the day, tales were told and songs sung. Robinson writes that some of the older mountaineers came "to criticize the younger shooters and tell marvellous tales of what they could do and had done in bygone years."[14] Gran'ther Hill criticizes the caplocks and flintlocks, relates his adventures "tu Hubbar't'n with Ethan Allen, Seth Warner, Remember Baker, John Stark, and Benedict Arnold, whom he calls "the damned traitor." He then sings "in a voice half croak and half whistle, to a small but appreciative audience," a traditional song, "Marching to Quebec."[15] The Danvis turkey shoot reminds Antoine of a turkey shoot he attended in Canada, where the turkeys were not placed on a box but were hidden behind a hill. In this tall tale, however, Antoine shoots over the top of the hill at the turkey's gobble and hits the bird "raght bit tween hees backs!"[16]

Robinson does not say much about other holidays, but he does refer to the "glories of the Fourth of July at Vergennes" in *Sam Lovel's Boy*,[17] and in an essay, "In Search of Nothing," he writes that churches are decorated with arbutus at Easter. Speaking of the arbutus, he says, "Every one who cares for it knows where it grows now, and people come in troops to rob the woods of it for the decoration of churches at Easter. They might better leave it in these first temples."[18] Thanksgiving and Christmas, of course, are days of family reunions and feasting in Robinson's stories, and naturally when members of a family visit on these holidays gossip and stories are exchanged. For instance, in a short story, "Uncle Gid's Christmas Tree," Uncle Gid and Aunt Milly Corbin invite their daughter Nancy and her husband Nathan for Christmas dinner. After the guests arrive, Aunt Milly and Nancy talk mainly of marriages, births, and deaths, while Uncle Gid tells Nathan tales of the chase and Nathan relates a few fishing stories.[19]

In Robinson's fiction a custom even stronger than the annual festivities is that of washing the family's clothing each Monday. As Harold W. Thompson suggests, among the folk a woman is considered a thrifty housewife only if she washes clothes on Monday.[20] The importance of complying with this custom is emphasized in the following traditional rhyme:

> If you wash on Monday,
> You have all week to dry.
> If you wash on Tuesday,
> You are not so much aware.
> If you wash on Wednesday,
> You wash for shame.

If you wash on Thursday,
You are not so much to blame.
If you wash on Friday,
You wash for need.
If you wash on Saturday,
O, you are sluts indeed.[21]

Washing on Monday is such a regular event in the lives of the Danvis folk that in their calculating a week's time the days are counted from wash day. In Robinson's short story "A Housewife's Calendar," Betsey Blake's wash boiler springs a leak on Monday while she is boiling water for her washing, and she is forced to postpone her weekly washing until her boiler is repaired the following day. When wash day is delayed until Tuesday, a second Monday is added to the Blake's calendar, and the Blakes nearly miss their Thanksgiving dinner. It is nearly noon on Thanksgiving Day when John Blake learns from a friend that his calendar has been upset. When John discovers the error, he exclaims, "Good gracious Peter! If Betsey an' me hain't done it! . . . . Most noon Thanksgivin' Day, Betsey's father an' mother an' sister a-comin', an' the turkey a-hangin' up in the cellar if she's kep' a-dreamin' as long as I have. It all come o' that plaguey ol' wash b'iler springin' a leak Monday, so she could n't wash till Tuesday, an' we counted from that."[22]

NOTES

[1]Robinson, "Glimpses of New England Farm Life," p. 523.

[2]Robinson, *Sam Lovel's Boy with Forest and Stream Fables*, p. 144.

[3]Robinson, *Sam Lovel's Boy with Forest and Stream Fables*, p. 146.

[4]Robinson, *Danvis Folks and A Hero of Ticonderoga*, p. 181.

[5]Robinson, *Danvis Folks and A Hero of Ticonderoga*, pp. 174, 177-178.

[6]Robinson, *Uncle Lisha's Outing and Along Three Rivers*, p. 226.

[7]Robinson, *Sam Lovel's Boy with Forest and Stream Fables*, pp. 166-167.

[8]Robinson, *Vermont*, p. 301.

[9]Robinson, *Sam Lovel's Boy with Forest and Stream Fables*, pp. 167-168.

[10]Robinson, *Sam Lovel's Boy with Forest and Stream Fables*, p. 171.

[11]Robinson, *Vermont*, p. 301.

[12]Robinson, *Sam Lovel's Boy with Forest and Stream Fables*, p. 171.

[13]Robinson, *Uncle Lisha's Shop and A Danvis Pioneer*, p. 168. For an account of the legend of Mary Dyer see Samuel Adams Drake, *New England Legends and Folk-Lore* (Boston, 1901), pp. 36-46.

[14]Robinson, *Uncle Lisha's Shop and A Danvis Pioneer*, p. 160.

[15]Robinson, *Uncle Lisha's Shop and A Danvis Pioneer*, p. 167. For annotated variants of "Marching to Quebec" see *The Frank C. Brown Collection*, I, 118.

[16]Robinson, *Uncle Lisha's Shop and A Danvis Pioneer*, p. 167. Antoine's tale is Motif X1122.4* (f), "Hunter shoots over top of hill at turkey's gobble, kills turkey," in Ernest W. Baughman, *Type and Motif Index of the Folktales of England and North America* (The Hague, 1966).

[17]Robinson, *Sam Lovel's Boy with Forest and Stream Fables*, p. 147.

[18]Robinson, *In New England Fields and Woods*, pp. 148-149.

[19]Robinson, *Out of Bondage and Other Stories*, p. 203.

[20]Harold W. Thompson, *Body, Boots and Britches* (Philadelphia, 1940), p. 487.

[21]Harry M. Hyatt, *Folklore from Adams County Illinois* (Hannibal, Mo., 1965), p. 554, No. 12500. See *The Frank C. Brown Collection*, VI, 380, No. 1941.

[22]Robinson, *Out of Bondage and Other Stories*, p. 159.

CHAPTER 8

THE RITES OF PASSAGE AND THE PERFORMANCE OF FOLKLORE

Celebrations and customs associated with the rites of passage—notably with courtship and marriage and with death and burial—also serve as settings for the performance of folklore. The traditional day for courting in Robinson's Danvis stories is Sunday. In *Uncle Lisha's Shop* it was on Sunday nights that Lisha Peggs as a young man courted the fair Jerusha Chase.[1] In "A September Election," in his effort to win Malvina Piper from Tom Farr, Andrew Colby mounts his gray mare every Sunday and wends his way to the Piper homestead, where the usual diversion is sitting with Malvina on the sofa in the Pipers' square room.[2] Throughout the year, of course, there were also village activities which gave the young people opportunities to meet. During the winter months, for instance, there were the "singing schools" in the town house and the "donation parties" at the minister's house. Of these two gatherings Robinson says in "Glimpses of New England Farm Life":

One night in the week, it may be, the young folks all pack off in the big sleigh to the singing-school in the town-house, where they and some scores of others combine to murder psalmody and break the heart of their instructor.

At these gatherings are flirtations and heart-burnings as well as at the "donation parties," which occur once or twice in the winter, when with kindly meant unkindness the poor minister's house is taken possession of by old and young, whose gifts too often but poorly compensate for the upturning and confusion they have made with their romping games.[3]

There were also flirtations at most of the bees. Robinson says in *Vermont*:

Very naturally, weddings often came of these merry-makings [the various bees], and were celebrated with as little ostentation and as much hearty good fellowship. The welcome guests brought no costly and useless presents for display; there were no gifts but the bride's outfit of home-made beds, homespun and hand-woven sheets, table-cloths, and towels given by parents and nearest relations. The young couple did not parade the awkwardness of their newly assumed relations in a wedding journey, but began the honeymoon in their new home, and spent it much as their lives were to be spent, taking up at once the burden that was not likely to grow lighter with the happiness that might increase. But if the burden became heavy, and the light of love faded, there was seldom separation or divorce. If there were more sons and daughters than could be employed at home, they hired out in families not so favored without loss of caste or sense of degradation in such honest service. They often married into the family of the employer, and their position was little changed by the new relation.[4]

Robinson describes country weddings in the fifteenth chapter of *Sam Lovel's Camps*, where he details the marriage of Sam Lovel and Huldah Purington. In this Danvis story, a Sunday before the marriage of Sam and Huldah notice of the approaching wedding "was 'published' at the town house in which, for lack of a church, all religious meetings but those of the Quakers were held."[5] On the following Sunday about forty guests, mostly relatives, attended a quiet wedding in the home of the bride. After the ceremony Sam "stood manfully at his post, while a dozen young men enjoyed their first and last opportunity of saluting his bride, and more girls offered him their lips than he had ever kissed before." Continuing his description Robinson writes:

There was no display of gifts, for there were none but the silver spoons given by the bride's parents, for in those days wedding guests were invited for their presence, not for their presents.

Later in the evening, by some chance a fiddle and fiddler came in conjunction, and those so disposed had an opportunity to prance with some regard to the time and tunes of "Money Musk," "Hull's Victory," the "Backside of Albany," and many another tune that has outlived its dancers of those days.

Wedding journeys were not the fashion in Danvis in those days, and that of Sam and Huldah was only from her father's house to that of his, and was quite uneventful. Perhaps it was made on foot across lots, or on top of one of the lumber-wagon loads of the bride's "settin' aout," of quilts, blankets, and linen, all homemade; feather beds, each with its thirty pounds of good live-geese feathers; the big and little wheels and the reel and many other articles that had long been set apart as Huldah's.[6]

The young people of Danvis are relatively free to marry whomever they wish; however, matchmaking, which is nearly universal in country marriages in Ireland as well as in Europe generally,[7] is not unknown in Danvis either, although it is not the rigid institution in Danvis that it is in Europe. In "A September Election" Levi Piper tries to arrange a marriage of convenience between his daughter, Malvina, and Andrew Colby to assure a Piper victory in an approaching election.[8] But to obviate the forced marriage, Malvina elopes with her own choice, Tom Farr, on the morning of the election. Such elopements are not common in the Danvis stories. Abductions are not present at all in the Danvis stories, but in an historical story, *In the Green Wood*, there are references to abductions of maidens by both Indians and whites.[9] In the most detailed account, Tom Pangborn abducts a Scottish girl, Lisbeth Cameron, who, along with her mother, was a party to the abduction, when the girl's father denies young Pangborn the privilege of marrying his daughter: "The custom of being stolen by lovers was common among her race, and Lisbeth took kindly to it, only it was too tame, with no risk of pursuit or being fought for."[10]

In connection with courtship and marriage, Robinson in one of his short stories, "Landlord Dayton's Shooting Match," makes use of one of the most common situations in folktales, the holding of a contest for the hand of a young lady.[11] The central motif in Robinson's story is "Suitor contest: shooting" (H331.4), a common form of competition for a bride in North American Indian tales, where the target involved is generally an eagle.[12] Baughman does not report this motif in Anglo-American folktales, so it may be only a coincidence that Robinson uses it as the central element for one of his short stories. At any rate, the parallel is interesting. In "Landlord Dayton's Shooting Match" two men, Tom Hale and Dick Barrett, both want to marry barkeep Phineas Dayton's daughter, Dorothy. Landlord Dayton likes both of the young men equally well and thinks his daughter does too. In order to determine which man shall wed his daughter, Dayton decides to hold a shooting contest between the two suitors. Dayton tells the young men, "Wal, then, I'll tell ye what I'm a-goin' tu du, an' give ye a equal chance. You both on ye start aout wi' your rifles at 10 erclock, percizely, an' the one 'at comes in at dark wi' the biggest string o' pa'tridges he'll hev my consent an' what help I can put in tu git Dorothy."[13] Since both men are good shots, the contest seems to be fair—except for one thing: Susan Crane, Landlord Dayton's niece and hired girl who would like to marry Dick Barrett herself, overhears the contest being planned. When Barrett leaves his rifle in the bar while he goes to the store for powder, Susan persuades a lame hostler who hopelessly admires her to move the rear sight of Dick Barrett's rifle to one side, which naturally prevents him from winning. Nevertheless, all ends happily. Dorothy prefers Tom Hale anyway, and Barrett finds that he prefers Susan Crane.[14]

Other important transitions in life mentioned by Robinson include beliefs and practices concerned with birth and death. An age-old question of children is, "Where do babies come from?" Parents, of course, generally put off answering the question truthfully as long as they can. Sometimes parents' answers are inventive, although usually they draw upon a stock of folklore even to this day. The adults in Robinson's works are typical. In *Sam Lovel's Boy*, for instance, when the time draws near for Huldah Lovel to bear her second child, neighborly women show up at the Lovel home to help with the household duties; Dr. Root, a self-taught herbalist, is present to superintend the steeping of herbs; and as soon as breakfast is over, little Sammy Lovel is hustled off to Joseph Hill's house to spend the morning listening to Gran'ther Hill's tales and to spend the afternoon playing "Injun" with the Hill children. When Sammy returns home the doctor has gone, but Aunt Jerusha and Maria Hill are still busy at the stove preparing food and boiling medicinal herbs. When Sammy inquires about his mother, Aunt Jerusha says, "Mammy's in the bedroom, an' she's got a leetle sister for him, 'at the darkter fetched in his saddlebags." Aunt Jerusha draws upon a widespread folk explanation to children concerning the origin of babies.[15]

Robinson reports a few customs and beliefs involving death. His best account of funeral customs appears in the fourteenth chapter of *Sam Lovel's Camps*. The day that Mrs. Lovel dies she is laid out in the square room of the Lovel's home. Almost immediately a group of Danvis women come to the house to get things in order for the other visitors, to prepare pie, nutcakes, and plums for the watchers who "set up" each night with the corpse, and to sit in the kitchen and gossip, "which was the chief compensation of their labors." When it is nearly time for the evening meal, most of the gossipers visit the square room to pay a "common mark of respect expected of all who came to the house of mourning," and then they leave to prepare supper for their own families. Two of the ladies, however, remain to fix supper for Sam Lovel and his father. The few visitors who came after supper "made transparent attempts at cheerful discourse, while decorously avoiding lightness of conversation, and discussed crop prospects and forecast the weather from the moon's signs and the last days of the past month."[16]

"On the third day after Mrs. Lovel's death," Robinson writes, "the Lovel house was filled with Danvis folks who met 'at ten o'clock at the house,' to pay the last tribute of respect to their deceased neighbor." Mrs. Lovel was laid to rest beside the grave of the first Mrs. Timothy Lovel on the hillside of the "uncared-for burying ground."[17] Thus, as Robinson points out in *A Hero of Ticonderoga*, the funeral rites in the pioneer communities were simple. In that historical story, for example, Seth Beeman is buried on his own soil with little ceremony. "They set at his head a rough slate stone," writes Robinson, "whose rude lettering could be read half a century later, telling his name and age, and the manner of his death."[18] Robinson comments briefly on Quaker burial practices in "The Mole's Path," saying that Quakers were buried in unmarked graves beside the Friends' meeting house.[19]

Robinson also mentions several superstitions concerning death. When Sam Lovel sees a cat prowling in front of the Lovel's home where the body of his stepmother is laid out, he chases the animal away. Perhaps Sam is merely chasing the cat away from the barrels that served as hen coops; however, it seems that the cat is interested in something other than baby chicks, for it passes the barrels and heads towards the house. Furthermore, the cat moved "with so much more than ordinary uncanny feline stealth that Sam's flesh crept as he watched her creeping, halting, listening, always intent on something unseen within the house."[20] Robinson must be referring to the popular belief that a "corpse in a house will attract the cats of the vicinity to gather around it and conduct themsleves in a very unearthly sort of way."[21] As Kittredge maintains in *Witchcraft in Old and New England*, the tame cat has some devilish traits in folklore. For instance, there is a widespread superstition "that cats must be kept away from a corpse or they may mutilate it. This turns up in our own country in an enlightening form: 'Never take a cat near a dead person, lest the cat take the soul of the dead.' The soul, we remember, often issues from the mouth of a sleeping man in the shape of a mouse!"[22] It is plausible, then, that Robinson was familiar with these superstitions.

About other beliefs concerning death Robinson is more explicit. In "The Gray Pine," for example, when Amos Brown mistakes his daughter for a witch or spirit and shoots at her to show his friend that "a bullit 'ont hurt it," he commits suicide after he discovers that he has killed his own daughter.[23] The next morning when Amos Brown's body is found lying on his kitchen floor, a candle with a "winding sheet" drooping from its sputtering wick is also found in the house.[24] This widespread belief that a "winding sheet"—a peculiar formation of wax on a burned candle—is prophetic of death also appears, along with other omens of death, in *A Danvis Pioneer* when Mrs. Purington, who is "an authority on mortuary affairs through frequent attendance at deathbeds and funerals," visits Gran'ther Hill's sickbed:

There was crowded standing-room for the solemn company between the bedstead, the oilcloth-covered light-stand, and the cherry-wood chest of drawers, whereon lay the worn and ancient family Bible, open at one of the stormiest chapters of the Old Testament. It might have seemed to some that a recently developed turn for Biblical research was one of the most alarming symptoms of Gran'ther Hill's illness. In an unstable position on the edge of the chest there was an unfinished axe-helve awaiting the last touches of the veteran's hands. Last night's candle stood on the stand, the extinguisher half revealing a portentous winding-sheet which had formed during the last burning; and even while Mrs. Purington silently called attention to this ominous sign still another was given. A phoebe bird hovered a moment at the open window, then flew in and caught a fly in an airy loop of flight that ended in a misjudged dash against the raised sash. . . .[25]

An axe carried into the house, a winding sheet formed on a candle, and a bird flying into the house are all familiar portents of death.[26]

Some of Robinson's characters—French-Canadians, Yankees, and Scotsmen—share the belief that the dead can return. In "The Gray

Pine" Amos Brown believes so strongly in spirits that he shoots his daughter, mistaking her for a ghost or a witch. In *Out of Bondage* a Negro escaping from slavery on the Underground Railroad is hidden in the barn of a Quaker farmer. While a French-Canadian hired man is working in the barn, he hears the hiding Negro cough, and the Canuck believes that he hears a ghost. The hired man tells his Quaker employer, "Yas, sah, bah jingo, Ah'm was hear nowse in de barn zhus' sem lak somebody cough, an' Ah b'lieve he was ghos' of dat hol' man come dead for 'sumption on de village las' week 'go."[27]

The returning-dead belief plays a much more important role in a folktale that Robinson includes in *In the Green Wood*. In this historical story, passing by the scene of British General Abercrombie's noted defeat to the French General Montcalm in July 1758, Donald McIntosh tells his wife that this is the very spot where her cousin, Duncan Cameron, lost his life:

"Here it was, Elspeth, your cousin, Duncan Cameron, died," said Donald very seriously to his wife.

"Wae's the day, for he was a bonnie gentleman," said she.

"Aweel, he had e'en mickle warnin' an' might hae keepit the breath in his body if he wad," said Donald.

"But he valued honor mair than life, like a true Cameron," she said proudly.

"An' gin he valued mair the opeenion o' mortal man ner what Gude gie him, 'twas his ain affair; but do ye think if 'twas made plain to me I'd be drooned if I went avont Ticonderoga, I'd nae bide here?"

"How was it, Uncle Donald?" said Lisbeth Cameron.

"E'en just this way. It was your father's cousin, Fergus Cameron, and Stewart of Appin fell into some clavers, an' Fergus gie Stewart the lee, an' Stewart oot wi' his dirk an' stabbed him to the heart. When his bluid cooled he was wae for the deed, for he kenned weel the claymore an' skean dhu o' every Cameron wad be thirsty for his ain bluid, an' so what did he do but rin to the house o' Duncan Cameron, the ain brother o' the dead, an' said he'd killed a man, an' if Duncan wadna save him he'd be murthered by the dead man's kin.

"He had nae mair nor gien his word when his brother's ghaist came till him an' tauld him his murtherer was lyin' in his house, an' he maun e'en gie him tae vengeance or kill him wi' his ain hand. But Duncan Cameron said he had gien his word, an' the man should be safe frae a' harm whiles he was under his roof. Then when that was a' the answer he wad gie, the ghost tauld him he should dee at Ticonderoga.

"That was a strange name he never heard afore, an' he didna ken where in a' the wide warld it might be. And when he went to the wars in Europe an' in India he was ae listenin' for the name, but ne'er did he hear the like o't. An' sae at last his regiment, the Forty-second, it was, cam till America, an' was sent wi' Abercrombie away against the French, an' at last he heard that the place they were marchin' against wad be Ticonderoga, an' he kenned weel the day o' his doom was nigh. An' it was the next day he fell wi' a dozen French bullets through his body, as he was leadin' his company in the charge against the abattis."[28]

In *Body, Boots and Britches* Thompson points out that this tale is "perhaps the most famous ghost story of York State" and reprints the "classic version" from Francis Parkman's *Montcalm and Wolfe.*[29]

In *In the Green Wood* Robinson writes that while ransacking the cellar of the Skene home in search of booty, "some rangers found the ghastly remains of Colonel Skene's unburied wife. She had been kept there for twelve years that an annuity might still be drawn, which was to continue while 'her body remained above ground.' "[30] Forty pages earlier in this story, belief in ghosts is attached to this same legend when Lisbeth Cameron and her mother shudder at a "half-crazed woman's wild tale" that in the Skenes' house there are "ghosts an' devils an' lost souls an' onbaried corpses."[31]

Antoine Bassette also believes in ghosts. In *A Danvis Pioneer* when Antoine thinks that Gran'ther Hill has died, he says to himself of Gran'ther, "He was so hugly Ah'll was 'fraid of it, me! An' Ah'll guess, seh, dis worl' was be more peaceably, for gat de hol' man aout of it! What dey goin' do where he gone prob'bly, hein? Wal, Ah'll be glad dey gat it, an' Ah'll hope dey an't send it back." But shortly Antoine sees Gran'ther Hill walking towards him and thinks that the old man has been sent back from the dead. Antoine hightails from the meadow to the house and tells Joseph Hill that he has seen something as awful as a *loup-garou.* "Hees ghos' come at me on de road," the Canuck gasps. "Oh, he scare me dead. Oh, mon Dieu! mon Dieu! Oh, what for you' fader an' let me 'lone wen he'll dead! He chase me on de road! Oh, he was awf'ly hugly hol' ghos'!" Joseph Hill, however, assures Antoine that "Father hain't half so dead as you be."[32]

NOTES

[1]Robinson, *Uncle Lisha's Shop and A Danvis Pioneer*, pp. 134, 146.

[2]Robinson, *Sam Lovel's Boy with Forest and Stream Fables*, p. 162.

[3]Robinson, "Glimpses of New England Farm Life," p. 519.

[4]Robinson, *Vermont*, pp. 296-297.

[5]Robinson, *Sam Lovel's Camps and In the Green Wood*, p. 203.

[6]Robinson, *Sam Lovel's Camps and In the Green Wood*, pp. 204-205.

[7]Conrad M. Arensberg, *The Irish Countryman: An Anthropological Study* (Gloucester, Mass., 1959), p. 72.

[8]Robinson, *Sam Lovel's Boy with Forest and Stream Fables*, p. 160.

[9]Robinson, *Sam Lovel's Camps and In the Green Wood*, pp. 222, 228.

[10]Robinson, *Sam Lovel's Camps and In the Green Wood*, p. 259.

[11]Stith Thompson, *The Folktale* (New York, 1946), p. 153.

[12]Stith Thompson, *The Folktale*, p. 337.

[13]Robinson, *Out of Bondage and Other Stories*, p. 179.

[14]Robinson, *Out of Bondage and Other Stories*, pp. 178-186.

[15]Robinson, *Sam Lovel's Boy with Forest and Stream Fables*, pp. 36-42. See *The Frank C. Brown Collection*, VI, 4, No. 6, for a variant of this tradition with comparative notes. Cf. Motif T589.6, "Where children come from."

[16]Robinson, *Sam Lovel's Camps and In the Green Wood*, pp. 200-202.

[17]Robinson, *Sam Lovel's Camps and In the Green Wood*, p. 203.

[18]Robinson, *Danvis Folks and A Hero of Ticonderoga*, p. 259.

[19]Robinson, *Out of Bondage and Other Stories*, p. 49.

[20]Robinson, *Sam Lovel's Camps and In the Green Wood*, p. 198.

[21]*The Frank C. Brown Collection*, I, 638.

[22]George Lyman Kittredge, *Witchcraft in Old and New England* (New York, 1929), p. 178. See Motif B766.1, "Cat mutilates corpses," and Motif B766.1.1, "Cat must be kept from dying person because it will catch the person's soul issuing (from mouth) in form of mouse."

[23]Robinson, *Out of Bondage and Other Stories*, p. 245. For variants of this belief see *The Frank C. Brown Collection*, VII, 132, No. 5691; VII, 148, No. 5763.

[24]Robinson, *Out of Bondage and Other Stories*, p. 246.

[25]Robinson, *Uncle Lisha's Shop and A Danvis Pioneer*, p. 109.

[26]For instance, see *The Frank C. Brown Collection*, VII, 76, No. 5391; VII, 44, No. 5165; VII, 21, No. 5006; VII, 61-62, Nos. 5280-5281.

[27]Robinson, *Out of Bondage and Other Stories*, p. 31. The Motif is E337.1, "Sounds of re-enacted actions."

[28]Robinson, *Sam Lovel's Camps and In the Green Wood*, pp. 223-224. The Motifs are E231, "Return from dead to reveal murder," and E545.2, "Dead predict death."

[29]Harold W. Thompson, *Body, Boots and Britches*, p. 321.

[30]Robinson, *Sam Lovel's Camps and In the Green Wood*, p. 260. Cf. Motif T211.4.1, "Wife's corpse kept after death."

[31]Robinson, *Sam Lovel's Camps and In the Green Wood*, p. 222.

[32]Robinson, *Uncle Lisha's Shop and A Danvis Pioneer*, pp. 115-116.

CHAPTER 9

HUNTING, FISHING, AND CAMPING TRIPS AND THE
PERFORMANCE OF FOLKLORE AWAY FROM THE VILLAGE

Although the Danvis folk depend largely on subsistence farming for their livelihoods, they sometimes supplement their tables and incomes by fishing, hunting, and trapping. These activities, however, serve primarily as diversion. They are not part of the economic agricultural cycle; fishing, hunting, and trapping—whether for a day or for an extended period—must be done during a lull in the essential farming activities. As Robinson points out in *Vermont*, "The laborious life of the farmer had an occasional break in days of fishing in lulls of the spring's work, and between that and haymaking; of hunting when the crops were housed, and the splendor of the autumnal woods was fading to sombre monotony of gray, or when woods and fields were white with the snows of early winter."[1] Similarly, in "Glimpses of New England Farm Life," he writes that "there comes a little lull in work betwixt planting and hoeing during which boys and hired men assert their right, established by ancient usage, to take a day to go a-fishing."[2] Since outdoor excursions can be taken only during occasional lulls, in *Uncle Lisha's Outing* Sam Lovel, Antoine Bassette, Uncle Lisha Peggs, and Joseph Hill must go on a short hunting trip between corn shucking and potato digging;[3] and in *Sam Lovel's Camps* the part-time Danvis fishermen must go on a brief fishing trip near Lake Champlain just before hoeing.[4]

On the other hand, Robinson reports that many Vermont farmers "made a considerable addition to their income by trapping the fur-bearers," mainly the muskrat and the mink.[5] But that the trapping of fur-bearing animals for profit is not an essential part of the Danvis economy is apparent in *Sam Lovel's Camps*, in which Robinson writes that "Sam had not much experience in trapping muskrats, those fur-bearers being not at all plenty in the rapid, weedless streams of the hill country, where all his hunting and trapping had until now been done."[6]

When Sam decides to go on a camping trip on the Slang to trap musk-rats, he takes Antoine along as partner and instructor. Robinson's comments on trapping, however, show that he, unlike Sam Lovel, was familiar with the sport. In his essay "Old Boats," for instance, in addition to describing a large, flat-bottomed, square-ended scow used for transporting logs, grain, sand, and hay, Robinson writes about an old trapping skiff:

In the shade of shore-lining trees that annually bathe ankle-deep in the spring floods, when the pickerel swim among their bolls and the painted plumage of the wood drake floats double beside their gray reflections, one stumbles upon the half-stripped bones of an old trapping skiff. Though of almost as primitive mold, she is of very different pattern from the scow. Short and narrow, sharp at both ends, her sides of three-lapped streaks fastened to a few knees of natural crook, she was as cranky as the other was steady, and more heavily burdened with one person than the other with as many as could find room in her. Yet the trapper, standing upright, a little abaft midships, adroitly humored her cranky tricks, as with his long setting pole he drove her over submerged logs and coaxed her through intricate passages of the flooded wood, or with sturdy ax-strokes chopped notches for his traps, or set them as he squatted by log, feedbed and house. Cruising within shot of a muskrat, duck or pickerel, he stooped and snatched his ready gun from the hooks that, with the leather flap that covered the lock, still hold their places.[7]

Steel traps, as we have seen in an earlier chapter, were handmade at nine dollars a dozen. In *Sam Lovel's Camps*, Sam "bargained for the making" of such traps, and he and Antoine set them "in the muskrat houses, chopping out a small opening to the bed, whereon the trap was set, and the covering carefully replaced. From the houses so taken possession of rose the tally sticks, to which the trap chains were fastened, like miniature flagstaffs." Antoine, however, has his own method of trapping the muskrat, which he says will net "forty, prob'ly twenty so in one day!" Indian fashion, he stealthily approaches a musk-rat house and drives a spear "into the centre of the rough cone of flags, mud, and sedges, a little below the top and on the south side." Then the "half-savage Canuck," as Robinson calls Antoine, chops into the house, removes the pierced muskrat, and happily watches it writhe in pain on the stick until the kindhearted Sam Lovel kicks the animal in the head to end its suffering. Sam does not care for Antoine's method of catching the muskrat and tells the Canuck that "it's too durn'd savage. The's too much Injun 'baout that for me." Sam prefers the deadfall, which "knocks the life aout on 'em fust dab," although the deadfall, he maintains, "hain't wuth shucks for mushrat."[8]

As Robinson suggests, the Canuck no doubt learned his "savage" method from the American Indian. As a matter of fact, although the European settler in the New World did not preserve the folktales of the American Indian, he certainly absorbed much from the Indian in the field of traditional material culture, especially that of subsistence. The general lack of interest on the part of most American folklorists in material culture, however, has resulted in an underestimation of the vital impact made by the Indian on American folk culture,[9] other than the usual enumeration of the obvious contributions of corn and potato cultivation. Since the Vermont pioneer lived in a wilderness where his nourishment depended heavily on hunting and fishing, the white settler borrowed a number of techniques and devices from the Indian.

Robinson does not slight this borrowing. When on the trail, for example, the Indian would travel "tuckernuck," an Algonquian word meaning "a picnic."[10] As Robinson suggests, the early Americans borrowed both the idea and the word. In *A Danvis Pioneer*, when Josiah Hill and Kenelm Dalrymple eat a tuckernuck supper in an inn, Robinson explains, "In those primitive times it was no offense to the innholder nor shame to the traveler to carry his own provisions and eat them by the bar-room fire, and this was called 'traveling tuckernuck,' a name that smacks of Indian origin, as the custom does of the practice of the red wayfarer, whose sole dependence was on his bag of no-cake, a parched, pounded corn, and his hunk of dried venison, eked out by such game as he chanced to kill. Our travelers also adopted this plan a little later, when the old ranger would strike into the woods skirting the road and pick up a partridge or a wild pigeon."[11]

The watercraft of the American Indian was a more important contribution to the pioneer traveler, hunter, trapper, and fisherman, for no other mode of transportation was more important in the New World than water. European settlers in New England adopted both the birchbark canoe of the north and the log canoe of the Chesapeake Bay area. Both types are mentioned in Robinson's works. Comments about either making or repairing birchbark canoes appear in *Sam Lovel's Boy*, "McIntosh of Vergennes," *Uncle Lisha's Outing, A Danvis Pioneer,* and *Uncle Lisha's Shop*.[12] In *A Danvis Pioneer*, Robinson says that canoes are repaired with "a patch of bark, a thread of split spruce-root, and a little turpentine and deer's tallow."[13] In "McIntosh of Vergennes," while convalescing in the home of Donald McIntosh, an injured Indian makes a birchbark canoe to carry him home again. Concerning this Robinson says, "Donald's sons would not have tired of watching the curious fashioning of this craft if it had taken thrice as long to peel off the long sheet of white birch-bark, to make the ash frame, to sew the seams with spruce roots, and make them water-tight with grease and turpentine, and then to drive in the lining of cedar splints."[14] The most complete account of canoe building appears in *Uncle Lisha's Shop* when Sam Lovel, while fishing along Beaver Meadow Brook, meets two Indians with a large roll of birchbark and dickers with them to build a canoe for him. Later Sam explains the craft of building a canoe:

". . . Furst thing they made a frame the len'th an' shape the canew 's goin' tu be on top—jes tew strips of ash fastened together tu the ends, an' bars acrost, so"— illustrating his description with a diagram drawn on the floor with a bit of coal while all gathered about him. "Then they laid it daown on a level place they'd fixed an' drove stakes clus to it agin the ends o' the cross-bars all raound, an' one tu each end o' the frame. Then they pulled up the stakes an' took the frame away, keepin' the stake-holes clear o' dirt very car'f'l, an' spread the bark daown on the place, an' then sot the frame back on jes' ezackly where it was afore, an' put some cedar strips on 't, an' big stuns top o' them. Then they slit the bark from the aidge up tu the frame every onct in a little ways, so, all raound, 'an bent up the bark an' sot the stakes back in the holes, an' tied a bark cord acrost from top to top. Then they sewed up the slits, lappin' the bark over, ye see, an' sewin' it wi' black spruce ruts peeled an' split in tew, 'n' they're jest as tough as rawhide; luther-wood bark hain't no toughter. That' as fur as they've got yit, but nex' thing, 's nigh 's I c'n make aout, they cal'late tu raise the frame tu the top an' put some raves on aoutside and fasten 'em together an' then line the hull consarn wi' flat strips o' cedar drove in tight. 'N' then when they git the seams all daubed wi' spruce gum an' taller melted together it'll be all ready fer me tu—" "tip over," said Lisha, completing the sentence for him.[15]

Log canoes also are worked into Robinson's stories and essays. In *A Danvis Pioneer*, Kenelm Dalrymple has a canoe that he made from a pine log,[16] and similarly in *A Hero of Ticonderoga*, Job Carpenter fashions one from the trunk of a great pine tree.[17] In the essay "Old Boats," Robinson reports that as late as when he was a boy the log canoe was yet the "commonest craft on our waters":

. . . I find the decaying hulk of one of the most primitive of water craft embedded in alluvial mold and bed-embowered in royal ferns. Quite at one with the un-wrought logs of driftwood that lie around it, is a log canoe. So clumsily made was she, an Indian might have fashioned a neater one with fire and stone tools, though the maker of this had an ax, adze and gouge of steel, in proof whereof their marks still endure. The butt log of a great pine, out of which a sawmill could have sliced material for a whole fleet of small craft, went to the wasteful construction of this one boat. When there was an end of chopping, hewing and gouging, the pile of chips was of greater bulk than the boat.

In spite of her crankiness and her trough-like model, it could be said in her praise that she was a solid, seamless shell, needing neither oakum nor pitch to make her water-tight, and the wholesome odor of the freshly hewn pine, sweating turpentine at every pore, was a pleasanter smell than that of paint. Her sort were the com-monest craft on our waters when I was a boy, yet I do not remember one so new that it had not taken on the weather-beaten gray of age, so scarce and precious had suitable trees for making them become. I recollect their accustomed navigators as men also bearing marks of age and long service—old men who were uncles to all younger generations. They were not fishing for sport, but engaging in it as a serious business of life, befitting their bent forms and intent faces.

"Ef you want tu ketch fish, you must bait your hook wi' necessity," Uncle Stafford would inform us as we gazed enviously over his gunwale at the fare of great pike lying thick on the canoe bottom. He used a lure composed of pork rind and red flannel . . .[18]

Thus, Robinson observed veterans of the War of 1812, such as Uncle Stafford, in their traditional watercraft, and he learned from them about the traditional fishing lure of pork rind and red flannel, which the part-time fishermen in his fiction, especially old-timers like Uncle Lisha and Uncle Tyler, also use for bait.[19] Robinson briefly mentions techniques of the American Indian for catching fish—the use of the fish weir, the bark net, and the wooden spear. In *A Danvis Pioneer*, for example, Joseph Hill and Kenelm Dalrymple visit some Indians who are salmon fishing on Lewis Creek, and Robinson writes, "Many women and children were all busy, some with bark nets at the weirs, others with curious wooden spears, others cleaning the fish, and others drying them on racks over smoking fires."[20]

Other important gifts of the American Indian to the early settlers that Robinson mentions include the toboggan and snowshoe. In *A Danvis Pioneer*, for instance, Kenelm Dalrymple makes both, "for he was skilled in all such Indian craft."[21] Kenelm, in turn, teaches his partner, Josiah Hill, to make and wear snowshoes, and Josiah perfects himself in the art of snowshoe weaving. In "McIntosh of Vergennes," while an injured Indian, Joe Wadso, is recuperating in the McIntosh home, he teaches the McIntosh boys to make snowshoes, "weaving the raw-hide filling of a snowshoe after the Indian fashion . . . [and] whittling the ashen bow of one of another pair of this indispensable winter foot-gear."[22] The snowshoe quite early had a wide distribution in almost every area of the Northern Hemisphere where snow is heavy. As Daniel Davidson points out, the snowshoe is a circumpolar trait;[23] thus, it is probably not an invention of the North American Indian. Nevertheless, the Indian version of the snowshoe laced with sinew or thong, as Robinson suggests, was borrowed by the New England pioneers and greatly aided the early travelers and hunters in the northern forests.

As Robinson's works suggest, the comparative study of the impact of the American Indian material culture on that of the European settler is certainly within the realm of the study of folklore, for the Indian's influence was manifested first of all at the folk level. The pioneer observed the Indian at work, and the white settler integrated the Indian's techniques into his own material culture and by nonacademic means passed them on. Although Robinson's works are not theoretical treatises with closely argued central ideas, nevertheless one is able to discern from Robinson's writings that acculturation is a two-way process, as most anthropologists agree.[24]

The authentic hunting, fishing, and camping excursions that Robinson describes also provide occasions for the performance of folklore away from the village. In "The Raccoon," for instance, he reports that songs are sung and tales and jokes are told on coon hunts when the raccoon hides in a tall and limbless tree under which the hunters keep vigil until daylight. "A huge fire enlivens the long hours of guard keeping," writes Robinson. "A foraging party repairs to the nearest cornfield for roasting ears, and the hunters shorten their watch by munching scorched corn, sauced by joke and song and tales of the coon hunts of bygone years."[25]

On camping trips tale swapping occurs on rainy days and lazy days. In "A Rainy Day in Camp," Robinson suggests that on such a day the camper can listen to his guide's "stories of hunting, fishing, and adventure, or learn woodcraft of him and the curious ways of birds and beasts. He may fashion birch-bark camp-ware, dippers, cups and boxes, or whittle a paddle from a smooth-rifted maple."[26] Folklore is also performed around the campfire before, during and after supper.[27] From his own camping experience he writes in "Mingo—A Silhouette" that the Robinsons' hired man, Mingo Niles, told riddles during meals on a camping trip. "When our tidbits were roasted and we sat snatching hot morsels of them from burning fingers," he reports, "Mingo propounded riddles that he alone could answer, for who could ever guess 'A hill full, a hole full, can't ketch a bowl full' was dew, or others equally blind and senseless? If the secret had been previously imparted to one, he declared it with the pride of an original discoverer, otherwise Mingo divulged it with the air of an inventor."[28]

On camping, hunting, and fishing trips away from the village, the setting for folklore in Robinson's works is invariably the campfire, as in "Story-telling," the sixteenth chapter of *Uncle Lisha's Outing.* Robinson points out in "The Reluctant Camp-Fire" that this fire "dispels every sullen look, warms every heart to genial comradeship; jokes flash back and forth merrily, and the camp pulses again with reawakened cheerful life."[29] Robinson feels that storytelling is so essential to camp life that the very sight of a dead campfire recalls storytelling sessions: "You laugh again at the jokes that ran around that merry circle and wonder again and again at the ingenuity with which small performances were magnified into great exploits, little haps into strange adventure, and with which bad shots and poor catches were excused."[30] Indeed, for Robinson the open campfire is such an important part of the ritual of storytelling that he doubts that the new way of "camping out" in a well-built lodge is congenial to tale telling. In "Camping Out," he writes, "What can make amends for the loss of the camp-fire, with innumerable pictures glowing and shifting in its heart, and conjuring strange shapes out of the surrounding gloom, and suggesting unseen mysteries that the circle of darkness holds behind its rim? How are the wells of conversation to be thawed out by a black stove, so that tales of hunters' and fishers' craft and adventure shall flow till the measure of man's belief is overrun?"[31] In "A New England Woodpile," he writes that an open fire in a fireplace is nearly as effective as the campfire:

The Yankees who possess happy memories of the great open fires of old time are growing few, but Whittier has embalmed for all time, in "Snow-Bound," their comfort and cheer and picturesqueness. When the trees of the virgin forest cast their shadows on the newly risen roof there was no forecasting provision for winter. The nearest green tree was cut, and hauled, full length, to the door, and with it the nearest dry one was cut to match the span of the wide fireplace; and when these were gone, another raid was made upon the woods; and so from hand to mouth the fire was fed. It was not uncommon to draw the huge backlogs on to the hearth with a horse, and sometimes a yoke of oxen were so employed. Think of a door wide enough for this: half of the side of a house to barricade against the savage Indians and savage cold! It was the next remove from a camp-fire. There was further likeness to it in the tales that were told beside it, of hunting and pioneer hardships, of wild beasts and Indian forays, while the eager listeners drew to a closer circle on the hearth, and the awed children cast covert scared backward glances at the crouching and leaping shadows that thronged on the walls, and the great samp-kettle bubbled and seethed on its trammel, and the forgotten johnny-cake scorched on its tilted board.[32]

In "The Summer Camp-Fire," Robinson points out that the camp-fire in summer "is not, like the great hospitable flare and glowing coals of the autumn and winter camp-fires, the centre to which all are drawn, about which the life of the camp gathers, where joke and repartee flash to and fro as naturally and as frequently as its own sparks fly upward, where stories come forth as continuously as the ever-rising volume of smoke."[33] During the coldest of the winter months camping for pleasure is interrupted, but storytelling goes on. For Robinson writes in "The Home Fireside," when the sportsman sits near the fireplace mending his tackle and cleaning his gun on a cold day, the children watch and play at camping out. "The callow campers," he says, "assail him with demands for stories, and he goes over, for their and his own enjoyment, old experiences in camp and field."[34]

NOTES

[1]Robinson, *Vermont*, pp. 298-299.

[2]Robinson, "Glimpses of New England Farm Life," p. 522.

[3]Robinson, *Uncle Lisha's Outing and Along Three Rivers*, p. 24.

[4]Robinson, *Sam Lovel's Camps and In the Green Wood*, p. 187.

[5]Robinson, *Vermont*, p. 300.

[6]Robinson, *Sam Lovel's Camps and In the Green Wood*, p. 21.

[7]Robinson, *In New England Fields and Woods*, p. 222.

[8]Robinson, *Sam Lovel's Camps and In the Green Wood*, pp. 21-22.

[9]For an important exception see A. Irving Hallowell, "The Impact of the American Indian on American Culture," *Folklore in Action*, ed. Horace P. Beck (Philadelphia, 1962), pp. 120-138.

[10]H. L. Mencken, *The American Language: Supplement One* (New York, 1962), p. 171.

[11]Robinson, *Uncle Lisha's Shop and A Danvis Pioneer*, p. 29.

[12]Robinson, *Sam Lovel's Boy with Forest and Stream Fables*, pp. 58-60; *Out of Bondage and Other Stories*, pp. 111-112; *Uncle Lisha's Outing and Along Three Rivers*, p. 89; *Uncle Lisha's Shop and A Danvis Pioneer*, pp. 60, 68, 231-232.

[13]Robinson, *Uncle Lisha's Shop and A Danvis Pioneer*, p. 68.

[14]Robinson, *Out of Bondage and Other Stories*, pp. 111-112.

[15]Robinson, *Uncle Lisha's Shop and A Danvis Pioneer*, p. 232.

[16]Robinson, *Uncle Lisha's Shop and A Danvis Pioneer*, p. 36.

[17]Robinson, *Danvis Folks and A Hero of Ticonderoga*, p. 235.

[18]Robinson, *In New England Fields and Woods*, pp. 223-224.

[19]Robinson, *Uncle Lisha's Shop and A Danvis Pioneer*, p. 226; *Sam Lovel's Camps and In the Green Wood*, p. 113. For similar traditional baits compare *The Frank C. Brown Collection*, VII, 481, Nos. 7833, 7838.

[20]Robinson, *Uncle Lisha's Shop and A Danvis Pioneer*, p. 41.

[21]Robinson, *Uncle Lisha's Shop and A Danvis Pioneer*, p. 37.

[22]Robinson, *Out of Bondage and Other Stories*, p. 114.

[23]Daniel Sutherland Davidson, *Snowshoes*, Memoirs of the American Philosophical Society, VI (Philadelphia, 1937), 4.

[24]Ralph Beals, "Acculturation," *Anthropology Today*, ed. A. L. Kroeber (Chicago, 1953), p. 628.

[25]Robinson, *In New England Fields and Woods*, pp. 78-79.

[26]Robinson, *In New England Fields and Woods*, p. 68.

[27]Robinson, *Sam Lovel's Camps and In the Green Wood*, pp. 59-60.

[28]Robinson, *Out of Bondage and Other Stories*, p. 68. For a discussion of this and other traditional riddles in Robnison's works see Chapter 14 of the present work.

[29]Robinson, *In New England Fields and Woods*, p. 81.

[30]Robinson, *In New England Fields and Woods*, p. 90.

[31]Robinson, *In New England Fields and Woods*, p. 63.

[32]Robinson, *In New England Fields and Woods*, pp. 121-122.

33Robinson, *In New England Fields and Woods*, p. 75.
34Robinson, *In New England Fields and Woods*, p. 23.

CHAPTER 10

SUGARING AND BEE HUNTING

"Many families," Robinson points out in *Vermont*," saw no sweetening, from one end of the year to the other, but maple sugar and syrup, the honey from their few hives, or the uncertain spoil of the bee-hunter."[1] Tapping the maple tree and hunting the honeybee were important aspects of early folk economy of which Robinson has much to say throughout his works. European settlers clearly learned the art of making maple sugar and syrup from the American Indians, for no European tree yields a sweet sap comparable to that of the maple tree.[2] In "A New England Woodpile," Robinson acknowledges the white man's debt to the Indian, and he briefly traces the evolution of techniques for tapping the maple:

. . . Here is a sugar-maple, three feet through at the butt, with the scars of many tappings showing on its rough bark. The oldest of them may have been made by the Indians. Who knows what was their method of tapping? Here is the mark of the gouge with which early settlers drew the blood of the tree; a fashion learned, likely enough, from the aboriginal sugar-makers, whose narrowest stone gouges were as passable tools for the purpose as any they had for another. These more distinct marks show where the auger of later years made its wounds. The old tree has distilled its sweets for two races and many generations of men, first into the bark buckets of Waubanakis, then into the ruder troughs of Yankee pioneers, then into the more convenient wide-bottomed wooden sap-tubs; and at last, when the march of improvement has spoiled the wilderness of the woods with trim-built sugar-houses and patent evaporators, the sap drips with resounding metallic tinkle into pails of shining tin. . . .[3]

Robinson through his observation of nature suggests quite plausibly that the Indian might have gotten the idea to tap the maple by watching the red squirrel. In "In the Spring Woods" Robinson writes:

If you wade into the woods—and it is easier wading without a gun than with it—about the time the sugar-makers are beginning their work, you may see that some-one has been before them, tapping nearer the sky than their augers bore, and where the sap has a finer and more ethereal flavor. You can see little trickles of it darkening some of the smaller smooth branches, and if your eyes are sharp enough, the incisions it flows from. These are the chisel marks of the red squirrel, the only real sap-sucker I know of, excepting the boy. Make yourself comfortable on some patch of ground that the spring ebb of the snow has left bare and keep still long enough, and you may see him stretch himself along a branch and slowly suck or lap the sap as it oozes from the wound. Evidently he enjoys it greatly, and it must be grateful to his palate, for all winter save in a thaw or two, he has had nothing to quench his thirst but snow, and eating one's drink is a hard and poor way of taking it. Was he the first to discover the sweetness of the maple, and did the Indians take the hint of sugar-making from him? If so we are under obligations to him . . .[4]

The white settler promptly borrowed the idea of maple sugar making from the American Indian, and as soon as the pioneer began clearing his land and building his house, he began preparations to tap the maple trees.[5] In *A Danvis Pioneer*, young Josiah Hill is depicted as spending much of his time "hollowing out sap troughs and making spouts for the coming spring sugar-making."[6] In *Uncle Lisha's Shop*, Robinson writes that with the first warm days of spring "most of the 'men folks' were away in the sap works gathering their great harvest of the year."[7] In "The Nameless Season," he describes the sugar camp "with its mixed odors of pungent smoke and saccharine steam, its wide environment of dripping spouts and tinkling tin buckets, signs that at last the pulse of the trees is stirred by a subtle promise of returning spring."[8] In *Out of Bondage*, a Negro escaping in winter on the Underground Railroad is hidden in the sugar house, for "No one ever goes there till sugaring-time, after the wood is hauled, and that's just finished."[9]

Other material on sugar making can be found in the chapter on "Old Time Customs and Industries" in *Vermont* and in "Glimpses of New England Farm Life." In *Vermont* he briefly describes an early method of making sugar:

When the first touch of spring stirred the sap of the maples, sugar-making began, a labor spiced with a woodsy flavor of camp life and small adventure. The tapping was done with a gouge; the sap dripped from spouts of sumach stems into rough-hewn troughs, from which it was gathered in buckets borne on a neck-yoke, the bearer making the rounds on snowshoes, and depositing the gathered sap in a big "store trough" set close to the boiling place. This was an open fire, generously fed with four-foot wood, and facing an open-fronted shanty that sheltered the sugar-maker from rain and "sugar snow," while he plied his daily and nightly labor, now with the returning crow and the snickering squirrel for companions, now the unseen owl and fox, making known their presence with storm-boding hoot and husky bark. The sap-boiling was done in the great potash kettle that in other seasons seethed with pungent lye, but now, swung on a huge log crane, sweetened the odors of the woods with sugar-scented vapor. . . .[10]

In "Glimpses of New England Farm Life," he tells of pioneer techniques of sugaring, too, but he also includes material on later methods:

The blood of the maples is stirred, and in sugar-making regions the tapping of the trees is begun. A warm day following a freezing night sets all the spouts a-dripping merrily into the bright tin "tubs," and once or twice a day the oxen and sled go winding through the woods, hauling a cask to which the sap is brought from the trees with buckets and neck-yoke, and then taken to the sugar-house. This is set, if possible, at the foot of some hill-side or knoll, on which the sled may be driven so that its burden overtops the great holders standing beside the boiling-pans within. Into these holders the sap is discharged, through a pipe. Now the boiling begins, and the thin sap thickens to rich sirup as it seethes and bubbles in its slow course from the first pan to the last, while the woods about are filled with the sweet odor of its steam.[11]

Robinson incorporates his intimate knowledge of sugar making into his creative writing, and his use of folklore contributes to his theme of self-sufficiency and to the verisimilitude of his fiction. For example, consider the following three paragraphs from one of Robinson's historical novelettes, *A Hero of Ticonderoga*:

Seth tapped the huge old maples with a gouge, and the sap, dripping from spouts of sumac wood, was caught in rough hewn troughs. From these it was carried in buckets on a neck-yoke to the boiling place, an open-fronted shanty. Before it the big potash kettle was hung on a tree trunk, so balanced on a stump that it could be swung over or off the fire at will. Sugaring brought pleasure as well as hard labor to Nathan. There were quiet hours spent in the shanty with his father, with little to do but mend the fire and watch the boiling sap walloping and frothing, half hidden beneath the clouds of steam that filled the woods with sweet odor.

Sometimes Job joined them and told of his lonely scouts in the Ranger service, and of bush fights with Indians and their French allies, and of encounters with wild beasts, tales made more impressive in their relation by the loneliness of the camp-fire, with the circle of wild lights and shadows leaping around it in the edge of the surrounding darkness, out of which came, perhaps from far away, the howl of a wolf or the nearer hoot of the great horned owl.

Sometimes Martha spent part of day in camp with her brother, helping in womanly ways that girls so early acquired in the training of those times, when every one of the household must learn helpfulness and self-reliance. But the little sister enjoyed most the evenings when the syrup was taken to the house and sugared off. The children surfeited themselves with sugar "waxed" on snow, and their parents, and Job, if he chanced to be there, shared of this most delicious of the few backwoods luxuries, and the five made a jolly family party.[12]

Although this brief passage communicates much of the same information about making sugar that one finds in Robinson's expository prose, these paragraphs offer more than just a few technical facts. Robinson reveals something of the solitary hard work of the sugar maker who often found himself with nothing to do but fix the fire and watch the boiling sap. In *Out of Bondage*, Robinson writes that in one sugar house there was "a small loophole in the door, made to afford the sugar-maker the amusement of shooting crows when time hung heavy on his hands."[13] Accordingly, the sugar maker would indeed welcome a storyteller like Job in his camp to help while away the hours while the fire burned and the sap boiled. As a matter of fact, as Van Wagenen points out, "Sugaring time has long been (perhaps still is) something of a rural spring festival. When sap is running freely, it is often necessary to boil all day and far into the night. A snug sap house with a roaring fire and a pleasant aroma of boiling sap easily becomes a place of evening resort, more especially for the young folks."[14] Such is the case in *Uncle Lisha's Shop*, although not all of the participants are by any means "young folks." In a chapter entitled "In the Sugar Camp," Uncle Lisha misses the evening storytelling sessions in his shop when all of his companions are away in their sugar camps:

Among the tall maples that grew on some hillside of every farm the smoke of the sugar camp drifted upward, and the daily and nightly labors there of all Lisha's friends had for some time prevented their customary visits to the shop. Lisha having, as he said, "got tew ol' an' short-winded tu waller raound in the snow, an' never could git the heng o' showshoein'," had hired Pelatiah to do his sugar-making, while he attended to his shoemaking and mending. But getting very lonely with his solitary labors, during a slack run of sap he sent his henchman out among his friends with a verbal "invite" to a sugaring off at his camp on a certain evening. Accordingly at "airly candleligh'in'," the guests came straggling in, and were loudly and warmly welcomed by their host. "I'm dreffle glad tu see ye, boys! I hain't sot eyes on ye fer a month o' Sundays, seems 'ough. Make yerselves tu hum, an' I'll sweeten ye up tu rights." . . .

"Wal, boys," the old man said, after testing the syrup for the twentieth time by pouring it slowly out of his dipper, "it begins tu luther-ap'n, an' I guess it's baout ready. Peltier, you put aout an' git tew three buckets o' clean snow; Samwill, ketch a holt o' that 'ere stick an' help me histe this 'ere kittle off. Naow then, fetch up some seats, the' is sap tubs 'nough layin' raound. Samwill, Jezeff, Solon, some o' ye, the' 's a baskit of biscuit in back there under my cut, an' a bowl o' pickles; won't ye jes' fetch 'em aout?"

So bustling about, he at last got his guests seated around the kettle of hot sugar and the buckets of snow, and they fell to, each in turn dipping out some syrup, and pouring it in dabs upon the snow, when it presently cooled into waxy clots ready for eating.[15]

The "sugaring off," or sugar party, was the "earliest picnic of the season."[16] Generally, it was for young people. As Robinson says, "All the young folks of a neighborhood were invited to the 'sugaring off,' and camp after camp in turn . . . rung with the chatter and laughter of a merry party . . ."[17] In "Glimpses of New England Farm Life," he adds that the sole refreshment at the sugar parties is "hot sugar poured on clean snow, where it cools to a gummy consistency known as 'waxed' sugar."[18] The pickles that Uncle Lisha served at his sugar party were, of course, to cut the sweetness of the waxed sugar in order to allow the party goers to eat more sugar.[19]

Naturally the sugaring off party afforded the opportunity for the young men and young ladies of the village to get together and become better acquainted. "The duty of the rustic gallant," Robinson explains, "is to whittle a little maple paddle (which is held to be the proper implement for sugar eating) for his mistress, and to keep her allotted portion of the snow-bank well supplied with the amber-hued sweet."[20] In fact, it was after such a sugaring off party that Uncle Lisha proposed to Aunt Jerusha:

. . . Goin' hum in the moonshine, I ast her to jine me in a sugarin' for life, an' 'fore we got to the chips in the do' yard she 'greed she would, an' here we be! Me on this 'ere shoebench, an' she," lifting his voice and pointing a waxy forefinger at the door that opened into the kitchen, "an' she a-peekin' through the crack o' that 'ere door!" The door squeaked suddenly to, and the wooden latch clicked rather spitefully.[21]

Sugaring time, then, was an important part of village life in Vermont, for both subsistence and enjoyment, and lasted until the first peep of the frogs. As Robinson points out, "Sap-flow and sugar-making slacken, so that a neighbor finds time to visit another at his sugarworks, and asks, 'Have you heard the frogs?' Only one 'run' of sap after the frogs peep, is the traditional rule. So the frogs having peeped, the last run comes, and sugar-making ends."[22] The result of the spring sugaring, the maple sugar, along with honey, was, as Van Wagenen asserts, "the housewife's answer to what must have been a chronic sugar shortage."[23] It was almost imperative that a man do his own sugaring, as most of the Danvis folk did, or hire someone to do it for him, as Uncle Lisha did, or do his sugaring "on share," as Antoine did with Joel Bartlett's son-in-law. In "Antoine Sugaring" Antoine explains the concept "on share": "He'll furnishin' noting but de tree and de hwood. Ah'll furnishin' all de res', de spout, de sap buckle, de bilin' kettly, an' de man, dat was de bes'."[24]

Although the pioneer industries of bee hunting and beekeeping did not contribute especially to occasions for the performance of oral folklore, as sugaring did, the bee is the subject of considerable lore, so both bee hunting and beekeeping propagated traditional beliefs and practices. In A Danvis Pioneer when Antoine Bassette and Pelatiah are helping Joseph Hill with his July haying, they hear an untimely blast of the dinner horn, and Antoine says that either Maria Hill's clock is fast or the bees are swarming. But Pelatiah replies, "If it's bees, they hain't wuth fussin' with. 'A swarm in July hain't wuth a fly.' "[25] Pelatiah is referring to a widespread folk belief concerning the success of swarming bees, which is usually formulated in a verse, such as:

> Swarm in May, worth a load of hay;
> Swarm in June, worth a silver spoon;
> Swarm in July, not worth a fly.[26]

In "Hunting the Honey-Bee" Robinson refers to two legends explaining why the bees left their hives for the woods:

. . . There is a tradition that an Indian wizard was feasted on bread and honey, and strong water sweetened with honey, by the wife of a Puritan magistrate, to the great satisfaction of the inner red man. Learning whence the lucent syrup came, he told the bees such tales of the flowers of the forest, blooming from the sunny days of mid-April till into the depth of winter (for he bethought him that the sapless yellow blossoms of his own witch-hazel would in some sort bear out his word), that all the young swarms betook themselves to the wild woods and made their home therein. Another legend is that the wizard, in some way learning the secret of the bees, took on the semblance of their queen, and led a swarm into the woods, where he established it in a hollow tree, and so began the generations of wild bees.[27]

Lured by an Indian wizard or not, the fact is that the honeybee left his domestic hive for the woods shortly after he was brought to the New World by the early settler. As Robinson puts it, honeybees, "when the freak takes them, utterly refuse to be charmed or terrified into abiding with their owners by any banging of pans or blowing of horns."[28] It is a widespread folk belief that making noises, such as beating on pans and blowing horns, will prevent bees from swarming.[29] The bees soon took to the woods, and Robinson says much about hunting the honey-bee.

In "Hunting the Honey-Bee" Robinson reports that sometimes the bee tree is found by accident, but in most cases by the more sophisticated technique of using the beebox and crosslining. Generally, the bee hunter chooses either August or September to set out with beebox, axe or knife, sometimes a compass, and a dinner pail. The beebox, about six inches on each side, has a hinged lid in which is set a small square of glass. Between the lid and the bottom is a slide that divides the box into two compartments. In the lower part the bee hunter places a small piece of honeycomb partly filled with a thin syrup of white sugar and water.

With his few implements the bee hunter seeks his bee along meadow fences or in the field. When he finds a bee he slips his open box under it, slaps the lid down, and captures it. Then he covers the glass with his hand to darken the bee's chamber till the bee stops buzzing and settles on a piece of comb that the hunter has put on the slide. When the hunter sees through the glass that the bee is taking the bait, he sets the box on a stump, boulder, fence or stake and opens the lid. For about five minutes or so the bee hunter must sit or stand a little distance from the box until the bee fills itself, comes out of the box, and flies homeward.

On the bee's first trip to the bee tree, the bee hunter does not attempt to determine its course. Instead, he puts the comb on top of the beebox, adds a bit more syrup, and awaits the return of the honey-bee. The bee keeps returning to the box, and at each return brings with it a few more bees. Now the bee hunter tries to determine their line of flight. If the bees' journey is short, the hunter knows the bee tree is not far. If the bees are long in returning, he moves the comb to the bottom of the beebox. When some of the bees settle on the comb, he closes the lid, shakes the box until the bees come to the top of it, and closes the slide to shut the bees off from the comb so that they will not besmear themselves with the syrup as the bee hunter moves up the line.

Carefully keeping his course, the bee hunter walks quickly with his box of bees into the woods until he finds a convenient opening. Again, he lets the bees on the comb, and the bees come and go as before. At this point, crosslining is sometimes done by setting the box a short distance from the line already established and getting a new line. Where the new line intersects the old line, the bee tree should be near. The point is still not well-defined, for there are probably a number of trees around the bee tree. With a little more observation, however, the bee tree can be easily located.[30]

As he does with most aspects of traditional life, Robinson incorporates his intimate knowledge of bee hunting into his fiction. In *Uncle Lisha's Shop*, for example, Sam Lovel sets out one September day to hunt bees among the asters and goldenrods in the little graveyard that overlooks Uncle Lisha's old homestead. Shortly after Sam puts his beebox on top of one of the gravestones, one bee after another finds the box and flies straight toward the deserted house. When the bees return with their companions, Sam tells his dog, Drive:

"All right," said Sam. "Le's move up," and going cautiously to it, he shut the lid, tapped the side till the bees arose from the comb in the bottom, when he shut the lower slide, took up the box and moved on in the direction the bees had taken to within a few rods of the house. Then he opened the slide and then the cover, and when the bees had filled themselves again, they sailed away with their freight as before. They soon returned and were again imprisoned till Sam had set the box on one of the posts of the garden-fence. Again he gave them their liberty, and in ten minutes a hundred bees were buzzing to and fro between the box and a knot-hole high up in the gable of the shop.

"Yes, sir," said Sam, laughing softly, "the's a swarm under the cla'b'rds o' the shop, jes' as sure 's your name's Drive! Wal, they c'n stay there for all o' me."[31]

Sam Lovel is, of course, more interested in the sport of hunting the honeybee than he is in the honey. In a second place in *Uncle Lisha's Shop*, after finding a bee tree, Sam says, "Tu easy faound for fun . . . but bee-huntin' 's better 'n no huntin', an' more fun 'n fencin' stacks 'at c'n jes' 's well wait a spell while the rowen grows . . . An' it helps tol'able well ter keep a feller's mind off 'm onprofitable thinkin'."[32] Furthermore, in a third place in *Uncle Lisha's Shop*, when Uncle Lisha asks Sam if he enjoys bee hunting, Sam answers, "Sartainly

I du. 'Tain't so excitin' as fox-huntin' an' sech, but it takes a feller int' the woods in a pleasant time o' year, an' it's interestin' seein' the bees a-workin' an' seein' haow clust you c'n line 'em and cross-line 'em, an' a feller's got tu hev' some gumption, an'—wal, I'd a good deal druther hunt bees 'an tu lug sap."[33] The sentiments of an old bee hunter, Uncle Jerry, in "A Bee Hunter's Reminiscences," are similar to those of Sam Lovel:

"So you like to hunt bees, Uncle Jerry?" I asked my old friend, who had mentioned that pastime with a glow of animation.

"Of course I du," he answered, "anything that's huntin' an' that comes the fust on't when the' hain't no other huntin'. It's a pleasant time o' year tu be a-shoolin' 'raound the aidge o' the woods an' intu 'em, an' you're like tu run ontu signs o' young foxes bein' raised, that'll be hendy tu know 'baout, come fall. An' it hain't every dodunk 't c'n hunt bees, le' me tell ye. If you think so, you jest try it.

"A feller's got tu hev sharp eyes, an' use 'em, an' be pooty well l'arned in the critter's ways, an' hev some gumption, in a gin'ral way. An' it hain't all lazin' 'raound, nuther. I've lined bees nigh ontu three mild, an' when a feller done that an' fetches up ag'in a tame swarm in someb'dy's do' yard it makes him feel kinder wamble-cropped.

* * * * * * * * * * * * * *

"You sh'ld like tu go a-bee huntin', hey? Wal, 't ain't much use nowerdays, the's so many tame ones tu bother a feller. An' I guess y' eyes hain't good 'nough. Nighsighted, hain't ye? An' it hain't ev'y dodunk 'at c'n hunt bees. But come nex' summer, we'll try it a hack if you wantu."[34]

Accordingly, Robinson says so much about the techniques and the attitudes relevant to pioneer bee hunting that from stories and essays like "A Bee Hunter's Reminiscences," "Bee Hunting," "Hunting the Honey-Bee," and *Uncle Lisha's Shop*, one can learn enough about bee hunting to practice it himself.

NOTES

[1]Robinson, *Vermont*, p. 295.   [2]Van Wagenen, p. 169.

[3]Robinson, *In New England Fields and Woods*, p. 122.

[4]Robinson, *In New England Fields and Woods*, pp. 151-152.

[5]Van Wagenen, p. 169.

[6]Robinson, *Uncle Lisha's Shop and A Danvis Pioneer*, p. 38.

[7]Robinson, *Uncle Lisha's Shop and A Danvis Pioneer*, p. 221.

[8]Robinson, *In New England Fields and Woods*, pp. 15-16.

[9]Robinson, *Out of Bondage and Other Stories*, pp. 41-42.

[10]Robinson, *Vermont*, p. 295.

[11]Robinson, "Glimpses of New England Farm Life," p. 520. For another good account of sugaring in Vermont see Needham and Mussey, pp. 33-45.

[12]Robinson, *Danvis Folks and A Hero of Ticonderoga*, pp. 231-232.

[13]Robinson, *Out of Bondage and Other Stories*, p. 46.

[14]Van Wagenen, p. 174.

[15]Robinson, *Uncle Lisha's Shop and A Danvis Pioneer*, p. 222.

[16]Robinson, "Glimpses of New England Farm Life," p. 520.

[17]Robinson, *Vermont*, pp. 295-296.

[18]Robinson, "Glimpses of New England Farm Life," p. 520.

[19]Beverly Drake, "In New England It's Time for Sugar on Snow," *The Christian Science Monitor*, March 14, 1968, p. 5.

[20]Robinson, "Glimpses of New England Farm Life," p. 521.

[21]Robinson, *Uncle Lisha's Shop and A Danvis Pioneer*, p. 146.

[22]Robinson, "Glimpses of New England Farm Life," p. 521.

[23]Van Wagenen, pp. 174-175.

[24]Robinson, *In New England Fields and Woods*, p. 229.

[25]Robinson, *Uncle Lisha's Shop and A Danvis Pioneer*, p. 104.

[26]*The Frank C. Brown Collection*, VII, 435, No. 7515.

[27]Robinson, *Silver Fields and Other Sketches of a Farmer-Sportsman*, p. 245.

[28]Robinson, *Silver Fields and Other Sketches of a Farmer-Sportsman*, p. 245.

[29]For example, see Hyatt, p. 53, No. 1354.

[30]Robinson, *Silver Fields and Other Sketches of a Farmer-Sportsman*, pp. 243-255.

[31]Robinson, *Uncle Lisha's Shop and A Danvis Pioneer*, p. 247.

[32]Robinson, *Uncle Lisha's Shop and A Danvis Pioneer*, p. 188.

[33]Robinson, *Uncle Lisha's Shop and A Danvis Pioneer*, p. 223.

[34]Robinson, *Out of Bondage and Other Stories*, pp. 213-214, 217.

CHAPTER 11

HOUSEHOLD CRAFTS

Although Robinson's comments on the traditional material culture of Vermont are often incidental, they show that certain items were current in tradition, and they certainly round out the social context of the verbal folklore that he includes in his fiction. Moreover, from a literary point of view, Robinson's faithful reporting of most aspects of folklife contributes to the credibility of his stories. However, of the three general categories of traditional material culture—folk arts, folk crafts, folk architecture—he mentions folk arts least. Of course, most of the Danvis stories are set in either Uncle Lisha's shop or in the field, where one would not expect to find many of the traditional arts. Consequently, Robinson is not actually neglecting the traditional arts; he merely accurately depicts the milieu on which he is focusing. Accordingly, other than some casual remarks about painted curtains, a painted vase, a japanned tobacco box, gayly painted caravan wagons, and whittling,[1] virtually the only extensive references in Robinson's works to anything that might be considered folk art are his comments on carved powder horns. Powder horns, of course, are more related to activities in the field than to those in the home. As one might expect, references to powder horns are found only in stories of Vermont pioneer life. In *A Danvis Pioneer,* for instance, an old ranger draws from his pocket "a flat powderhorn engraved in black outlines with a rude map of Champlain and its tributaries."[2] Similarly, in *In the Green Wood* Tom Pangborn also has "a flat powder-horn, upon which a map of the lake and its tributaries was etched in black lines."[3] In "A Story of the Old Frontier" Simeon Draper has an engraved powder horn that he brought with him from Connecticut.[4]

Robinson has more to say about folk crafts and represents most of the traditional crafts in his writings. For example, in addition to those crafts and craftsmen mentioned earlier, there are references to the crafts of the pewterer, the tinsmith, the cooper, the hatter, the wainwright, the clockmaker, the pump log maker, the clay pipe maker, the treenware maker, and the horn comb maker.[5] Furthermore, Robinson refers to traditional baskets in a number of places. In *Sam Lovel's Boy* when Lisha and Sammy meet three Indians in the woods, one of the male Indians is making basket splints from a peeled ash log, while a female Indian is "weaving a pretty basket of red, blue, and yellow splints."[6] As Allen H. Eaton points out, of the many varieties of baskets made in New England, the best known and most widely used is the ash splint basket, which is also the one that Robinson mentions most frequently. Eaton explains that the first step in making an ash splint basket involves selecting the proper tree and cutting its trunk into logs from five to eight feet long. Then one log is placed across another and pounded to loosen the layers. After the log is pounded, the craftsman simply cuts down the full length of the log and peels off the strips of ash.[7] According to Eaton, the best craftsmen make their baskets in a traditional way without nails or metal; and he indicates that basket making is truly a traditional craft learned, in part, from the Indians.

Robinson observed similar basketmaking techniques of both the Indian and the European settler; the materials used in making baskets in the New World were different from those in Europe, and the European settler had to learn something about making baskets from the Indian. In "Given Away," he tells of visiting an old French-Canadian couple, John and Marie Cherbineau, whose chief industries were making baskets and braiding straw hats for neighbors and storekeepers. Robinson reports that upon arriving at the Cherbineau home, "I found old John, the lean and agile opposite of his ponderous spouse, engaged in the primary process of basket making, pounding an ash log and stripping off the thin splints."[8]

As might be expected of an author interested mainly in the masculine activities, Robinson's comments on the traditional techniques for preserving and cooking foods are sketchy. For the most part, he simply gives a brief inventory of some of the foods preserved and served in nineteenth-century Vermont. He mentions that strings of apples and rings of pumpkins were dried: "Hooks and poles over the stove supported a few strings of late-dried apples and some shriveled rings of pumpkin-like necklaces of old gold . . ."[9] Similarly, in *A Danvis Pioneer* he mentions that wild moose meat is smoked, dried, and then stored in the low loft of the log cabin of Josiah Hill and Kenelm Dalrymple.[10] He mentions that pork is stored in a cellar, fried nutcakes are kept in a stone jar, meal is stored in a barrel, and plums are merely "put up," but the techniques for preserving the plums, for instance, are not explained.[11]

About food preparation, however, Robinson says more. A typical breakfast, for example, he describes in "Glimpses of New England Farm Life" as "fried pork, or sausages, or beefsteak,—let us hope not fried,— or cold roast beef, left from yesterday's dinner, the potatoes, the wheaten and 'rye-'n'-injun' bread, the johnny-cake or buckwheat-cakes, the apple-sauce, the milk and the butter . . ." All these, reports Robinson, are homegrown, "nothing 'boughten' but the tea or coffee, and the pepper and salt."[12] In "A New Year's Swearing-off," the Folsoms have a similar breakfast of coffee, sausages, and baked potatoes.[13] In fact, no meal in Danvis, at home or on a camping trip, is complete without potatoes. Indeed potatoes are such an important part of every meal that even on a camping trip Joseph Hill finds it necessary to apologize when he does not have them to serve his fellow campers for breakfast. Potatoes are, in fact, "as much missed at a Yankee feast as they would be at a banquet of the descendants of Irish kings."[14]

Potatoes are also an important ingredient in traditional fish chowder. "Pork, fish, potatoes, crackers, and onions furnished all the requisites for a chowder," writes Robinson, "a dinner all in one pot, and one that needed no constant tending."[15] In addition, in *Sam Lovel's Boy* Robinson tells about an Indian technique for cooking fish. Speaking of an Indian woman, Robinson writes, "She slipped six dressed trout crosswise into the cleft of a green wand, tied the cleft end together with a strip of bark, thrust the other end into the ground and slanted this primitive broiler at the proper angle over the coals . . ."[16] The Yankees, however, have their own method of cooking fish over an open fire. In *Sam Lovel's Boy*, for example, "Four trout were dressed, a fire burned to a rosy bed of coals, the fish spitted on sharpened sticks, each with a slice of pork laid inside him, and so broiled . . ."[17] Sammy Lovel, for one, prefers this method to that without seasoning of Indian women.[18]

Pork is a popular meat in Robinson's fiction, both for table and for seasoning. In *In the Green Wood*, frizzled pork and rye and Indian bread are served for supper, but Robinson terms this a "rude repast," apparently since potatoes are not served.[19] In *Sam Lovel's Boy,* Ruby Hill serves a typical Danvis meal of boiled pork, potatoes, Indian pudding, and dandelion greens.[20] Of all the foods gathered in Robinson's writings—greens, nuts, and berries—greens are the most frequently mentioned and invariably are served with boiled pork. For instance, in *A Danvis Pioneer* in the spring "caowslops an' dand'lierns" are gathered and served with boiled pork, and when spring greens are no longer available to the Danvis folk, beet greens are picked and also served with boiled pork.[21] In addition, partridges are fried "'long wi' a slice o' pork,"[22] although pigeons are generally made into pies, as in *Sam Lovel's Boy* when thirteen pigeons make a pigeon pie.[23] And in *Uncle Lisha's Outing* Sam Lovel remarks, "Pa'tridge is pooty dry meated, but pidjins

makes tol'able pidjin pies, aour folks thinks."[24]   The dish eaten by
French Canadians all over the continent, pea soup, is generally seasoned
with pork.[25]

For the special holiday meals on Thanksgiving and Christmas,
turkey is in order in Danvis. Thus, in *Danvis Folks* Mrs. Purington asks
Huldah to "come over tu Thanksgivin' tu-morrer tu aour haouse. We
hain't goin' tu hev no gret, jest turkey an' some high bush cranb'ry sass
an' punkin pie an' sech . . ."[26] In "Uncle Gid's Christmas Tree," however, when Gideon and Pamela Corbin cannot find a turkey for their
Christmas dinner, they serve a "mysterious roast" to their guests. For
along with the more traditional holiday dishes of baked potatoes, hot
johnnycake, biscuits, cider apple sauce, honey, and pumpkin pies, Aunt
Pamela serves roasted raccoon, which she and her husband pass off as a
"coshaw," or pig, since their guests "might spleen ag'in 'coon."[27]
Roasted raccoon, obviously, is not a typical Danvis dish.

In addition to pumpkin pie and apple sauce, other desserts and
treats include molasses candy, sweet flag candy, "popple bark bitters,"
"seek-no-further," a lump of maple sugar moulded in an eggshell, sliced
calamus root candied in maple sugar, gingerbread, spruce gum, maple
sugar "waxed" on snow, and hasty pudding.[28] Of these traditional
candies and treats, however, only hasty pudding is treated at length by
Robinson, when in *Danvis Folks* Huldah and Aunt Jerusha decide to
make some pudding for lunch. Concerning the making of hasty pudding, Aunt Jerusha asks Huldah:

". . . Du you wet your meal in col' water fust er stir it right in when the water
biles?"

"Oh, I stir it right int' the kittle as soon as it biles," said Huldah, bringing the pud-
ding-stick and the basin of meal, "an I salt it well when it's abaout as thick as
gruel."

"So du I," and the old woman nodded emphatic approval of the dry meal method.
"It's more partic'lar work and there's more danger of it's bein' lumpy; but it need
n't be, if you're keerful tu sprinkle in slow an' keep a-stirrin' the same way all the
time. . . ."

She critically watched Huldah as she sifted the meal into the seething kettle with
one hand and stirred it with rapid turns of the other, while the wholesome fragrance
of the boiled meal and the parching of a few grains scattered on the stove began to
diffuse itself through the room. Then when the stick was lifted and dripped its
burden in an even stream, her face relaxed to an expression of satisfaction.

"It's smooth as 'lasses, Huldy. Naow be you goin' to make a lawful puddin'?"

"I never heard abaout no law fer puddin'."

"Wal, there was in Connect'cut in an airly day. Ye see most ev'ybody 'at was anyways forehanded useter hev 'printice boys an' gals bound tu 'em till they come of
age, an' some on 'em useter keep th' 'printices on hasty puddin', an' made it so thin
'at it wa'nt much more 'n gruel an' starved the poor creeturs so 't they would't

sca'cely make a shadder; an' so the Leegislatur passed a law 'at they got tu make
hasty puddin' so thick 'at the puddin' stick 'ould stan' right up in the middle of the
kittle. But I'd ruther not have it quite so thick fer me tu eat, bein' 'at I hain't a
'printice gal. You got it thick 'nough. Naow set it on the back o' the stove an' let
it blubber a spell. . . ."[29]

Other than hasty pudding, the food about which Robinson says
most is bread. In his stories of the early days, johnnycake is the bread
generally eaten. In "McIntosh of Vergennes," for example, a Scottish
housewife, Bessie McIntosh, while knitting keeps "an eye to the venison
stewing in the pot hanging high on the trammel and to two great johnny-
cakes baking on their boards atilt before the fire—one trick of Yankee
cookery that the gudeman favored."[30] In *In the Green Wood*, Mrs.
Pangborn bakes a johnnycake "on its board before the open fire," and
in *A Hero of Ticonderoga*, Ruth Beeman "mixed a johnnycake with hot
water and salt, and set it to bake on its board, tilted before the fire."[31]
But the best description of johnnycake, along with the best accounts of
no-cake and samp, appears in *Danvis Folks* when Aunt Jerusha tells
Huldah about these pioneer foods:

". . . You never hearn o' no-cake? Wal, that was parched corn paounded up in a
mortar an' eat wi' milk ef they hed it, an' ef they had n't, jest mixed up wi' water.
They l'arnt that of Injins, an' they lowed it 'ould stan' by a man longer 'n any other
Injin corn fixin's. Then they uster make samp in the Plumpin' mill, big mortars
they was, 'at went wi' a spring pole, an' they'd change off ontu samp when they
got sick o' no-cake. Hasty puddin' an' johnny-cake they couldn't hev, 'thout gittin'
the corn graound tu a reg'lar mill, an' them was mebby forty miled off. Bimeby
they got tu raisin' wheat, an' then some folks begin to stick up the' noses at Injin.
But aour folks did n't, 'case they come f'm Rho' Dislan' an' allers sot gret store by
all sorts o' Injin victuals. Father allers would hev his johnny-cake fer breakfus' an'
hev it baked on a board, long after they hed 'em a stove. You never eat a johnny-
cake baked on a board? You don't say. Wal, then, you do know what johnny-cake
is, Huldy. Haow did they make 'em? Wal, jest stirred up the meal wi' b'ilin' water
an' salt, not tew thick ner tew thin, an' then spread it ontu a oak board 'at was made
a-puppus, an' sot it up afore the fire, tilted a leetle mite at fust ag'in' a flat iron, an'
kep' a-settin' it up stretter an' stretter till that side was done, an' then turn it over
an' bake t' other side, an' all the time keep a-bastin' on 't wi' sweet cream, an' then
eat it an' be thankful 'at the Lord made Injin corn tu grow an' give his creeturs the
knowledge tu use it proper. . . ."[32]

That Aunt Jerusha must explain the processess of making johnny-
cake, no-cake, and samp to Huldah indicates that by Huldah's generation other breads and techniques of bread-making had become popular.
Robinson refers to some of the latter in *Uncle Lisha's Shop* when Mr.
Purington tips over a pot of "emptin's" while "pokin' raound in the
suller," and Mrs. Purington must set out to borrow some emptyings,
used as a leavening agent, in order to bake bread:

"I've ben all 'raound Robin Hood's barn tu borry them emptin's. Fust I went tu Joel's, though I might ha' knowed better 'n tu, for Jemimy she allers uses milk risin'; mis'able flat tasted bread it makes tew. Ketch me a-makin' bread wi' milk risin'! . . . Arter I sot an' talked wi' Jemimy a spell I went on tu Briggses; but Miss' Briggs she hain't got nothin' but yeast cakes, an' I hain't uster usin' them. So arter I'd sot an' rested me a spell . . . I went on tu Hillses', and Miss' Hill she'd jest sot a mes tu workin', 'n' so she hedn't got none. . . . Then I went along over tu Uncle Lisher's, an' there I made aout tu git me some emptin's. . . . Wal, . . . we've got us some emptin's tu start with, an naow we've got tu set tu work an' make some. Hope yer father won't tip over the pot again, pokin' raound in the suller. You've skum the milk, I s'pose, an' got the pans washed an' scalded?"[33]

In most of Robinson's stories there is a definite division of labor based on sex; consequently, while the farmer is tending his crops or stock, his wife is generally busy at one or another of the household crafts. Other than cooking and preserving food, among the most important and most time consuming of the household crafts were textile making and needlework, and Robinson most frequently portrays women in his stories as either spinning, carding, darning, knitting, quilting, braiding rugs, or, in short, performing one of the textile crafts.

Not all of Robinson's Danvis women make all of the clothing for their families. In "A September Election," for instance, Mrs. Piper tells her husband, Levi, that he might as well purchase "some fine shirt timber an' have Ann 'Lizer make 'em when she makes aour dresses." Mrs. Piper tells her husband that for three shirts he will need to buy "nine yards o' linen and Ann 'Lizer won't charge over'n above fifty cents apiece if she comes right int' the haouse an' makes 'em up 'long wi' me an' Malviny's dresses."[34]

The folk culture Robinson depicts is simultaneous to that called the "homespun age" by Jared Van Wagenen, Jr., in *The Golden Age of Homespun*. The "homespun age," as Van Wagenen defines it, was certainly not static, for it "began with our earliest settlements, . . . reached its fullest fruition during the generation following the Revolution, and . . . drew definitely toward its close about the time of the Civil War."[35] Similarly, Robinson depicts the textile crafts from their beginnings during the earliest settlement of Vermont through their fullest fruition a generation after the Revolution to their decline near the close of the Civil War.

Robinson points out that the matron of nearly every pioneer household in Vermont taught both her daughters and her maids, if she had them, how to spin and weave flax and wool. "The beat of the little wheel, the hum of the great wheel, the ponderous thud of the loom," Robinson reports, "were household voices in every Vermont homestead, whether it was the old loghouse that the forest had first given place to, or its more pretentious framed and boarded successor. All the womenfolk knitted stockings and mittens while they rested or visited, the click of the needles accompanied by the chirp of the cricket and the buzz of gossip."[36] For both work and holiday, Robinson says, everyone in the household "was clad in homespun from head to foot, save what the hatter furnished for the first and the traveling cobbler for the last."[37]

The importance of textile making as a pioneer industry is illustrated in the historical story *A Hero of Ticonderoga* when a pioneer family, the Beemans, comes from Connecticut to live in Vermont. While Seth Beeman and his son, Nathan, are busy clearing the land and piling logs for the spring burning, Mrs. Beeman, with her daughter as companion, remains inside the newly occupied log house, where she "plied cards and spinning-wheel, with the frugal store of wool and flax brought from the old home. So their busy hands kept loneliness at bay, even amid the dreariness of the wintry wilderness."[38] Throughout *A Hero of Ticonderoga*, Mrs. Beeman is frequently portrayed either with her wool cards or near her spinning wheel.[39] In *A Danvis Pioneer*, the textile crafts play an important part in the lives of the Danvis women. Robinson writes that after Josiah Hill settles in his new home in Danvis with his wife, "No house was better provided nor more neatly kept than his, nor resounded more constantly with the musical droning of the great wheel and the livelier whir and beat of the flax wheel."[40]

A generation later in the Danvis stories textile making is still an essential craft. In *Uncle Lisha's Shop*, Huldah Purington before her marriage one day borrows Aunt Jerusha's wool cards. "I wanter borry your wool caards, Aunt Jerushy," says Huldah, "to caard some rolls for father some socks. Aourn is lent, we do' know where."[41] Another step of the textile making process, the operation of the spinning wheel, is briefly described in "The Purification of Cornbury," when Robinson writes that Mrs. Dana "drew the big wheel, with its white saddle of rolls, from the corner, and set it to humming its musical song while she stepped back and forth beside it; now twirling the wheel swiftly in one way, now slowly the other."[42] By degrees the manufacture of wool passed from the Vermont home to a mill. In *Along Three Rivers*, Robinson reports that at Dover, or Walker's Falls, on Otter Creek there was a carding machine, and he adds, "I think there was another carding machine in the neighborhood of the upper forges. In these establishments wool was carded into rolls for spinning, and cloth dressed after the spinning and weaving had been done at the homes of the farmers. The quietude of complete desertion pervades these places now, and scarcely a vestige of any of the works remains to memorialize the days when they were astir with busy life."[43] A woolen factory on Otter Creek, however, was well within Robinson's memory:

The woolen factory was forty or more rods above the bridge. Robert Hazard, son of the first Vermont Robert, carried it on for a time, followed by Theodore Lyman, who for many years manufactured the tag locks and pulled wool of the neighboring farmers into flannel and "sheep's gray," which was the ordinary wear of our country folk forty years ago, and very good and substantial wear it was too. I suppose it was this gray fullcloth that Thoreau calls "Vermont gray," but with us it was always "sheep's gray," and many a well-to-do farmer wore it to "mill an' to meetin'." My earliest and most vivid recollection of Theodore Lyman is that he had but one hand, having lost the other by the bursting of a gun in the ceremony of "wakin' up off'sers," which at early dawn ushered in June training day. He sold the factory to E. Daniels, who continued running it till it was burned a few years ago.[44]

If one reads the Danvis stories in historical order, he will observe a gradual decline of the textile crafts in the Vermont household and will notice a gradual dependence on the mills for textile making. In fact, in the last of the Danvis stories, *Sam Lovel's Boy,* textile making has all but disappeared. Speaking of the big and little wheels, Robinson writes:

. . . for the wheels and the reel that clicked at every fortieth turn, most coveted plaything of children, were shoved close to the wall as if symbolic of their retreat into the background of the passing years, where the cards and the loom had already taken their places. The rolls were made by the carding machine; most of the cloth woven at the factory where much of the woolen spinning was beginning to be done. So the arts of hand-carding and hand-weaving were no longer indispensable parts of a girl's education and even the beautiful and graceful art of wool-spinning was no longer taught to every girl. Old folks mourned the degenerate days when the musical hum of the great wheel should be no longer heard.

"If Polly does up an' git married, I do' know what she'll do for a settin' aout," Uncle Lisha said, as his eyes wandered over to the silent wheels and reel. "I don't s'pose she could spin a run o' yarn tu save her."

"Law sakes! Her mother 's got a 'stro'nary settin' aout all pervided—more 'n as much agin as Huldy ever had; stuff 'at she's saved up, an' stuff 'at she's spun, an' wove no eend o' linen sheets an' woolen sheets for winter, an' tew thirty-paound live-geese feather beds!"

"Wal, Huldy's Polly 'll know haow tu spin an' weave. I'll warrant ye, an' not be beholden tu nob'dy for her beddin'," Uncle Lisha said.

"I d' know 'baout that," said Timothy, shaking his head dubiously. "It 's all for bein' pop'lar naowerdays, an' mebby Huldy 'll foller the fashi'n wi' Sis. She 's a-cuttin' an' sewin' rags tu weave her a carpet for the square room, an' fust ye know, a h'us'mat won't be good 'nough for the front door."[45]

Accordingly, as Robinson points out in *Vermont,* "Wool-carding machines were erected at convenient points, and hand-carding made no longer necessary. Presently arose factories which performed all the work of cloth-making (carding, spinning, weaving, and finishing), . . . and the use of the spinning-wheel and hand-loom became lost arts."[46] As his treatment of the household crafts suggests, in writing about the passing folklore of Vermont in its social context, Robinson was more than a regional enthusiast or an antiquarian, for he saw the traditional arts, crafts, beliefs, customs, stories, and songs of the Vermonters in their historical perspective.

NOTES

[1]Robinson, *Sam Lovel's Boy with Forest and Stream Fables*, p. 162; *Out of Bondage and Other Stories*, p. 214; *Uncle Lisha's Outing and Along Three Rivers*, p. 198; *Danvis Folks and A Hero of Ticonderoga*, pp. 171, 184.

[2]Robinson, *Uncle Lisha's Shop and A Danvis Pioneer*, p. 20.

[3]Robinson, *Sam Lovel's Camps and In the Green Wood*, p. 227.

[4]Robinson, *Out of Bondage and Other Stories*, p. 98.

[5]Robinson, *Danvis Folks and A Hero of Ticonderoga*, pp. 117, 250, 255; *Uncle Lisha's Outing and Along Three Rivers*, pp. 54, 120, 122, 242; *Sam Lovel's Camps and In the Green Wood*, pp. 81, 118; *Out of Bondage and Other Stories*, pp. 73, 118, 161-162, 165.

[6]Robinson, *Sam Lovel's Boy with Forest and Stream Fables*, p. 58.

[7]Eaton, pp. 47-48.   [8]Robinson, *In New England Fields and Woods*, p. 182.

[9]Robinson, *Sam Lovel's Boy with Forest and Stream Fables*, p. 133.

[10]Robinson, *Uncle Lisha's Shop and A Danvis Pioneer*, p. 36.

[11]Robinson, *Danvis Folks and A Hero of Ticonderoga*, pp. 201, 255, 256; *Sam Lovel's Camps and In the Green Wood*, p. 201.

[12]Robinson, "Glimpses of New England Farm Life," p. 513.

[13]Robinson, *Out of Bondage and Other Stories*, pp. 207-208.

[14]Robinson, *Sam Lovel's Camps and In the Green Wood*, p. 120.

[15]Robinson, *Sam Lovel's Camps and In the Green Wood*, p. 58. For a variant of this traditional recipe see Imogene Wolcott, *The Yankee Cook Book* (New York, 1939), pp. 8-9.

[16]Robinson, *Sam Lovel's Boy with Forest and Stream Fables*, p. 61.

[17]Robinson, *Sam Lovel's Boy with Forest and Stream Fables*, p. 32.

[18]Robinson, *Sam Lovel's Boy with Forest and Stream Fables*, p. 61.

[19]Robinson, *Sam Lovel's Camps and in the Green Wood*, p. 239.

[20]Robinson, *Sam Lovel's Boy with Forest and Stream Fables*, p. 41.

[21]Robinson, *Uncle Lisha's Shop and A Danvis Pioneer*, p. 106.

[22]Robinson, *Uncle Lisha's Shop and A Danvis Pioneer*, p. 169.

[23]Robinson, *Sam Lovel's Boy with Forest and Stream Fables*, p. 52.

[24]Robinson, *Uncle Lisha's Outing and Along Three Rivers*, p. 123.

[25]Robinson, *Uncle Lisha's Shop and A Danvis Pioneer*, p. 56.

[26]Robinson, *Danvis Folks and A Hero of Ticonderoga*, p. 70.

[27]Robinson, *Out of Bondage and Other Stories*, pp. 202, 206.

[28]Robinson, *Out of Bondage and Other Stories*, p. 196; *Uncle Lisha's Outing and Along Three Rivers*, p. 200; *Sam Lovel's Boy with Forest and Stream Fables*, pp. 39, 46, 99, 100; *Uncle Lisha's Shop and A Danvis Pioneer*, p. 201; *Danvis Folks and A Hero of Ticonderoga*, p. 232.

[29]Robinson, *Danvis Folks and A Hero of Ticonderoga*, pp. 116-117. See Thomas Robinson Hazard, *The Jonny-Cake Papers of "Shepherd Tom"* (Boston, 1915), pp. 61-62.

[30]Robinson, *Out of Bondage and Other Stories*, p. 114.

[31]Robinson, *Sam Lovel's Camps and In the Green Wood*, p. 209; *Danvis Folks and A Hero of Ticonderoga*, p. 209.

[32]Robinson, *Danvis Folks and A Hero of Ticonderoga*, p. 118. See Mrs. Earle's comments on johnnycake, no-cake, and samp, p. 149. But for a better account of johnnycake see Hazard, pp. 17-18, 28-30.

[33]Robinson, *Uncle Lisha's Shop and A Danvis Pioneer*, pp. 179-180.

[34]Robinson, *Sam Lovel's Boy with Forest and Stream Fables*, p. 163.

[35]Van Wagenen, p. x.   [36]Robinson, *Vermont*, p. 293.

[37]Robinson, *Vermont*, p. 293.

[38]Robinson, *Danvis Folks and A Hero of Ticonderoga*, p. 231.

[39]Robinson, *Danvis Folks and A Hero of Ticonderoga*, pp. 236, 275.

[40]Robinson, *Uncle Lisha's Shop and A Danvis Pioneer*, p. 95.

[41]Robinson, *Uncle Lisha's Shop and A Danvis Pioneer*, p. 178.

[42]Robinson, *Out of Bondage and Other Stories*, p. 173.

[43]Robinson, *Uncle Lisha's Outing and Along Three Rivers*, pp. 242, 245.

[44]Robinson, *Uncle Lisha's Outing and Along Three Rivers*, pp. 231-232.

[45]Robinson, *Sam Lovel's Boy with Forest and Stream Fables*, pp. 133-134.

[46]Robinson, *Vermont*, p. 303.

CHAPTER 12

FOLK ARCHITECTURE

Robinson's main contribution to the study of folk architecture is found in his article on traditional New England fences. His interest in fences is especially important since most American folklorists have ignored fences in their research. Raup points out fencing "is an increasingly significant element of material culture, indicative of its physical surrounding, having special social significance, and acquiring different forms which may stem from culture contact and traditions":

The materials of which fences are built are usually indicators of vegetation and climatic conditions, from the cactus of the Southwest to the tropical bamboo fences of Japan. The type of fence is often a measure of the ingenuity of its builder, for he builds his enclosure at a minimum cost and for maximum protection. Since the cost element is involved, the fence becomes an index of wealth, whether it be the well-trimmed hedge of the English estate or the makeshift barrel-hoop fence seen occasionally in Lower California. . . .[1]

Further, as Austin E. Fife maintains, "Fencing is a necessity wherever land is to be reserved for specialized use or for particular individuals or groups. It is thus absolutely essential in any culture which assigns value to the concept of private property, or which wishes to reap the benefits of the specialized use of land."[2]

Although Robinson mentions only the rail fence and the pole fence in his fiction,[3] he saw fit to devote a whole article to the fences of New England. Since this article, entitled "New England Fences," appeared, in *Scribner's*, early in 1880, it must be considered a landmark in the history of folklife studies in the United States. Robinson points out that he wrote this most specifically in order "to make some record of such fences as we now have, and some that have already passed away."[4] He describes ten types of traditional fences as well as several combined forms.

The early fences he describes are the pole fence,[5] the brush fence,[6] and the log fence.[7] According to Robinson, when the early settlers bought a patch of ground they often fenced it in with poles. This pole fence, he says, resembles the rail fence, but the poles are longer than rails. There are also cross-staked pole fences, which are laid straight, each pole being upheld "by two stakes crossing the one beneath, their lower ends being driven into the ground."[8] Pole fences were still made during Robinson's life, and such a fence surrounds the garden patch of a Negro family in *Uncle Lisha's Outing*.[9] Another early type described by Robinson is the brush fence. He points out that according to unwritten law the brush fence must be a rod wide with no specification as to its height. In building the brush fence the small trees that stand along the fence line are chopped down, although not severed from the stump, and are made to fall lengthwise of the fence. Other trees are then cut and brought to the fence line to give the fence its required width and the desired height. Brush fences, too, were still being constructed during Robinson's lifetime.[10] Robinson remembers seeing only one example of another early fence, the log fence, which could be made only when timber was plentiful. More substantial than either the pole fence or the brush fence, the log fence, according to Robinson, was made of pine and built three logs high. The logs were laid straight, "overlapping a little at the ends, on which were placed horizontally the short cross-pieces, which upheld the logs next above."[11] The completed log fence resembles a solid wooden wall.

After these early fences came the rail fence, sometimes called the snake fence, from its contour resembling a snake's meandering trail, and sometimes called the Virginia fence, "perhaps because the Old Dominion was the mother of it as of presidents, but more likely for no better reason than that the common deer is named the Virginia deer, or that no end of quadrupeds and birds and plants, having their home as much in the United States as in the British Provinces, bear the title of Canadensis." Robinson feels that the rail fence is American in origin and "probably has enclosed and does yet enclose more acres of our land than any other fence."[12] Robinson was not in a position to speak with any authority about the origin of the rail fence, and unlike modern objective folklife research, his discussion of the rail fence tends to be subjective. Nevertheless, his comments aptly illustrate that the fence is more than mere utility. The recurrent theme of many of Robinson's writings, that those things closest to nature are best, is found once again in his discussion of traditional fences. He says a new rail fence is ugly until it is weather-stained and covered with mosses, vines, and lichens.

This idea that nature improves upon man's creations finds its way into his discussion of another New England fixture, the board fence. He asserts that it is uglier than the rail fence because the board fence "is more prim and glaring, as there is no alternation of light and shade in its straight line. But age improves its appearance also . . ."[13] His account of the stone wall is essentially subjective too. According to Robinson, the stone wall, the most enduring of fences, is also the most appealing to the eye.[14]

He discusses other New England fences such as the stump fence, the slab fence, the water fence, and the slate fence.[15] The stump fence, he says, looks like a barricade "of mighty antlers." An excellent photograph of a stump fence near Robinson's home is included in *Vermont: A Guide to the Green Mountain State*.[16] The protruding roots of the stumps indeed look like "mighty antlers," as he observed. He notes that during his life many fields of old pine-bearing land were surrounded by stump fences.[17] As late as 1945 H. H. Chadwick, a publicity director of Vermont, wrote to Mamie Meredith about stump fences in Vermont:

In regard to stump fences. They used to be a familiar sight in Vermont. In early days of settlement many trees were cut down and burned to clear the land and it was considerable part of a job to get rid of the stumps. Often these were dug out by hand and hauled to the boundary line and laid up. Occasionally in recent years I have seen the remains of one of these fences but most of them have rotted away or have been burned by the owners.[18]

Another fence, the slab fence, is neither picturesque nor enduring, according to Robinson. Slab fences, which are made from the slabs from the sawmill, are seldom seen anywhere but near sawmills. One end of each slab rests on the ground, and the other end is upheld by cross stakes.[19] A fence with an even more restricted area of distribution is the slate fence. Fences, of course, are made of whatever materials are abundant, and in the slate region of Vermont, Robinson observed a peculiar fence made of slabs of slate "set in the earth like a continuous row of closely planted headstones."[20] H. R. Raup reports that in the slate belt of eastern Pennsylvania slate is also used in fence building, but in Pennsylvania the slabs of slate are mortised for rails and used only as fence posts.[21]

The simplest fence discussed by Robinson is what he calls the water fence, which consists of only a pole spanning a stream. Robinson points out that one end of the pole might be fastened by a link and staple to a tree near the water. He says that in shallow streams the pole often has a central support, which might be either a large stone that is conveniently located in the right place or a pier made like a large bench.[22] In addition to these clear types of fences, Robinson notes that there are also combined forms in New England. For example, although he has rarely seen them, Robinson writes that some New England fences are half wall and half board or half wall and half rail. The half wall and half rail fence he calls a regional form of the post and rail fence, which he says is common in northern New England. In the Vermont variant the low wall is topped with rails that rest on cross stakes slanted across the walls, or the ends rest in rough mortises cut in posts that are built into the wall.[23]

In addition to Robinson's remarks on traditional fences, throughout his writings there are incidental comments on both house and barn architecture. Although no specific dates and no exact specifications are given, one can trace generally the development of architecture in Vermont from pioneer days until just after the Civil War. For example, in his local history, *Along Three Rivers,* Robinson writes that in pioneer Vermont "the forested banks were notched with clearings" and "stout log houses arose where never had been dwellings more stable than the Indian's bark wigwam."[24] Of course, by the time Vermont was settled log architecture was firmly established, especially on the frontier, where there were no sawmills at first and where the trees had to be cleared. The pioneer's attitude toward the forests of Vermont is aptly expressed in *In the Green Wood* when Robinson writes that as John Pangborn struck his axe into a tall pine, he "had the backwoodsman's love of warfare with trees, those giants that stood in the way."[25] In *A Danvis Pioneer* Josiah Hill's attitude toward trees is similar. After Josiah settles in the almost uninhabited township of Danvis after the Revolution and begins clearing his land to build a log house, Robinson writes, "Again the quick resonant strokes of his axe were echoed from side to side of a widening clearing. He rejoiced in the conquest of the forest giants, venerable patriarchs, concerning whose fate he felt no sentimental emotion."[26] Antoine Bassette's pragmatic attitude toward trees, in *Uncle Lisha's Outing* is no doubt typical, for where Sam Lovel saw the beauties of nature in the forest growth, Antoine merely "saw the axe helves in the hickory, the baskets in the ash, and plank in the hemlock and pine, and the medicinal virtues of the prettiest plant were more to him than its beauty."[27]

Virtually all of the references to log architecture in Robinson's works are in the historical stories of Vermont pioneer life and *A Danvis Pioneer.* In *A Danvis Pioneer,* for instance, when Josiah Hill and Kenelm Dalrymple set out from Connecticut to Vermont they spend their first nights in a farmhouse or in an inn, but as they draw closer to Vermont, "They came to poorer nightly quarters in one-roomed loghouses, and at last to camping in or under the body of the cart by out door fires, and so, by degrees, passed out of civilization into the wild, rude life of the pioneer."[28] One such house where Josiah and Kenelm spent a night was a "bark-roofed loghouse" that had a "primitive plumping mill; a hollowed stump, spring pole and pestle."[29] In most cases in Robinson's works, however, bark roofs are found mainly on temporary dwellings, such as a trappers' "shanty of logs roofed with bark" in *In the Green Wood.*[30] Shanties are also mentioned in the short story "Saved by an Enemy" and in *Sam Lovel's Camps.* John Gardener, a hunter and trapper in the short story lives alone in "an open-fronted log shanty on Otter Pond" as late as 1868, and in *Sam Lovel's Camps* Sam Lovel and Antoine Bassette sleep in "a shanty of freshly riven logs with the upper ends slanted together in the form of an A tent."[31]

But the most typical log house described by Robinson has one room, although there is generally an upper sleeping chamber (reached by a ladder), with a roof generally of puncheon, not bark. In *A Hero of Ticonderoga*, the Beemans have such a log house—a small, one room, clay-chinked, log house with a ladder that served as a stair to the upper room.[32] Similarly, in *Danvis Folks*, Aunt Jerusha recalls that as a child she lived in such a log house with a ladder to an upper chamber.[33] One of the most concise statements of log house construction in Robinson's works is in *A Danvis Pioneer*. Upon arriving in Vermont Josiah Hill and Kenelm Dalrymple search for a suitable site for their cabin and finally find one near a small creek "with a convenient landing for boats, and yet out of sight of the main stream, though but a little way from it." Upon finding such an ideal site, Josiah and Kenelm "at once set to felling trees for their house; cut the logs of proper length; hauled them to the spot; rolled them up; notched them and set them in place; cut a place for a door and window; split and hewed puncheons for floor and roof, and in a few days had a substantial house, all the crevices warmly chinked with moss and clay; a stone fireplace at one end; a one-posted bedstead in a corner with a luxurious bed of marsh grass and cedar twigs . . ." The log house of Josiah and Kenelm has a "wooden hinged door . . . with wooden latch lifted from the outside by a string, and a wooden shutter of the same sort."[34]

Apparently Robinson observed firsthand either the log houses or the remains of log houses that he describes. In a footnote to his description of the log house of Josiah Hill and Kenelm Dalrymple, Robinson says that "In 1860, the traces of their cabin, with its fireplace, were plain to be seen."[35] It was around 1860 that Robinson was doing the research for his local histories, "A Sketch of the Early History of Ferrisburgh" and *Along Three Rivers*. And at that time he observed, among other things, near a small cove on the right bank of Little Otter the ruins of a log house, which was perhaps the model for the log house of Josiah Hill and Kenelm Dalrymple:

. . . the stone fireplace under the leaf mould and under the same covering and mouldered to the like consistency, the log walls of a house or cabin in a plainly defined parallellogram of low banks, on one of which stood a well-grown beech tree. In the fireplace, which was a double one, for the accommodation of two apartments, there was a heap of ashes containing bones and broken clay pipes. . . .

. . . from the traces remaining when I saw it first, it must have been built very long ago and I have no doubt was the first domicile of white men on the shores of the creek.

It was built with some care and trouble, for the stones were evidently brought from the lake shore, no small labor, whether by boat or sledge. The site was well chosen for hiding from casual voyagers on the creek, as well as for easy observation of them and ready access to wider lookout. Perhaps it was the quarters of some adventurous party of fur-trappers or a post of colonial scouts, but one may be sure it antedated the invasion of the lumberman and the pioneer husbandman, for either would have left some sign in the primeval forest that still held the ground when I first saw the place. It is now part of a bushy pasture and every trace of its ancient occupance is obliterated.

I remember well the green old age of the great hemlock that marked the corners of this and three other lots. It was a famous landmark, long known as the "Hemlock Corner." It bore the numbers of the lots with some initials that are forgotten . . .[36]

In an essay, "Given Away," Robinson points out that he visited the log house of a French-Canadian couple, John Cherbineau and his wife: "Stumps, young saplings, raspberry and blackberry briers held a far larger part of the deforested acres than did John's potato patch and cornfield, in the midst of which stood the little log cabin that, with its whitewashed walls and notched eaves, looked as little native to the soil as its tenants."[37] Evidently the small log house of the Cherbineaus served as the model for the log house of a French-Canadian family, Antoine Bassette's parents, in *Sam Lovel's Camps*, "a small log-house with whitewashed sides and notched shingles along its eaves."[38]

In addition to dwellings, other examples of log architecture mentioned by Robinson include a log prison, a log schoolhouse, and log barns. As Shurtleff points out in *The Log Cabin Myth*, a prison constructed of rounded logs with moss-filled chinks would not have held prisoners for very long.[39] Similarly, when Robinson writes of a log prison in *A Danvis Pioneer*, the prison is not of the cabin type construction, for the log prison "had been specially built for the confinement of Tories. It was a double-walled log house, the space between the walls being filled with earth . . ."[40] In *A Danvis Pioneer*, Robinson writes that the first schoolhouse in Danvis was of log, "furnished with rough desks and seats for the larger scholars, while the smaller ones were provided with two long benches of slabs supported on rough-hewn logs driven into holes on the bark sides of the slab. There was a huge stone fireplace in one end of the room, by which an attempt was made to warm it . . ."[41]

Robinson mentions log barns also. In *A Danvis Pioneer*, for example, he says that Timothy Lovel has a log barn, and in "An Old-Time March Meeting" Gran'ther Hill says that the first town meeting in Danvis was held in a log barn and that the townspeople sat around the log mangers in it.[42] Also in "The Gray Pine," set in 1855, he writes of "a small house with unglazed windows, and the ruins of a log barn."[43] Robinson's comments on log barns are merely incidental; he says more about frame barns. For instance, speaking of a frame barn in "Glimpses of New England Farm Life," Robinson says:

Inside, is the broad "barn floor," with grain scaffolds above it, and, on one side, a great "bay" filled with hay, on the other, the stable for cows, and, over this, a "mow." In the mysterious heights above, whose dusty gloom is pierced by bolts of sunshine, are dimly seen cobwebbed rafters and the deserted nests of the swallows.

On this floor, in winter days, the threshers' flails are beating out the rye, with measured throb. Chanticleer and Partlet and all their folk come to the wide-open southern doors to pick the scattered kernels, and the cattle "toss their white horns" in their stanchions and look with wonder in their soft eyes on this unaccountable pounding of straw. Then, when the "cave" (as the long pile of unwinnowed grain on one side of the floor is called) has become so large as to narrow too much the threshing-room, the fanning-mill is brought from its corner, and amid clatter and clouds of dust the grain is "cleaned up" and carried away to the granary. . . .[44]

Emerson, who maintained that he liked "a man who likes to see a fine barn as well as a good tragedy,"[45] certainly would have seen eye to eye with the Vermonter, for Robinson writes, "A pleasant thing to look upon is an old gray barn with its clustering sheds, straw-stacks and well-fenced yards; in this, the cattle taking their day's outing from the stable; in that, the sheep feeding from their racks or chewing the cud of contentment or making frequent trips to the water-trough in the corner."[46]

In *Uncle Lisha's Outing*, Robinson's description of the interior of a woodshed serves as a kind of verbal folk museum, giving a fairly complete inventory of the tools in it. Sam Lovel takes some game birds to the Bartletts and helps Rebecca Bartlett pick the birds in the Bartletts' woodshed:

Sam . . . followed Rebecca to the woodshed. Half of this was floored with plank, neatly swept, but thickly scarred with axe wounds where misdirected blows had fallen along the border nearest the chip-littered ground, on which the tiers of wood arose to the base of the cobwebbed rafters, to which phoebe-birds' nests of past summers clung in various stages of dilapidation. The cheese-press stood at one end of the floor, the lever weighted with worn-out plow-points, making occasional spasmodic, creaking descents, presently followed by an increased trickle of whey into the keeler. A workbench stood at the other end, with a vise and a few tools upon it, under a dusty window, a rack of augers and a sickle, and a corn-cutter made from a broken scythe. Along the walls between the cheese-press and the workbench hung various utensils of the dairy and the kitchen, divided by the kitchen and cheese-room doors. Elderly hens made cautious incursions into this debatable ground between indoors and out, where nests were tolerated if once established.

Rebecca sat down on the chopping-block and Sam on the saw-horse, and they stripped the feathers from the birds into the same basket; and so, with hands and tongues employed together, economized time like two gossips at their knitting.[47]

Other incidental references to architecture abound. For instance, in *Danvis Folks* he refers to "the afterthought of builders known as a lean-to," which is attached to the Lovels' house and serves as Uncle Lisha's shop when he returns from Wisconsin to live with the Lovels.[48] In *Sam Lovel's Camps* he writes of "the gray and brown shingled sides of the old meeting house" where the Friends hold their Sunday meetings.[49] And in "An Old-Time March Meeting," he describes the Danvis townhouse in the 1840's: "an unpainted, weatherbeaten, clapboarded building of one story, with one rough, plastered room, furnished with rows of pine seats, originally severely plain, but now profusely oranmented with carved initials, dates, and strange devices. A desk and seat on a platform at the farther end, for the accommodation of the town officers, and a huge box stove, so old and rusty that it seemed more like the direct product of a mine than of a furnace, completed the furniture in the room . . ."[50]

Throughout Robinson's writings are references to some of the typical rooms in a New England farm dwelling. Most frequently mentioned are the square room, the buttery, and the kitchen. Of these rooms Robinson says most about the kitchen:

Though every farm-house now has its sitting-room and parlor, and most a dining-room, the kitchen continues to be a favorite with farming folk,—a liking probably inherited from our grandfathers. In many of their houses this was the only large room, in which the family lived, and where all meals were taken, guests entertained, and merry-makings held. At one end was the great fire-place wherein back-log and fore-stick burned, sending forth warmth and light, intense and bright over the broad hearth, but growing feebler toward the dim corners where Jack Frost lurked and grotesque shadows leaped and danced on the wall. On the crane, suspended by hook or trammel, hung the big samp-kettle, bubbling and seething. The open dresser shone with polished pewter mug and trencher. Old-fashioned, splint-bottomed chairs, rude but comfortable, sent their long shadows across the floor.

The tall clock measured the moments with deliberate tick. The big wheel and little, the one for wool, the other for flax; the poles overhead, with their garniture of winter crooknecks and festoons of dried apples; the long-barreled flint-lock that had borne its part in Indian fight, at Bennington, and in many a wolf and bear hunt, hanging with powder-horn and bullet-pouch against the chimney,—all these made up a homely interior, far more picturesque than any to be found in modern farm-houses. Those who remember old-time cookery aver that in these degenerate days there are no Johnny-cakes so sweet as those our grandmothers baked on a board on the hearth, no roast meats so juicy as those which slowly turned on spits before the open fire nor any brown bread or baked beans to compare with those which the old brick ovens and bake-kettles gave forth.

In those old kitchens that have partly withstood the march of improvement, the great fire-place has fallen into disuse. Oftener it has been torn down, chimney, oven and all, to make room, now deemed better than its company, and its place supplied by the more convenient cook-stove. The wood-work is painted, the smoke-stained whitewash is covered by figured wallpaper; andirons, crane, pot-hook and trammel have gone for old iron; the place of the open dresser is usurped by a prim, close cupboard; big and little wheel, relics of an almost lost and forgotten handicraft, have long since been banished to the garret. There, too, has gone the ancient clock, and a short, dapper time-piece, on whose lower half is a landscape of startling colors, hurries the hours away with swift, loud tick.

Everything has undergone some change; even the old gun has had its flint-lock altered to percussion.

Of all the rooms in our farm-house, the kitchen chamber is probably the least changed. Its veined and blistered whitewashed ceiling, low sloping at the sides, still bumps unwary heads. The great trunk that held grandmother's bedding when she and grandfather, newly wedded, moved into this, then, wild country, and the sailor great-uncle's sea-chest, occupy their old corners. The little fire-place is un-changed and on the chimney above it hang, as of old, bundles and bags of boneset, catnip, sage, summer savory, elder-root, slippery-elm and no end of roots and herbs for sick men's tea and well men's seasoning. There are the same low beds with patch-work covers and by their side the small squares of rag carpet,—little oases for naked feet in the chill desert of the bare floor; and the light comes in through the same little dormer-windows through which it came seventy years ago. To this dormitory the hired man betakes himself when his last pipe is smoked and soon, in nasal trumpet-blasts, announces his arrival in the Land of Nod, to which by nine o'clock or so all the household have followed.[51]

Obviously, Robinson's casual remarks on the traditional architecture in his area of Vermont in no way meet the desires of modern folklore research, and much of the material he includes on folk architecture
will not serve as a substitute for systematic research. But many of the
traditions that he reports were fading when he was writing; therefore,
many of his comments on folklife are virtually all we have from an age
and area in which scientific folklore research was nonexistent. Robinson's incidental comments on dwelling and barn architecture help round
out his rather complete picture of Vermont folklife; the references to
architecture lend verisimilitude to his stories and give authenticity to
the folk milieu of his storytelling scenes. Moreover, his treatment of
folk architecture, especially his fine essay on traditional fences, shows
that he was as interested in preserving material folklore as he was in
preserving verbal folklore.

NOTES

[1]H. F. Raup, "The Fence in the Cultural Landscape," *Western Folklore*, VI (1947), 7.

[2]Austin E. Fife, "Jack Fences of the Intermountain West," *Folklore International*, ed. D. K. Wilgus (Hatboro, Pa., 1967), p. 51.

[3]Robinson, *Out of Bondage and Other Stories*, p. 168; *Danvis Folks and A Hero of Ticonderoga*, p. 34; *Uncle Lisha's Outing and Along Three Rivers*, p. 42.

[4]Robinson, *Silver Fields and Other Sketches of a Farmer-Sportsman*, p. 224.

[5]See Mamie Meredith, "The Nomenclature of American Pioneer Fences," *Southern Folklore Quarterly*, XV (1951), 132.

[6]See Meredith, pp. 116-117; Raup, p. 1.   [7]See Meredith, p. 127.

[8]Robinson, *Silver Fields and Other Sketches of a Farmer-Sportsman*, p. 225.

[9]Robinson, *Uncle Lisha's Outing and Along Three Rivers*, p. 42.

[10]Robinson, *Silver Fields and Other Sketches of a Farmer-Sportsman*, pp. 225-226.

[11]Robinson, *Silver Fields and Other Sketches of a Farmer-Sportsman*, pp. 226-227.

[12]Robinson, *Silver Fields and Other Sketches of a Farmer-Sportsman*, pp. 227-228. See Meredith, p. 134; Raup, p. 3.

[13]Robinson, *Silver Fields and Other Sketches of a Farmer-Sportsman*, pp. 230-232. See Raup's comments on the board fence, pp. 2, 6.

[14]Robinson, *Silver Fields and Other Sketches of a Farmer-Sportsman*, pp. 232-235. See Meredith, p. 140; Raup, p. 2.

[15]These traditional fences, except the water fence, are discussed by Meredith, pp. 5, 136, 141; and Raup, p. 2.

[16]Workers of the Federal Writers' Project of the Works Progress Administration for the State of Vermont, *Vermont: A Guide to the Green Mountain State* (Boston, 1937), p. 202.

[17]Robinson, *Silver Fields and Other Sketches of a Farmer-Sportsman*, pp. 235-236.

[18]Quoted in Meredith, p. 141.

[19]Robinson, *Silver Fields and Other Sketches of a Farmer-Sportsman*, pp. 236-237.

[20]Robinson, *Silver Fields and Other Sketches of a Farmer-Sportsman*, p. 238.

[21]Raup, p. 5.

[22]Robinson, *Silver Fields and Other Sketches of a Farmer-Sportsman*, pp. 237-238.

[23]Robinson, *Silver Fields and Other Sketches of a Farmer-Sportsman*, p. 232. For variants of these combined forms see Meredith, pp. 133, 144.

[24]Robinson, *Uncle Lisha's Outing and Along Three Rivers*, p. 251.

[25]Robinson, *Sam Lovel's Camps and In the Green Wood*, p. 243.

[26]Robinson, *Uncle Lisha's Shop and A Danvis Pioneer*, p. 91.

[27]Robinson, *Uncle Lisha's Outing and Along Three Rivers*, p. 41.

[28]Robinson, *Uncle Lisha's Shop and A Danvis Pioneer*, p. 27.

[29]Robinson, *Uncle Lisha's Shop and A Danvis Pioneer*, p. 30.

[30] Robinson, *Sam Lovel's Camps and In the Green Wood*, p. 235.

[31] Robinson, *Out of Bondage and Other Stories*, p. 226; *Sam Lovel's Camps and In the Green Wood*, p. 20.

[32] Robinson, *Danvis Folks and A Hero of Ticonderoga*, pp. 230, 246, 249.

[33] Robinson, *Danvis Folks and A Hero of Ticonderoga*, p. 117.

[34] Robinson, *Uncle Lisha's Shop and A Danvis Pioneer*, pp. 35-36.

[35] Robinson, *Uncle Lisha's Shop and A Danvis Pioneer*, p. 35.

[36] Robinson, *Uncle Lisha's Outing and Along Three Rivers*, pp. 234-235.

[37] Robinson, *In New England Fields and Woods*, p. 181.

[38] Robinson, *Sam Lovel's Camps and In the Green Wood*, pp. 151-152.

[39] Shurtleff, p. 210.

[40] Robinson, *Uncle Lisha's Shop and A Danvis Pioneer*, p. 90.

[41] Robinson, *Uncle Lisha's Shop and A Danvis Pioneer*, p. 97.

[42] Robinson, *Sam Lovel's Boy with Forest and Stream Fables*, p. 147.

[43] Robinson, *Out of Bondage and Other Stories*, p. 233.

[44] Robinson, "Glimpses of New England Farm Life," p. 512.

[45] Quoted in Matthiessen, p. 173.

[46] Robinson, "Glimpses of New England Farm Life," p. 512.

[47] Robinson, *Uncle Lisha's Outing and Along Three Rivers*, p. 124.

[48] Robinson, *Danvis Folks and A Hero of Ticonderoga*, p. 57.

[49] Robinson, *Sam Lovel's Camps and In the Green Wood*, p. 170.

[50] Robinson, *Sam Lovel's Boy with Forest and Stream Fables*, p. 145.

[51] Robinson, "Glimpses of New England Farm Life," pp. 516-518.

CHAPTER 13

FOLK BELIEFS AND FOLK MEDICINE

"In a sense," writes American folklorist Wayland D. Hand, "superstitions and popular beliefs may be regarded as the least common denominators of folklore. Like items of folk speech, which are also short and turn up everywhere, folk beliefs are found in several genres of folklore, particularly in folk legend and related narrative forms."[1] By placing his folk beliefs in realistic stories, Robinson aptly shows how beliefs intermingle with the other areas of folklore. Folk beliefs are so closely related to some of the other genres of folklore in Robinson's writings that arranging his works by genre is virtually impossible without some repetition.

Beliefs are often closely related to oral prose narratives. Harold W. Thompson points out that just across Lake Champlain from Vermont there are numerous legends about treasure that has been hidden by members of retreating or fleeing armies.[2] Robinson refers to two such tales in his Danvis stories. These two accounts of buried treasure not only show that Robinson was acquainted with several folk beliefs concerning the treasure hunt, but the material he includes in *Sam Lovel's Camps* shows that Robinson was also familiar with the widespread folk belief in second sight.[3] In his local history, *Along Three Rivers*, Robinson tells of "some of old Jesse's sons" who found the remains, including a fireplace, of a log cabin while digging medicinal roots. One of old Jesse's sons—Jesse, Junior—was an acquaintance of Robinson's. "Jesse, Jr.'s sister-in-law," Robinson reports, "was gifted with second sight, whereby it was revealed to her that there was buried treasure under the hearthstones" of the remains of the old cabin.[4] Apparently, Robinson's friend, Jesse, Jr., becomes Job, Jr., in *Sam Lovel's Camps*. While fishing alone on the East Slang, Pelatiah Gove meets a lowlander who claims that he is gathering herbs for his wife, who is a mesmerist. The lowlander tells Pelatiah that "I come a-lookin' arter some rhuts 't I want-ah. My womern she's a feemale doctor, messmericle. My brother, Job,

Junyer, he gives her the in-flew-ence 'n' puts her to sleep. 'N' then she can look right inter yer insides an' read 'em just like a book-ah. Terms, half a dollar for examernation, one dollar for proscription, cash on delivery-ah. Sleepin' Sairy, probably you've hearn tell on her."[5]

Later Pelatiah and Sam Lovel discover that the lowlander, John, is far more interested in finding buried treasure than he is in finding medicinal roots. For Pelatiah and Sam see John and his two brothers, Jethro and Job, Jr., tramping through the thicket of an island where Sam and Pelatiah are stranded. The two Danvis friends hear Jethro call out that he has found "seas an' oceans an' thaousen's o' Seneky snake rhut, I vaow!" But Sleepin' Sairy's husband replies, "Oh, dum your Seneky snake rhut-ah! We got suthin' 'at's more 'caount 'an or'nary rhuts to tend tu; what the Bible calls the rhut of all evil is what we're arter-ah." Then Sam and Pelatiah overhear that the three brothers are searching for money hidden by Benedict Arnold when he was retreating, and they also overhear that John's wife told the three brothers where to find Arnold's treasure after Job, Jr., had given her the influence. In spite of the power of John's wife, however, the three lowlanders fail to find any treasure. But John explains to Jethro that "we would ha' hed it 'f you'd hel' your plegged gab-ah. A-speakin' jest 's the crowbar hit the chist, an' then of course it moved, jest 's any tarnal fool might ha' knowed it would-ah."[6] John, of course, is referring to the international folk belief that if the treasure-seeker speaks before he gets his hands on the treasure, the treasure will move, and he will lose it.[7]

In *Danvis Folks* Uncle Lisha tells a story that is based on a legend concerning treasure hidden by soldiers. In this case, the reference is to the well-known tradition of Rogers' Rangers and the silver image of St. Francis.[8] As Uncle Lisha tells the story, an old, half-cracked veteran of the French war, Bart Johnson, along with Major Rogers and his soldiers, retrieved a lot of money, gold, and silver, including "a silver idolatry imidge 'at weighed more 'n twenty paounds—jest clean silver," from some Canadian Indians during the war. After the attack on the Indians, according to Lisha, Rogers' soldiers headed toward the Connecticut River but ran short of provisions and divided into small parties. More concerned with saving their lives than with anything else, most of the rangers threw away their plunder; however, Bart Johnson kept his treasure and buried it on a mountain he thought was Tater Hill. Each year after the war until he died old Bart searched for the buried treasure on Tater Hill, but he never found it. Lisha says that on one occasion when Bart searched for his treasure until after dark, suddenly he heard some howling wolves coming his way. Bart felt around in the dark for a tree to climb, finally found one he could get his arms around, and stayed awake all night clinging to a limb and listening to the wolves howl. The next morning, however, when Bart tried to climb down the tree, he found he had spent the night sitting on the roots of a large tree.

When Uncle Lisha finishes his tale, Solon Briggs shows that he is acquainted with the ritual of treasure hunting by suggesting that perhaps Bart Johnson spoke before he got his hand on the treasure, enabling the spirit guarding the treasure to move it.[9] Solon claims that, at any rate, Bart should have used a witch stick to locate the buried treasure:

"I should admire tu know if he ever tried the myraculous paower of a witch hazel crotch," said Solon. "I c'n find veins of water with 'em on falible, an' the' hain't no daoubt 'at they hev jest as paowerful distraction tow-ards gold and silver, hid artificial, or growin' nat'ral in the baowels of the airth. Mebby he did find it an' spoke afore he got his hand on 't an' it moved. It sartinly will, ef you speak a audible laoud word. The' is allers a sperit a-guardin' bairied treasure, an' ef you speak afore you lay you hand on 't, it gives the sperit paower to move it, the' 's no tellin' haow fur."[10]

The use of a forked twig to locate water, of course, is widespread in folklore;[11] and the use of the same twig with metallic objects attached to the end, or else the use of a metal rod, is also a common means of finding buried treasure.[12]

Uncle Lisha's tale of Bart Johnson's treasure results in a treasure hunt by Solon Briggs and Antoine Bassette, but Solon uses a plain witch hazel divining rod without metallic attachments. Solon tells Antoine, "You're useter to the woods 'an I want you tu du the ingineerin' an' I'll work the divinin' rod. I've got me a superguberous one 'at I cut from the north side of a witch hazel bush." So as the two treasure seekers seek old Bart's buried booty, Antoine carries the tools and Solon works the witch stick, walking slowly, "holding his forked divining rod with the point upward, a prong in either hand, with his palms turned inward." After much laborious traveling over ankle-deep moss, piles of rocks, and prostrate trunks of decaying trees, Solon and Antoine come upon a colony of yellow birches around a giant yellow birch. With divining rod before him, Solon marches around the large birch until the tip of his hazel twig points straight down. Solon orders Antoine to start digging and warns the Canuck about the tabu of speaking before they get their hands on the treasure. The portentous Briggs tells the Canuck that "if ever we du strike the money you mustn't speak a audible, laoud word afore we git a holt on 't er it 'll slide intu the baowls o' the airth." But as Antoine's crowbar strikes something that gives forth a metallic sound, the Canadian cannot hold back an exclamation. Solon Briggs angrily maintains it is for this reason that they fail to find Bart Johnson's buried treasure.[13] All in all, then, Robinson's material on buried treasure shows that he was thoroughly familiar with a number of beliefs connected with treasure hunting.

Supporting Hand's assertion that folk beliefs may be considered the least common denominators of folklore is a supernatural tale told by Uncle Lisha in *Uncle Lisha's Shop*. In this tale the New England belief that the Gray Pine is a bad omen is important, for the tale involves a number of disasters that befell Noah Chase when he stood under an unlucky tree. According to Lisha, Noah Chase encouraged Amos Jones to go along with him to club starving deer that were yarding on crusted snow. Finding about twenty deer yarding around a small spruce tree, Noah clubbed about ten of the deer and cut their throats. Amos begged Noah to stop slaughtering the helpless animals, but Noah merely laughed and clubbed a fawn-laden doe, boasting that he would "kill tew tu one shot." Noticing that Noah was standing under an unlucky tree, Amos warned his companion that something terrible would happen to him. But Noah simply laughed again and called Amos "a sup'stitious chicken-hearted ol' granny," and then Noah slit the doe's throat. Unable to endure the cruelty of Noah, Amos left for home, while Noah pursued a buck. Chasing the buck, however, Noah caught the toe of his snowshoe in the limb of a fallen tree, and he fell, breaking his leg and knocking himself unconscious. It was nearly dark when Noah finally pulled himself to his feet and discovered that he could not walk. While he was deciding what to do, he saw an apparition of the fawn-laden doe that he killed earlier. He threw his club at the doe, but the club went right through the deer, as if she were a puff of smoke.[14] As Noah crawled toward a clearing, the doe always remained just ahead of him. Pursued by howling wolves, Noah finally reached the clearing a little after dark. Unable to go any farther, he sat down and yelled for help, while the howling wolves remained between him and the ghost. At last help arrived, and Noah was taken home, where his leg was set by a doctor. But Noah remained ill for three months, during which he constantly saw the vision of the fawn-laden doe and heard the howling of the wolves. Although Noah got a little better, his son was killed by Indians out west, his older daughter ran away with a worthless drunk, and his other daughter married an Irishman. After all these misfortunes, Amos Jones visited Noah and told him, "I tol' yer so!" Soon after that Noah fell ill of consumption, of which he died after suffering ten years.[15] When Lisha finishes his tale, Joseph Hill remarks that he does not know what an unlucky tree is, and Uncle Lisha must explain:

"Wal," said Lisha, "what some calls an onlucky tree, an' thinks is, is a sca'se kind of a tree, half way 'twixt a cat spruce an' a pitch pine. The leaves is longer 'n a spruce 'n' shorter 'n a pine, an' the branches grows scraggider 'n any spruce. They hain't no size—never seen one more 'n ten inches 't the butt. They hain't no good, 'n' I d' know's they be any hurt, but some folks think they be, an' you couldn't git 'em tu go a-nigh one for nuthin'. Think if they du the' 'll suthin' dreffal happen tu 'em or some o' their folks. . . ."[16]

Another of Robinson's stories, "The Gray Pine," one of his best, also makes extensive use of the folk belief in an unlucky tree.[17] In Part I of "The Gray Pine," the narrator tells of a trip he took from his home in the Champlain Valley to the Adirondacks to hunt deer. He joins a small hunting party on his arrival, and guided by Uncle Harvey Hale, the hunters take individual stations along a runway by a river. After an hour or so of maintaining his station with no sight of a deer, the narrator is forced to take shelter from a pelting snowstorm under a solitary evergreen. Later, during a lull in the storm, he hears the baying of dogs and suddenly sees a large buck coming towards him. But the deer veers away, and the hunter's shot misses. Uncle Harvey comes running and is angry to learn that the shot missed its mark. Noticing the tree under which the narrator was standing, however, the old guide exclaims, "It's no wonder 't ye missed! It's more a wonder 't yer gun didn't bust er suthin' an kill yer! Why, man alive, that 'ere 's an *onlucky tree*! Come 'way from it." When the curious narrator asks Harvey about the unlucky tree, the old guide explains: "It's what I tell ye, an onlucky tree, 'at no man, much less a woman, is safe to go anigh! I wouldn't stand under that 'ere tree ten minutes for half o' York State! I didn't know 't the' was one o' the cussed things left here, 'r I'd ha' burnt it 'fore naow. I c'n tell ye no end o' hurt an' trouble they've made; no end on 't!"[18]

Uncle Harvey, indeed, knows a number of stories about misfortunes caused by unlucky trees, and in Part II of "The Gray Pine," Uncle Harvey tells his "wust story of the onlucky tree": Amos Brown, "a shiftless and thriftless farmer," lives alone with his pretty and industrious daughter, Polly, who has many admirers but prefers to care for her drunken father. One summer an artist, Walter White, comes to the valley to sketch, and boards with the Browns. Polly falls for Walter, and he grows fond of her, too, although he is somewhat uncertain of marrying such an uncultured girl. At the end of the summer when Walter is leaving, he tells Polly that if at dusk the next evening a wagon stops by a certain unusual evergreen tree and the driver alights and plucks a sprig from the branches, then she will know that Walter has sent for her to join him at a small lake port. On the appointed day Amos Brown leaves to go hunting, which Polly knows will ultimately take him to Bell's tavern. While spending the afternoon with her household duties and preparing her father's favorite dish, she realizes how desolate the house will be for her father if she leaves. She writes a note to Walter stating that she will remain with her father, dons a light-colored dress, and goes to meet the wagon driver at the appointed evergreen tree. Meanwhile, Amos Brown has gotten drunk on rum at Bell's, and the barkeep asks Hiram Hall to help Amos home. Near Amos's house Hiram halts and points out a dim whiteness in the shadow of an evergreen. "By the Lord, it's a sperit, Hiram, er les a witch!" says the old drunk. "Le' go my arm 'n' I'll show ye 'at a bullit 'ont hurt it!" Amos fires at the ghostly figure; the two men hear a cry and see the white shape fall to the earth. When Amos investigates, he finds the lifeless body of his daughter near the unlucky tree. That night Amos shoots himself.[19]

Robinson himself annotates the folk belief of the unlucky tree on the first page of "The Gray Pine" in a footnote referring to an article on trees by John H. Sears. In this article Sears says of the Gray Pine:

Pinus Banksiana ("Gray" or "Scrub Pine") is quite a rare tree in New York. Seldom more than four or five growing within ten miles of each other. Solitary ones are most common. As to size, they are seldom over 8 feet high though one was found in Altona 15 feet high and 8 inches in diameter, but this tree was partially decayed on one side of the trunk. In appearance, at a short distance, this tree resembles the black spruce more than it does a pine. The bark on the trunk is exactly like a spruce; the foliage is 1½ inches long and from 1/8 to 1/6 of an inch wide; the cones grow in pairs and close to the limb; and they are different in shape from all other pines. This tree is known as the "unlucky tree" by the people in this part of the country. The more observant ones call it a cross between the pine and spruce.

I met several men of good general education, who were convinced of the danger arising from this tree, and who cited cases of its malignant influence (similar to the stories told of the Upas tree of Java). It is considered dangerous to pass within ten feet of its limbs and more so to women than to men. It is equally dangerous to cattle; so that whatever ill befalls a man, his family or his cattle, if there is one of these trees on his land it must be destroyed,—burned down by wood being piled around it, for no one would venture to cut it down.[20]

Robinson had firsthand acquaintance with the Gray Pine. In an entry dated September 27, 1876, in a journal still at the Robinson home in Ferrisburg, Robinson writes, "This day I found on a ridge, north of 'Ruey Hill' a little colony of *Gray or Lerut Pine*, the first and only I have ever saw." In addition, Robinson's wife writes in her journal, also still at Rokeby, on June 6, 1902, that there was a colony of Gray Pine trees at the edge of Monkton: "On the edge of the woods are the curious trees. The 'Unlucky Tree' of early settlers. Their whole appearance is strange . . . R. E. R. discovered these trees which are not known by botanists to grow anywhere else . . . so far south as this . . . R. E. R. went with Mr. Wild after he was totally blind and guided him directly to the spot—which shows his marvellous memory."

A good example of how folk beliefs and material culture go hand in hand in living tradition is found in Robinson's account of the folk household craft of soapmaking in *Uncle Lisha's Outing,* when some of the Danvis folk encounter a woman making soap. The making of soap from fats boiled with lye from wood ashes was, of course, a necessary housecraft of the pioneer housewife; and since either too much or too little lye poured in the melted grease would easily spoil the soap, the uncertainty of the soapmaking process gave rise to a number of superstitions, such as the belief that witches spoil the soap. In the following passage Robinson skillfully works in some of the techniques of soapmaking and some of the beliefs connected with soapmaking:

As they drew near they sniffed a familiarly pleasant and pungent odor of smoke and lye which led them to an outdoor fire where Uncle Lisha's yesterday acquaintance was boiling soap. Uncle Lisha introduced his companions who were cordially welcomed by the mistress, without an apology for the man's hat and coat she wore, except to say:—

"If you ever made soap you know folks don't want tu dress up much for it, an' you c'n see I hain't.

"I guess you don't want tu," said Aunt Jerusha sympathetically. "It is turrible messin', clarifyin' the grease, an' the lye 'll take the color aout 'n eve'ything it teches."

"An' so onsartain," Huldah added. "You never know whether it 's a-goin' tu be soap."

"I know it," cried the housewife. "It is the provokin'est! Your lye 'll bear an aig like a cork, an' your grease 'll be all right, an' yit they won't be soap. I wonder what 's come of my man. If you men folks could find him, mebby it 'could be more in'erestin' 'an aour gabbin'. He went tu git some chunks. Soapb'ilin' 's a good time to burn up chunks. Gid—Gid-eon! Where be ye? I guess he 'll come," she said, after listening a moment; and then returning to the subject of soap-making, "Some says it's 'cause the wind 's north, but I do' know. Anyways, it does act onaccountable."

"I believe the witches or the Ol' Cat hisself gits into 't," Aunt Jerusha declared.

"Same as intu cream sometimes," said Huldah. "Solon Briggs says 'at a piece o' silver money 'll drive the witches aout o' that, an' mebby it 'ould aout of soap."

"Wal, I'm goin' tu see whether it 's soap or not," the soapmaker said, tucking her dress between her knees, pulling her hat over her eyes, and blowing the steam away while she dipped a few spoonfuls of the contents of the kettle into an old saucer. This she stirred and cooled with her breath, watching it anxiously, while her feminine guests looked on with almost as much interest, as the liquid dribbled in a thin stream from the spoon.

"Mebby they was beech ashes," Uncle Lisha suggested, regarding it and the disappointed and vexed face of the matron.

"No, they was most all ellum," she answered. "Plague on 't, it don't look like nothin'."

"Wal, the' hain't no better ashes than ellum, so it ain't that," said the old man.

"Try a leetle dash o' water in 't," Aunt Jerusha suggested, and when this was done the liquid at once thickened in the saucer and the face of the fair soapmaker relaxed to an expression of supreme satisfaction, which was sympathetically repeated in the countenances of her visitors.[21]

Furthermore, outdoor sports and camping trips not only provide opportunities for the performance of folklore away from the village, but since the men of Danvis devote a considerable amount of their time to hunting, trapping, and fishing, a number of folk beliefs are associated with these activities. Several beliefs in Robinson's writings are connected with fish or fishing. In *Sam Lovel's Camps*, Robinson writes that when Antoine Bassette decides to improvise a fishing pole and line and to hunt some worms to catch some bullpouts, Antoine's success in bait hunting is "an encouraging sign of future luck."[22] Moreover, Antoine always spits on the fishing worm for good luck when he baits his hook. This widespread folk belief was actually practiced by the Robinsons' hired man, Mingo Niles, who taught Robinson himself to never forget to spit on the angleworm when baiting a hook.[23]

In Robinson's works beliefs about individual fish concern the bowfin, the eel, and the sheepshead. In *Sam Lovel's Camps* when Antoine learns that Joseph Hill has caught and cooked an inedible bowfin, the Canuck says, "O Zhozeff, don't you shame mek us heat dat? Ant you'll see where de dev' put hees t'umb w'en he'll peek it an' t'row 'way cause he so bad he won't have it hese'f?"[24] Baughman reports this folklore motif, "Marks on certain fish from devil's fingerprints," from England only.[25]

Different folk beliefs dealing with the reproduction of eels motivate a heated argument between Antoine Bassette and a Yankee lowlander, Time, in *Sam Lovel's Camps*:

. . . Once Antoine hauled up an ugly ling, which Sam told Joseph was "one o' his bowfins 'at had forgot his scales," but Antoine oracularly informed them that this "was de mudder of de heel," for thus he had long since settled to his own satisfaction the vexed question of the generation of the eel.

"You're sartin 'at eels come f'm lings, be ye?" Time asked in a tone that plainly indicated his unbelief in this theory.

"Yes, sah! Ah'll seen it!" said Antoine.

"Wal, they don't! Du ye want I sh'ld tell ye where eels come from?"

"Ah'll ant want you. Ah'll know all of it," Antoine said, but the others signified their willingness to be informed.

"Wal, then," said Time, "eels comes f'm clams, them freshwater clams 'at you c'n see thaousan's on any day daown yunder in the shaller water to the san'bar. I know it, 'cause I've seen hundreds o' little eels in 'em, not bigger 'n pin points."

"Haow you'll know he was heel 'f he ant more bigger as pint pins?" Antoine roared in the big voice the Canuck assumes when he would make himself terrible.

"Where du eels come from, then?" Time loudly demanded.

"L—l leeng, ant Ah'll tol' you?" Antoine roared again, lifting himself from his seat with a grip of both hands on the seat of his trousers.

"Clams! clams! clams!" Time bellowed in a crescendo so vociferous that it frightened the skimming swallows from their pretty sport in the neighborhood of the boats.[26]

Robinson also includes in essays both of these beliefs concerning the reproduction of the eel. In "Portraits in Ink," he refers to the belief that eels are generated in mussels,[27] and in "On a Glass Roof," he mentions that the ling is the mother of the eel. In the latter essay Robinson reveals his Canuck informant for the belief that the ling is "de mudder of de eel": "If this theory will help settle the vexed question of the generation of the eel, the scientists are welcome to it, if they will only give credit therefor to my friend Joseph Gerard of Vermont, commonly known as Joe Gero."[28] As Robinson suggests, the folk have given considerable thought to the reproduction of eels. For example, speaking of his own neck of the woods, the Ozarks, Vance Randolph writes that "many hill folk believe there is something supernatural about the reproduction of eels; this is doubtless because no little eels are seen in the stream, and eels are never found to contain spawn."[29]

In "The Path of Boatless Generations," Robinson mentions a traditional belief that he held as a youngster concerning the "lucky bones" found in the heads of sheepshead fish: "These last valiant fighters we valued only for the fun of catching, the show they made on our strings and the 'lucky bones' which were the inner adornment of their heads, perhaps carried by them, as by us, for luck. I have no knowledge that these charms ever brought us good luck, but we felt that the chances were better with a pair of them rattling in our trousers pockets."[30] This same belief has been reported from North Carolina, and a similar belief concerning lucky bones in the head of the codfish has been reported from New England as well as from North Carolina.[31]

Robinson mentions several other familiar beliefs about luck that the Danvis outdoorsmen, among others, would know. Other lucky signs that he refers to include looking over one's shoulder at the thin crescent of a new moon[32] and finding a four-leaved clover.[33] Furthermore, hunting guide Uncle Harvey Hill in "The Gray Pine," says that "they say 't the's luck in odd numbers,"[34] and the narrator in "An Underground Railroad Passenger," blows away at one breath globes of seeded dandelions for luck.[35] Robinson also recounts beliefs about fur and turtles that the trapper and fisherman would know. In "What the November Woods Gave," when Jacob Bennett finds a coon asleep in a hollow tree, he tells his son, Isaac:

". . . Now, we'll just have his pelt nailed up on the woodshed door. I shouldn't wonder if it was pretty nigh prime, for it's had three r's to get so in."

"How do you mean, father?" Isaac asked.

"Why, they say fur 's good in ev'ry month that 's got an r in it, but it ain't, not in September nor sca'cely in October, an' it begins to git faded in April, some kinds does. But now it's most December . . ."[36]

Apparently this belief is an analogue to the more familiar popular belief that oysters are not good except in the months having an "R" in them, a belief that Robinson also mentions in *Uncle Lisha's Shop.*

In this Danvis story John Dart tells barkeep Hamner that oysters "don't bite, they say, in no month 'at hain't got an R in 't."[37] Another common belief that Robinson includes concerns the variety of meat found in a turtle. In *Uncle Lisha's Outing*, Antoine mentions that a turtle contains five kinds of meat, "pirk an' beef, an' . . . Ah'll fregit toder, 'cep' cheekin."[38] Another belief that Robinson mentions about the turtle, although not as familiar as the belief above, is that it takes a turtle nine days to die.[39] Nine, a magic number in folklore, suggests the well-known belief that cats have nine lives, a belief that Robinson also uses in *Sam Lovel's Boy*.[40] Other familiar beliefs about animals in Robinson's works are well-known ones concerning frogs and toads. In *Sam Lovel's Boy*, Uncle Lisha tells Sammy that killing frogs will make the cows give bloody milk, and Lisha adds that killing toads will cause warts to appear on one's hands.[41]

In *A Hero of Ticonderoga*, Robinson refers to the familiar mythical mermaid. In this historical story Job Carpenter shows his guests "an odd-looking spotted and coarse-haired skin stuffed with moss into some semblance of its form in the flesh." Job says that he killed the creature on the ice of the lake early one winter and that a soldier at the fort said it was a saltwater seal fish. But Job maintains that "it don't look no ways reasonable that sech a creatur' could come all the way up the St. Lawrence, an' the Iroquois River, an' most the len'th o' this lake. My idee is, it's a fresh-water maremaid, an' nat'ral to this lake." Job continues, "An ol' Injun told me that there's always ben one o' these cretur's seen in this lake a spell afore every war that's ever ben. But I hope the sign 'll fail this time." But the sign does not fail, and later as the war approaches, Job points out, "The sign o' that fresh water maremaid is comin' true ag'in."[42] Baughman gives only British and Irish variants of this motif in which a mermaid appears as an omen of a tragic event.[43]

As we have seen, the people depicted in Robinson's stories depend on farming for their livelihoods, so several beliefs in Robinson's works are concerned with animal and plant husbandry. These beliefs, too, are based on the observation of the moon and wildlife. For example, in *Uncle Lisha's Shop*, Solon Briggs maintains that "I wouldn't kill my hawgs or my beef crutter in the old o' the moon onless I wanted the meat to shrink in the cookin', ner sow my peas in the wanin' o' that lunimary 'f I wanted 'em tu grow luxuberant."[44] Another traditional belief concerning spring planting is in "Glimpses of New England Farm Life": "The hickory has given the sign for cornplanting, for its leaves are as large as a squirrel's ear (some say, a squirrel's foot)."[45] In North Carolina corn is planted when poplar leaves are as large as a squirrel's ear, while Ray B. Browne reports that in Alabama corn is planted when elm or oak leaves get as large as a squirrel's ear.[46]

The weather beliefs of Robinson's characters are also based in part on a close observation of natural phenomena. The following debate takes place at a Danvis town meeting:

"Wal, I cal'late we're goin' tu git an airly spring," said one of a knot of elderly men and middle-aged wiseacres. "When the ol' bear come aout he did n't see no shadder."

"What, the twenty-sixt' o' Febwary?" one of the latter chuckled. "Why, good land o'massy, the sun was er—shinin' jest as bright as 'tis today!"

"The twenty-sixt' hain't the day! It's the secont, an' it snowed all day!"

"Sho! It's the twenty-sixt'," the other asserted. "Ev'ybody knows that 'at knows anythin' abaout signs."

"Wal, I know it's the secont."

"No, 'tain't nuther!"

"'Tis tuther!"

"Wal," drawled big John Dart, "s'posin' the' wan'n't no bear ary day? What then?"[47]

Here Robinson shows us in fiction what other writers, such as Vance Randolph, tell us in exposition: the day that the groundhog, or bear, is supposed to make his prognostications varies. Although February 2 is recognized as Groundhog Day on most of our calendars today, oldtimers often hold that another day, frequently February 14, is actually Groundhog Day. But most of the Danvis folk maintain that February 26 is the day that the bear, not the groundhog, comes out to prophesy the weather. For example, one February day when Uncle Lisha's friends visit him in his shop, they find the old shoemaker "studying his almanac by the light of his little candle." Paying more attention to his pamphlet than to his guests, Uncle Lisha turns from an anecdote by his favorite author to weather prophecy in his almanac and runs his finger down the columns of days of the month until he comes to February 26. Then suddenly the old cobbler shouts, "Boys, did ye know 't this was the twenty-sixt' of Febewary? This is the day 't the ol' bear comes aout! He's seen his shadder, 'n' he won't poke his nose int' the daylight agin fer forty days. We sh'll hev' a col' March, 'n' like 'nough the wind 'll be north when the sun crosses the line, 'n' then we'll hev' a back'ard spring 'n' poor corn year."[48]

Although Solon Briggs, "who was weatherwise as well as wise in other things,"[49] doubts that "bears an' woo'chucks know whether the spring 'll be back'ard or for'ad," he adds, "I du not deny there bein' signs gi'n whereby an' by which we can tell suthin' more or less haow the weather's a-goin' tu be, sech f'r instance as hawg's melt an' the hus's o' corn, the haighth o' weeds an' et cetery."[50] Moreover, the oracular Solon Briggs shows his knowledge of weather lore in other places. For example, one November evening when it has snowed, Solon asserts, "I knowed 'at 't was goin' to snow, an' said 't was, an' it does snow, but . . . when the snow comes on ter the graound when it's conjoled—that is, when it's froze, it hain't a-goin' t' stay on an' en-dure long."[51] Solon can foretell the weather by the condition of his rheumatism and by the hooting of owls. He maintains that his rheumatism is always worse before a storm, and he agrees with Tom Hamlin, Uncle Lisha, Sam Lovel, and Ruth Beeman in other stories by Robinson that the hooting of owls warns that a storm is near.[52] Whereas the hooting of owls is a sign of bad weather, the singing of bluebirds is a sign of good weather. In one tale, *In the Green Wood*, John Pangborn holds that when a bluebird is heard singing "spring's a-comin' kind o' mod'rate."[53] In folklore, weather beliefs are often associated with dog days, too. For instance, it is frequently believed that if it rains on the first dog day, it will rain for forty days.[54] Mrs. Purington displays her characteristic negative attitude in *Uncle Lisha's Shop* when she maintains that "nob'dy never knows what the weather's a-goin' t' be in dog-days."[55] But even the negative Mrs. Purington would probably agree with Donald McIntosh that when there is "a stepmither's breath i' the air" a guest should be invited to move away from the drafty door and offered a seat by the warm fireside.[56] In folklore, a "stepmother's breath" is the cold wind blowing through the door.[57]

References to folk medicine appear throughout Robinson's writings. In "McIntosh of Vergennes," an Indian, Wadso, gathers "medicinal herbs to cure his inward and outward hurts" while he is recuperating at the McIntosh home from injuries he suffered when he fell through an icy river while trapping.[58] In this same story Robinson suggests that the European settler learned the medicinal value of certain native American plants from the American Indians. Young Donald McIntosh "was a studious boy, much given to wandering alone in the woods and finding out the medicinal virtues of roots and herbs, learning them of the Indians . . ."[59] An Indian also plays an important role in the administering of folk medicine in *A Danvis Pioneer*, when both Josiah Hill and Kenelm Dalrymple fall ill with ague. Josiah concocts hot drinks of herbs and hemlock twigs, but their fevers and chills continue until an Indian to whom they had given food repays their kindness by bringing a squaw to their camp to administer a mixture of rum and prickly ash berries to the two pioneers:

. . . The woman produced a package of dried red berries, giving out an aromatic odor like lemon peel. She called for liquor of some sort, and they brought out a quart bottle of hoarded New England rum. The Indian and squaw each took a drink from it to make room for the berries, which were then added, with the result of producing a mixture which was liquid fire. When Josiah, whose ague fit was on, took a mouthful of it, it burned its way into his interior with such effect that the ague was banished from his body, and a few doses made him well again; and with Kenelm the effect was the same, though at first he swore the Indians had poisoned him out of revenge for his share in the Rogers raid. . . .[60]

Since the squaw requests liquor for the remedy she mixes, apparently her cure is not native American, although liquor is frequently used in Anglo-American folk remedies. Sometimes it is mixed with poplar bark or wild-cherry bark and drunk to cure chills.[61] When other pioneer Vermonters in Robinson's stories find their knowledge of folk medicine insufficient, they must summon help. For instance, when James Pangborn (*In the Green Wood*) is ill, his son, John, says to himself, "We've tried every root and herb we ever heard of, and they don't do any good." So he goes after a doctor but finds Seth Warner instead, who tells young Pangborn, "I'm as good a doctor as you're likely to find this side of Bennington, and I'm going with you." On the way Seth Warner gathers herbs, which he immediately brews and administers to James Pangborn on arrival. Before departing Warner gives the Pangborns a plentiful supply of herbs and complete directions for administering them.[62]

Robinson's stories illustrate the scarcity of physicians in early Vermont and indicate the importance of learning traditional cures from both the Indians and frontiersmen. Robinson himself points out in "Mingo—A Silhouette" that he learned much folk medicine from the Robinsons' hired man, Mingo Niles. In another place Robinson writes that Mingo cared nothing for the sights of the forest, "but only for what was edible, medicinal or in some way practically useful."[63]

In his stories set after the early occupation and settlement of Vermont, Robinson offers essentially the same information about folk medicine in fiction that modern folklorists report in exposition. Robinson's Danvis characters rely on teas and poultices, and the village physician competes with the more popular backwoods yarb doctor, who in *Sam Lovel's Boy*, is appropriately called Dr. Root.[64] Thus, in *Danvis Folks*, when Maria Hill is ill with fever, the root doctor is summoned after considerable debate between those in favor of the regular physician and those in favor of the root doctor. Speaking of Maria Hill and her illness, Robinson writes:

. . . Their mother, who lay in the bedroom beyond, had been ill for weeks with an intermittent fever, but was now "on the gain," thanks to the treatment of the keen-eyed, blue-coated man with the hair trunk full of roots and herbs and their tinctures.

He was a disciple of Dr. Samuel Thompson, a self-taught mediciner, who, many years before, had brought upon himself the wrath, bitterer than his own concoctions, of the regular physicians of New England by his unauthorized practice and his denunciations of their methods. In time they enlarged and improved their pharmacopoeia by availing themselves of his discoveries, but gave him no credit, and few know to what "noted empiric" they are indebted for them. Joseph was conservative, and would rather have employed the old regular physician of Danvis than this innovator, or perhaps both, and his father was bitter "agin Injin an' ol' woman ways o' darkterin';" but this unlicensed practitioner had cured Maria's mother of "newrology," and him she was set upon having, and Joseph consented, according to his usual custom when "M'ri" insisted.

"Mis' Hill," said the doctor, looking over his spectacles and his trunk at Joseph, "is sights better. The reg'lar course we've gi'n her, lobele 'metics, steamin' an' sofuth, has hove off the agur spells an' the fever. All she wants naow is strenth'nin', suthin' tu give her an appetite t' eat, an' suthin' nourishin' t' eat. We're goin' tu leave her these here spice bitters, tu take a small spoo'f'l steeped up in a teacup o' hot water three times a day; an' you must git some popple bark, and steep up a big han'f'l on 't in a gallern o' water, an' hev her drink a ha' pint on 't most any time when she's dry, or a dozen times a day; an' it would be a good thing for her tu take a leetle pennyr'yal tea, say a teacupful three, four times a day, kinder 'tween times, an' then eat nourishin' victuals."[65]

The root doctor's prescriptions—lobelia, bitters, poplar bark, and pennyroyal—are all familiar folk remedies.[66] Lobelia is frequently mentioned in Robinson's stories as a medicinal plant.[67] In *Out of Bondage,* for example, Julia Peck, persuading a Canuck that he is ill in order to confine him to the house to prevent him from informing on a runaway slave, gives him a tincture of lobelia, which is called a "Thompsonian treatment."[68] "Tinctur' o' lobele," Julia Peck asserts, will clean out the Canuck's stomach "an' du him good."[69] In *Danvis Folks,* Mrs. Purington mentions that Sammy Lovel "was fetched through the whoopin' cough an' the measles wi' Hive surrup an' lobele an' pennyrile tea . . ."[70] In *Uncle Lisha's Shop*, Joseph Hill maintains that an alum curd poultice is the best remedy for sore eyes, "thaout 't was lobele steeped intu speerits."[71]

Pennyroyal, too, a mint well known to folk medicine practitioners, is mentioned several times. In addition to the places discussed above, it is named in "The Gray Pine," as a cure for a cold.[72] Furthermore, in an autobiographical essay Robinson writes that when he and Mingo found pennyroyal in the woods, it "went home to join the congregation of bundles and bags of healing roots and herbs on the garret rafters, each marked with its name and date of gathering in my mother's neat handwriting."[73]

A perennial frequently used in folk medicine that is mentioned by Robinson is boneset. In *Danvis Folks,* Mrs. Purington observes that Uncle Lisha looks "wore aout an' tuckered," diagnoses that he is coming down with fever, and prescribes "boneset er pennyrile er suthin'."[74] In *Uncle Lisha's Shop*, Mrs. Purington tells her moonstruck daughter, Huldah, "You be dreffle mumpin' this summer . . . I b'lieve I'd orter steep up some boneset an' hev ye take some; I b'lieve yer stomerk's aouten order."[75] In "A September Election," Harriet Piper notices her daughter, Malvina, behaving similarly and prescribes the same remedy.[76] In *A Danvis Pioneer,* when Gran'ther Hill is sick, Mrs.

Purington asks Joseph Hill, "I s'pose you give your father bwunset?"
Joseph replies that his headstrong father took some boneset himself.
Joseph explains, "Ye can't ezackly give him nothin'. He won't let
ye."[77] Gran'ther Hill's faith in blood-letting is elaborated upon in
Danvis Folks, when the Danvis patriarch carries on a debate with the
local root doctor. Here Robinson is able to work in a number of other
folk remedies:

"Ye'll draownded her wi' yer cussed slops!" Gran'ther Hill growled, turning in his
chair and thumping the floor with rapid blows of his cane. "'F you'd ha' gi'n her
some callymill an' bled her 'n the fust on 't, she 'd ha' ben all right naow! You've
roasted her an' biled her, an' naow yer goin' tu draownded her wi' yer pailfuls o'
spice bitters an' popple soup, an' the Lord knows what tarnal slops!"

"Callymill is pizon, an' tew much bleedin' is what kills hawgs," said the doctor
with calm emphasis.

"Pizon is good when it's took proper," Gran'ther Hill retorted, "an' folks hain't
hawgs, not all of 'em hain't. I wish 't Darkter Stun 'could come along an' gi' me a
dost o' callymill an' bleed me; I know it 'ould make me feel better this tarnal
roastin' weather. It's a feller's blood 'at heats him. I c'n feel mine a chuggin' up
ag'in the top o' my skull every beat o' my pult, an' I wish I was red of a quart on
't!"

"You don't look, Kepting Hill," the doctor said, after a brief survey of the old
man's gaunt figure, "as if you hed a grea' deal o' blood tu spare."

"I know't I've shed lots on 't for my country," said Gran'ther Hill. "But I've got
'nough left tu fill up tew, three pepper darkters wi' better 'n they've got!"

"No daoubt on 't, Kepting, no daoubt on 't," the good-natured mediciner answered,
"but you don't wanter waste it. Tew much good blood no man can't hev, an' aour
remedies make bad blood good. You take some pepsissiway an' put it in some ol'
Medford, an' take a swaller three times a day, a good big swaller, Kepting, an' see
what it'll du for yer blood."

"That saounds sensibler 'n the water swash you was talkin' on, an' I begin tu think
you know suthin' arter all. Jozeff, nex' time you go over tu Hamner's, you git me
a quart, 'n' I'll gether me some pepsissiway, an' I'll put in three, four sprigs, an' try
it."

"Reason is aour guide," said the doctor, "an' aour remedies is what Natur p'ints
aout tu us. We don't make no secret o' what she tells us. Naow, these 'ere spice
bitters is compaounded of several nat'ral plants, but the main ingrejencies is feverbush an' bayberry. We hain't no secrets; all we're after is the trewth."

"Go tu' thunder!" growled Gran'ther Hill. "You're arter yer livin' jes' as all on us
is. Nothin' on this livin' airth riles me wus'n herin' darkters an' preachers gabbin'
baout the raslin' raound jes' for the sake o' duin' other folks good, when they an
ev'ybody knows it's theirselves they're workin' for. Who they tryin' tu fool,—God
amighty, or folks, or the' ownselves?"

"Sartainly, we've got tu live whilest we're raslin' for the trewth, Kepting. You
drawed pay when you was fightin' fer your kentry, an' you fit a leetle better,
proberbly, 'n you would for nothin' but glory. Starvin' fodder that is, for livin' on
in this world. An' that reminds me 't Mis' Hill wants suthin' nourishin' t' eat.
The' hain't nothin' better 'n pa'tridge meat, which it is victuals an' medicine to

oncte, for a pa'tridge is continerly a-feedin' on a hulsome diet, feverbush berries, wintergreen, pepsissiway, blackberries, popple-buds, and birchbuds, an' I do' know what all, of Nature's pharmycopy, which is dissimerlated through the meat. . . .[78]

Pipsissewa, mentioned by the root doctor, in addition to other traditional remedies, is also named in Robinson's short story "A Letter from the 'Hio." In this story a letter from Susan Ward of Buckeye, Ohio, to her Vermont friends enables Robinson to work in folk tonics for the blood and a traditional cure for asthma:

" 'I set down this afternoon to write a few lines to you to inform you of our health and welfare. We air all well as we ever was except mother, she enjoys considerable poor health this spring.' "

"There now," Aunt Charity broke in, "I allers tol' Marier she 'd ortu commence a-takin' picry jest afore spring opens, but she never would, not faithful."

"I do' know 'baout picry," said Mrs. Perkins, with slow impressive wags of her head, "picry's pooty ha'sh. Naow, I should say pepsisiway steeped up in cider or sperits. The' hain't a fall but I hev him go int' the woods an' git me a hull lot o' pepsisiway. It's good for the blood, and it's good for the stomerk; an' gives ye an appetite t' eat."

"Gosh, yes! More 'n a ton on 't in the garret," chuckled her husband, boring Jared's ribs with a forefinger.

"Naow, Mr. Perkins," his wife said reproachfully.

"Wal," he insisted, "you take an' put in a hull mess on 't every identical fall, an' never take none out; it 'cumulates, I tell ye."

"You can't say 'at I would n't ha' took some this very spring if the 'd ben sperits in the haouse an' the cider had n't all been put in the vinegar baril."

"Dumb yer picry an' things!" Uncle Peter burst out. "Be ye goin' to read that 'ere letter, Phoeb' Ann?"

"Yes, why don't ye? We're all a-waitin'," Aunt Charity urged, and Phoebe Ann, having kept her place with her finger while awaiting opportunity, went on: " 'this spring, and father which he is troubled some with his asmy' "—

"Why don't he smoke mullein leaves? Take an' dry 'em an"—Mrs. Perkins interrupted, but Uncle Peter's chair gave a sharp, ominous squeak, and the reading continued.[79]

In addition to pipsissewa, picra, and mullein leaves—all well known to practitioners of folk medicine—Robinson refers to other traditional remedies.[80] In *Out of Bondage*, Robert Ransom gives herb tea to an ill Negro who is escaping from slavery. "It's old woman's medicine," says Ransom, "but it's all I have."[81] In *Sam Lovel's Camps*, some treasure seekers find "seas an' oceans an' thaousen's o' Seneky snake rhut," which Robinson calls a medicinal herb.[82] In *Out of Bondage*, after a Canuck complains of stomach pains, Deborah Barclay offers him some pepper tea or some salt and water to relieve his pain.[83] In *Danvis Folks*, Robinson writes about "the sturdy houseleeks—hens and chickens their mistress called them, and nursed them in their box in doors and out the year round, for their oddity and their repute for curing corns."[84]

Traditional cures for coughs and colds are also found in Robinson's writings. In *Out of Bondage*, a runaway Negro slave is given "hive syrup" to cure his cough,[85] while in *Uncle Lisha's Shop*, "some sets gret store by wild turnips dried an' grated an' took in 'lasses fer a hackin' cough."[86] In *Uncle Lisha's Outing*, Sam Lovel orders for a nearly-drowned boy a handful of catnip steeped in boiling water as a preventive of cold. Addressing the mother Sam says, "You give him a good lot on 't, hot as he c'n take it."[87] When Sam returns to his camp, his wife, Huldah tells him, "Folks hain't half so apt tu ketch cold if they let the' clo's dry on 'em."[88]

Other of Robinson's folk cures make use of animal life instead of plant life. Skunk oil "was a soverign remedy for croup and rheumatism, and therefore in demand by youth and age."[89] In *Uncle Lisha's Shop*, Lisha tells his cronies that "when I was a leetle chap they cured me o' croup with skunk's ile, which they gi'n it ter me spoo'ful arter spoo'ful, an' greased my stomerk with it outside, tew. An' then arter I'd got growed up, skunk essence cured me of azmy."[90] Other traditional cures involve eels and snakes. A widespread cure for rheumatism is to tie a dried eelskin around the rheumatic limb or, according to Clifton Johnson, around the waist, in New England.[91] Robinson uses this folk cure in *Sam Lovel's Camps*; Antoine Bassette says that if you'll wear an eelskin around your back "you'll ant never had lame backaches!"[92] Sam Lovel growls out another folk cure: "Humph! I've hearn tell o' folks wearin' snakes in the' hats tu cure headache, an' I'd jest livs as tu hev that pesky thing waound 'raound my body. Ugh!"[93]

NOTES

[1]Wayland D. Hand, "American Superstitions and Popular Beliefs," *Folklore In Action,* ed. Horace P. Beck (Philadelphia, 1962), p. 151.

[2]Harold W. Thompson, p. 300. Motif N511.1.7, "Treasure hidden by retreating army."

[3]Motif D1825.1, "Second sight."

[4]Robinson, *Uncle Lisha's Outing and Along Three Rivers,* p. 234.

[5]Robinson, *Sam Lovel's Camps and In the Green Wood,* pp. 49-50.

[6]Robinson, *Sam Lovel's Camps and In the Green Wood,* pp. 161-162.

[7]Motif C401.3, "Tabu: speaking while searching for treasure."

[8]For other accounts of the tradition of Rogers' Rangers and the silver image, see Dorson's note in *Jonathan Draws the Long Bow,* p. 225, and Robinson, *Vermont,* p. 38.

[9]Motif F494.1, "Guardian spirit of land." Cf. Motif F494.1.1, "Swamp spirit guards buried treasure."

[10]Robinson, *Danvis Folks and A Hero of Ticonderoga,* pp. 121-122.

[11]See *The Frank C. Brown Collection,* VII, 175, No. 5871.

[12]*The Frank C. Brown Collection,* VII, 190-181. Nos. 5892-5894. Motif D1314.2, "Magic wand (twig) locates hidden treasures."

[13]Robinson, *Danvis Folks and A Hero of Ticonderoga,* pp. 161-164.

[14]Motif E520, "Animal ghosts."

[15]Robinson, *Uncle Lisha's Shop and A Danvis Pioneer,* pp. 205-207. Motif Q211.6, "Killing an animal revenged."

[16]Robinson, *Uncle Lisha's Shop and A Danvis Pioneer,* p. 209.

[17]Robinson, *Out of Bondage and Other Stories,* pp. 231-246.

[18]Robinson, *Out of Bondage and Other Stories,* p. 236.

[19]Robinson, *Out of Bondage and Other Stories,* pp. 231-246.

[20]John H. Sears, "Notes on the Forest Trees of Essex, Clinton and Franklin Counties, New York," *Bulletin of the Essex Institute,* XIII (October-December, 1881), 186-187.

[21]Robinson, *Uncle Lisha's Outing and Along Three Rivers,* pp. 193-194. Motifs D2084, "Industrial processes magically interrupted"; D2084.2, "Butter magically kept from coming"; G265.8.1, "Witch bewitches household articles"; Cf. Hyatt, pp. 543-544, Nos. 12240-12249; *The Frank C. Brown Collection,* VI, 362-364, Nos. 2806-2817; *The Frank C. Brown Collection,* VII, 441, No. 7542, "To drive witches out of milk which can't be easily churned, drop a piece of silver in the churn."

[22]Robinson, *Sam Lovel's Camps and In the Green Wood,* p. 72. Cf. *The Frank C. Brown Collection,* VII, 480, No. 7827.

[23]Robinson, *Out of Bondage and Other Stories,* p. 67. See *The Frank C. Brown Collection,* VII, 481, No. 7833; VII, 482, No. 7844.

[24]Robinson, *Sam Lovel's Camps and In the Green Wood,* pp. 121-122.

[25]Motif A2217.3.2 (Baughman).

[26]Robinson, *Sam Lovel's Camps and In the Green Wood,* pp. 137-138.

[27]Robinson, *Silver Fields and Other Sketches of a Farmer-Sportsman,* p. 199.

[28]Robinson, *Silver Fields and Other Sketches of a Farmer-Sportsman,* p. 134.

[29]Randolph, *Ozark Superstitions,* p. 250. Cf. *The Frank C. Brown Collection,* VII, 408, No. 7330.

[30]Robinson, *In New England Fields and Woods,* pp. 168-169.

[31]*The Frank C. Brown Collection,* VII, 162-163, Nos. 5810-5811; Clifton Johnson, *What They Say in New England* (Boston, 1896), p. 88.

[32]Robinson, *Sam Lovel's Camps and In the Green Wood*, p. 167. See *The Frank C. Brown Collection*, VII, 185, No. 5920.

[33]Robinson, *Out of Bondage and Other Stories*, p. 76. For parallels see *The Frank C. Brown Collection*, VII, 491-492, Nos. 7909-7912.

[34]Robinson, *Out of Bondage and Other Stories*, p. 232. In "Vermont Proverbs and Proverbial Sayings," *Vermont History*, XXVIII (July, 1960), 202, Muriel J. Hughes gives "There is luck in odd numbers."

[35]Robinson, *Out of Bondage and Other Stories*, p. 60. For similar beliefs see Hyatt, p. 40, Nos. 1060-1064.

[36]Robinson, *Out of Bondage and Other Stories*, p. 152.

[37]Robinson, *Uncle Lisha's Shop and A Danvis Pioneer*, p. 170. For a version see *The Frank C. Brown Collection*, VI, 364, No. 2820.

[38]Robinson, *Uncle Lisha's Outing and Along Three Rivers*, p. 112. Cf. *The Frank C. Brown Collection*, VI, 364, No. 2822.

[39]Robinson, *Sam Lovel's Camps and In the Green Wood*, p. 75.

[40]Robinson, *Sam Lovel's Boy with Forest and Stream Fables*, p. 89. Motif D1273.1.3.1, "Nine as magic number." See *The Frank C. Brown Collection*, VII, 380-381, No. 7157, "A cat has nine lives."

[41]Robinson, *Sam Lovel's Boy with Forest and Stream Fables*, p. 64. See *The Frank C. Brown Collection*, VI, 310, No. 2414; VII, 437, No. 7524.

[42]Robinson, *Danvis Folks and A Hero of Ticonderoga*, pp. 228, 272.

[43]Motif B81.13.7 (Baughman), "Mermaid appears as omen of catastrophe." Cf. Motifs D1812.5.1.9, "Sight of mermaid bad omen"; B81.9.5, "Skin of mermaid."

[44]Robinson, *Uncle Lisha's Shop and A Danvis Pioneer*, p. 218. See *The Frank C. Brown Collection*, VII, 466, No. 7715; VII, 531, No. 8201.

[45]Robinson, "Glimpses of New England Farm Life," p. 522.

[46]*The Frank C. Brown Collection*, VII, 523, No. 8138. Ray B. Browne, *Popular Beliefs and Practices from Alabama* (Berkeley and Los Angeles, 1958), p. 247, No. 4165.

[47]Robinson, *Sam Lovel's Boy with Forest and Stream Fables*, p. 146. For a well annotated variant of this popular belief see *The Frank C. Brown Collection*, VII, 210, No. 645.

[48]Robinson, *Uncle Lisha's Shop and A Danvis Pioneer*, pp. 214-217.

[49]Robinson, *Uncle Lisha's Shop and A Danvis Pioneer*, p. 142.

[50]Robinson, *Uncle Lisha's Shop and A Danvis Pioneer*, p. 217.

[51]Robinson, *Uncle Lisha's Shop and A Danvis Pioneer*, p. 149. Cf. Hyatt, p. 11, No. 286.

[52]Robinson, *Uncle Lisha's Shop and A Danvis Pioneer*, p. 142; *Sam Lovel's Camps and In the Green Wood*, p. 51; *Uncle Lisha's Outing and Along Three Rivers*, p. 66; *Danvis Folks and A Hero of Ticonderoga*, p. 248. For variants of these widespread folk beliefs, see *The Frank C. Brown Collection*, VII, 304, No. 6647; VII, 316, No. 6719.

[53]Robinson, *Sam Lovel's Camps and In the Green Wood*, p. 210. See Hyatt, p. 21, No. 564.

[54]*The Frank C. Brown Collection*, VII, 270, No. 6437.

[55]Robinson, *Uncle Lisha's Shop and A Danvis Pioneer*, p. 180. Cf. *The Frank C. Brown Collection*, VII, 200, No. 6009.

[56]Robinson, *Out of Bondage and Other Stories*, p. 116.

[57]*The Frank C. Brown Collection*, VI, 46, No. 268; VII, 353, No. 6968.

[58]Robinson, *Out of Bondage and Other Stories*, p. 111.

[59]Robinson, *Out of Bondage and Other Stories*, p. 114.

[60]Robinson, *Uncle Lisha's Shop and A Danvis Pioneer*, pp. 40-41.

[61]Browne, p. 47, No. 722.

[62]Robinson, *Sam Lovel's Camps and In the Green Wood*, pp. 240-241.

[63]Robinson, "Reminiscences," p. 285.

[64]Robinson, *Sam Lovel's Boy with Forest and Stream Fables*, p. 36.

[65]Robinson, *Danvis Folks and A Hero of Ticonderoga*, pp. 18-19.

[66]For folk cures using bitters and poplar bark, see *The Frank C. Brown Collection*, VI, 116, No. 796; VI, 145, No. 1060; VI, 248, No. 1915; VI, 354, No. 2743.

[67]Lobelia is given as a folk cure in *The Frank C. Brown Collection*, VI, 250, No. 1937; VI, 309, No. 2402.

[68]A New England folk cure is also called a "Thompsonian treatment" in B. A. Botkin, *A Treasury of New England Folklore* (New York, 1965), p. 352.

[69]Robinson, *Out of Bondage and Other Stories*, pp. 39-40.

[70]Robinson, *Danvis Folks and A Hero of Ticonderoga*, p. 203. Pennyroyal tea is given as a cure for measles in *The Frank C. Brown Collection*, VI, 234, No. 1817.

[71]Robinson, *Uncle Lisha's Shop and A Danvis Pioneer*, p. 166. Cf. *The Frank C. Brown Collection*, VI, 182, No. 1382.

[72]Robinson, *Out of Bondage and Other Stories*, p. 239. See *The Frank C. Brown Collection*, VI, 114, No. 785, "Pennyroyal tea is used as a cure for diseases."

[73]Robinson, "Reminiscences," p. 285.

[74]Robinson, *Danvis Folks and A Hero of Ticonderoga*, p. 66. See *The Frank C. Brown Collection*, VI, 145, No. 1056; VI, 150, No. 1105.

[75]Robinson, *Uncle Lisha's Shop and A Danvis Pioneer*, p. 180. See *The Frank C. Brown Collection*, VI, 221, No. 1703, "Boneset [*Eupatorium perfoliatum*] tea is good for the stomach."

[76]Robinson, *Sam Lovel's Boy with Forest and Stream Fables*, p. 158.

[77]Robinson, *Uncle Lisha's Shop and A Danvis Pioneer*, p. 102. For folk cures involving phlebotomy, see *The Frank C. Brown Collection*, VI, 129, No. 912; VI, 188, No. 1423; VI, 254, No. 1966.

[78]Robinson, *Danvis Folks and A Hero of Ticonderoga*, pp. 19-21.

[79]Robinson, *Out of Bondage and Other Stories*, p. 78.

[80]See, for example, *The Frank C. Brown Collection*, VI, 119, No. 820, "Mullein will cure asthma." Browne, p. 36, No. 518, "A tea made from pipissewa leaves will cure any kind of blood trouble." "Hiera picra," sometimes called "hickery-pickery" by the folk, is a "purgative drug composed of aloes and canella bark, sometimes mixed with honey"—*The Oxford Universal Dictionary on Historical Principles*, ed. C. T. Onions (London, 1955), p. 900.

[81]Robinson, *Out of Bondage and Other Stories*, p. 46.

[82]Robinson, *Sam Lovel's Camps and In the Green Wood*, p. 161. Randolph, in *Ozark Superstitions*, p. 107, writes, "Seneca-root or rattlesnake weed (*Senega*) is said to make a mighty fine chills-and-fever medicine."

[83]Robinson, *Out of Bondage and Other Stories*, p. 39. See *The Frank C. Brown Collection*, VI, 222, No. 1724, "Drink salty water to cure indigestion." Red-pepper tea is given as a cure "for stomach cramps or bellyache" in Randolph, *Ozark Superstitions*, pp. 95-96.

[84]Robinson, *Danvis Folks and A Hero of Ticonderoga*, p. 18. Cf. Hyatt, pp. 225-227, Nos. 5903-5144.

[85]Robinson, *Out of Bondage and Other Stories*, p. 23. Apparently "hive syrup" is a cough syrup made with honey, a common ingredient in traditional cough

syrups. See Randolph, *Ozark Superstitions*, p. 93; *The Frank C. Brown Collection*, VI, 162, No. 1211.

[86]Robinson, *Uncle Lisha's Shop and A Danvis Pioneer*, p. 211. Cf. *The Frank C. Brown Collection*, VI, 308, No. 2391.

[87]Robinson, *Uncle Lisha's Outing and Along Three Rivers*, p. 166. See *The Frank C. Brown Collection*, VI, 150, No. 1106, "Catnip tea is good for colds."

[88]Robinson, *Uncle Lisha's Outing and Along Three Rivers*, p. 184. For similar beliefs compare Hyatt, p. 278, Nos. 6108, 6109, 6110.

[89]Robinson, "Reminiscences," p. 285.

[90]Robinson, *Uncle Lisha's Shop and A Danvis Pioneer*, p. 145. According to Randolph, *Ozark Superstitions*, p. 93, "Many Ozark youngsters are dosed with large quantities of skunk oil for throat ailments, particularly croup."

[91]Johnson, p. 49. See *The Frank C. Brown Collection*, VI, 256, No. 1977.

[92]Robinson, *Sam Lovel's Camps and In the Green Wood*, pp. 130-131.

[93]Robinson, *Sam Lovel's Camps and In the Green Wood*, p. 131. For versions of this traditional cure, see *The Frank C. Brown Collection*, VI, 207, No. 1588; VI, 208, No. 1589.

CHAPTER 14

TRADITIONAL NONSINGING GAMES, RHYMES, AND RIDDLES

Since Robinson concentrates on the masculine activities of Danvis, the folklore of children and women is held in the background. He does include some material on the toys, games, rhymes, and riddles of interest to children and gives some information on the activities of women. As for folk toys, Robinson mentions the rag dolls of the Danvis girls and the homemade balls of the Danvis boys.[1] The toy ball of young Sammy Lovel, according to Robinson, was "tightly wound of raveled stocking yarn about a core of India rubber made of strings cut from one of the shapeless overshoes of those days," and covered with a woodchuck hide. "According to some occult rule," Robinson says, "the old shoemaker cut the skin into oval quarters and sewed them over the ball with waxed ends." With the ball the boy can play "tew ol' cat" or "barnbase."[2] "Two Old Cat" is also played by a group of Danvis boys at a raising bee in *Danvis Folks*.[3] Newell explains in *Games and Songs of American Children* that in the game of "Old Cat" there are two goals, one for the batter and another for the pitcher. Runs, then, are made from the batter's goal to the pitcher's goal. The game gets its name, "One Old Cat" or "Two Old Cat," from the number of batters.[4]

Robinson describes in more detail the popular traditional game, "I Spy."[5] In "An Underground Railroad Passenger" there is a fairly complete description of the game, including a traditional counting-out rhyme:

Finding the boys at leisure, a game of "I Spy"—or as we had it, perhaps by inheritance from our English ancestors, "hi-spy"—was presently arranged. We were "counted out" by our favorite formula, "Wire, brier, limber lock, six geese in a flock," and it fell to Tom's lot to blind.

Before his loud announcement of the first ten of the hundred,—which he was so rapidly counting that there was but a continuous mumble between the tens,—Jim, Billy and I scattered in search of hiding-places. I was at no loss to find one, for I knew every nook and corner of the premises; and as neither of the others went that way, I tiptoed up the stairs that led to the hayloft over the stable. This place af-

130

forded a good outlook to the "gool," as well as a good hiding place.

[At last] . . . Tom Sherman sang out, "One hundred!" and the warning, "One, two, three, look out for me!"

. . . Tom spied the other boys, and I got a safe run to the "gool" . . .[6]

The counting-out rhyme to which Robinson refers is a fragment of the familiar "William a Trembletoe."[7] A version of this traditional rhyme from the American oral tradition runs:

> William, William Trembletoe
> He's a good fisherman'
> Catches hens, put them in pens;
> Some lay eggs, some lay none.
> Wire, briar, limber lock,
> Three geese in a flock;
> One flew east, one flew west,
> One flew over the goose's nest.
> O-U-T spells out and begone,
> You old dirty dish rag.[8]

Two other traditional rhymes Robinson mentions are "Old King Cole" and "Jack a Nory." Robinson twice refers to "Old King Cole" in *Sam Lovel's Camps* but gives no texts. In *Sam Lovel's Boy*, he gives a fragment of "Jack a Nory," when one rainy day Sammy Lovel comes to Uncle Lisha's shop for stories from Uncle Lisha. "Wal, I'll tell ye a story," says Uncle Lisha,

> " 'Baout ol' Mother Morey
> An' naow my story's begun."[9]

But Sammy Lovel, who is familiar with this rhyme, says, "Oh, not that ol' story," so Uncle Lisha must tell another tale. Iona and Peter Opie report that "Jack a Nory" is often used exactly as Uncle Lisha uses it—to put off children's demands for stories.

In "Mingo—A Silhouette" Robinson describes a riddle session in which he participated as a boy. One of the riddles propounded by Mingo by a campfire was "A hill full, a hole full, can't ketch a bowl full." Robinson includes a version of this riddle as well as versions of six other traditional riddles in *Sam Lovel's Boy*. The riddles are told around a warm stove in Uncle Lisha's shop, not around a campfire; but they are told for the same reason—to entertain a boy. When Sammy becomes bored, he asks Uncle Lisha to tell some riddles, and telling riddles Uncle Lisha "was nothing loath to do, as it would not hinder his listening to propound the unguessable questions nor give the time-worn answers."[10] One riddle, a version of the above riddle that Robinson heard from Mingo Niles, runs:

> Hill full,
> A hole full,
> You can't ketch a bowl full.[11]

The answer to this riddle is not given, but since it is a version of the riddle that Robinson learned from Mingo, the answer is probably the same, "dew."[12]

Another riddle in *Sam Lovel's Boy* for which Robinson also fails to give an answer is a variant of a widespread traditional riddle, too:

> Over the water,
> Under the water,
> Never teched the water.[13]

Although the answer to this riddle is lacking, versions of it from Great Britain, the West Indies, Canada, and the United States have the same answer: "A woman crossing a bridge with a pail of water on her head."[14]

For the other five riddles Robinson supplies answers. Robinson writes that Lisha propounds "that masterpiece of poetry and mystery":

> Chink, chink,
> Through the brook,
> And never stops to drink.[15]

The solution given is "a chain dragged through a brook by oxen."

In *Sam Lovel's Boy* Uncle Lisha asks Sammy a version of "Little Nancy Etticoat":

> Nitty crout,
> Netty crout,
> Wears a white petticrout
> And a red nose;
> The longer she lives the shorter she grows.[16]

The answer is a candle.

Another traditional riddle reported from Nova Scotia, Tennessee, and New Orleans describes a barrel as having two heads and one body.[17] An Ontario analogue in F. W. Waugh's collection, "Canadian Folklore from Ontario," runs, "Boddy, Noddy,/Two heads and one body"; but the answer given is wheelbarrow,"[18] which is not as intelligible as a North Carolina version with the same answer that goes, "Niddy, niddy, noddy, two arms and one body."[19] The form of a riddle that Uncle Lisha asks Sammy in *Sam Lovel's Boy* is similar to the Ontario riddle; however, the answer, "barrel," agrees with the version from Nova Scotia, Tennessee, and New Orleans. Uncle Lisha's version is, "Niddy, noddy, tew heads an' one body."[20]

In *English Riddles from the Oral Tradition* Archer Taylor writes, "English riddlers of the seventeenth century know the description of snow as a person who goes around the house and leaves a white glove."[21] Although this popular English riddle seems to lack parallels in continental Europe, it has been relatively popular in the United States and Canada. Taylor lists versions, for instance, from the Ozarks, North

Carolina, New York, Ontario, and Nova Scotia. A version listed by Taylor runs, "Round the house and round the house,/And leaves a white glove i' the window."[22] A very close variant is asked by Uncle Lisha in *Sam Lovel's Boy*; it is: "Raoun' the haouse an' raoun' the haouse, an' leave a white glove in the winder."[23]

Another variant of a traditional riddle in *Sam Lovel's Boy* runs:

> Chic, Chic, Cherry, O,
> All the men in Derry, O,
> Can't climb Chic, Cherry, O.[24]

This riddle, to which the answer is "smoke," has parallels in Africa, in the West Indies, in the southern United States, and in Scotland.

NOTES

[1]Robinson, *Uncle Lisha's Shop and A Danvis Pioneer*, p. 181; *Danvis Folks and A Hero of Ticonderoga*, p. 254; *Sam Lovel's Boy with Forest and Stream Fables*, p. 69.

[2]Robinson, *Sam Lovel's Boy with Forest and Stream Fables*, pp. 43, 46.

[3]Robinson, *Danvis Folks and A Hero of Ticonderoga*, p. 161.

[4]William Wells Newell, *Games and Songs of American Children* (New York, 1883), p. 185.

[5]See Newell, p. 160; *The Frank C. Brown Collection*, I, 38; Alice B. Gomme, *The Traditional Games of England, Scotland, and Ireland* (London, 1894-98), I, 212-213.

[6]Robinson, *Out of Bondage and Other Stories*, pp. 60-61.

[7]Henry Carrington Bolton, *The Counting-Out Rhymes of Children, Their Antiquity, Origin, and Wide Distribution* (London, 1888), pp. 3, 102-103, 117.

[8]*The Frank C. Brown Collection*, I, 160.

[9]Robinson, *Sam Lovel's Boy with Forest and Stream Fables*, p. 34. See Opie, p. 233, No. 260.

[10]Robinson, *Sam Lovel's Boy with Forest and Stream Fables*, pp. 112-113.

[11]Robinson, *Sam Lovel's Boy with Forest and Stream Fables*, p. 113. See Taylor, *English Riddles*, pp. 661-663.

[12]Robinson, *Out of Bondage and Other Stories*, p. 68.

[13]Robinson, *Sam Lovel's Boy with Forest and Stream Fables*, p. 113.

[14]Taylor, *English Riddles*, p. 60, No. 165b.

[15]Robinson, *Sam Lovel's Boy with Forest and Stream Fables*, p. 113. See Taylor, *English Riddles*, p. 86, No. 253.

[16]Robinson, *Sam Lovel's Boy with Forest and Stream Fables*, p. 113. See Taylor, *English Riddles*, pp. 221-224, Nos. 607-631.

[17]Taylor, *English Riddles*, p. 17, No. 30a.

[18]F. W. Waugh, "Canadian Folklore from Ontario," *Journal of American Folklore*, XXXI (1918), 70, No. 804. See Taylor, *English Riddles*, p. 184, No. 518.

[19]*The Frank C. Brown Collection*, I, 294, No. 34.

[20]Robinson, *Sam Lovel's Boy with Forest and Stream Fables*, p. 113.

[21]Taylor, *English Riddles*, p. 76.

[22]Taylor, *English Riddles*, p. 76, No. 210a.

[23]Robinson, *Sam Lovel's Boy with Forest and Stream Fables*, p. 112.

[24]Robinson, *Sam Lovel's Boy with Forest and Stream Fables*, p. 113. See Taylor, *English Riddles*, pp. 656-657.

CHAPTER 15

PROVERBS AND PROVERBIAL PHRASES

Because of his avowed interest in preserving the folk language of his area[1] and his use of such a large number of traditional words, phrases, and exclamations from nineteenth century rural Vermont, Robinson's writings should prove useful to the dialectologist interested in regional vocabulary and structure, perhaps even pronunciation, current when no systematic field collection was attempted. Countless regional words, phrases, and exclamations can be found throughout the Danvis stories. For example, when one of the Danvis folk speaks of the whole lot or of the whole group, he uses the phrase "the hull caboodle."[2] When someone is told to move swiftly or to hurry, he is told either to "clipper"[3] or to "hyper."[4] When a character has a fit of rage or a fit of compassion, he is said to have a "conniption fit."[5] Those who are not very bright are called "dumb'd do-dunks."[6] Anything that is not working properly is "aout o' kilter."[7] When something is average, the Danvis people say it is "middlin'."[8] When a citizen of Danvis walks slowly, he is said to be "a-moggin' ";[9] when he walks idly, he is "traipsin'."[10] When the Danvis folk revolt against something, they "spleen ag'in" it.[11] There are also many examples of traditional exclamations, including: "Good airth an' seas,"[12] "By the Lord Harry,"[13] "Thunder in the winter,"[14] "I swan,"[15] "Pshaw,"[16] "By hokey,"[17] "By the gret horn spoon,"[18] "Gosh all fishhooks,"[19] and "By gum."[20]

The traditional words, expressions, and names that Robinson uses are within the domain of verbal folklore. As folklorist Louise Pound points out, "Surely dialect is a species of folklore, though the two subjects are usually treated independently. Dialect, in the sense in which we now ordinarily use the word, is *lore*, linguistic lore, and linguistic lore exists in tradition alongside the folk beliefs and folkways, the folk legacies that we usually term lore."[21] On the other hand, although the general folklorist is naturally interested in the traditional naming and pronunciation habits of homogeneous groups, only trained linguistic geographers have the specialized knowledge needed to study folk dialect scientifically. As Jan Brunvand maintains, the study of folk speech, strictly speaking, belongs to the highly specialized area of linguistics.[22] Accordingly, Robinson's use of folk speech should be examined by a trained dialectologist in a separate study. A linguist might well study the dialect in Robinson's writings in the same manner as Sumner Ives studied the dialect in the stories of Joel Chandler Harris.[23]

Although the systematic study of the folk speech in Robinson's writings must necessarily be relegated to the trained dialectologist, the study of more complex forms of verbal folklore—proverbs and proverbial phrases, which truly abound in these stories—is clearly within the realm of general folkloristics. Robinson's intimate relationship with the village folk, his accurate portrayal of a traditional milieu, his admitted purpose of preserving folk sayings, and his unique ability to reproduce folk speech make the study of the proverbial material in his writings exceedingly valuable to anyone interested in the texts and context of nineteenth century proverbial sayings. In his realistic stories, Robinson clearly shows proverbs and proverbial phrases functioning in an artistically reconstructed folk society. Unlike the other genres of verbal folklore, such as tales and riddles, the proverbs spoken by Robinson's Danvis folk are not told in storytelling or riddling sessions but are an integral part of the lives of the Danvis citizens. Proverbs occur in their everyday speech whenever the occasion demands a terse statement to size up a situation or to pass judgment on behavior. At the Lovels' paring bee, for example, after the young people have spent considerable time playing kissing games while their elders looked on, Uncle Lisha aptly sizes up the situation with a proverb and announces that it is time to turn from singing games to country dancing. "Come," says Lisha, "you young folks orter be abaout cl'yed wi' bussin' an' we ol' folks has eat saour grapes long 'nough, so le' 's all turn tu an' hev a leetle sensible enj'yment a-dancin'."[24] When Uncle Lisha and Aunt Jerusha return to Vermont after three years in Wisconsin and fellow New Englanders on the canal boat constantly degrade their native soil and glorify the West, Uncle Lisha passes judgment on the attitude of his fellow passengers with an appropriate proverb: "It's a dirty bird 'at faowls his own nest."[25] In short, the proverbs in Robinson's stories are set in an authentically reconstructed milieu and function as proverbs do in an actual folk society. As folklorist Roger D. Abrahams says of the function of proverbs:

Proverbs are traditional answers to recurrent ethical problems; they provide an argument for a course of action which conforms to community values. They arise in the midst of a conversation, and are used by speakers to give a "name" to the ethical problem confronting them, and to suggest ways in which it has been solved in the past (though the suggestion is not necessarily directed immediately to the ones confronted by the problem). The use of a proverb invokes an aura of moral rightness in a conversation; the comfort of past community procedure is made available to the present and future. Proverbs may be used directly to teach or to remind and measure those who already know them. The proverb says at once, "This is the way things are and have been," and "This is the way of responding properly to such a situation." The strategy of the proverb, in other words, is to direct by appearing to clarify; this is engineered by simplifying the problem and resorting to traditional solutions.[26]

Generally speaking, the proverbs used by the Danvis folk serve to instruct, to sanction behavior, to amuse, and to enhance ordinary conversation. For instance, in *Uncle Lisha's Shop,* Lisha draws upon two traditional proverbs to teach young Sammy Lovel the virtues of rising early in the morning: "It's the airly bird 'at gits the worm, you know; an' I've heard your father say time an' agin, 'An haour 'fore sunup 's wuth tew arter.' "[27] A proverb also sanctions behavior at Hamner's turkey shoot in *Uncle Lisha's Shop,* when John Dart hits a turkey on the very first shot of the match and Hamner, not happy to let a turkey go for so little money, refuses to let John shoot at another turkey. Hamner justifies his action with a proverb—"You s'pose I'm a goin' tu hev the bread took aouten my maouth that way?"—and the marksmen at the shoot respect Hamner's decision.[28] Some of the proverbs in Robinson's stories are amusing comments on a situation. When Sam Lovel tells of the fun of coon hunting in cornfields at night with dogs, Uncle Lisha confesses that he finds "no gret fun in stumblin' raound in the dark 'n' fightin' skeeters half the night." Still, Lisha humorously acknowledges Sam Lovel's point of view by citing a well-known Wellerism. "Wal," Uncle Lisha says, "everybody tu their notion, 's the ol' woman said when she kissed her kyow."[29] Furthermore, innumerable proverbial phrases and similes intensify or add color to the everyday speech of the Danvis folk. One is not simply parsimonious in the Danvis stories; he is "tighter 'n the bark tu a tree." One is not merely destitute; he has "not a red cent in his pocket." When it is cold in Danvis, it is "colder 'n charity"; and when it is hot, it is "hotter 'n blazes." A Negro is not simply dark, but he is "so black a coal would make a white mark on him." When it is quiet in Danvis, it is "stiller 'n last year's bird's-nest." When a Danvis citizen speaks in a low inarticulate voice, he does not simply mutter, but he mumbles "his words as if they were so many hot potatoes."

The study of proverbs in Robinson's stories is important not only because he shows the texts of proverbs in context, but also because his material supplements Taylor and Whiting's collection of proverbs from nineteenth century (i.e., 1820-1880) American literature. Comparing Jan Brunvand's collection of 1500 separate proverbial sayings from the writings of 39 nineteenth century Indiana authors to Robinson's 400 traditional sayings, or about one-fourth of the proverbial sayings in Brunvand's important collection, one concludes that Robinson's books are a major source of nineteenth century proverbs.

The content of the proverbial material in Robinson's stories corroborates what other students of American proverbs have observed. That is, as Brunvand points out, "On the whole, judging from several representative collections, the subjects of well-known American proverbs tend to come from homey, simple, familiar, natural, and domestic topics. Nouns like 'dog,' 'man,' 'cat,' 'bird,' 'wind,' 'bear,' and 'day' appear more frequently than any others; a somewhat contradictory fact, however, is that references to the Devil in American proverbs usually outnumber those to God in collections by about four to one."[30] The content of the proverbs and proverbial sayings in Robinson's stories agrees almost wholly with the content of the proverbial material in other collections of American proverbs. For example, in Taylor and Whiting's collection among the most common key words are "bear," "bird," "cat," "Devil," "dog," "hen," and "horse." In the proverbs and proverbial sayings in Robinson's writings the most common key words are also concerned with either things domestic, familiar, and natural or with the Devil. Thus, the most common words in the proverbs that Robinson uses are "bear," "bee," "bird," "cat," "Devil," "dog," "hen," "horse," "time," and "wolf."

Since the proverbial material in Robinson's stories contributes significantly to our knowledge of proverbial sayings in tradition in Vermont during the nineteenth century, the proverbs and proverbial phrases are listed and annotated separately. Following the arrangement of the material in Archer Taylor and Bartlett Jere Whiting's *Dictionary of American Proverbs and Proverbial Phrases, 1820-1880,* the texts are arranged alphabetically according to the first noun or according to the first important word if the noun is lacking. Whereas Taylor and Whiting culled proverbs from the works of many American authors, excluding Robinson, and arranged their variants of proverb texts in chronological order, the Robinson list was compiled from the writings of a single author, and no attempt was made to separate his works. Representative parallels from major collections of Anglo-American proverbs have been cited; however, no attempt has been made to cite all the possible references for each item. Only texts with parallels in other collections have been included.

NOTES

[1] See Robinson's note preceding *Danvis Folks* in *Danvis Folks and A Hero of Ticonderoga*, p. 16.

[2] Robinson, *Uncle Lisha's Shop and A Danvis Pioneer*, p. 186. See "caboodle" in Muriel Joy Hughes, "A Word-List from Vermont," *Vermont History*, XXVII (April 1959), 131.

[3] Robinson, *Uncle Lisha's Shop and A Danvis Pioneer*, p. 186. Cf. Hughes, "A Word-List from Vermont," p. 130, "clip along."

[4] Robinson, *Sam Lovel's Boy with Forest and Stream Fables*, p. 173. See Hughes, "A Word-List from Vermont," p. 143, "hyper."

[5] Robinson, *Danvis Folks and A Hero of Ticonderoga*, p. 208. See Hughes, "A Word-List from Vermont," p. 136, "a conniption fit."

[6] Robinson, *Uncle Lisha's Outing and Along Three Rivers*, p. 94. See "dodunk" in Hughes, "A Word-List from Vermont," p. 133.

[7] Robinson, *Uncle Lisha's Shop and A Danvis Pioneer*, p. 212. See Hughes, "A Word-List from Vermont," p. 145, "out of kilter."

[8] Robinson, *Sam Lovel's Camps and In the Green Wood*, p. 35. See "middling" in Hughes, "A Word-List from Vermont," p. 35.

[9] Robinson, *Uncle Lisha's Outing and Along Three Rivers*, p. 47. Cf. "mog along" in Hughes, "A Word-List from Vermont," p. 149.

[10] Robinson, *Uncle Lisha's Shop and A Danvis Pioneer*, p. 213. See Hughes, "A Word-List from Vermont," p. 164, "traipse."

[11] Robinson, *Uncle Lisha's Shop and A Danvis Pioneer*, p. 213. See "spleen" in Hughes, "A Word-List from Vermont," p. 159.

[12] Robinson, *Uncle Lisha's Outing and Along Three Rivers*, p. 24. See Hughes, "A Word-List from Vermont," p. 134, "Good earth an' seas!"

[13] Robinson, *Uncle Lisha's Outing and Along Three Rivers*, p. 201. Cf. "By George Harry" in Hughes, "A Word-List from Vermont," p. 163.

[14] Robinson, *Sam Lovel's Camps and In the Green Wood*, p. 187. See Hughes, "A Word-List from Vermont," p. 163, "Thunder in the Winter!"

[15] Robinson, *Sam Lovel's Camps and In the Green Wood*, p. 61. See Muriel J. Hughes, "Vermont Exclamations of Early Days," *Vermont History*, XXII (October 1954), p. 294, "I swan."

[16] Robinson, *Uncle Lisha's Outing and Along Three Rivers*, p. 35. See "Pshaw" in Hughes, "Vermont Exclamations of Early Days," p. 295.

[17] Robinson, *Out of Bondage and Other Stories*, p. 201. See "By Hokey" in Hughes, "Vermont Exclamations of Early Days," p. 292.

[18] Robinson, *Sam Lovel's Camps and In the Green Wood*, p. 82. See Hughes, "Vermont Exclamations of Early Days," p. 293, "By the great horn spoon."

[19] Robinson, *Sam Lovel's Camps and In the Green Wood*, p. 34. See "Gosh all Fishhooks" in Hughes, "Vermont Exclamations of Early Days," p. 294.

[20] Robinson, *Uncle Lisha's Shop and A Danvis Pioneer,* p. 196. See Hughes, "Vermont Exclamations of Early Days," p. 293, "By Gum."

[21] Louise Pound, "Folklore and Dialect," *Nebraska Folklore* (Lincoln, 1959), p. 211.

[22] Jan Harold Brunvand, *The Study of American Folklore* (New York, 1968), p. 28.

[23] See Sumner Ives, "Dialect Differentiation in the Stories of Joel Chandler Harris," *American Literature*, XXVII (March 1955), 88-96.

[24] Robinson, *Danvis Folks and A Hero of Ticonderoga*, p. 91. The proverbs

140 /

and proverbial phrases in Robinson's writings are annotated in the index at the end of this chapter.

[25]Robinson, *Danvis Folks and A Hero of Ticonderoga*, p. 37.

[26]Roger D. Abrahams, "Introductory Remarks to a Rhetorical Theory of Folklore," *Journal of American Folklore*, LXXXI (1968), 150.

[27]Robinson, *Uncle Lisha's Shop and A Danvis Pioneer*, p. 114.

[28]Robinson, *Uncle Lisha's Shop and A Danvis Pioneer*, p. 164.

[29]Robinson, *Uncle Lisha's Shop and A Danvis Pioneer*, p. 214.

[30]Brunvand, *The Study of American Folklore*, p. 43.

INDEX OF PROVERBS

ABBREVIATIONS USED TO IDENTIFY ROBINSON'S BOOKS

DF: *Danvis Folks and A Hero of Ticonderoga,* ed. Llewellyn R. Perkins. Rutland, 1934.

INEFW: *In New England Fields and Woods,* ed. Llewellyn R. Perkins. Rutland, 1937.

OB: *Out of Bondage and Other Stories,* ed. Llewellyn R. Perkins. Rutland, 1936.

ULO: *Uncle Lisha's Outing and Along Three Rivers,* ed. Llewellyn R. Perkins. Rutland, 1934.

ULS: *Uncle Lisha's Shop and A Danvis Pioneer,* ed. Llewellyn R. Perkins. Rutland, 1937.

SLB: *Sam Lovel's Boy with Forest and Stream Fables,* ed. Llewellyn R. Perkins. Rutland, 1936.

SLC: *Sam Lovel's Camps and In the Green Wood,* ed. Llewellyn R. Perkins. Rutland, 1934.

OTHER ABBREVIATIONS

vb.: verb

sb.: substantive

REFERENCE WORKS

Apperson: George L. Apperson. *English Proverbs and Proverbial Phrases: A Historical Dictionary.* London, 1929.

Boshears: Frances Boshears. "Proverbial Comparisons from an East Tennessee County," *Bulletin of the Tennessee Folklore Society,* XX (1954), 27-41.

Brunvand: Jan Harold Brunvand. *A Dictionary of Proverbs and Proverbial Phrases from Books Published by Indiana Authors Before 1890.* Bloomington, 1961.

Halpert (1951):   Herbert Halpert. "Proverbial Comparisons from West Tennessee," *Bulletin of the Tennessee Folklore Society,* XVII (1951), 49-61.

Halpert (1952):   Herbert Halpert. "More Proverbial Comparisons from West Tennessee," *Bulletin of the Tennessee Folklore Society,* XVIII (1952), 15-21.

Hardie: Margaret Hardie. "Proverbs and Proverbial Expressions Current in the United States East of the Missouri and North of the Ohio River," *American Speech,* IV (1959), 461-462.

Hughes "Comparisons":   Muriel J. Hughes. "Vermont Proverbial Comparisons and Similes," *Vermont History,* XXVI (October 1958), 257-293.

Hughes "Proverbs, I":   Muriel J. Hughes. "Vermont Proverbs and Proverbial Sayings: Part I, A-K," *Vermont History,* XXVIII (April 1960), 113-142.

Hughes "Proverbs, II":   Muriel J. Hughes. "Vermont Proverbs and Proverbial Sayings: Part II, L-Z," *Vermont History,* XXVIII (July 1960), 200-230.

Hughes "Word-List":   Muriel J. Hughes. "A Word-List from Vermont," *Vermont History,* XXVII (April 1959), 123-167.

Hyamson: Albert M. Hyamson. *A Dictionary of English Phrases.* London, 1922.

NC: *The Frank C. Brown Collection of North Carolina Folklore,* ed. N. I. White. Durham, N. C., 1952. Vol. I.

Oxford: W. G. Smith and Janet Heseltine. *The Oxford Dictionary of English Proverbs.* Oxford, 1935.

Pearce: Helen Pearce. "Folk Sayings in a Pioneer Family of Oregon," *Western Folklore*, V (1946), 229-242.

Person: Henry A. Person. "Proverbs and Proverbial Lore from the State of Washington,"*Western Folklore*, XVII (1958), 176-185.

Randolph and Wilson: Vance Randolph and George P. Wilson. *Down in the Holler: A Gallery of Ozark Folk Speech*. Norman, Oklahoma, 1953.

Stevenson: Burton Stevenson. *The Home Book of Proverbs, Maxims and Familiar Phrases*. New York, 1948.

Taylor *Comparisons*: Archer Taylor. *Proverbial Comparisons and Similes from California* Berkeley, 1954.

Taylor *Index*: Archer Taylor. *The Proverb and An Index to "The Proverb."* Hatboro, Pa., 1962.

Taylor and Whiting: Archer Taylor and Bartlett Jere Whiting. *A Dictionary of American Proverbs and Proverbial Phrases, 1820-1880*. Cambridge, Mass., 1958.

Thompson *Body, Boots and Britches*: Harold W. Thompson. *Body, Boots and Britches*. Philadelphia, 1940.

Tilley: Morris P. Tilley. *A Dictionary of the Proverbs in England in the Sixteenth and Seventeenth Centuries*. Ann Arbor, 1950.

Wilstach: Frank J. Wilstach. *Dictionary of Similes*. New York, 1924.

—A—

Adder. Biteth like a serpent and stingeth like an adder (SLC 180; ULS 210 Biteth even like a serpent and stingeth like an adder). Stevenson 2343:12.

All. He would not abide by the terms of the match unless it resulted in his favor, which was hardly fair, save as all things are so in love and war (OB 182). Taylor and Whiting 5 All (3).

Anvil. I noticed you held her stiddy as an anvil (OB 190). Cf. Stevenson 76:9.

—B—

Baby. See Bairns.

Bandbox. It was as neat as a new bandbox (ULS 174). Taylor and Whiting 15 Bandbox.

Bairns. As helpless as bairns (OB 109). Hughes "Comparisons" 259 As helpless as a baby.

Bark. Tighter 'n the bark tu a tree (DF 49). Taylor and Whiting 16 Bark.

Barn. See Barn door.

Barn door. Ye couldn't hit a barn-door tew rod off whilst ye 're a-puffin' that way (DF 34; ULS 165 He *hes* hit a barn with it bein' 'at he was on the inside on 't an' all the doors shet). Taylor and Whiting 17 Barn door (3).

Bat. Blind as a bat (DF 168). Taylor and Whiting 18 Bat (1).

Beans. He do' know beans 'baout anything (ULS 240; DF 106 Th' hain't a man jack on 'em 'at knows beans about wolf huntin'). Taylor and Whiting 18 Bean (3).

Bean-pole. His father . . . now came forth . . . a queer figure in a short red flannel shirt astilt on long bare legs, bringing to mind the old simile of a "shirt on a bean-pole" (SLC 87). Taylor and Whiting 19 Bean-pole.

Bear. 1. Crosser 'n a bear wi' a sore head (SLC 35). Taylor and Whiting 19 Bear (5).

2. Hungrier 'n a bear (ULS 175, 229). Taylor and Whiting 19 Bear (11).

3. As tough as a bear (ULS 180). Taylor and Whiting 20 Bear (22).

4. He . . . c'ld rastle like a bear (ULS 145-46). Taylor and Whiting 20 Bear (30).

5. You're as bad off as the feller 'at ketched the bear . . . Ye see, he follered a bear track intu a hole, an' the feller 'at was a-huntin' along with him he stayed aoutside. "I've ketched a bear," he hollered from inside. "All right," says t' other feller, "fetch him aout an' le' 's see him." "I can't fetch him," says he. "Wal," says t' other feller, "come aout yourself." "I can't," says he, "he's got a holt on me an' won't let me," says he (ULO 95). Taylor *Index* 14 "I have caught a bear." "Bring it here." "It won't come." "Then come yourself." "It won't let me go."

Beasts. Sleeping like gorged beasts (ULS 74). Cf. Stevenson 2132:5 He sleeps like a pig.

Beat. vb. It does beat all (OB 127, 136). Taylor and Whiting 21 Beat, vb. (1).

Bee. 1. A swarm in July hain't wuth a fly (ULS 104). Apperson 32; NC 368 Bee (1); Oxford 634.

2. Busy 's a bee (DF 98). Taylor and Whiting 22 Bee (2).

3. Busy as a bee in a tar barrel (OB 158). Taylor and Whiting 22 Bee (3).

4. He got drunk as a bee on 't (ULO 132; SLC 66 Drunker 'n a bumble bee). Cf. Apperson 33:9 His head is full of bees.

5. Jes' as straight as a bee was (DF 163). Cf. Bee line.

Bee line. Haow does a haoun' dog strike a bee line fer hum when he's done a-huntin' (ULS 218). Taylor and Whiting 23 Bee line (1).

Bell. It's clear as a bell (DF 248). Taylor and Whiting 24 Bell (1).

Best. We'll e'en hae to tak what they'll gie us an' mak the best o't, be it sweet or saur (SLC 250). Cf. Taylor and Whiting 26 Best (4).

Betty Martin. O my eyes an' Betty Martin (ULS 187). Cf. Taylor and Whiting 26 Betty Martin.

Bird. 1. It's a dirty bird 'at faouls his own nest (DF 37). Taylor and Whiting 28 Bird (17).

2. I tell ye it 's the airly bird 'at gits the worm (ULO 135; ULO 169 After threescore years of partial disproof he was still a believer in the maxim that inculcates the benefits of early rising; SLB 114 It's the airly bird 'at gits the worm, you know). Taylor and Whiting 28 Bird (19).

3. But Noer he on'y laughed 'n' said haow t' he was goin' ter kill tew tu one shot (ULS 206). Taylor and Whiting 29 Bird (21).

4. See Bobolink.

Blaze. Hotter 'n blazes (OB 215). Taylor and Whiting 32 Blaze (7).

Blue. Yes, he's true blue (ULS 49). Taylor and Whiting 34 Blue (3).

Bobolink. Sing like a bobolink (ULS 49). NC 371 Bird (23) Sings like a bird.

Bone. The punk in my wa'scut pocket's dry's bone (SLC 160). Taylor and Whiting 36 Bone (3).

Book. 1. He knows the woods julluk a book (ULS 186). Taylor and Whiting 37 Book (4).

2. She can look right inter yer insides an' read 'em just like a book-ah (SLC 49). Taylor and Whiting 37 Book (6).

Boy. 1. Aunt Jerusha said he was "in a bigger hurry 'n a boy a-goin' a-fishin'." (DF 84). Hughes "Comparisons" 261 As happy as a boy going fishing.

2. Faster 'n a boy a-killin' snakes (SLB 169). Hughes "Comparisons" 279 As busy as a man killing snakes.

Bran. Don't ye s'pose I know brand when the bag's ontied? (ULO 189). Taylor and Whiting 41 Bran.

Bread. You s'pose I'm a goin' tu hev the bread took aouter my maouth that way? (ULS 164; SLC 48 A-takin' the bread right outen my mouth-ah). Tilley B629.

Breed. A diff'ent breed o' cats (ULS 236). Hughes "Proverbs, I" 118 Breed.

Bridge. Don't you cross no bridges till ye come tu 'em (DF 194). Taylor and Whiting 43 Bridge (2).

Brier. Keener 'n a brier (SLC 205; DF 78 Keen as a brier). Taylor and Whiting 43 Brier.

Brook. It's longer 'n a brook (DF 29). Hughes "Comparisons" 262 As long as a brook.

Brush heap. You look's 'ough you'd ben dragged through a brush heap (ULS 186). Cf. Randolph and Wilson 180 I feel like a bobcat that's been drug tail-first through a brierpatch.

Bucket. I guess I'd ha' kicked th' bucket if it hedn't b'en for her (ULS 58). Taylor and Whiting 45 Bucket.

Buckle. I must buckle tu (ULS 103). Stevenson 251:3.

Bud. He shan't be nipped in the bud if I can help it (SLB 29). Taylor and Whiting 45 Bud (3).

Bush. I'll say it right naow wi'aout no beatin' 'raound the bush (ULS 24). Taylor and Whiting 48 Bush (3).

Business. You see what comes o' not tendin' t' y' own business (ULS 105). Taylor and Whiting 49 Business (3).

Button. They don't care a button for huntin' (OB 208). Taylor and Whiting 50 Button (3).

—C—

Cart. Puttin' the cart afore the hoss (ULS 210). Hughes "Proverbs, I" 120 Cart.

Cat. 1. Scairt 's a strange cat (DF 126). Taylor *Comparisons* 24 I'm a cat in a strange garret—I'm scared.

2. J'rome loves colored folks as a cat loves hot soap (OB 37). Taylor and Whiting 60 Cat (39) Dreads them . . . as a cat hates hot soap.

3. Honly you got for be sure you keel it 'nough, 'cause cat gat nan life (SLB 89). Taylor and Whiting 58 Cat (4).

4. Darker 'n a stack o' black cats wi' the' eyes put aout (DF 121). Taylor and Whiting 58 Cat (8).

5. As stealthily as a cat (OB 64). Cf. Taylor and Whiting 59 Cat (22).

6. So that 's the way the cat jumps, is it? (SLB 132). Taylor and Whiting 60 Cat (47).

7. I "whipped the cat" winters (ULS 245). Taylor and Whiting 62 Cat (61).

8. See Way.

Cent. An' not a red cent in his pocket (ULO 132). Taylor and Whiting 63 Cent (2).

Charity. It's colder 'n charity (OB 90). Taylor and Whiting 65 Charity (1).

Chase. She led him a wil'-goose chase (SLB 122). Taylor and Whiting 65 Chase (2).

Cherry. His fur was as red as a cherry (SLB 123). Taylor and Whiting 66 Cherry (1).

Child. A thump of the grandfather's cane reminded the boy of the often-repeated maxim that such as he were to be seen, not heard (DF 21; "Recollections of a Quaker Boy" 104 Remembering the oft-repeated maxim that children were to be seen, not heard). Taylor and Whiting 68 Child (13).

Chip. He's a chip o' the ol' block (ULS 113; OB 179 She's a chip o' the ol' block). Taylor and Whiting 69 Chip (2).

Christian. Jist as clear 's a Christian's eye (ULO 62). Hughes "Comparisons" 264 As clear (shiny) as a Christian's eyeball.

Clock. He's comin' daown the road naow along wi' bub, smokin' his pipe as carm as a clock (ULS 117; DF 190 He's carm as a eight-day clock). Taylor and Whiting 72 Clock (1).

Coal. He was so black a coal would make a white mark on him (OB 24). Taylor and Whiting 73 Coal (1).

Coast. The coast is clear (OB 65). Taylor and Whiting 74 Coast.

Cock. 1. Be you cock o' the walk this time? (ULS 218). NC 385 Cock (1); Hyamson 90.

2. Someb'dy nuther is cock sure to git a shot (OB 231). Hyamson 91.

Conscience. Stretch like a deacon's conscience (ULO 200). Apperson 111 His conscience is made of stretching leather; Cf. Tilley C599, C606.

Cooky. I'll bet a cooky (OB 224). Taylor and Whiting 79 Cooky.

Creation. But you men folks du beat all creation (ULS 176). Taylor and Whiting 84 Creation.

Cricket. Jest as smart as a cricket (DF 81). Hughes "Comparisons" 266 As smart as a cricket.

Crow. As black as a crow's wing (SLB 57). Taylor and Whiting 85 Crow, sb. (2).

Cry. sb. What comes of pig-shearing is proverbial ("Glimpses of New England Farm Life" 525). Taylor and Whiting 86 Cry, sb.; NC 393 Devil (1) Great cry but little wool, as the devil said when he sheared his hogs.

Cud. He's a tough cud fer someb'dy to chaw (DF 193). Apperson 94.

Cure. Wal, what can't be cured must be endured (SLB 136). Taylor and Whiting 87 Cure (2).

Cut. Everything 's all cut an' dried (ULS 236). Taylor and Whiting 89 Cut, vb. (1).

—D—

Dan. He'll foller a fox from daniel to Bashaby (ULS 197). Taylor & Whiting 90 Dan.

Dander. Father's got his dander up (OB 210). Taylor and Whiting 90 Dander (1).

Death. It comes as sure as death an' taxes (SLB 148). Taylor and Whiting 95 Death (18); Hughes "Comparisons" 267 As sure as death and taxes.

Deed. Shine like a good deed in a naughty world (ULS 137). Stevenson 541:14.

Devil. 1. He pull back more harder as de dev' (DF 124). Cf. Taylor and Whiting 97 Devil (7).

2. The devil is nighest when you're speakin' on him (SLC 64; OB 116 Speak o' the deil an' he'll be at your log; SLC 249 Name the deil, an' he'll aye be at your lug; SLB 173 The devil's allers nighest, an' so fo'th). Taylor and Whiting 98 Devil (16).

3. Run as if Aunt Hornie was chasin' ye (OB 110). Taylor and Whiting 100 Devil (38).

4. The handsome devil-may-care face of Dick Barrett (OB 180). Taylor and Whiting 100 Devil (40).

5. More hugly as dev' (ULO 39). Apperson 768; Hyamson 350; NC 392 Devil (10); Wilstach 439.

6. He swore it beat the devil, if 't wa'n't the devil hisself (ULS 151). Brunvand 35 Devil (5); Cf. Taylor and Whiting 98 Devil (10).

7. The country's goin' tu the divil (SLB 149). Brunvand 36 Devil (10); Stevenson 558:11.

8. Col' lak a dev (ULS 205). Cf. NC 392 Devil (4) As hot as the devil.

9. See Old Scratch.

Dirt. They looked cheaper'n dirt (OB 214). Taylor and Whiting 102 Dirt (2).

Dog. 1. I hain't hed a chance tu speak tu ye 'lone 'fore in a dawg's age (ULS 176). Taylor and Whiting 105 Dog (3).

2. Tew old a dog tu l'arn new tricks (ULS 20). Taylor and Whiting 105 Dog (6).

3. I'm shameder 'n a licked dawg (SLC 81). Taylor and Whiting 105 Dog (8).

4. There's a lot 'at I've took on a debt an' can sell dog cheap for cash (ULS 21). Taylor and Whiting 105 Dog (9).

5. I'm tireder 'n a dawg (OB 162). Taylor and Whiting 105 Dog (19).

6. I hate to see white men whipped like dogs (DF 252). Cf. Taylor and Whiting 107 Dog (41), 108 Dog (52); Apperson 159.

Doornail. He was deader 'n a door nail (ULS 140). Taylor and Whiting 109 Doornail.

Duck. Waddled like a hurried duck (ULS 196; DF 46 Waddled like a thirsty duck). Hughes "Comparisons" 268 To waddle like a duck.

Dutch. A-drivin' your needle to beat the Dutch, this mornin', hain't ye? (OB 188). Taylor and Whiting 114 Dutch (3).

—E—

Eel. As crooked as an eel (SLC 71). Cf. Taylor *Comparisons* 30 As crooked as a snake.

Egg. 1. So weak it won't sca'cely bear an egg (OB 97). Cf. Hughes "Comparisons" 269 Strong enough to bear up an egg.

2. Fuller o' the devil 'an an egg is o' meat (SLC 220). Taylor and Whiting 117 Egg (3).

Egypt. It's darker 'n Egypt (DF 185). Taylor and Whiting 119 Egypt.

Elm. Tougher 'n a ellum gnurl (ULS 236). Hughes "Comparisons" 269 Tougher than green elm.

End. 1. I didn't scarcely know which eend my head was on (DF 44). Taylor and Whiting 120 End (2).

2. He'd sarch tu the eend o' the airth if you ast him (ULS 186; ULS 238 You're a goin' to the end o' the airth; ULO 61 Hunted to de eends of de airth). Brunvand 43 End (3).

3. That feller's got pretty nigh the len'th o' his rope (DF 178). Taylor and Whiting 120 End (5).

Everything. Ev'ryt'ing come to de feller dat waitens (INEFW 228). Hughes "Proverbs, I" 129 Everything (1).

Eyes. Four eyes is better 'n tew (DF 31). Stevenson 730:3.

—F—

Face. 1. It's jest flyin' in the face o' Providence (ULO 202). Stevenson 1908:10.
2. See Tony.

Fair. He promised me fair and square (SLB 169). Taylor and Whiting 127 Fair (2).

Fat. 1. Dat mus' be w'ere de folkses leeve on de fat of de lan' (OB 33). Stevenson 765:4.
2. It tackles fat and lean (ULS 102). Cf. Person 182:221 You have to take the fat with the lean.

Fiddle. I don't cal'late tu hev ary one on ye play secont fiddle tu anybody up tu Montpelier (SLB 162). Taylor and Whiting 131 Fiddle (5).

Fight. sb. Spilin' for a fight (ULS 122). Taylor and Whiting 132 Fight, sb.

Finger. I would n't 'a' missed hevin' a finger in this pie for a gov'nor's right o' land (ULS 53). Taylor and Whiting 133 Finger (3).

Flash. You hain't flashed in the pan (ULS 75). Pearce 236:102 He's (or It's) only a flash in the pan.

Flea. Snug as a flea in a blanket (SLB 123). Cf. NC 409 Flea (3) As snug as a flea under a shirt collar; Taylor and Whiting 13 Flea (4).

Flinders. I blowed my harnsome shirt . . . all to flinders (ULS 143). Cf. Taylor and Whiting 139 Flinders.

Flint. They'll fix yer flint (ULS 241). Taylor and Whiting 139 Flint (3).

Floor. Flat as this 'ere floor (ULS 20). Taylor and Whiting 139 Floor (2).

Folks. Light yer pipe like white folks (ULS 138). Taylor and Whiting 142 Folks (7).

Fool. The' 's ol' fools as well as young fools, an' it's hard tellin' which is the biggest (DF 191). Cf. Taylor and Whiting 142 Fool (8) Old fools is the biggest fools there is.

Foot. 1. A man at your time o' life, wi' one foot in the grave (ULS 110). Taylor and Whiting 143 Foot (3).
2. I jest hypered right over the maountain, best foot fo'ard (OB 217). Taylor and Whiting 143 Foot (4).

Fox. 1. As cunning as a fox (*Silver Fields and Other Sketches of a Farmer-Sportsman* 200; ULS 55 More cunning than a fox). Taylor and Whiting 145 Fox (2).
2. Sly as foxes (ULS 62). Taylor and Whiting 145 Fox (7).

Frog. Take your col' feet off'm me. They're julluk tew frawgs (DF 174). Wilstach 61 Cold as a frog.

Fun. It was snowin' like fun (DF 89). Taylor and Whiting 148 Fun (3).

—G—

Galley-west. This 'ere's knocked me gally west (SLC 200; SLC 66 I'll come aout there an' knock ye gally west; SLC 41 I'll knock ye gally west; DF 31 You . . . knocked him gally west; DF 195 It 'could knock me gally west). Taylor and Whiting 149 Galley-west.

Gate. A-bobin' up an' down ju' like a sawmill gate (ULS 92). Cf. Halpert (1951) 55:175 Swings like a rusty gate.

Get out. Looks like all git aout (ULS 174; SLC 153 Blow like all git aout). Taylor and Whiting 151 Get out.

Ghost. 1. But the worm presently gave up the ghost (SLB 205). Taylor and Whiting 152 Ghost (3).

2. Silently, as a ghost (DF 283). NC 413 Ghost (2); Wilstach 352.

Gilderoy. Tew drinks on't clear 'ould knock a feller higher 'n Gilderoy's kite (ULS 158; ULO 33, 202; OB 193). Taylor and Whiting 152 Gilderoy.

Girl. He's as tender-hearted as a gal (ULO 127). Taylor and Whiting 12 Baby (4) For all his grand looks, he's tender hearted as a baby.

Gizzard. Don't fret yer gizzard (SLC 23). Taylor and Whiting 153 Gizzard (1).

Glove. As pliable as a glove (SLB 46). Wilstach 296 Pliant as a glove.

Gods. The gods of the valleys are not the gods of the hills (DF 250). Cf. Stevenson 985:8 The deities of one age are the bywords of the next.

Gold. As yellow as old gold (DF 178). Taylor and Whiting 155 Gold (6).

Goose. 1. I'm a gone goose (SLB 169). Taylor and Whiting 156 Goose (2).

2. Fooler as a geese (SLC 131). Hughes "Comparisons" 272 Sillier than a goose.

Goose Grease. Slicker 'n goose grease. Taylor and Whiting 157 Goose grease (2).

Gospel. It 's gospel truth (OB 163). Taylor and Whiting 157 Gospel (2a).

Grain. Work kinder goes ag'in the grain (ULO 105; OB 166 But I swan it goes agin my grain). Taylor and Whiting 158 Grain (2).

Grape. We ol' folks has eat saour grapes long 'nough (DF 91). Taylor and Whiting 158 Grape (2).

Grass. You go tu grass (SLC 187; ULS 226 Oh, naow you go tu grass). Taylor and Whiting 159 Grass (4).

Grease. I hain't grease ner pitch. I guess I sha'n't melt (ULS 112). Cf. Taylor and Whiting 360 Sugar (2) I know he is neither sugar nor salt (i.e., can go out in the rain).

Grindstone. See Stone (3).

Growth. Scairt me aouten a year's growth (DF 213). Taylor and Whiting 163 Growth.

Gruel. I salt it well when it's about as thick as gruel (DF 116). Cf. Apperson 624 As thick as porridge; Taylor *Comparisons* 81 As thick as hasty pudding.

Gun. Sure as guns (OB 187; SLB 161). Taylor and Whiting 164 Gun (2).

—H—

Hail Columbia. He gave me Hail Columby (OB 215; DF 53 He'll gi' me Hail

Columby; OB 169 Givin' us Hail Columby; ULS 103 Give her Hail Columby). Taylor and Whiting 166 Hail Columbia.

Hammer. 1. Dead as a hammer (SLC 38). Taylor and Whiting 168 Hammer (1). See Mallet.

2. So at it we went, hammer an' tongs (OB 215). Taylor and Whiting 168 Hammer (3).

Hand. 1. Thicker 'n tew hands in a mitten (SLC 146). Cf. Halpert (1951) 61:699 Thick as two peas in a pod.

2. A way of making work light with many hands (ULS 97). Taylor and Whiting 169 Hand (7).

3. See Palm.

Handsome. Harnsome is 'at harnsome does (OB 163). Taylor and Whiting 171 Handsome (1).

Haste. More haste, less speed (OB 189). Taylor and Whiting 173 Haste (4).

Hat. Ye don't weigh no more 'n a straw hat (DF 54). Thompson *Body, Boots and Britches* 495 Four ounces lighter 'n a chip (straw) hat.

Hatter. Drunker 'n a hatter (ULO 132; ULS 19 The hatter, already proverbially drunk). Cf. Taylor and Whiting 174 Hatter: "The saying 'mad as a hatter' and the Mad Hatter of 'Alice in Wonderland' both derive from the lurching gait, the tangled tongue, and the addled wits of mercurialism (caused by the mercury used in the processing of felt hats)."

Have. It's aour'n tu hev an' tu hol' (SLC 164). Stevenson 1989:11.

Hay. Deader 'n hay (SLC 37, SLC 59, ULS 151, DF 30; SLB 40 Dead as hay). Hughes "Comparisons" 273 Deader 'n hay.

Heel. Bob's shakin' his heels in Canada (ULO 168). Cf. Stevenson 1123:1 To cool one's heels; Oxford 505; Brunvand 68 Heel (3).

Hell. 1. Quicker 'n ever hell scorched a feather (ULS 167). Taylor and Whiting 180 Hell (4).

2. I'd as lief be in hell wi'aout claws (ULS 74). Cf. Hughes "Word-List" 142 Rather be in hell with my neck (back) broke.

Hen. 1. You do' know no more 'baout a bwut 'an a hen (ULO 148). Cf. Taylor and Whiting 181 Hen (16) These greasers don't know as much as a farrer hen.

2. Fusster raoun' more as one hol' sheekin' wid one hen (ULO 71). Taylor and Whiting 181 Hen (19) She made more fuss nor er settin' hen with one chicken.

3. Mad as a settin' hen (SLB 169; SLC 188 Madder 'n settin' hens; DF 29 Madder 'n tew settin' hens). NC 423 Hen (7).

4. You hain't spunk 'nough tu break up a settin' hen (ULO 173). Cf. Hughes "Comparisons" 274 As still as a settin' hen.

5. It hain't no more like talk 'an a passel o' hens hevin' a cacklin' bee in the mornin' (ULO 57). Hughes "Comparisons" 269 No more like talk than a passel of hens having a cackling bee in the morning.

6. Clucking like a hen bringing home her brood (ULO 129). Cf. Boshears 33:276.

Hide. Can't find hide ner hair on 't (SLB 148). Taylor and Whiting 183 Hide (1).

Hog. 1. Lazier 'n a fattin' hawg (SLC 145). Hughes "Comparisons" 275 As lazy as a hog; NC 425 Hog (7).

2. Contrayer 'n a hawg (ULO 136). Hughes "Comparisons" 275 As contrary

as a hog on ice.

3. Harkin' julluk a hawg in a cornfiel' (DF 126). Tilley H502.

Hole. See Ladder.

Hollow. That beats us all holler (ULS 176). Taylor and Whiting 186 Hollow (1).

Hook. 1. He was determined to get a fox by hook or by crook (SLB 109). Taylor and Whiting 187 Hook (1).

2. He . . . cleared out, hook an' line, bob an' sinker, 'fore noon (OB 230; SLB 39 It was gone, bob an' sinker). Taylor and Whiting 187 Hook (2).

Horse. 1. Strong lak leetly hosses (ULS 57). Taylor and Whiting 190 Horse (11).

2. You must n't look a gift hoss in the mouth (OB 154). Taylor and Whiting 191 Horse (16).

3. It is an old saying, "that a good horse cannot be of a bad color" (INEFW 248). Apperson 311; Stevenson 1181:6.

4. That 'ere Harris 'll lie faster 'n a hoss c'n trot (ULO 187). Taylor and Whiting 190 Horse (7).

5. It's ridin' a free hoss tew fur (ULO 178). Hughes "Proverbs, I" 139 Horse (7); NC 428 Horse (19).

6. Beeg lak hosses (ULO 109). Hughes "Comparisons" 275 Big like a hoss.

7. It's hard paying for a dead horse (OB 156). Hughes "Comparisons" 282 Like paying for a dead horse.

Hour. An haour 'fore sunup 's wuth tew arter (SLB 114). Hughes "Proverbs, I" 140 Hour (2) One hour in the morning is worth two at night.

How de do. Well, that's a pretty haow de du (DF 91). Taylor and Whiting 194 How de do.

Hunter. "Samwell," said Solon Briggs, "is a reg'lar Ramrod, so tu speak; a mighty hunter afore the Lord (ULS 197). Stevenson 1202:9.

—I—

Ice. As cold as ice (ULO 184; ULS 107 As col' as chunks o' ice). Taylor and Whiting 197 Ice (2).

Image. I be dryer 'n a graven image (ULO 98; DF 46 Drier 'n a gravern image). Taylor and Whiting 198 Image (1).

Industry. Industry brings plenty (OB 214). Cf. Oxford 223 Industry is fortune's right hand, and frequently her left.

Iron. Wear julluk iron (ULS 128). Brunvand 77 Iron (5).

—J—

Jack-in-the-box. Springing up like a gigantic jack-in-a-box (ULS 124-25). Cf. Halpert (1952) 19:809; Boshears 33:197 Jumps like a jumping jack.

Jug-full. I hain't a-findin' no fault wi your roas' beef an' turkey, by a jug full (SLC 35; SLC 162 Twan't you, not by a jug full; OB 191 No, sirree, not by a jugful). Taylor and Whiting 206 Jug-full.

Jumping Jack. See Jack-in-the-box.

—K—

Kettle. This is a pretty kettle of fish (DF 283). Taylor and Whiting 207 Kettle (1).

Kill. Ye might's well kill me as skeer me tu death (DF 74). Taylor and Whiting 208 Kill (2).

Kite. Some on 'em 'll git blowed higher 'n a kite (OB 141). Taylor and Whiting 209 Kite (2), 1. See Gilderoy.

Kith. I useter 'most wish, when I was wanderin' hither an' yon wi' aout kith or kin or friend, I could come tu my own ag'in (ULS 98; SLB 123 Wal, this un was all alone in the world wi'aout kith or kin). Brunvand 81 Kith; Stevenson 1295:11.

Knee-high. I knowed your father when he wa' n't knee high tu a grasshopper (OB 127; DF 30 Wa'n't knee-high tu a tudstool). Taylor and Whiting 210 Knee-high.

—L—

Live. 1. As true as I live an' breathe (OB 40; ULO 182 Yes, they be, true 's you live; ULO 97 Jest as true as you live). Taylor and Whiting 225 Live (3).

2. Never . . . again so long 's I live an' breathe (ULS 178). Randolph and Wilson 180 Sure as I live and breathe. See Live, 1.

3. You'll ketch your death jest as sure as you live (ULO 184; ULS 43 Sure as you live). Taylor and Whiting 225 Live (2).

Lock. Without lock, stock or barrel (INEFW 156). Taylor and Whiting 226 Lock.

Log. 1. Julluck rollin' off 'm a lawg (ULO 24; DF 134 As easy as rollin' off a lawg). Taylor and Whiting 227 Log (1).

2. As lifeless as a log (OB 109). Taylor and Whiting 227 Log (2).

3. He lays there julluk a lawg (ULS 107). Boshears 33:205 Lying like a log.

Long. sb. That's the long an' short on't (ULS 236; OB 166 The long an' short on 't is). Taylor and Whiting 227 Long, sb.

Looks. You can't allers tell by the looks of a toad how fur he'll jump (OB 60). Hughes "Proverbs, II" 200 Looks.

Loon. Holler like a loon (DF 111; SLC 146; SLB 127). Hughes "Comparisons" 278 To holler like a loon.

Lots. I put 'crost lots (ULS 146; SLB 122 She put her cross lots). Taylor and Whiting 229 Lots.

Luck. They say 't the's luck in odd numbers (OB 230). Hughes "Proverbs, II" 202 Luck (2); Oxford 394.

Lynx. Sharper eyed 'n a lynk (DF 30; DF 31 Eyes julluck a lynk). Taylor and Whiting 231 Lynx (1).

—M—

Mad. Leakin' like mad (OB 156). Cf. Taylor *Comparisons* 56 To run (to work) like mad.

Maggot. Stiff as a maggit (OB 226). Taylor and Whiting 232 Maggot (1).

Major. You stood it like a major (DF 24). Taylor and Whiting 233 Major.

Mallet. Deader 'n a mallet (DF 31). Taylor and Whiting 168 Hammer (1). See Hammer.

Man. 1. As independent as a man on the taown (ULO 139). Cf. Hughes "Comparisons" 279 As busy as a man on the town.

2. A-sweatin' like a man a-mowin' (ULS 207; ULS 219 Sweat like a man a-mowin'). Hughes "Comparisons" 279 To sweat like a man a-mowin'.

Meat-axe. It was pant'er, hol' big feller, hugly lak meat-axe (ULO 106). Taylor and Whiting 240 Meat axe (2).

Meeting house. Couldn't hit a meetin' house a-standin' still (OB 212). Cf. Taylor and Whiting 241 Meeting house (1).

Middle. 'T 'ould kick ye int' the middle o' next week (DF 22). Taylor and Whiting 242 Middle (2).

Milk. The' hain't no use o' cryin' over spilt milk (DF 198; ULO 54; DF 283 Well, there's no use crying over spilt milk). Taylor and Whiting 243 Milk (5).

Might. The strong making might right ("Glimpses of New England Farm Life" 512). Taylor and Whiting 242 Might.

Molasses. 1. It's as smooth as 'lasses (DF 116). Taylor and Whiting 247 Molasses (1) Slick ez molasses.

2. Slower 'n col' m'lasses (SLC 145). Hughes "Comparisons" 279 As slow as cold molasses.

Month. I hain't sot eyes on ye fer a month o' Sundays (ULS 222). Taylor and Whiting 248 Month.

Moonshine. No more taste in 't 'n moonshine (DF 37; OB 197 It hain't got no more scent then moonshine). Cf. Taylor and Whiting 249 Moonshine (2); Stevenson 1623:3.

Mouse. 1. It would be as useless to search for them as for a mouse in a straw stack (OB 101). Cf. Taylor and Whiting 260 Needle (2). See Needle.

2. As still as mices (SLC 60; SLC 21 Not mek it no more nowse as leetly mouses; ULO 68 Softle as leetly maouses). Taylor and Whiting 252 Mouse (5).

Mouth. Pike an' pick'ril 'at 'ould make a man's maouth water tu see (SLC 146). Taylor and Whiting 253 Mouth (5).

Mud. 1. You're as deep in the mud as I be in the mire (ULS 73). Taylor and Whiting 253 Mud (2).

2. Richer 'n mud (OB 127). Taylor and Whiting 254 Mud (3).

—N—

Name. Jes' as sure 's your name's Drive (ULS 247). Taylor and Whiting 257 Name (1).

Nature. It does beat all natur' (DF 64; ULO 195 It beats all natur'). Taylor and Whiting 258 Nature (9).

Needle. Ye might as well hunt fer a needle in a hay maow (DF 159). Taylor and Whiting 259 Needle (2). See Mouse, 1.

Nest. Stiller 'n last year's bird's-nest (OB 56). Hughes "Comparisons" 281 As empty as last year's bird nest.

Nick. In the nick of time (OB 161). Tilley N160.

Nip. You an' Dick has bin a-hevin' on 't, nip an' tuck, for my Dorothy (OB 179). Taylor and Whiting 262 Nip (2).

Nothing. 1. Nothin' like tryin' (SLC 47). Taylor and Whiting 265 Nothing (7).
2. See Work.

Now. Chuse your pardners naow or never (DF 91). Taylor and Whiting 266 Now.

—O—

Old Scratch. Ol' Scratch owed me a gretch (SLB 136). Taylor and Whiting 270 Old Scratch (1).

Opossum. It's no use playin' 'possum (OB 48). Taylor and Whiting 271 Opossum (6).

Otter. Slick 's an otter (DF 51; SLC 186 The ol' feller 's slick as an auter). Hughes "Comparisons" 281 As sleek as an otter.

Owl. Tougher 'n a biled aowl (ULS 163, 219; SLC 72). Hughes "Comparisons" 281 Tougher 'n a b'iled owl.

—P—

Palm. Smooth as the palm o' my hand (ULO 199). Hughes "Comparisons" 273 As smooth as the palm of my hand.

Pancake. Flatter 'n a pancake (SLC 83). Taylor and Whiting 275 Pancake.

Parings. Hain't no more 'caount tu em 'n the parin's o' the nails (OB 241). Cf. Tilley W924 The worth of a thing is best known by the want.

Peacock. If I'd made it, I sh'd be proud as a peacock (DF 214). Taylor and Whiting 278 Peacock (2).

Peg. The's sights o' women folks 'll like tu see Mis' Peck took daown a peg (SLB 159). Taylor and Whiting 279 Peg (3).

Penny. Here the surveyor comes again, like a bad penny as he is (DF 251). Taylor and Whiting 280 Penny (6).

Picture. She was harnsome as a pictur (SLC 146; SLC 182; SLC 204). Taylor and Whiting 282 Picture (2).

Pig. 1. As heavy as a pig (OB 153). Cf. Taylor and Whiting 283 Pig (2) She is as fat as a pig.

2. It squeaks an' grunts ju' luk a litter o' hungry pigs (SLB 134). Cf. Wilstach 189 Grunts like a hog; NC 458 Pig (12) Grunts like a pig; NC 458 Pig (14) Squeals like a pig; Taylor and Whiting 284 Pig (20) Squeak, squeak, went the fiddle . . . like a pig when he's being yoked.

3. Perlite 's a pig (SLC 166). Cf. Taylor and Whiting 283 Pig (4) As good natured as a sucking pig.

Plummet. The bird dropped like a plummet (OB 199). NC 460 Plummet; Wilstach 103.

Post. sb., 1. You might as well talk to a post (DF 94; SLB 158 No more int'res' in what's a-goin' on 'an a post in the fence; SLB 161 You might's well argy wi' posts). Taylor and Whiting 292 Post, sb. (1).

2. I jes' stood still as a post (DF 142). Taylor and Whiting 292 Post, sb. (3).

3. 'Twixt you an' me an' the whippin' pos' (DF 114). Taylor and Whiting 293 Post, sb. (5).

Pot. A watched pot won't never b'ile (INEFW 238; SLC 53 The proverbial perverseness of watched pots). Hughes "Proverbs, II" 211 Pot (1); NC 461 Pot (2); Oxford 694.

Potato. Mumbling his words as if they were so many hot potatoes (ULS 125). Taylor and Whiting 294 Potato (15).

Powder. See Priming.

Pride. Pride goeth before a fall (ULS 168). Taylor and Whiting 296 (1).

Priming. I did n't keer a primin' o' paowder (SLB 25; ULS 66 Not as I care the primin' of a rifle for that). Hughes "Word-List" 153 Not to care a priming of powder; Cf. Taylor and Whiting 294 Powder (2) He ain't worth the powder that would kill him.

Pucker.   What be you in such a pucker for. . . ? (OB 207). Taylor and Whiting 297 Pucker.

Pudding.   Stuny Brook 's thick 's puddin' (DF 152; ULS 235-36 Thicker 'n puddin'). Hughes "Comparisons" 284 Thicker than hasty pudding; NC 463 Pudding.

Pussley.   Ev'ybody's mean, meaner 'n pusley (OB 54). Taylor and Whiting 299 Pusley; Hughes "Comparisons" 284 Meaner 'n pusley (purslane).

Purslane.   See Pussley.

—Q—

Quaker.   Jest one night on 't hes made me sleepier 'n a Quaker meetin' (DF 98). Cf. Taylor and Whiting 300 Quaker (1) They were all as mum as a Quaker Meetin'.

Queen of Sheba.   We'll feed Lyddy like the Queen o' Sheby (OB 194). Cf. Taylor and Whiting 300 Queen of Sheba; Boshears 32:138.

—R—

Rack.   It has gone tu rack an' ruin (DF 62). Brunvand 116 Rack (1).

Ramrod.   Standing stiff as a ramrod (DF 177). Taylor and Whiting 303 Ramrod (1).

Rats.   It means, sir, that we're not to be caged like rats (ULS 77). NC 466 Rat (8); Wilstach 431.

Rawhide.   They're jest as tough as rawhide (ULS 232). Cf. Taylor *Comparisons* 83 As tough as leather; NC 435 Leather; Apperson 642; Tilley L166.

Riddance.   Good riddance to bad rubbage (DF 237). Hughes "Proverbs, II" Riddance.

Robin Hood.   I've ben all 'raound Robin Hood's barn (ULS 179; ULS 219 All raound Robin Hood's barn). Taylor and Whiting 308 Robin Hood.

Rock.   1. Steady as a rock (ULS 94; OB 186 As stiddy as a rock; SLB 40 Steddy as a rock). NC 468 Rock (4); Wilstach 387.
   2. The road was hard as a rock (OB 233). Taylor and Whiting 309 Rock (3).

Rocket.   The bird took alarm and went off like a rocket (OB 183). Taylor and Whiting 309 Rocket (2).

Rose.   1. Lowizy was there, blushing like a June rose (SLC 168). NC 468 Rose (6) Blushes like a rose.
   2. Blushing red as a rose (OB 32). Taylor and Whiting 312 Rose (5).

Row.   I hedn't no idee . . . 'at Huldy keered a row o' pins (ULS 178; DF 139 Don't . . . keer a row o' pins; OB 161 I hain't wuth a row o' pins). Hughes "Comparisons" 285 Not worth a row of pins.

—S—

Sam Hill.   Wal, it does beat Sam Hill (ULO 146; ULO 201 If this don't pooty nigh beat Sam Hill; DF 24 It'll hurt like Sam Hill; SLC 82 But why in Sam Hill; ULO 27; ULS 170 Sam Hill!). Taylor and Whiting 317 Sam Hill.

Sauce.   What's sass for gander 's sass for goose (ULO 195). Taylor and Whiting 318 Sauce.

Sawmill.   "Cold as a saw-mill" being a New England proverb; and it is often said of one who leaves outer doors open in cold weather, "Guess he was brought up in a saw-mill, where there wa'n't no doors." (*Silver Fields and Other Sketches of a Farmer-Sportsman* 54). Hughes "Comparisons" 286 As cold as a sawmill; Randolph and Wilson 180 Tommy acts like he was raised in a sawmill.

Scat. Quicker 'n scat (ULO 73). Taylor and Whiting 319 Scat.

Scratch. sb. You'd strike fire true when it come tu the scratch (ULS 75). Taylor and Whiting 320 Scratch, sb. (1).

Senses. What's the use o' scarin' anybody aouten the' seben senses? (ULS 101; ULS 186 Scairt aouten your seben senses; OB 94 Scairt a gal onct aouten her seben senses). Stevenson 2072:1.

Serpent. See Adder.

Shank's horses. Each riding as he did, "Shank's horses" (ULS 233; DF 141 I guess my shank's hosses 'll fetch him). Taylor and Whiting 324 Shank's mare.

Sheep. I do' know but I sh'd feel as mean 'f I'd ben stealin' sheep an' got ketched at it (OB 172). Cf. Taylor and Whiting 325 Sheep (14) Looking after me as if I'd been stealing sheep.

Shirt. Quicker 'n you can git off a wet shirt (SLB 102). Cf. Taylor *Comparisons* 72 To take off like a dirty shirt, i.e., in a hurry.

Shoe. 1. Ye look jest as nat'ral as an ol' shoe (ULO 141). Cf. Taylor *Comparisons* 29 As common as an old shoe.

   2. I putty nigh jumped aouten my shoes (ULS 101). Cf. Taylor and Whiting 337 Skin (6).

Shooting. As sure as shootin' (ULS 177; OB 188 Sure as shootin'). Taylor and Whiting 329 Shooting (3).

Shucks. Don't ye wait till he sheds his fur, er the cub won't be wuth shucks (DF 139 'T won't 'mount tu shucks; SLC 22 Hain't wuth shucks). Taylor and Whiting 331 Shucks (3).

Side. We'd show 'em which side their bread was buttered on (OB 173). Taylor and Whiting 332 Side (11).

Silver. Brighter than burnished silver (ULS 215). Taylor and Whiting 334 Silver (2).

Sin. They was uglier 'n sin (OB 216). Taylor and Whiting 335 Sin (8).

Smelt. He's deader 'n a smelt (ULO 96). Taylor and Whiting 339 Smelt.

Snail. Ol' hoss is gittin' bunged an' slower 'n a snail (OB 51). Hughes "Comparisons" 287 As slow as a snail.

Snag. I'm most afeered he's run ag'in' a snag tu Hamner's (DF 91). Taylor and Whiting 340 Snag.

Snake. 1. She's decaitful as a snake (SLC 146). Cf. NC 478 Snake (12) As treacherous as a snake; Taylor and Whiting 341 Snake (1) A guileful snake in the grass.

   2. They're poorer 'n snakes (DF 144). NC 478 Snake (9).

Sneezed. A good fat duck hain't tu be sneezed at (ULO 156; OB 200 Tew 'coons hain't to be sneezed at). Taylor and Whiting 342 Sneezed.

Snow. As white as the snow (OB 152). Taylor and Whiting 342 Snow (6).

Squirrel. As spry 's a squirrel (ULS 224). Taylor and Whiting 349 Squirrel (1) As chipper as a squirrel.

Stake. 1. I knawked him stiffer 'n a stake (DF 21). Taylor and Whiting 350 Stake (1).

    2. You an' Uncle Lisher is r'ally goin' tu pull up stakes an' go t' the West? (ULS 238). Taylor and Whiting 350 Stake (3).

Star. Thank your stars they hain't Injuns (ULS 32). Taylor and Whiting 350 Star (5).

Steamboat. He'll smoke lak stimboat (DF 123). Cf. Taylor and Whiting 351 Steam-engine; Hardie 470:155 Puffing like a steam engine.

Steel trap. 1. Smarter 'n a steel-trap (SLC 204; ULO 109 Smart boy, lak steel traps). Taylor and Whiting 352 Steel trap (5).

    2. See Trap.

Stick. sb. 1. More . . . n' you could shake a stick at in a fortnight (ULS 226; SLB 173 The' was more 'n you can shake a stick at in a fortni't; SLB 64 More . . . 'n you can shake a stick at; SLB 72 More 'n you could shake a stick at). Taylor and Whiting 352 Stick, sb. (2).

    2. It al'ways made Bijer crosser 'n two sticks tu see him raound (ULS 211). Hughes "Comparisons" 288 Crosser than two sticks; Hardie 467:30 As cross as two sticks.

Stone. 1. It's jest as cold as a stun (ULS 107; ULS 110 Cold as stuns; SLB 67 Cold as stone). Taylor and Whiting 355 Stone (3).

    2. Ah! the bird was stone dead (DF 29). Taylor and Whiting 355 Stone (6).

    3. I can't swim no more 'n a grin'stun (ULO 138). Oxford 545 To swim like a stone.

Swarm. See Bee, 1.

—T—

Tales. I du hope it 'll du good . . . an' keep you f'm tellin' tales out o' school (OB 39). Taylor and Whiting 365 Tales.

Taxes. See Death.

Teazles. She'd stick tu it like teazles (SLC 184; SLB 122 Stick tu her ju' like teazles). Cf. Taylor and Whiting 48 Bur (3).

Tender-hearted. See Girl.

Thick. Sticks tu ye through thick an' thin (ULO 156). Taylor and Whiting 368 Thick, sb.

Thunder. An' bose of it faght so hard dat way lak hol' t'under (INEFW 241). Cf. Taylor and Whiting 371 Thunder (11), (15).

Tickle. Tickled tu death tu git back hum again (DF 81). Taylor and Whiting 372 Tickle (2).

Tiger. I expected to see him pounce upon the crouching figure of my companion like a tiger on his prey (OB 64). Taylor and Whiting 373 Tiger (8).

Time. 1. Haow time does fly (ULS 101). Taylor and Whiting 374 Time (10).

    2. Tam was money (SLC 76). Taylor and Whiting 374 Time (12).

    3. Time cuts daown all, bwuth gre't an' small (ULS 192). Taylor and Whiting 374 Time (14).

    4. It's about time 't honest folks was abed an' rogues locked aout, but you

needn't hurry none 'baout goin' t' bed, Ann Twine (ULS 140; SLC 38 It's high time all honest folks was abed; ULO 69 A'rarin' raoun' . . . when honest folks ortu be abed; ULO 70 Wal, it's high time honest folks was abed). Hughes "Proverbs, II" 222 Time (2).

    5. Shoolin' 'raound in the woods jest tu kill time (SLC 145). Cf. Hughes "Proverbs, II" 222 Time (9) The right way to kill time is to work it to death.

Tobey. See Tony.

Tony. Blacker 'n Tony's face (OB 202). Cf. Hughes "Comparisons" 290 As black as tobey's behind (boot, foot).

Tongue. She had a tongue, hung in th' middle an' sharp both eends (SLC 195). Taylor and Whiting 378 Tongue (1).

Tooth. When the roast was done the Indians fell to it tooth and nail like a pack of hungry wolves (ULS 73). Taylor and Whiting 378 Tooth (9).

Tophet. The sun a-blazin' daown hotter 'n Tophit (DF 61). Hughes "Comparisons" 290 As dark (Hotter) as Tophet.

Track. Le's make tracks quick an' fur apart (ULS 75; ULS 43 Makin' tracks, quick! and fur apart). Taylor and Whiting 380 Track (5).

Trap. 1. Shutting his mouth like a steel trap (OB 179). Stevenson 1634:13 She's as tight-mouthed as a bear trap.

    2. See Steel trap.

Tripe. I carc'late he'll be tougher 'n tripe (ULO 100). Hughes "Comparisons" 290 Tougher than tripe.

Trivet. You'll be right as a trivet (ULS 37; OB 149, 159). Taylor and Whiting 382 Trivet (1).

Turtle. Slow as turtles (ULS 74). NC 490 Turtle; Boshears 39:796.

—W—

Water. 1. He . . . would druther see folks in hot water 'n aout on 't (ULS 211). Taylor and Whiting 395 Water (13).

    2. Cold Water Quenches Valor (SLC 38). Cf. Taylor and Whiting 394 Water (7); Tilley W112.

Way. 1. There's more'n one way to skin a cat (DF 160). Taylor and Whiting 396 Way (12); Hughes "Proverbs, I" 121 Cat (7).

    2. The' ha' no tew ways 'baout it (ULS 236; ULO 98 But there ain't no tew ways 'baout it). Taylor and Whiting 397 Way (16).

Weed. Jul'us a-growin' so fast—grows lak a weed, he does (ULO 109). Taylor and Whiting 398 Weed, sb.

Weight. I would n't part wi' that 'ere spring fer its weight in gold (OB 166). Taylor and Whiting 398 Weight (1).

Whistle. Wet your whistle (SLC 247). Taylor and Whiting 401 Whistle, sb. (5).

Whitehead. Clipper like a whitehead (ULS 113). Taylor and Whiting 401 Whitehead (2).

Wind. 1. They 're all fickleder 'n the wind that blows (DF 82). NC 497 Wind (3) As fickle as the wind.

    2. More deceivin' 'an the wind that blows (ULS 38). Cf. Taylor and Whiting 403 Wind (5).

3. Runnin' pretty clus to the wind, I should think (OB 158). Taylor and Whiting 405 Wind (21).

Wink. Quicker as you mek some wink (DF 124). Taylor and Whiting 406 Wink (1).

Witches. There, you've taowsled my hair till it looks as if the witches hed been in it (ULS 25). Stevenson 2549:8.

Wolf. 1. Hear the damned wolf in black sheep's clothing (ULS 22). Taylor and Whiting 407 Wolf (1).

2. It's darker 'n a wolf's maouth (DF 52). Taylor and Whiting 408 Wolf (5).

3. Hungry as wolves (OB 100; SLC 60 I'm a-gittin' wolfish; ULS 73 Like a pack of hungry wolves). Taylor and Whiting 408 Wolf (7).

4. Haowl lak some wolf (INEFW 229). Taylor and Whiting 408 Wolf (15).

5. Oh, they're bad ones, wuss'n wolves they be (SLC 221). Cf. Taylor and Whiting 408 Wolf (3), (8).

Woman. 1. Everybody tu their notion, 's the ol' woman said when she kissed her kyow (ULS 214). Taylor and Whiting 409 Woman (15); NC 441 Man (17); Oxford 178; Tilley M103.

2. A-lyin' an' gossipin' wus'n a passel o' women tu a quiltin' (ULS 233). Cf. Wilstach 231 Swere and lye as a womman kan.

Wool. As thick as wool (OB 153). Wilstach 420 Thick, like wool.

Word. Naow there won't be a chance tu put in a word aidgeways (DF 68). Taylor and Whiting 413 Word (10).

Work. It's nothin' but work an' chore an' git jawed to pay for it (OB 141). Cf. Taylor and Whiting 413 Work (1).

World. I thought more on her 'an all the hull world (DF 82). Cf. Taylor and Whiting 414 World (1).

CHAPTER 16

FOLKSONGS

Folksongs play a much smaller role in Robinson's writings than some of the other genres of verbal folklore, such as folktales, folk beliefs, and proverbs. Thirty years after his death, however, one of the finest collections of regional folksongs was begun in Vermont by Helen Hartness Flanders under the auspices of the Vermont Commission on Country Life.[1] The efforts of Mrs. Flanders and her collaborators— Phillips Barry, George Brown, and Elizabeth Flanders Ballard—resulted in an excellent archive of traditional songs at Middlebury College and in several important published collections of folksongs, including *Vermont Folk-Songs and Ballads* (1931), *A Garland of Green Mountain Song* (1934), *Country Songs of Vermont* (1937), *The New Green Mountain Songster* (1939), *Ballads Migrant in New England* (1953), and *Ancient Ballads Traditionally Sung in New England*, (four volumes, 1960-1965).

Consequently, compared to the field work in the area of folksongs by Mrs. Flanders and her associates, Rowland Robinson's contribution to folksong studies seems negligible. Nevertheless, Robinson was acquainted with a number of traditional songs, and his use of these folksongs in his writings to round out his picture of nineteenth-century Vermont folklife indicates his extreme sensitivity to oral traditions and suggests his overall concept of folklore. Folksongs in Robinson's works include native American ballads, French-Canadian songs, play-party songs, and country dance songs.

Although nearly all the sessions in the shop of Uncle Lisha are devoted to swapping tales, one of the gatherings in a chapter of *Danvis Folks* entitled "A Morning of Song" is devoted to singing songs. The same Danvis cronies who spin yarns in other Danvis stories contribute mostly traditional songs at this songfest. But unlike the complete versions of folktales that Rowland Robinson gives throughout his Danvis stories, the folksongs he gives are almost all fragments—sometimes a stanza, sometimes a line, sometimes only a title. Accordingly, some of the fragments cannot be precisely identified. For example, Pelatiah Gove takes his turn at the songfest by singing of a heartbroken young man who "went to sea to drown himself and his sorrows." Other than paraphrasing the conclusion of the ballad, however, Robinson gives only the first two stanzas of the song, which run:

> 'T is of a poor young man,
>   Distraghted quite by love,
> His storee I'll relate,
>   Your tears all fer to move.
>
> Conven-iunt a damsel lived,
>   No rose it could compare
> A-with the damask of her cheek,
>   The color of her hair.[2]

Of course, there are traditional ballads that tell of tragedies similar to this one. For instance, "Willie Down By the Pond,"[3] a native American ballad found only in the South, tells of heartbroken Willie, who drowns himself in a mill pond when his sweetheart teasingly says she will not marry him.[4] But it does not seem likely that Pelatiah's fragment is "Willie Down By the Pond."

In addition, Robinson gives fragments of both of the only native colonial ballads that have survived in the oral tradition, "Springfield Mountain" and "Brave Wolfe."[5] Perhaps *the* oldest native American ballad, "Springfield Mountain" tells of a young man who is bitten by a snake while mowing a field. The young man calls for help; however, his cries are not answered, and he dies. Evidently the event described in the ballad actually occurred in Massachusetts in 1761. But although "Springfield Mountain" was at first a serious ballad relating an actual tragedy, the folksong became a humorous stage song, which subsequently became better known than the earlier serious form in the American oral tradition. Phillips Barry extensively studied "Springfield Mountain" and found four main types of the ballad—two serious types, the Myrick and Curtis types, and two humorous types, the Sally and Molly types. Barry writes:

> One fact, fully documented, has been established: Timothy Myrick of Wilbraham, Mass., formerly Springfield Mountain, died of snakebite in Farmington, Connecticut, August 7, 1761, the date recorded on his grave monument in Wilbraham. It has also been shown that the presence of families named Curtis, in Springfield and Weathersfield, Vermont, may account for the name "Curtis" in ballad tradition, side by side with "Myrick." Of the four types, the first two, Myrick and Curtis, belong to domestic tradition not traceable back of the year 1849 . . . the last two, "Sally" and "Molly," are of professional tradition, caught up by the folk, of which the former has a copyright record of 1836, the latter 1840. There is no evidence that the ballad is of earlier date than the second quarter of the last century.[6]

Commenting on Barry's statement, however, G. Malcolm Laws has pointed out that it is unlikely that "Springfield Mountain" was created over fifty years after the event it describes. "Furthermore," Laws asserts, "the evidence that the youth died at Farmington is not conclusive. My belief is that this ballad, like many others, was locally composed soon after the tragedy it recounts."[7] At any rate, one of the serious types, the Myrick, was collected from the Vermont oral tradition by George Brown and printed in *Vermont Folk-Songs and Ballads* in 1931. A headnote to the variant Brown collected reads: "Recorded by Mr. Brown in Townshend, Vermont, from the singing of Mr. Josiah S. Kennison. Mr. Kennison's version of this truly New England folksong differs from almost all others in that it is entirely serious, and without a trace of the caricature and clownishness that usually characterize this piece."[8] The first stanza of Mr. Kennison's version goes:

> On Springfield mountain there did dwell
> A handsome youth, was known full well,
> Lieutenant Merrill's only son,
> A likely youth, near twenty-one.

Apparently, the fragment of "Springfield Mountain" that Robinson includes in *Sam Lovel's Camps* is a version of this same Myrick type, although in Robinson's variant Springfield Mountain has been localized, becoming Mansfield Mountain, and Lieutenant Myrick (or Merrill in the version above) has been garbled, becoming Colonel "Maaryit." The single stanza of "Springfield Mountain" that Robinson gives is sung by Joseph Hill as he drives a baggage wagon to the camp of Sam Lovel and Antoine Bassette:

> Odn Maadnsfield Maounting onct didn ndwell-ell,
>   N-a likeli you-ugh-th I-ee knowed full well-n.
> Cur-d-nell Maaryit's noli sodn,
>   N-a-a-abaout the aage of twentnti-wodn-n-n.[9]

A version of the first stanza of "Brave Wolfe,"[10] the other colonial ballad that has survived in the American oral tradition, is found in two of Robinson's Danvis stories. The ballad of "Brave Wolfe" commemorates the death of Major-General James Wolfe, who died September 13, 1759, of wounds suffered during the siege of Quebec. According to G. Malcolm Laws, "Brave Wolfe" is of broadside origin. Laws asserts, "This laudatory account of the general's gallant death at the Battle of Quebec is in 18th century broadside style. It is clearly not of folk origin, but the folk accepted it and cherished it."[11] In the ballad Wolfe's sweetheart forsakes him for another, so Wolfe gives her a gold ring and goes to Quebec "to free America from its commotion." There Wolfe and his party meet the French in battle, and Wolfe is fatally wounded. When the brave general learns from his aide-de-camp that the French have been defeated, however, Wolfe replies, "I die with pleasure." "Brave Wolfe" is still current in the oral tradition, and in *Body, Boots and Britches* Harold W. Thompson gives a complete text from Corinth, New York. The first stanza of the New York version runs:

> Cheer up, ye young men all, let nothing fright you;
> Though at your love's pursuits, let that delight you;
> Don't let your fancy move when come to trial,
> Nor let your courage fail at the first denial.[12]

Rowland Robinson's two fragments of "Brave Wolfe" are found in *Sam Lovel's Camps* and *Danvis Folks*. In *Sam Lovel's Camps* Robinson writes that "Sam sang from the ballad of 'Brave Wolf,'" and Sam sings the following version of the first stanza of the ballad:

> Chee-er up your hearts, young men,
>   Let naw-thing fright you;
> Be a–w–v a galiant mind,
>   Let tha-a-at delight you![13]

In *Danvis Folks* Solon Briggs sings the other fragment of "Brave Wolfe," which, except for the dialect, is the same as Sam Lovel's version. Solon's fragment of "Brave Wolfe" runs:

> Cheer up your hearts, young men;
>   Le-at noth-ing fright yeou,
> Be o-of a galliant mind,
>   Le-at that delight yeou.[14]

After Solon's fragment, though, Robinson adds that "the hero of Quebec at last 'died with pleasure' in the arms of his 'Eddy Konk.'" Apparently Wolfe's "Eddy Konk" is a corruption of his "aide-de-camp," who generally appears in the last stanza of the ballad.

In *Danvis Folks* Robinson writes that after Solon's version of "Brave Wolfe," Joseph Hill "lifted up his voice in commemoration of another humbler and fairer victim of the great destroyer." Then Robinson gives the following fragment of Joseph's song:

> It was all by the banks of a beauchiful river,
>   As I walked aout in the sweet month of June,
> A pretty fair maid I chanced to diskiver,
>   As calmly she strayed by the light of the moon.
>   Nya—sing derry daown derry,
>   Nya—derry daown day.[15]

Of course, sometimes the attempt to identify a ballad by a single stanza is a risky business because of the use of conventional expressions and situations in folksongs. Joseph's song, for instance, remotely suggests one of the few native American ballads having a supernatural theme, "Lost Jimmie Whalen," a lumberjack ballad still current in Maine.[16] The first stanza of a Maine version of "Lost Jimmie Whalen" goes:

> As lonely I strayed by the banks of the river,
> I was watching the sunbeams as evening drew nigh;
> As onward I rambled, I spied a fair damsel;
> She was weeping and wailing with many a sigh.[17]

In the remainder of the ballad of "Lost Jimmie Whalen," the grieving girl cries for her drowned sweetheart, Jimmie Whalen, who then rises from his watery grave. When she begs him to stay, he replies that "death is the dagger that keeps us asunder," though promising from his grave to guide her and keep her from danger. Jimmie vanishes "straight to the skies," and his sweetheart is left alone wailing in sorrow. As the ballad ends, she sinks to the ground and vows, ". . . Oh, my lost Jimmie Whalen,/I will sigh till I die by the side of your grave." Whether Joseph Hill's fragment is actually "Lost Jimmie Whalen," however, is not certain.

The fullest text of an Anglo-American ballad that Robinson gives is Uncle Lisha's version of "High Barbary," a British broadside ballad relating an English victory over a pirate ship.[18] Lisha's version of "High Barbary," with Robinson's commentary, goes:

Then Uncle Lisha roared a song commemorating the gallant exploits of

> "Tew Lofty ships that from ol' England sailed,
> One was the Prince o' Luther, one was the
> Prince o' Lee,
> Crewsin' raoun' the coast of Barboree."

If he ran amuck among the titles of English princes, the bold Briton, in quest of pirates, could not have shouted his orders louder than the Yankee cobbler sang:—

> " 'Go aloft,' cried aour Cap'n, 'go aloft,'
> shaouted he,
> 'Look ahead, look astarn, look a-weather,
> look a-lee'
> Crewsin' raoun' on the coast o' Barboree;"

nor the corsairs have answered more boldly the hail,

> " 'We aire no men o' war, no privateers,'
> says they,
> 'But we aire some jolly pierutts a-seekin'
> arter prey,
> Crewsin' raoun' on the coast o' Barboree,"

nor could the victorious British sea dogs have announced with greater zest the just retribution that overtook the pirates.

Except for three omitted stanzas, Uncle Lisha's version of "High Barbary" compares favorably with a text collected from the Maine oral tradition, which runs:

There were two lofty ships from Old England came,
  Blow high, blow low, and so sailed we;
One was the Queen of Russia and the other Prince of
  Wales,
  Cruising down along the coast of the High Barbaree.

"Aloft there, aloft!" our jolly boatswain cried,
  Blow high, blow low, and so sailed we;
"Look ahead, look astern, look aweather, look alee,
  Look down along the coast of the High Barbaree."

"There's nought upon the stern, there's nought upon
  the lee,"
  Blow high, blow low, and so sailed we;
"But there's a lofty ship to windward and she's sailing
  fast and free,
  Sailing down along the coast of the High Barbaree."

"Oh, hail her, oh, hail her!" our gallant captain cried,
  Blow high, blow low, and so sailed we;
"Are you a man-of-war, or a privateer," said he,
  "Cruising down along the coast of the High Barbaree?"

"Oh, I'm not a man-of-war, nor a privateer," said he,
  Blow high, blow low, and so sailed we;
"But I'm a salt-sea pirate a-looking for a fee,
  Cruising down along the coast of the High Barbaree."

Oh, 'twas broadside to broadside a long time we lay,
  Blow high, blow low, and so sailed we,
Until the Queen of Russia shot the pirate's mast away,
  Cruising down along the coast of the High Barbaree.

"Oh, quarter, oh, quarter!" those pirates then did cry
  Blow high, blow low, and so sailed we,
But the quarter that we gave them, we sunk them in
  the sea,
  Cruising down along the coast of the High Barbaree.[20]

The authors of *British Ballads from Maine* suggest that "High Barbary" is a secondary form of "The George Aloe and the Sweepstake" (Child 285).[21] But Laws, while recognizing certain points in common in the two ballads, asserts that "High Barbary" and "The George Aloe and the Sweepstake" are very different in content and phraseology. Laws believes that "High Barbary" was probably written by Charles Dibdin (1745-1814), an author of naval songs, who was perhaps inspired by the older Child ballad.[22]

As we have seen in the second chapter of the present work, the biographical evidence indicates that Rowland Robinson "knew many old songs." But it is certain that Robinson went to sources other than the oral tradition for some of the folksongs that he uses in his stories. He especially went to other sources for French-Canadian songs. In *Danvis Folks,* for example, Robinson gives the following version of a common French-Canadian folksong, "A la claire fontaine," which is sung by Antoine's father:

> A la claire fontaine
> M'en allant promener,
> J'ai trouve l'eau si belle
> Que je m'y suie baigne.
> Il y a longtemps que je t'aime,
> Jamais je ne t'oublierai.

Then following the French version of "A la claire fontaine" Robinson gives an English translation, which runs:

> Down to the crystal streamlet
> I strayed at close of day,
> Into its limpid waters
> I plunged without delay.
> I've loved thee long and dearly,
> I'll love thee, sweet, for aye.[23]

In a footnote in *Danvis Folks* Robinson acknowledges that he took this French version of "A la claire fontaine" with its English translation from William McLennan's *Songs of Old Canada.*[24] It is significant that of the many items of folklore Robinson uses in his fiction, this French-Canadian folksong is the only one he acknowledges borrowing from print. It seems likely that if Robinson was honest enough to document the source of this song, he would have done the same for other items of folklore if he had taken them from books.

"A la claire fontaine" is also mentioned in one of Robinson's short stories, "Antoine Sugaring." Antoine says that sometimes he passes the time in his sugar camp singing "La Claire Fontaine" at the top of his voice.[25] Regardless of Robinson's source, by using it he has added a touch of realism to his fiction. "A la claire fontaine," according to McLennan, "heads our Canadian songs," and the song apparently enjoyed as great a popularity in France as in Canada.[26] This is substantiated by Marius Barbeau. Barbeau says of this popular folksong, "For French Canada it has been used as a national anthem. It came to the shores of the New World with the seventeenth-century colonists, and has followed them wherever they went, in their labors and adventures."[27]

Another French-Canadian song that Robinson uses is "Papineau."[28] In *Uncle Lisha's Shop,* as the storytellers leave Lisha's shop after an evening of spinning yarns, Antoine sings " 'Papineau' at the top of his sonorous voice," and the others join "in the ringing refrain,

'Hurrah, pour Papineau!' "[29] At one of the gatherings in Lisha's shop, too, Lisha says, "Wal, Ann Twine, it's your turn naow. You got to tell a story or sing a song. Le's hev Pappy no, come. 'Pappee no sa bum payraow.' " Then Robinson adds that this is "the first line of that once popular Canadian revolutionary song."[30] Robinson mentions "Papineau" in his short story "Antoine Sugaring," also. Antoine says, "Somtam Ah sing de song of Papineau, but de hecho come from de maountain lak some voice from Canada w'en Ah'll was boy, 'fore Ah mos' spilt mah bloods in de Papineau war, an' mek more lonesick Ah'll was 'fore. Sem lak hol' song say, "Ah'll never ant freegit.' "[31] The "old song" of this last sentence, however, apparently refers to a line in "A la claire fontaine," which goes, "Jamais je ne t'oublierai."

It is possible that Robinson went to sources other than the oral tradition for "Papineau," although it is unlikely since he gives only the title and anglicized fragments of the song. Two texts of the same version of "Papineau," however, can be found in one of Robinson's notebooks, dated from 1896 to 1899, which is still at Rokeby. This notebook, kept by Robinson after he became blind, includes ideas for stories, drafts of letters, and observations about birds he could hear singing from his window. Robinson wrote his notes in an unsteady backhand with pencil on paper placed over a 6 3/4" x 4 1/8" piece of stiff, grooved cardboard. However, the two versions of "Papineau" in this notebook are not in Robinson's hand. One text, French with English translation, is written into the notebook; the other text, French only, is written on the back of a prescription form from the office of Dr. William Gilpin Robinson, 341 Lexington Avenue, New York, New York, and has been inserted in the notebook. The stories in which Robinson refers to "Papineau," however, were written earlier than the dates in the journal. Consequently, it is conceivable, although highly conjectural, that Robinson had actually heard the French song but did not recall all of it since it was outside of his Yankee tradition. Then perhaps later he collected a complete text of the song from another source and placed it in his notebook for future use.

Another popular French-Canadian folksong that Robinson uses in his fiction is a paddle song with double entendre lyrics, "En roulant ma boule." For instance, at the songfest in Uncle Lisha's shop, Antoine's father, "without much persuasion, . . . sang 'Roulant ma Boule.' "[32] In addition, in "Antoine Sugaring" Antoine says that often he gets lonely at the sugaring camp, and the Canuck adds, "Sometam Ah'll try for feel better for sing some hol' French song on de top of mah voice, 'La Claire Fontaine,' 'Roulant ma Boule.' "[33] Robinson gives only the refrain of "En roulant ma boule," and both Antoine and his father sing the same version, which runs:

Rouli, roulant, ma boule roulant,
En roulant ma boule roulant.
En roulant ma boule.[34]

The refrain of "En roulant ma boule" that McLennan gives in *Songs of Old Canada*, a book with which Robinson was familiar, is exactly the same as the version sung by Antoine and his father.[35] Marius Barbeau, however, points out that "the refrain 'Rouli, roulant, ma boule roulant, en roulant ma boule' is the only one extensively known in Canada."[36] Speaking of two French-Canadian work songs, "En roulant ma boule" and "A Saint-Malo," Barbeau says:

Familiar at first among canoemen, these ditties have for more than a generation passed into the small repertory of every household, school, and shop. They were among the earliest to be published, back in the 1850's, and have since obstinately occupied the forefront—the shop-window, we might say—of every Canadian songbook, large or small. They have taken on a significance somewhat analogous to that of the maple leaf or the beaver on our national flags. But what they gained on the surface they lost in depth. At one time they had many variants in tune and text. They shared in the inimitable musical quality of the best folk melodies unspoiled by the sluggish throats of the "educated" class. But it is almost too late to find them in uncontaminated form even in their former haunts. A blighting uniformity has come over them.[37]

Although print has to a large extent standardized the text of "En roulant ma boule," Barbeau gives an uncontaminated version of the folksong, which was collected in 1916 from Edouard Hovington, a 90-year-old canoeman of Tadoussac, Quebec. The refrain of this orally collected text, which differs slightly from the uniform versions generally found today, goes:

Roulite roulant,
Ma boule roulant.
Roulite roulant,
Boule roulant.
En roulant ma boule qui roule,
En roulant ma boule.[38]

Again with "En roulant ma boule" Robinson has chosen a typical French-Canadian folksong, which when sung by his Canuck characters helps make them credible. McLennan writes of "En roulant ma boule," "As a popular song in Canada, it ranks next to 'La claire fontaine.' "[39] Likewise, Barbeau says that "En roulant ma boule" is so characteristically Canadian "that we are apt to forget that it is an old-country possession as well. Our list of versions, though still incomplete, includes at least twenty-nine versions from France and a large number from Canada; and parallels have been published by C. Nigra for northern Italy."[40]

Besides Anglo-American ballads and French-Canadian folksongs, Robinson uses several songs generally associated with play-party games. B. A. Botkin, who provides the fullest treatment of the American play-party song, says of the play-party:

> The play-party (at its height a generation or two ago) was a rural American social gathering for playing games, distinguished by the manner in which it was "got up," by the age of its participants, and by the character of the games played. In its typical form it was not an "invitation affair" but was open to the whole country-side. Attended by the entire family for the same reason that they attended the singing school and the literary society because they had no other place to go, it had for its active participants the young people of high school and marriageable age and young married couples, with the old folk and the children present chiefly as spectators, although the former might serve as leaders or have their square dances (if they were not conscientious objectors) and the latter might play their own games off at one side or before the regular party began. The most important differentia, however, was the character of the games played. Play-party or party games (to give them their generic name) were, with few exceptions, singing-games, including both dramatic choosing or marching games (which may conveniently be known as "party *plays*") and dancing games, in which the dancers swung each other by the hands or, if permitted, by the waist, with no music save their own singing ("swinging plays"). Synonyms for the play-party include "party," which meant a play-party as distinguished from a "dance," and "bounce-around" or "frolic" to distinguish the more boisterous and rollicking fun of the play-party from the milder diversions of the social or evening party, "social," or "sociable," which was for invited guests and, although it might include swinging plays, was largely restricted to parlor and school games.[41]

Accordingly, Botkin uses the term "play-party" strictly in limiting it "to country or country town gatherings of young people from the teens on up, for the sole purpose of playing games with words, tune, dance figures, and dramatic action."[42] Botkin points out, however, "that party games were played at other gatherings than the play-party proper," too.[43] And in the writings of Rowland E. Robinson, the singing games are played not at the play-party proper but at other gatherings. For example, in "Glimpses of New England Farm Life" Robinson mentions that "The Needle's Eye," "Marching to Quebec," and "Philander's March" were familiar tunes to which games were played by young people at paring bees.[44] Likewise, at the Lovels' paring bee in *Danvis Folks* the singing games played are "The Needle's Eye," "Marching to Quebec," and "Philander's March," all of which are common American play-party songs.[45]

In "The Needle's Eye," a singing game that is played somewhat like "London Bridge," two players, a boy and a girl, raise their clasped hands above their heads, forming an arch. The rest of the players form a line and march through the arch while "The Needle's Eye" is sung. As the song ends, the clasped hands of the leaders fall around the neck of the person beneath the arch at the time. If the player caught is a boy, the girl who helped form the arch kisses him; if a girl is caught, the boy who helped form the arch kisses her. Then the person caught replaces the one of his sex in the arch, and the game continues.[46] Robinson's version of the song "The Needle's Eye" goes:

> The needle's eye, that doth soffy
> The thread that runs so treue,
> It has caught many a smiling lass
> And naow it has caught yeou![47]

In *Folk Songs of Old New England*, Eloise Hubbard Linscott reports a similar version from Maine:

> The needle's eye no one can pass,
> The thread that's drawn so true;—
> It has caught many a lovely lass,
> And now it has caught you.[48]

Another song that Robinson uses, "Marching to Quebec," has been collected as both a game song and as an ordinary folksong in the American oral tradition.[49] In his fiction Robinson uses "Marching to Quebec" in both genres. As Botkin points out, American historic folksongs of national conflict sometimes were adapted for play-party use. Botkin says:

. . . The theme of the separation of lovers by war and their reunion by peace has the dramatic utility of suggesting marching games, in which a player or a couple in the center chooses another to enter the center, and joins the marching ring or ranks, or a boy and a girl march down the aisle under raised arms. Played according to the former method is "We're Marching Down to Old Quebec," based on a war ballad which has variously been assigned Revolutionary and War of 1812 origin . . .[50]

Rowland Robinson refers to the song "Marching to Quebec" in several places. He writes in *Danvis Folks* that at the Lovels' paring bee when the young people engage in games, almost everyone joined in to sing "We're marching onward tow-ard Quebec."[51] In *Danvis Folks* Gran'ther Hill, walking across a pasture from partridge hunting, whistles toothlessly "We're marching onward toward Quebec," and Robinson adds that Gran'ther Hill's "rheumatic footsteps fell to the time of the old martial air."[52] Only once, however, does Robinson give more than a line of "Marching to Quebec." In *Uncle Lisha's Shop* at a turkey shoot Gran'ther Hill gets a little high on Hamner's rum and begins to sing "Marching to Quebec" to "a small but appreciative audience," Gran'ther Hill's version of "Marching to Quebec" goes:

> We're a-marchin' on tow-wards Quebec,
> Whilst the drums is loudli bea--tin,

> For Americay hes gained the day
> An' the British is retrea-tin'![53]

In *Games and Songs of American Children,* William Wells Newell gives
the following New England version of "Marching to Quebec":

> As we were marching to Quebec,
> The drums were loudly beating;
> The Americans have won the day,
> The British are retreating.
> March! march! march! march![54]

In *Danvis Folks* another game played at the paring bee at the
Lovels' home is timed to the words of "Come, Philander, le' 's be a-
marchin'."[55]   In *Danvis Folks,* upon the return of Uncle Lisha and
Aunt Jerusha from Wisconsin, the old shoemaker is elated to see once
again such familiar landmarks as Potato Hill, and both sing a version of
"Come, Philanders," which runs:

> Come, Philander, le' 's be a-marchin',
> Ev'ry one his treu love a-sarchin';
> Chuse your treu love, now or never,
> See that you don't chuse no other.
> Fol de rol de fol de rol de day.[56]

Newell reports that "Come, Philanders" is familiar throughout New
England and gives a variant of the song close to the one that Robinson
uses:

> Come, Philanders, let's be a-marching,
> Every one choose from his heartstrings;
> Choose your true love now or never,
> And be sure you choose no other.[57]

In addition to the play-party songs, Robinson mentions a number
of hoedown songs, which unlike the play-party songs are primarily
instrumental.   Whereas the play-party games were the main form of
song-dance entertainment for the young people a century ago, the
country dances served the same function for older adults. Mrs. Linscott
says:

> The country dance was the regular pastime of our grandmothers—when piety
> did not intervene—and was enjoyed usually once a week, unless a special occasion
> called for celebration.   According to the occasion, the dance was held in the
> kitchen, front room, barn, or town hall, where old and young danced to the
> strains of "Honest John" and "Hull's Victory."   Then, as in some areas today, a
> corn husking, a harvest, or the laying of the new barn floor, all required due
> recognition.   They came by wagon or shank's mare, sometimes from as far as
> twenty-five miles, to the kitchen junket and kitchen knockdown of Vermont, the
> kitchen whang of Maine, the barn dance, or, as some strenuous participants call it,
> the hog-wrasslin' . . .[58]

In Robinson's writings, the country dance songs, like the play-party songs, are performed at various gatherings and bees after the work is over. This coincides with the findings of contemporary folklorists. For instance, Bruce R. Buckley says, "The growth and development of traditional dances and play-parties during the early part of this century were tied very closely to a tradition of sharing the work of your neighbors. The philosophy of 'more hands make lighter work' was a common one held by the small rural communities, and neighbors would work together and use each of these occasions to play together. . . . After the work was over, all would have a meal together, clear out the kitchen or the parlor (many times both rooms), and the dance would begin."[59] Accordingly, in "Glimpses of New England Farm Life" Robinson writes that after work is done at New England paring bees, the fiddle songs of "French Four" and "Twin Sisters" "set all feet to dancing."[60] Both "French Four" and "Twin Sisters" are traditional New England country dance songs, apparently of British origin.[61]

Other country dance songs that Robinson mentions are "Money Musk," "Hull's Victory," and "Backside of Albany." Writing of the wedding day of Sam Lovel and Huldah Purington, Robinson says, "Later in the evening, by some chance a fiddle and fiddler came in conjunction, and those so disposed had an opportunity to prance with some regard to the time and tunes of 'Money Musk,' 'Hull's Victory,' the 'Backside of Albany,' and many another tune that has outlived its dancers of those days."[62] In addition, in an essay, "The Path of Boatless Generations," Robinson mentions that "Money Musk" is a fiddle tune played at paring bees, and he incorporates this knowledge of folk-life into his fiction, when in *Danvis Folks*, "Money Musk" is played by the drunken fiddler Wat Palmer at the Lovels' paring bee.[63] Mrs. Linscott reports that "Money Musk"—coming from the village of Money Musk, Aberdeenshire, Scotland—is a traditional New England dance tune known as "The Countess of Airly" in the early eighteenth century. As for "Hull's Victory," Mrs. Linscott reports that "no country dance would be complete without it."[64] "Hull's Victory" is the alternate title of the American war ballad "The Constitution and the Guerriere," a native American ballad relating Captain Isaac Hull's victory over Captain R. Dacres and the British frigate Guerriere on August 19, 1812.[65] Similarly, "Backside of Albany" was based on a song commemorating Commodore Thomas McDonough's naval victory at Plattsburg in October 1812. But "Backside of Albany," originally called "The Siege of Plattsburg," was a stage song performed in Albany in 1815 in the play *The Battle of Lake Champlain*. The text of "Backside of Albany" was first published in the same year, 1815, in a songster, *Columbian Harmonist*.[66] Harold W. Thompson in *Body, Boots and Britches* gives a version of "The Siege of Plattsburg" from the *Diamond Songster*

(1817). This version, in Negro dialect, begins:

> Back side Albany stan' Lake Champlain,
> One little pond half full a' water,
> Plat-te-burg dare too, close pon de main,
> Town small—he grew bigger do hereafter.
> On Lake Champlain,
> Uncle Sam set he boat,
> Massa M'Donough, he sail 'em;
> While Gen'ral M'Comb
> Make Plat-te-burg he home,
> Wid de army, who courage nebber fail 'em.[67]

Other songs Robinson mentions include "Bonaparte's March," "The Road to Boston," "The White Cockade," and "Yankee Doodle." In his essay "Mingo—A Silhouette," Robinson writes that Mingo Niles hummed "the plaintive measure of Bonaparte's march, in a deep, mellow voice that was the sweetest music to our untrained Quaker ears."[68] In addition, in *Along Three Rivers* Robinson reports a fiddle arrangement of this same song. Speaking of "Joe Denoir, a gigantic Frenchman, who was one of Napoleon's old Guard," Robinson says, "Once, as he was walking past the tavern, a fiddler in the bar room was playing 'Bonaparte's March,' and when his ear caught the air, he halted, erect and motionless, in the attitude of attention, and so stood till the last note was played."[69] Apparently, the fiddle tune of Bonaparte's march that Robinson refers to is the march "Bonaparte Crossing the Rhine," which was very popular around 1800 as a country dance tune.[70]

"The Road to Boston," "The White Cockade," and "Yankee Doodle" are tunes played at militia meetings in Danvis.[71] In addition, Gran'ther Hill whistles "The Road to Boston" in *Danvis Folks* when he marches Uncle Lisha and Aunt Jerusha to Sam Lovel's home; and again he whistles "The Road to Boston" in *Uncle Lisha's Shop* when he marches himself to Uncle Lisha's house.[72] "Boston," or "Going to Boston," conceivably the song Robinson refers to, has a tune resembling that of the familiar "Pawpaw Patch" and was widely used as a marching play-party song.[73] Similarly, the military tune of "The White Cockade" that Robinson mentions was used as a country dance song, too.[74] The very familiar "Yankee Doodle," of course, has become America's unofficial national song, although originally the British redcoats' lyrics during the early part of the American Revolution mocked the bumpkin Yankee militia.[75]

Another song that Robinson uses is "The Girl I Left Behind Me," a common song in both print and the oral tradition in Great Britain and the United States. Moreover, the song has been popular in many versions as a marching song, country dance song, play-party song, and ordinary folksong.[76] In Robinson's stories, too, "The Girl I Left Behind Me" does double duty as a marching song and as a folksong. In the historical story *In the Green Wood*, Robinson uses the song as a marching song when he writes, "The green-coated regiment of Colonel Herrick's Rangers marched away in three ranks to the tune of 'The Girl I Left Behind Me,' shrieked and rattled at their loudest by fife and drum, echoed from hillside and woodland, and reechoed in the heart of many a wife, mother, and sweetheart who with pride and sorrow saw their loved ones departing."[77]   In *Uncle Lisha's Shop*, Robinson uses "The Girl I Left Behind Me" as an ordinary folksong when Huldah Purington sings:

> If ever I chance to go that way,
>   And she has not resigned me,
> I'll reconcile my mind and stay
>   With the girl I left behind me.[78]

In addition, Robinson uses "The Girl I Left Behind Me" in another Danvis story, *Danvis Folks,* where he writes that Antoine strikes up "more tunefully than intelligibly, 'The girl I left behind me'." Antoine's version runs:

> De bee growl an' weesh for save hees store,
>   De dove he shall turn over
> An' fall in de water, mek it roar,
>   If Ah'll fregit for love her.
> If ev'ree chance Ah'll gat dat way,
>   An' she ant gat for sign me,
> Ah'll reckon up mah min' for stay,
>   To de gal Ah love behine me.[79]

Here again Antoine shares the Anglo-American folksong tradition, as he does in other places in Robinson's fiction. For instance, in another Danvis story, "A September Election," when Antoine is walking to Burtontown, he "added a snatch of an old Canadian song, or his own rendering of some popular ballad of his adopted land."[80]

NOTES

[1]See the following articles by Helen Hartness Flanders: "The Quest for Vermont Ballads," *Proceedings of the Vermont Historical Society*, VII (June 1939), 53-72; "Index of Ballads and Folk-Songs in the Archive of Vermont Folk-Songs at Smiley Manse, Springfield, Vermont," *Proceedings of the Vermont Historical Society*, VII (June 1940), 214-251; "List of Folk-Songs Recorded in Vermont in November, 1939," *Proceedings of the Vermont Historical Society*, VII (September 1940), 302-311.

[2]Robinson, *Danvis Folks and A Hero of Ticonderoga*, p. 136.

[3]Laws G19. The standard work identifying and discussing ballads native to the United States is G. Malcolm Laws, *Native American Balladry* (Philadelphia, 1964). The note "Laws" followed by a number having a prefix A to I refers to a ballad in this book.

[4]See *The Frank C. Brown Collection*, II, 638-39.

[5]Laws, *Native American Balladry*, p. 13.

[6]Quoted in Laws, *Native American Balladry*, p. 220. See the *Bulletin of the Folk-Song Society of the Northeast*, No. 12 (1937), p. 7.

[7]Laws, *Native American Balladry*, p. 220.

[8]Helen Hartness Flanders and George Brown, *Vermont Folk-Songs and Ballads* (Brattleboro, 1931), pp. 15-16.

[9]Robinson, *Sam Lovel's Camps and In the Green Wood*, p. 77. Laws G16.

[10]Laws A1.

[11]Laws, *Native American Balladry*, p. 13.

[12]Harold W. Thompson, p. 323.

[13]Robinson, *Sam Lovel's Camps and In the Green Wood*, p. 20.

[14]Robinson, *Danvis Folks and A Hero of Ticonderoga*, p. 134.

[15]Robinson, *Danvis Folks and A Hero of Ticonderoga*, p. 135.

[16]Laws C8.

[17]MacEdward Leach, ed., *The Ballad Book* (New York, 1955), p. 726.

[18]Laws K33. The note "Laws" followed by a number having a prefix J to Q refers to a ballad of broadside origin in G. Malcolm Laws, *American Balladry from British Broadsides* (Philadelphia, 1957).

[19]Robinson, *Danvis Folks and A Hero of Ticonderoga*, pp. 135-36.

[20]Phillips Barry, Fannie H. Eckstorm, and Mary W. Smyth, *British Ballads from Maine* (New Haven, 1929), p. 413.

[21]Barry, Eckstorm, and Smyth, p. 413. See Francis James Child, ed., *The English and Scottish Popular Ballads* (New York, 1965), V, 133-35.

[22]Laws, *American Balladry from British Broadsides*, p. 158.

[23]Robinson, *Danvis Folks and a Hero of Ticonderoga*, p. 23.

[24]See William McLennan, *Songs of Old Canada* (Montreal, 1886), pp. 2-3.

[25]Robinson, *In New England Fields and Woods*, p. 231.

[26]McLennan, p. 2.

[27]Marius Barbeau, *Jongleur Songs of Old Quebec* (New Brunswick, 1962), p. 93.

[28]Louis Joseph Papineau (1786-1871) was a French-Canadian political hero who was instrumental in the Lower Canada Rebellion of 1827. Papineau became a popular hero, and the Folklore Division of the National Museum of Man in Ottawa has several folksongs in its archives about Papineau.

[29]Robinson, *Uncle Lisha's Shop and A Danvis Pioneer*, p. 196.

[30]Robinson, *Uncle Lisha's Shop and A Danvis Pioneer*, pp. 192-93.

[31] Robinson, *In New England Fields and Woods*, p. 231.

[32] Robinson, *Danvis Folks and A Hero of Ticonderoga*, p. 134.

[33] Robinson, *In New England Fields and Woods*, p. 231.

[34] Robinson, *Danvis Folks and A Hero of Ticonderoga*, p. 134.

[35] See McLennan, pp. 20-25.

[36] Barbeau, p. 99.

[37] Barbeau, p. 101.

[38] Barbeau, p. 97.

[39] McLennan, p. 20.

[40] Barbeau, p. 99.

[41] B. A. Botkin, *The American Play-Party Song* (New York, 1963), pp. 16-17.

[42] Botkin, *The American Play-Party Song*, p. 18.

[43] Botkin, *The American Play-Party Song*, p. 19.

[44] Robinson, "Glimpses of New England Farm Life," p. 527.

[45] Robinson, *Danvis Folks and A Hero of Ticonderoga*, pp. 90-91.

[46] Newell, pp. 91, 241; *The Frank C. Brown Collection*, I, 108-109; Eloise Hubbard Linscott, *Folk Songs of Old New England* (London, 1962), pp. 43-44.

[47] Robinson, *Danvis Folks and A Hero of Ticonderoga*, p. 91.

[48] Linscott, pp. 43-44.

[49] See *The Frank C. Brown Collection*, I, 118.

[50] Botkin, *The American Play-Party Song*, p. 70.

[51] Robinson, *Danvis Folks and A Hero of Ticonderoga*, p. 91.

[52] Robinson, *Danvis Folks and A Hero of Ticonderoga*, p. 33.

[53] Robinson, *Uncle Lisha's Shop and A Danvis Pioneer*, p. 167.

[54] Newell, p. 125.

[55] Robinson, *Danvis Folks and A Hero of Ticonderoga*, p. 91.

[56] Robinson, *Danvis Folks and A Hero of Ticonderoga*, p. 50.

[57] Newell, p. 58.

[58] Linscott, pp. 59-60.

[59] Bruce R. Buckley, " 'Honor Your Ladies': Folk Dance in the United States," *Our Living Traditions*, ed. Tristram Potter Coffin (New York, 1968), p. 139.

[60] Robinson, "Glimpses of New England Farm Life," p. 527.

[61] Linscott, pp. 77-78, 114-115.

[62] Robinson, *Sam Lovel's Camps and In the Green Wood*, p. 204.

[63] Robinson, *In New England Fields and Woods*, p. 165.

[64] Linscott, pp. 86, 97-98.

[65] Laws A6.

[66] Hans Nathan, *Dan Emmett and the Rise of Early Negro Minstrelsy* (Norman, Oklahoma, 1962), p. 35.

[67] Harold W. Thompson, p. 67.

[68] Robinson, *Out of Bondage and Other Stories*, p. 66.

[69] Robinson, *Uncle Lisha's Outing and Along Three Rivers*, p. 240.

[70] Linscott, p. 70.

[71] Robinson, *Danvis Folks and A Hero of Ticonderoga*, pp. 177, 181.

[72] Robinson, *Danvis Folks and A Hero of Ticonderoga*, p. 62; *Uncle Lisha's Shop and A Danvis Pioneer*, p. 239.

[73] Botkin, *The American Play-Party Song*, pp. 148-49, 289-90.

[74] Linscott, p. 120.

[75] See Alan Lomax, *The Penguin Book of American Folk Songs* (Baltimore, 1964), p. 23.

[76]Laws P1A, P1B; Linscott, pp. 79-80; Botkin, *The American Play-Party Song*, pp. 49-50; *The Frank C. Brown Collection*, II, 378-85.

[77]Robinson, *Sam Lovel's Camps and In the Green Wood*, p. 260.

[78]Robinson, *Uncle Lisha's Shop and A Danvis Pioneer*, p. 173.

[79]Robinson, *Danvis Folks and A Hero of Ticonderoga*, p. 134.

[80]Robinson, *Sam Lovel's Boy with Forest and Stream Fables*, p. 164.

CHAPTER 17

TALL TALES

In *Jonathan Draws the Long Bow* Richard Dorson observes that folktales in the United States "run to the comic anecdote and the local legend, the tall story and trickster yarn, rather than to the creation myths, prose sagas, animal fables, aetiological tales, *Marchen*, and novelle familiar in medieval, classical, and primitive cultures."[1] The Yankee folktales that Robinson uses in his writings follow the main forms of American storytelling that Dorson describes above: tall tales, comic anecdotes, trickster stories, and local legends. In addition, Robinson uses several supernatural tales, mostly French-Canadian, and three etiological tales, all North American Indian.

Most of the folktales that Robinson uses in his writings, however, are tall tales. Following the main themes of American oral tales, these tales deal mainly with fishing, hunting, extraordinary skills, and remarkable phenomena. In *Uncle Lisha's Shop*, for example, Antoine tells a variant of a popular American tall tale, "The Breathing Tree."[2] Antoine contends that once when he was tracking a coon he discovered a large number of coon tracks all leading to the same place. Following the tracks, he began to hear a steady noise like a big hammer pounding very slowly, and as the noise intensified, he became more afraid. At last, however, Antoine saw that all the coon tracks led to small holes under a large rock, and there he found the source of the noise. So many coons were sleeping under the large rock that it rose and fell with the breathing of the raccoons.[3] Vance Randolph reports that "The Breathing Tree" is known throughout the Ozarks,[4] and Dorson notes variants from Vermont, Tennessee, and Indiana.[5]

Antoine tells a number of yarns involving unorthodox or ingenious methods of catching or killing game.[6] In *Sam Lovel's Boy*, for instance, when Sammy Lovel bags his first fox everyone praises him for his marksmanship—everyone but Antoine, that is. And Antoine, of course, has a whopper to tell about his own fox hunting talents when he was a

177

boy in Canada:

". . . Oh, Ah'll de boy for keel de fox w'en Ah leeve in Canada, jes' wid club. Ah'll see fox on de lot, hunt some mices, den Ah'll hid mase'f behin' stump an' shreek jes' lak mices. 'Speep! Speep!' "—drawing in his breath between his com- pressed lips,—"an' dat foxes he'll stick his ear an' come raght where Ah'll be, an' one tam ah'll skreek so preffic Ah'll fool de fox so bad, he'll come jomp raght hover de stomp an' touch hol' mah back neck an' an't le' go 'fore Ah'll holler lak loons. 'F you'll an't b'leeve dat you look dat scars. What you t'ink for dat, hein?"[7]

At one of the tale-swapping sessions in Lisha's shop Antoine tells how he caught a partridge by an unorthodox method, too. The Canuck asserts, "Bah gosh! 'todder day, seh, when Ah'll was be choppin' in de hwood dey was one of it flewed raght in ma face, an' Ah'll bite hees head wid ma mouf! Ah'll peek ma toof more as two nour fore Ah'll got de fedder off of it. Bah gosh! Ah'll got all de patridge Ah'll wan' for heat more as dis year, dat tam, me."[8] Furthermore, once in Canada while deer hunting with his brother-in-law Antoine caught a panther by an ingenious method. The two hunters found some unusual tracks in the snow and followed them a long time until they saw the tracks go into a hole in a large rock. Leaving his brother-in-law to guard the hole, Antoine went around to the back of the rock, where through a crack in the rock he found protruding a panther's tail. The ingenious Canuck found a strong stick, tied the panther's tail to it, and returned to the front of the rock. Then much to the alarm of his brother-in-law, Antoine went into the hole and shot the howling panther right between the eyes.[9] Antoine's whopper suggests an international tall tale in which the tail of a wolf is nailed to a tree.[10]

Another tale that Antoine tells is similar to the international tale "The Great Rabbit-Catch," in which a number of rabbits freeze their feet into ice at night and are taken by a lucky hunter.[11] In *Uncle Lisha's Outing* when Sam Lovel returns to camp with nineteen ducks, Antoine says contemptuously, "Pooh, dat ant nothings." Then Antoine proceeds to tell how he killed forty geese with a club when he was in Canada. According to Antoine, the geese landed on a muddy field, "an' he steek hees foot on de mud so he can' pull it, an' den he froze heem fas' 'cause it mos' winter; so den Ah'll ant not'ing for do honly knock hees head of it."[12] Antoine also tells a whopper about extraordinary luck in shooting pigeons in a short story, "Antoine Sugaring." One spring day when the pigeons were returning to Danvis to nest, the flock was so large that the birds hid the sun, and it got so dark that Antoine could not see the sight of his gun. Consequently, the Canuck just pointed his gun into the air and fired, and the pigeons began to fall on him until they covered him. After Antoine finally crawled out from under the pile of pigeons he looked into the sky and saw the sun shining through the hole he made in the flock. With a single shot Antoine got enough pigeons to supply everyone in Danvis with pigeon pie for two weeks.[13] Versions of this tale in which pigeons darken the sky have been reported from Vermont by Masterson and from Missouri and Arkansas by Randolph,[14] while the motif of falling birds covering the hunter has been attributed to both Gib Morgan and Paul Bunyan.[15]

In *Uncle Lisha's Shop* Antoine tells of an ingenious method he used to shoot a turkey. At one of the turkey shoots at Hamner's tavern the Canuck is reminded of a turkey shoot held in Canada, where the turkey was hidden behind a hill, and he had to fire into the air at the sound of the turkey's gobble:

"Bah gosh! Ah'll goin' help it!" cried Antoine, who had been prancing from group to group in search of listeners to what he had to tell concerning shooting. "Dat mek me rembler one tam dey have it shoot-turkey in Canady, an' dey'll ant let you see dem turkey, bah gosh no! Dey'll have it 'hind a hill of it, an' you'll gat for guess where he'll was an' den shoot. Yes, sah! Well, boy, Ah'll was be dere, an' Ah'll hear dat turkey beegin for boggler. Houkle, houkle, houkle! Den Ah'll pant up ma gun up so Ah'll tink de ball was drop off where he'll hit dat nowse, an' Ah'll shot off, pluck! 'Squowk!" Ah'll hear dat turkey said, an' bah gosh! You'll ant b'lieved me, dat ball stroke it raght bit tween hees back."[16]

Antoine is by no means the only citizen of Danvis who catches game by unusual methods. In *Sam Lovel's Boy* Gran'ther Hill tells Sammy Lovel and Uncle Lisha how he ingeniously caught a den of wolf cubs after he had trapped the bitch. Speaking of the cubs, Gran'ther Hill says, "When I reckoned they'd got hungry 'nough tu be keerless I baited a hook wi' mutton, an' when they'd grab it I'd yank 'em aout, till I got three."[17] In Aarne and Thompson's *The Types of the Folktale* only a single version of this tale, "Hunting the Wolves with Rod and Line," is cited, and it is from Norway.[18]

Antoine, however, tells most of the tales involving unorthodox methods of catching animals, and in *Danvis Folks* he tells a wolf story that matches Gran'ther Hill's yarn. The hero of Antoine's tale this time, though, is not the Canuck himself but his uncle, who killed ten wolves and wounded five others with a single shot. Antoine maintains:

. . . You Yankee tink it was be awfly beeg for feefty mans keel one wolf, but Ah goin' tol' you what mah fader's broder-law was be do, one tam. One naght, he'll load off hees gaun wid four, prob'ly tree ball an' han'ful of shot-buck an' he'll took twenty-fav' foot rope, an' he'll rrrubby rrrrubby all wid hawg blood, he jes' be keel, an' he'll jomp on hees traine, hees cutters, you know, an' he'll drove off on de hwood, wid mah fader for drove, an' drag dat ropes behin' de traine of it. An' bambye de wolfs beegin fer feel smell of it, an' he'll scratter togedder an' foller dat traine, more as twenty, t'irty of it, an' den he'll touch hol' dat ropes, one, two, tree, ten, feefteen, so many, de hoss he mos' can' pull it. Wal, seh, den mah fader's broder-law, he pant hees gaun raght long dat ropes, an' he'll shot, *poom*, an', seh, haow many you s'pose he'll keel, ten of it, an' fav', he'll go off flap, flap, guer-a-ouou, wid hees laig broke off an' hees jaw spile up for bit some more. Dat was de way in Canada, two mens keel ten wolfs, not feefty fer keel one, an' hol' mos'-dead-mans do it den."[19]

Harold W. Thompson, in *Body, Boots and Britches*, reports a variant of this tale from Ogdensburg, New York. A mighty hunter there decided to rid the North Country of bears and poured several barrels of honey in a long, straight line. He stood at one end of the line until there was a long row of bears gulping the honey. Then with one shot of his special gun he killed 144 bears.[20]

The bear—a favorite character in New England tales, according to Dorson—figures into several of the Danvis yarns.[21] The occasion for one bear story is in *Uncle Lisha's Outing* when Joseph Hill shoots a marsh hawk. As Joseph grabs the dying bird, the talons of one of its feet close upon his wrist. Then as he tries to free himself from the clutch of the bird, he is caught by the other foot. When Joseph turns to Uncle Lisha for relief, Lisha tells Joseph he is "as bad off as the feller 'at ketched the bear." Lisha explains:

". . . Ye see, he follered a bear track intu a hole, an' the feller 'at was a-huntin' along with him he stayed aoutside. 'I've ketched a bear,' he hollered from inside. 'All right, says t'other feller, 'fetch him aout an' le' 's see him.' 'I can't fetch him,' says he. 'Wal,' says t'other feller, 'come aout yourself.' 'I can't' says he, 'he's got a holt on me an' won't let me,' says he. . . .[22]

This short anecdote that Uncle Lisha tells is classified as a dialogue proverb by Archer Taylor, who points out that it is widely distributed in Europe. Taylor offers a modern version, which runs: " 'I have caught a bear.'—'Bring it here.'—'It won't come.'—'Then come yourself.' —'It won't let me go.' "[23]

Another bear story in the Danvis stories involves the motif concerning the hunter in danger.[24] In *Uncle Lisha's Outing* while Joseph Hill, Uncle Lisha, and Antoine gather nuts, Antoine relates a tale about a Frenchman in Canada who followed some bear tracks to where they went into a hole. For two or three hours the Canuck waited for the bear to come out of the hole, but the hunter got thirsty and leaning his gun against a tree went to a brook for a drink. But when his back was turned the bear came out of its hole and got between the man and his gun. According to Antoine, the Canuck ran home and left his gun in the forest.[25]

One bear folktale in Robinson's works is not told within a frame story set in Lisha's shop or on a camping trip, but the tale is presented as if it really happened to Uncle Lisha. In *Uncle Lisha's Shop* Lisha sets a spring gun in his cornfield in hopes that he will catch a bear that has been eating his corn. Later when Lisha is about to tell Antoine a tale, the gun goes off, and Lisha runs to the field, with Antoine stumbling along behind. Lisha charges the wounded bear, and after a short fray the bear finally falls to the ground. In the excitement, however, Lisha mistakes the bear's insides for his own entrails, and he gathers them in his apron. The old shoemaker believes he is dying and sends Antoine for the doctor, who upon examination of the contents of the apron angrily enlightens Lisha as to the owner of the entrails.[26] Dorson reports the same theme of the mistaken entrails in a bear story from Maine. This variant—printed in the Portland, Maine, *Telegram* on August 5, 1934—runs:

> We heard a growl and a scream. When we arrived, we heard groans and moans. We had nothing for defence but an old axe, which we used upon the bear with no response. The bear was dead, and poor Jack underneath. We got hold of the bear and dragged him off. Jack was a sad sight but still alive. There was gore a-plenty. We soon made a litter from barrel staves and poles, and moved him to camp, where poor Jack would often say to Aleck, "Tell Mother, I died aisy."
>
> There was still life, and a doctor was needed next, so we were debating which should go and who should stay. It occurred to us that Jack should not die in such a bloody condition. I heated some water and we went to work to make him more respectable. Gently we began around the edges. Things looked better. Little by little we removed the blood and then the intestines 'till at last neither blood nor intestines—not a scratch, not a bruise. The charge had scattered when the musket busted, and most of the old iron entered said bear's bay window. With the bear's dying spring, he had knocked Jack into a brush pile, then fell dead upon him emptying the bay window into Jack's pants and under his shirt tail. We convinced Jack that he was not dead after a spell.[27]

During one of the sessions in Uncle Lisha's shop the conversation about the pros and cons of marriage encourages Uncle Lisha to tell a bear story about an old couple who after thirty years of marriage fell out about something and maintained a long period of silence. Each wished the other would break the silence, but neither would speak first. Finally, one night they heard a rumpus among the sheep in the yard, and the old man went out to investigate. When he failed to return, the old woman followed and found her husband clinched with a large bear. "Go it, ol' man, go it, bear," she said, "it's the fust fight ever I see 'at I didn't keer which licked." After a while, however, when the old lady saw that her husband was tiring, she picked up a stake and walloped the bear on the head. But she had not only saved her husband, she had broken the silence. And Lisha concludes that the couple "lived together as folks ortu, tu the eend of the' days."[28] Dorson has traced this tale to a nineteenth-century jokebook, *The American Joe Miller* (London, 1865); and he also points out that it "persists in Wisconsin, and is credited to the 'walking, stalking library of stories,' Abe Lincoln."[29]

Sam Lovel lies about a bear, too. Sam maintains that he weighed a bear by lifting it:

. . . "Ah, wal, Uncle Lisher, I ketched a-nuther bear t'day."

"Du tell!" said Lisha, drawing hard on the waxed ends with which he was closing up a ripped boot-leg. "Wal, Sam, was he 's heavy 's ole Cap'n Powerses hawg was? 'Killed tew hawgs terday," says 'e, 'both on 'em good ones, but one on 'em was a sollaker, I tell ye—weighed ninety!' Was ye' bear's heavy's that, Sam?"

"Wal," Sam asked, "haows three hund'ed an' seventy-seven? That's his heft ezackly."

"Real weight or guess weight?" some one asked.

"Why, real weight, 'f course, an' no guessin' 'baout it."

"Where 'd ye weigh him?"

"T' hum," Sam replied shortly.

"Sho!" sneered the doubter, "ye hain't got no scales nor bolances! Haow could ye weigh 'im t' hum?"

"Wal, naow, I did weigh 'im fair an' hones', an' he weighed jist ezackly what I tell ye. I c'n lift jist three hund'ed an' fifty paound, an' I couldn't lift him inter j-e-s-t twenty-seven paound. Naow 'f that don't make three hund'ed and seventy-seven, I hain't got no 'rethmytic."[30]

As a matter of fact, four other tales in the Danvis stories include motifs of remarkable skills or strength. In *Uncle Lisha's Shop*, for example, Uncle Lisha tells Antoine and a half score of his other neighbors a tall tale about a shoemaker who was so skillful with his knife that he was hired at all the great occasions to slice bread until he got excited slicing bread at a shearing and cut himself and another man in two and wounded a third man. The two truncated men were stuck together again, but the incident spoiled the shoemaker's breadcutting business.[31] In *Sam Lovel's Camps* Joseph Hill tells Antoine about a man who was a skillful chewer. "I've hearn tell o' some ol' fishin' critter," says Joseph, " 'at c'ld put his hunks o' fish int' one corner o' his maouth an' let the bones run aout o' t'other corner, an' keep on fillin' up comf'able."[32]

A couple of tall tales in the Danvis stories involve the motif of remarkable jaws or teeth.[33] In *Uncle Lisha's Outing* after the Danvis cronies find a campsite and unload their provisions and utensils from the wagon, Sam drives the horses to the nearest farmhouse to find keeping for the animals. On Sam's return to camp he says that he found a place to keep the horses; but he adds that he hopes they can keep Antoine from the farm, "fer I'm afeared if he hears much o' the ol' feller's talk 'at owns the place he'll larn tu lie." The old farmer, Sam says, "tol' me, a-lookin' as honest as the cooper's caow, haow 'at he was a-patchin' the ruff of his barn, today, an' somehaow er nother he begin tu slip, an' kep' a-slippin', an' could n't stop himself no way, till jest as he went over the eaves, feet fust an' face daown, he ketched a holt o' the aidge o' the shingles with his teeth, an' there he hung till they fetched a ladder an' he clumb daown."[34] In *Jonathan Draws the Long Bow* Dorson reports a version of this folktale from Maine. In the Maine version a strong man fell while shingling a Baptist meeting-house and gripped the eaves with his jaws while still holding bundles of shingles under his arms. Moreover, he opened his mouth to yell for help without losing his hold on the eaves.[35]   As might be expected, Antoine matches Sam's story with a whopper about a Canadian brother-in-law with remarkable jaws. Antoine brags that one time his brother-in-law was driving a team of horses when the horses ran away and broke loose from the wagon. The brother-in-law, however, held the lines with his teeth, while he held the wagon with his hands, for more than a mile before he finally got the horses stopped.[36]

Other tall tales in the Danvis stories tell of remarkable fowls, mountain, river, and plants. In *Uncle Lisha's Outing* when Joseph tells Antoine that he is going to pluck a march hawk and save the feathers for a feather bed for his wife, Antoine maintains, "If you put de hawk fedder wid de dawk fedder he heat it all up."   And Antoine tells a whopper about when he was a boy in Canada. His mother was making a bed of goose feathers but needed a few more feathers to fill the tick. Consequently, Antoine's father shot a couple of hawks that were after the Bassettes' chickens. Mrs. Bassette plucked the hawks and put the feathers with her goose feathers to make a nice plump bed. In fact, it was such a nice bed that they used it only for company. About a year later Antoine's grandparents came to spend the night and were given the new bed. The next morning Antoine's grandmother complained that the tick was so thin that the bed ropes cut her. When the tick was examined only hawk feathers were found, for, according to Antoine, the hawk feathers had eaten the goose feathers.[37]   This tale has been reprinted in Botkin's *Treasury of New England Folklore*, but parallels from the field have not been located.[38]

Uncle Lisha's lies about the enormity of game and plants "out west" are more familiar than the hawk feathers tale. One November evening in Lisha's shop Uncle Lisha tells his friends that he would like to have "a turkey fer Thanksgivin' 's big 's what my boy 't lives in the 'Hio tells o' hevin' there, wild ones, tu, 't weighs thirty, forty paound!" When Sam Lovel and the other members of the audience question the truth of the statement, Uncle Lisha explains that out west "things grows bigger there 'n' what they does here. Why, the corn grows so high 't they have to climb up a ladder to bind the stocks, 'n' my boy writ 't the punkins grow'd so big in the 'Hio that a six-foot man stan'in' stret up couldn't tech the top on 'em!"[39]   As Dorson points out in a discussion of rich soil and big crops in New England tall tales, frequently "Yankee talk ran to lush bottoms, plenty, luxuriance, size and fertility of unexampled proportions."[40]

In a chapter of *Sam Lovel's Boy* entitled "Canadian Tales," Antoine Bassette shows up at the Lovel's home one morning to hoe in the garden, and young Sammy Lovel whiles away the morning listening to the Canuck's tales of wonderful things in Canada. Almost as soon as Antoine arrives he tells of remarkable hens that lay duck eggs; and when he notices that Sammy is eating a lump of maple sugar, the Canuck is prompted to tell a whopper about a remarkable mountain in Canada that is made of maple sugar. According to Antoine, at one time there were many maple trees growing on a large, volcanic mountain. One spring day lightning struck all the trees on the mountain, splitting them into kindling, and the sap ran off the trees into a large brook that flowed down the mountain. As the sap flowed down the mountain it boiled into maple syrup and overflowed the stream. When the syrup finally cooled, it formed a thick layer of maple sugar over the mountain. Now, according to Antoine, all one has to do is chop off the maple sugar with an axe and carry it off.[41]

Folk belief and folk hyperbole intermingle in a story about a remarkable river of milk that Antoine tells Sammy Lovel in *Sam Lovel's Boy*. Antoine tells Sammy that many years ago in Canada an old lame woman was traveling one night and stopped at a rich farmer's house for lodging; however, the farmer sent the old woman on her way. The old woman walked on until she came to a poor man's house; and although the poor man had very little to offer, he gave the old lady the best he had. The old lady was actually a witch, a familiar meddler in the dairy in folk belief,[42] and the witch caused all twenty of the rich man's cows to go dry and caused the poor man's cow to give so much milk that the milk formed a large river. Accordingly, the rude rich man became poor, and the courteous poor man became rich. Now, according to Antoine, if one goes to Canada he will find the river of milk, which also has a great waterfall that churns butter and produces buttermilk, all of which belong to the kind man.[43] Antoine's stories of a river of milk and of a mountain of maple sugar as well as Uncle Lisha's tale of the fertile soil and large crops of the Great West suggest the European mythical land of Cockaygne, where impossible things happen.[44] In *American Folklore* Dorson reports a similar instance of the paradise of Cockaygne grafted onto the Great West.[45]

Although not as numerous as the hunting tales, there are fishing yarns in Robinson's stories, too. In *Danvis Folks*, for instance, Antoine and Uncle Lisha swap fishing experiences that incorporate familiar tall tale motifs. As Antoine enters Uncle Lisha's shop one rainy day he hears Uncle Lisha mention something about fishing to Pelatiah Gove; and, of course, Antoine recalls a fishing experience he had one time in Canada. On that particular occasion Antoine threw his baited hook in the water, "an' de traout was so hongry in hees belly an' so crazy in hees head dey'll go after it so fas', de fus' one git it, de nex' one touch hol' hees mouf of dat one's tail an' de nex' de sem way till dey was twenty prob'ly 'f dey ant fifteen all in string." But as Antoine pulled in his fish, the string broke on a small fish, and he lost half the fish. The trout in the water were so hungry, however, that they began to jump at Antoine's dish of worms on the bank. Moreover, when Antoine picked up his dish of worms and started for home, the trout followed him to his door.[46] Dorson has found an anecdote similar to the first part of Antoine's tale in *The American Comic Almanac, 1833*, only the catch is wild geese and not fish. In the almanac story quoted by Dorson a gentleman tells an Irishman, "Tie a chord to the tail of an eel and throw it into the fens where the fowl haunt. One of the geese swallowing this slippery bait, it runs through him and is swallowed by a second and third, and so on till the cord is full. A person once caught so many in this way, that they actually flew away with him."[47] The last part of Antoine's tale is similar to a motif in Earl C. Beck's *Songs of the Michigan Lumberjacks*, in which a fish takes the bait of a fisherman a number of times and then follows him home.[48]

Upon hearing Antoine's whopper, Uncle Lisha maintains, "I s'pose I c'n pooty nigh match ye, Ann Twine, on'y my story's true." Then Lisha tells the following tale:

"Wal, oncte aout West, where I was in Westonstant, the' was a man went an' chopped a hole in the ice in a crik tu water his cattle, an' there was a dozen bull-paouts come up in the hole, an' he begin a-heavin' on 'em aout tu kerry 'em hum fer his dinner, but fust he knowed, it filled up full, an' he run tu git a baskit tu scoop 'em up, an' when he got back the hole was a-runnin' over wi' fish, jest a-b'ilin' over on 't the ice, an' kep' a-duin' so till they run over on t' the shore furder an' furder, till he begun to be afeared they'd kiver up his farm an' spile it. But the folks begun tu hear on 't an' come wi' their teams fm twenty mild off, an' hauled the bullpaouts away in reg'lar percessions, thirty forty sled-loads in a string, an' fed 'em to the' hawgs, an' m'nured the' land wi' them, till folks did n't know whether they was eatin' pork or fish, on'y fer bein' no bones, an' the hull country smelt like a fish kittle all summer."

Uncle Lisha looked around upon his audience, all of whom except Antoine, who asked:—

"You'll see dat, Onc' Lasha?"

"Wal, no; it happened the winter afore I went there, an' I didn't ezactly see it, but I smelt it."[49]

The same theme of the remarkable catch of bullheads appears in a letter by Robinson to the editor of *Forest and Stream*. Concerning a printed version of the tale in an earlier issue of *Forest and Stream*, Robinson writes:

It seemed to me when I read that Kekoskee fish story that I had heard something like it before from my neighbor Chase. Chancing to meet him a few days ago, I questioned him concerning it.

"Yes," he answered, "I read the story in the paper. I was there an' I can tell you what I seen. The hole was so full of bullheads that a man couldn't drive a spear to the bottom of it, an' when he pulled it up maybe there'd be a dozen on it all stuck together by the' horns. I rigged a bushel basket with ropes in the handles, an' we c'd push it just underneath the surface with a pole an' histe it right out again chuck full o' bullheads, with now and then a pickerel, till we filled a thirty-bushel sleigh box as full of 'em as it c'd hold. An' while we was there there was eighteen such sleighs loaded with 'em runnin' over full, and the road for a mile was black and read [sic] with bullheads that had spilled off and got smashed and trompled. Yes, sire, that's what I see myself; but they did tell the almightiest lies about it in that paper!"[50]

Apparently, then, Rowland Robinson learned the whopper about the bullheads from a neighbor. But in addition to his first-hand knowledge of oral tales, Robinson was also acquainted with long bow literature from the classic whoppers of Baron von Munchausen to the printed windies of nineteenth-century journalism. For instance, in "Major Joseph Verity: Some of His Sporting Adventures, as Modestly Set Forth By His Own Hand," Robinson makes explicit reference to Baron von Munchausen and to a definite Munchausen motif when he speaks of the "account of a famous German baron concerning his jacket made of the skin of a celebrated pointer, which, when he wore it, always led him to game."[51] Although Robinson's source is avowedly literary, this motif has been collected from the American oral tradition. For example, Vance Randolph reports that an Arkansas hunter was so heartbroken when his super coon dog died that he made a vest out of the animal's pelt. One night when the hunter took off his vest and lay down to rest in the woods, he fell asleep but suddenly was awakened by a loud noise coming from a hill not far from him. Upon investigation the hunter found that his vest had treed five coons.[52]

Furthermore, Llewellyn R. Perkins, the editor of the Centennial Edition of Rowland Robinson's works, notes, "There is little doubt that the Major Verity tales, an obvious parody upon Baron Munchausen, were written as a satire upon 'Adirondack' Murrey's hunting and fishing tales."[53] Internal evidence, too, indicates that Robinson was familiar with printed versions of traditional stories in popular journals. In "Major Joseph Verity," for example, the major points out that one of his friends told tales borrowed from newspapers as if they were his own adventures. To prove his point, Verity relates a tale that his friend told him and explains that "I have lately seen this story going the rounds of the papers as having happened somewhere out West, which appears to be the home of big stories as well as of other big things." The tale Verity speaks of is a traditional one. The major's friend, while fishing with another man, lost his powder horn overboard. The fishing partner volunteered to dive for the horn, but he stayed under the water for such a long time that Verity's friend became concerned and dived in to investigate, only to find the first diver on the bottom pouring powder out of the lost horn into his own.[54] In the Adirondacks this same folktale is attributed to old Mart Moody, a guide of the Tupper Lake Region,[55] while in Arkansas the same tale involves Davy Crockett.[56] But since Robinson has Major Verity say that the tale made the rounds of the newspapers, most likely Robinson was familiar with journalistic treatments of this folktale.

As a matter of fact, the tall tales in "Major Joseph Verity" represent Rowland Robinson's earliest attempt to use long bow motifs in literature, and his treatment of the yarns seems to have been regulated in part by the journalistic treatments of folk humor in vogue during the middle decades of the nineteenth century. At any rate, Robinson's purpose for writing the adventures of Verity apparently was different from his conscious effort in the Danvis stories to preserve oral stories and folk dialect in authentic rural settings. Unlike the folktales Robinson uses in his Danvis stories, the embroidered folklore motifs in "Major Joseph Verity: Some of His Sporting Adventures, as Modestly Set Forth By His Own Hand" are not related in realistic folk speech and are not set in authentic yarn-spinning situations. Instead, in "Major Joseph Verity" Robinson adopts the literary convention of the travelers' tale. As Dorson points out in "Legends and Tall Tales," "The tall tale grew naturally out of the travelers' tales that flourished in the seventeenth century when curious explorers visited the Americas and the Far East."[57] Dorson explains that the colonial travelers' tales were told as true adventures, but he adds that "by the nineteenth century these marvels are being told as tongue-in-cheek tall tales."[58] Such is the case with Robinson's Verity tales. Major Verity reports in first person wonders he has experienced or seen in another part of the country. Like other yarn-spinners in the tradition of the traveler, Verity boasts of his own prowess in hunting and fishing and tells of the remarkable climate and topography of a strange land, Adironda.

Moreover, unlike his handling of the folktales in the Danvis stories, within the tales told by Major Verity, Robinson sometimes imposes his own sympathy toward nature. Consequently, although the artistically wrought folktales retold in the Danvis stories certainly cannot be mistaken for faithful transcriptions of oral tales from the field, the tales incorporated into "Major Joseph Verity" are even farther removed from oral style. For example, one of Verity's tales in which Robinson moralizes and stylizes runs:

I was still-hunting on the first snow, which that season fell late for Adironda, it being then about the middle of September. I had tracked a fine buck, as I knew by the size of his footprints, only about twenty miles one morning, when I came upon him lying down to rest under a great hemlock. He was one of the largest I ever saw, and I stood a moment admiring his graceful pose and noble proportions before I should send the leaden messenger of death to lay him low, and must confess that I hesitated to speed it on its murderous errand. What sportsman worthy of the name has not at times, even in the ardor of the chase, had an almost overpowering softness of heart come upon him, a pity for the poor hunted object of his pursuit, a questioning of his conscience as to what right he has to take the life of a creature vastly his superior in innocence and harmlessness? Thus for a short space I stood, almost wishing that the buck were not so entirely at my mercy; but there were short commons in camp, and I had the butt of my rifle almost at my shoulder when somehow my attention was drawn to the great hemlock by a slight stir of a branch. Looking closer I saw an enormous panther crouching there, just ready for a spring upon the deer lying all unconscious of the two-fold danger lurking so near him. Now I saw the way out of my shedding the blood of the buck. How many of us are willing enough to see another commit, without lifting a hand to prevent, an act of cruelty we shrink from doing ourselves, and then holding ourselves conscience-free?

As the panther, assured of his aim, sprang out of the screen of evergreen branches in a great curve, I fired at his heart, and he fell upon the deer, crushing him beneath his weight, and rending the remaining life out of him in his terrible deaththroes. I rushed forward to give the panther a finishing shot, but it was not needed, for the first had done its work completely, and the giant cat lay dead stretched upon his intended prey. As I stood looking with some pride upon my handsome morning's work, my attention was called to a violent commotion in the undergrowth a little beyond, and going to see the cause of it, I found it to be a fine doe, whose back had been broken by the same bullet which killed the panther. Dispatching her with my knife, and turning her over to disembowel her, I found a grouse that, having burrowed in the snow, had been killed by the doe in her flounderings, and presently I stumbled over a hare that had been frightened to death by the noise, and the bloody scene which had been so suddenly enacted before him.

Now, of course all this, except the killing of the panther and the subsequent death of the buck, was purely fortuitous, and I claim no credit but for the well timed shot, yet I think it has seldom happened that one shot has brought one so much game, large and small, as did this.[59]

This tale is a variant of "The Lucky Shot," one of the most popular tales in the United States. "The Lucky Shot" is also well known in Europe, but in the European versions the game is usually killed by an accidental discharge of the gun, while Robinson's version conforms to the American variants in which the gun is used deliberately but luckily.[60] As Dorson has demonstrated in his article "Jonathan Draws the Long Bow," the tale of "The Lucky Shot" appeared in print in the United States as early as 1809 in a farmers' almanac. In this early American version of the tale—entitled a "Wonderful Story related by George Howell, a mighty Hunter, and known in the part of the country where he lived by the name of the Vermont Nimrod"— George Howell, with a single shot, bags a buck, a sturgeon, a rabbit, a woodcock, three partridges, and opens a honey tree. Dorson also gives versions of this popular tale from New England newspapers, local history, verse, and oral tradition.[61]

Dorson has pointed out, "The free-and-easy masculine society of the frontier and the back country relished tall tales of hunting, fishing, changeable weather, fast-growing crops, mythical animals, and the reversal of natural laws."[62] The familiar tall tale motifs in Robinson's "Major Joseph Verity" are clearly within this tradition. Like other heroes of American tall tales, such as Davy Crockett, Joseph Verity was a very precocious child who began his career with deeds of strength.[63] For instance, as a young man Verity could crush sap from a maple limb and could strangle a panther with a single hand, and even before that Verity shot houseflies on the wing with a popgun and caught minnows with a pin-hook of his own invention. At the age of ten he was an expert archer who could shoot an arrow upward and split it with another arrow as the first one descended. As a matter of fact, he could even shoot six arrows one after another, and each arrow would overtake the preceding one and strike it in the nock; consequently, when the six arrows fell they would be joined together into a single rod.[64] A similar feat is performed in Masterson's *Tall Tales of Arkansaw* when bullets shot at the same spot fuse together to form a rod, which is then used for a clothesline.[65]

Verity's skill in inventing did not end with his childhood. As a young man he invented a gun with an extremely long barrel, along which the ball was accelerated by relays of ignited powder. The gun could shoot so far that on one occasion when the major fired the gun, the ball traveled all the way around the world and struck Verity in the leg. In fact, the gun could reach game at such a distance that in hot weather a bird killed with the gun would spoil before Verity could pick it up.[66] In more recent years this motif has become associated with Paul Bunyan.[67] The motif of salting the bullet of a great gun to prevent spoilage of the game appeared about 1901 in a jokebook, Melville D. Landon's *Wit and Humor of the Age*,[68] and the same motif has been reported from the Kansas oral tradition as late as 1951. Clarence Sharp of Pittsburg, Kansas, told Vance Randolph that when he was a boy near Dutch Mills, Arkansas, he used to kill geese so high in the air that he put salt on the bullets to keep the birds from spoiling before they hit the ground.[69]

Other familiar folklore motifs can also be found in Robinson's "Major Joseph Verity." For instance, Major Verity had a red retriever that was so fast that the dog's hair flew off as it ran, leaving a red streak that enabled Verity to easily follow the dog. Furthermore, the dog brought back birds with such speed that they would be featherless when the retriever reached its master. In addition, Verity had a one-eyed hunting partner, who would help him take hold of a side of a hole of a fox, otter, or muskrat and turn the hole inside out, enabling their dogs to kill whatever animals were in the hole.[70]

When game became scarce in Major Verity's locality, he frequently took extended trips to Adironda, a remarkable region that in some ways resembles Schlaraffenland.[71] For Adironda, although not a glutton's paradise like the European Schlaraffenland, is certainly a hunter's paradise and a land where impossible things happen. For instance, in one place in Adironda, Verity saw a monkey, not at all indigenous to the region, disappear into a great pit, which upon investigation turned out to be a hole leading all the way to the other side of the earth, explaining the presence of a monkey in such an unnatural environment.[72] The motif of a remarkable passage through the center of the earth is familiar to readers of Munchausen. On one occasion, for instance, Munchausen passed from Mount Etna through the center of the earth to the South Seas.[73] According to Verity, though, even stranger than the passage to the other side of the earth was an extraordinary fountain of condensed water. Verity once drank the remarkable fountain, and when the condensed water expanded, it spurted from every pore in the major's body.[74]

Other common folklore motifs in "Major Joseph Verity" include lies about cold weather and thick fog. Verity reports that on certain elevated areas of Adironda the weather in midwinter equalled that of the Arctic. In fact, it sometimes became so cold in Adironda that food froze in one's stomach. Moreover, the blaze of the campfire even froze to the bottom of the camp kettle, and the frozen flames had to be chopped off.[75] In addition, the fog in Adironda was once so thick that Major Verity was unable to see his hand only a half-arm's length before him. Lost in the heavy fog, Verity fired his rifle into the air to summon help, and the rifle ball cut a hole through the dense fog to the blue sky above. But when Verity shot point-blank into the thick fog, the bullet traveled only about a hundred yards before halting mid-air. Major Verity tells of one unfortunate trapper who got caught in such a heavy fog during a sudden drop in temperature. The trapper became frozen in the fog and had to chop himself out.[76]

Other lies in the Verity adventures include tales of a thick flock of birds, mythical fish, and remarkable or great catches of fish. In Adironda Verity camped by a small lake that mysteriously raised about three feet each night and returned to its normal level at daybreak. Verity discovered the secret of the rising lake, however, when on one occasion he found the lake wedged with an enormous number of ducks, which settled on the lake each night, causing it to rise.[77] In another lake in Adironda Verity found singing fish, whose music served to attract insects. One winter Verity caught some of the fish by a remarkable trick. He tossed an artificial lure over the transparent ice, causing the fish to stun themselves on the ice as they struck at the hookless lure. Consequently, the major had only to chop through the ice, pick up the unconscious fish, and toss them behind him on the ice, where they soon froze. But that night when the fish thawed, Major Verity was awakened by singing coming from a bucket of water in which the fish had been placed.[78] From the Ozarks, Vance Randolph reports, "Old tales about fish humming or singing so loud that campers are unable to sleep on the gravel bars have often been repeated in newspapers and elsewhere."[79]

Besides the lake of the singing fish, another remarkable lake in Adironda was a small body of salt water within a rock-rimmed bowl of mountains. The basin, once a dry valley, was the site of a fierce conflict between two great Indian nations. During the battle many braves on both sides were slain, and a month after the war and each year after that for hundreds of years all the women of both nations gathered to weep for the slaughtered braves. From the tears of these Indian women was formed the remarkable inland salt water lake in Adironda.[80]

Of course, Major Joseph Verity also had a number of adventures with bears in Adironda. One time, for instance, a female bear chased the major around a large tree, and Verity was unable to get a shot at the bear until he bent the barrel of his gun to conform to the circumference of the tree. Verity hit the bear, but the bullet passed through the animal and kept sailing around the tree, barely missing Major Verity until at last a male bear came up to sniff his dead mate. Then the bullet hit the male bear and lodged into him, thus giving the major two bears with a single shot.[81] Here Robinson uses a widespread American tale in which a gun barrel is bent to make a spectacular shot. In the Adirondacks Mart Moody twisted his gun barrel, and the bullet traveled around a mountain three times killing two bears and a woodchuck.[82] A variant in the Ozarks tells of a man who had a blacksmith bend the barrel of his rifle so he could shoot a deer that always escaped him by dodging around a mountain before the hunter could fire.[83]

On another occasion Major Verity found himself facing a bear when he was without shot large enough to kill such a large animal. Luckily, however, the major had with him some unusual beans that swelled to an extraordinary size when cooked. As the bear approached him, Verity loaded both barrels of his gun with the beans and fired the beans right down the bear's throat. As the bear kept pursuing the major, the warmth and moisture in the animal's stomach caused the beans to swell until the bear finally burst.[84] Similar stories of hunters in danger who use unusual ammunition or other ingenious methods to kill an animal are abundant in folklore. Common substitutes for rifle balls are cherry pits or peach pits.[85] In other tales a hunter without ammunition or gun throws a stone in the open mouth of a bear and tosses a piece of flint in the rectum of the bear. When the stones meet the bear explodes.[86] Another time in Adironda Major Verity killed a remarkable bear that had nearly as much hair on the inside of its pelt as it had on the outside. In fact, even the bear's claws and eyeballs were coated with fur. According to Verity, a drop of oil from the bear would grow hair on the smoothest face or on the palm of the hand. Indeed, one man tasted the bear grease and hair even grew on his tongue. During one of the cold spells in Adironda the oil saved the major and a friend from freezing when after rubbing oil on their bodies they sprouted hair.[87]

With a clerical friend, Major Verity also had contests in canoeing and running up a waterfall in Adironda. In the canoeing contest neither the canoe of Verity nor that of his friend touched the water once in ten yards. The contest in running up the waterfall, however, was easily won by the major's friend, who took hold of the tail of a large trout as the fish was scaling the waterfall.[88]

Among other marvelous things that Major Joseph Verity observed in Adironda were worms as large as a man's wrist and a foot in length feeding on remarkable mulberries as large as saucers. Furthermore, Verity caught a fish so long that it could swim only endwise in a stream.[89] Vance Randolph reports that in Arkansas, too, some people say there is a catfish so large that it cannot turn around in White River.[90]

In Adironda, Major Verity also saw a panther chasing its tail, finally catching it between its teeth, and swallowing the tail until it finally swallowed itself. Another time Verity caught two sleeping panthers by tying their tails together and hoisting them to the top of a tree; however, when the panthers awoke they fought so fiercely that at the end of the fight only two tails and some shreds of skin were left. Major Verity's tremendous strength, however, finally led to a temporary disablement of the mighty hunter, for Verity was crippled while hunting a panther when he caught the animal's tail as it was climbing a tree. The major gave the tail such an awful yank that he pulled the tail off, and along with the tail came the spinal marrow, which paralyzed the panther and brought it down upon the major, breaking most of Verity's bones.[91] In *Jonathan Draws the Long Bow* Dorson gives a similar motif of a strong puller who grabbed a bull's tail and pulled it off.[92]

NOTES

[1]Dorson, *Jonathan Draws the Long Bow*, p. 3.

[2]This is Type 1916 in Antti Aarne and Stith Thompson, *The Types of the Folktale* (Helsinki, 1964). Motif X1116 (a), "Hunter notices crack in tree open and close. . . . finds great number of raccoons asleep in tree" (Baughman).

[3]Robinson, *Uncle Lisha's Shop and A Danvis Pioneer*, pp. 220-21.

[4]Vance Randolph, *We Always Lie to Strangers* (New York, 1961), pp. 100-101.

[5]Dorson, *Jonathan Draws the Long Bow*, p. 228.

[6]Motif X1124, "Lie: the hunter catches or kills game by ingenious or unorthodox method."

[7]Robinson, *Sam Lovel's Boy with Forest and Stream Fables*, p. 127.

[8]Robinson, *Uncle Lisha's Shop and A Danvis Pioneer*, p. 159.

[9]Robinson, *Sam Lovel's Camps and In the Green Wood*, pp. 59-60.

[10]Type 1896, "The Man Nails the Tail of the Wolf to the Tree."

[11]Type 1891, "The Great Rabbit-Catch."

[12]Robinson, *Uncle Lisha's Outing and Along Three Rivers*, p. 180. Motif X1606.2.4*, "Wild fowl are frozen into lake by quick, hard freeze" (Baughman). Cf. Motifs X1606.2 (Baughman); X1115 (b) (Baughman).

[13]Robinson, *In New England Fields and Woods*, pp. 232-33.

[14]James R. Masterson, "Travelers' Tales of Colonial Natural History," *Journal of American Folklore*, LIX (1946), 61. Randolph, *We Always Lie to Strangers*, pp. 95, 100. Motif X1119.1 (c), "Thick pigeons darken sky" (Baughman).

[15]See Baughman's notes for Motif X1121.2* (b), "Man shoots great gun at flock of birds; the falling birds cover hunter up."

[16]Robinson, *Uncle Lisha's Shop and A Danvis Pioneer*, p. 167. Motif X1122.4* (f), "Hunter shoots over top of hill at turkey's gobble, kills turkey" (Baughman).

[17]Robinson, *Sam Lovel's Boy with Forest and Stream Fables*, p. 39.

[18]Type 1896*. Motif X1124.4, "Hunting wolves with rod and line."

[19]Robinson, *Danvis Folks and A Hero of Ticonderoga*, pp. 122-23.

[20]Harold W. Thompson, p. 292. Motif X1124 (c), "Hunter pours barrels of honey on ground in long narrow, straight line" (Baughman).

[21]Richard M. Dorson, "Just B'ars," *Appalachia*, n.s., VIII (December 1942), 174.

[22]Robinson, *Uncle Lisha's Outing and Along Three Rivers*, p. 95.

[23]Archer Taylor, *The Proverb and An Index to "The Proverb"* (Hatboro, Pennsylvania, 1962), p. 156.

[24]Motif X1133, "Lie: the hunter in danger."

[25]Robinson, *Uncle Lisha's Outing and Along Three Rivers*, p. 171. Cf. Motif X1221 (bb), "Hunter is treed by bear, leaving gun on ground" (Baughman).

[26]Robinson, *Uncle Lisha's Shop and A Danvis Pioneer*, pp. 128-36.

[27]Dorson, "Just B'ars," pp. 178-79.

[28]Robinson, *Danvis Folks and A Hero of Ticonderoga*, pp. 191-92. Cf. Motif T272.1, "Silent wife brought to speech by dangers to her husband."

[29]Dorson, *Jonathan Draws the Long Bow*, pp. 226-27.

[30]Robinson, *Uncle Lisha's Shop and A Danvis Pioneer*, pp. 140-41. Motif X1015*, "Lie: remarkable ability to determine weight" (Baughman).

[31]Robinson, *Uncle Lisha's Shop and A Danvis Pioneer*, p. 139. Motif X980, "Lie: occupational or professional skill."

[32]Robinson, *Sam Lovel's Camps and In the Green Wood*, p. 131. Motif X933, "Lie: remarkable chewer."

[33]Motif X916 (c), "Remarkable jaws and teeth" (Baughman).

[34]Robinson, *Uncle Lisha's Outing and Along Three Rivers*, p. 30.

[35]Dorson, *Jonathan Draws the Long Bow*, p. 241. Motif X916 (cb), "Man with bale of shingles under each arm grabs eaves with teeth when ladder slips" (Baughman).

[36]Robinson, *Uncle Lisha's Outing and Along Three Rivers*, p. 30. Motif X916 (cc), "Man holds on to wagon with hands, holds lines of runaway horses in teeth until he gets horses stopped" (Baughman).

[37]Robinson, *Uncle Lisha's Outing and Along Three Rivers*, pp. 102-103, Cf. Motif X1267, "Lies about hawks" (Baughman).

[38]Botkin, *A Treasury of New England Folklore*, p. 161.

[39]Robinson, *Uncle Lisha's Shop and A Danvis Pioneer*, p. 150. The motifs are: X1265* (b), "Large turkey" (Baughman); X1402.3.4*, "Lie: length of great cornstalk" (Baughman); X1411.2, "Lies about large pumpkins" (Baughman).

[40]Dorson, *Jonathan Draws the Long Bow*, p. 127. Cf. Motif X1532, "Rich soil produces remarkable crop" (Baughman).

[41]Robinson, *Sam Lovel's Boy with Forest and Stream Fables*, p. 47. Motifs X1262*, "Remarkable chickens" (Baughman); X1528, "Mountain of unusual material" (Baughman).

[42]Kittredge, *Witchcraft in Old and New England*, pp. 163-173.

[43]Robinson, *Sam Lovel's Boy with Forest and Stream Fables*, pp. 48-49. Motifs Q2, "Kind and unkind"; X1547, "Lie: remarkable river."

[44]Type 1930, "Schlaraffenland." Motif X1503.

[45]Richard M. Dorson, *American Folklore* (Chicago, 1959), p. 52.

[46]Robinson, *Danvis Folks and A Hero of Ticonderoga*, pp. 171-72. Motifs X1307* (b), "Fish are so eager to be caught that one grasps tail of one already on hook; another grasps its tail, and so on" (Baughman); X1313* (a), "Fish jump at dish of worms on bank; the fisherman runs home, has to slam door to keep fish out" (Baughman).

[47]Quoted in Dorson, *Jonathan Draws the Long Bow*, p. 229.

[48]Earl C. Beck, *Songs of the Michigan Lumberjacks* (Ann Arbor, 1942), p. 286. Motif X1307* (a), "Fish takes bait of man several times, then follows him home" (Baughman).

[49]Robinson, *Danvis Folks and A Hero of Ticonderoga*, p. 172. Motif X1317 (a), "Fisherman cuts hole in ice; bullpouts spill out so fast and in such numbers that people come for miles around, take away loads for hog feed and fertilizer" (Baughman).

[50]*Forest and Stream* (November 18, 1893).

[51]Robinson, *Sam Lovel's Boy with Forest and Stream Fables*, p. 203. See Baron Munchausen, *The Adventures of Baron Munchausen* (New York, 1944), p. 215. Motif X1215.13* (b), "Man makes bottle of dog skin" (Baughman).

[52]Randolph, *We Always Lie to Strangers*, pp. 129-30.

[53]*Sam Lovel's Boy with Forest and Stream Fables*, p. 184. Apparently, Perkins is referring to William H. H. Murray, who wrote a number of books on Adirondack camp life and tales. See, for instance, his *Adventures in the Wilderness; or Camp-Life in the Adirondacks* (Boston, 1870), of which a copy is still in Robinson's library at Rokeby.

[54]Robinson, *Sam Lovel's Boy with Forest and Stream Fables*, p. 199. Motif X1737.2* (d), "Man pours gunpowder from another's horn into his own on lake

bottom" (Baughman).

[55]Harold W. Thompson, pp. 289-90.

[56]Randolph, *We Always Lie to Strangers*, p. 162.

[57]Richard M. Dorson, "Legends and Tall Tales," *Our Living Traditions*, ed. Tristram Potter Coffin (New York, 1968), p. 167.

[58]Dorson, "Legends and Tall Tales," p. 168.

[59]Robinson, *Sam Lovel's Boy with Forest and Stream Fables*, pp. 207-208.

[60]See Dorson, *American Folklore*, p. 45; and Stith Thompson, *The Folktale* (New York, 1946), p. 214. Type 1890, "The Lucky Shot." Motifs X1110, "The wonderful hunt"; X1124.3, "Accidental discharge of gun kills much game."

[61]Richard M. Dorson, "Jonathan Draws the Long Bow," *The New England Quarterly*, XVI (June 1943), 253-59.

[62]Dorson, "Legends and Tall Tales," p. 168.

[63]See Dorson, *American Folklore*, pp. 209-211.

[64]Robinson, *Sam Lovel's Boy with Forest and Stream Fables*, pp. 185-86. Motifs X912, "Lie concerning babyhood and boyhood of hero"; T585, "Precocious infant"; F611.3.2, "Hero's precocious strength."

[65]James R. Masterson, *Tall Tales of Arkansaw* (Boston, 1942), p. 69. Motif X981* (dd), "Man shoots series of bullets at same spot; the bullets fuse together into rod, are used for clothesline" (Baughman).

[66]Robinson, *Sam Lovel's Boy with Forest and Stream Fables*, pp. 187-88. Motifs X1121, "Lie: the great marksman's remarkable gun" (Baughman); X1121.1*, "Lie: great gun shoots bullet a great distance" (Baughman); X1121.1.1*, "Gun kills game so far away from hunter that the meat spoils by the time he picks it up" (Baughman); X1121.1.2*, "Hunter salts bullets of great gun so game will not spoil while he walks to get it" (Baughman).

[67]See Baughman's notes for Motif X1121.1.1*.

[68]Melville D. Landon, *Wit and Humor of the Age* (Chicago, c. 1901), pp. 181-82.

[69]Randolph, *We Always Lie to Strangers*, p. 119.

[70]Robinson, *Sam Lovel's Boy with Forest and Stream Fables*, pp. 187-88. Motifs X1215.7, "Lie: fast dog" (Baughman); X1761 (b), "Men pull up hole in which animals are living" (Baughman).

[71]Type 1930, "Schlaraffenland." Motif X1503. Cf. Motif X1531*, "Remarkable country" (Baughman).

[72]Robinson, *Sam Lovel's Boy with Forest and Stream Fables*, p. 193.

[73]Munchausen, pp. 191-92. Motif X1545.1, "Water passage through the earth"(Baughman).

[74]Robinson, *Sam Lovel's Boy with Forest and Stream Fables*, pp. 193-95. Cf. Motifs F716, "Extraordinary fountain"; X1543, "Lies about springs" (Baughman).

[75]Robinson, *Sam Lovel's Boy with Forest and Stream Fables*, pp. 192-93. Motifs X1620, "Lies about cold weather" (Baughman); X1622.3.2*, "Cold affects food" (Baughman); X1622.3.3*, "Cold affects liquids" (Baughman); X1623.3.1* (eb), "Frozen flames have to be cut off" (Baughman).

[76]Robinson, *Sam Lovel's Boy with Forest and Stream Fables*, pp. 195-196. Motifs X1651, "Lies about fog" (Baughman); X1623.5*, "Fog freezes (Baughman); X1606.2, "Lies about quick change in weather from warm to cold" (Baughman).

[77]Robinson, *Sam Lovel's Boy with Forest and Stream Fables*, pp. 196-97. Motif X1119.1, "Lie thick flock of birds" (Baughman).

[78]Robinson, *Sam Lovel's Boy with Forest and Stream Fables*, pp. 198, 209-

210. Motif X1153, "Lie: fish caught by remarkable trick." Cf. Motifs 1307* (h), "Fish strike at wooden minnows, knock themselves unconscious" (Baughman); B214.1, "Singing animal." Cf. Type 1889F, "Frozen Words (Music) Thaw."

[79]Randolph, We Always Lie to Strangers, p. 229.

[80]Robinson, Sam Lovel's Boy with Forest and Stream Fables, pp. 201-202. Motif A920.1.5.1, "Lakes originate from tears." Cf. Motifs F1051, "Prodigious weeping"; X1541*, "Remarkable salt content of water" (Baughman).

[81]Robinson, Sam Lovel's Boy with Forest and Stream Fables, pp. 190-91. Type 1890E, "Gun Barrel Bent to Make Spectacular Shot" (Baughman).

[82]Harold W. Thompson, p. 290.

[83]Randolph, We Always Lie to Strangers, p. 117.

[84]Robinson, Sam Lovel's Boy with Forest and Stream Fables, pp. 191-92.

[85]See Type 1889C, "Fruit Tree Grows from Head of Deer Shot with Fruit Pits."

[86]Randolph, We Always Lie to Strangers, pp. 110-111. Motif X1124 (e), "Hunter throws big stone in bear's open mouth" (Baughman).

[87]Robinson, Sam Lovel's Boy with Forest and Stream Fables, p. 193. Motif X1221, "Lies about bears." Cf. Motifs D1023.1, "Magic hair of bear"; F544.2.3, "Tongue with hair growing on it."

[88]Robinson, Sam Lovel's Boy with Forest and Stream Fables, p. 189. Motifs X971, "Lie: remarkable oarsman" (Baughman); X1303.1, "Big fish pulls man or boat" (Baughman).

[89]Robinson, Sam Lovel's Boy with Forest and Stream Fables, pp. 205-206. Motifs X1346, "Lies about worms" (Baughman); X1410, "Lie: remarkable fruits" (Baughman); X1301.2* (d), "Bass is so long that it must lie endwise in river" (Baughman).

[90]Randolph, We Always Lie to Strangers, p. 215.

[91]Robinson, Sam Lovel's Boy with Forest and Stream Fables, pp. 185, 190. Motifs X1213, "Lies about panthers" (Baughman); X953, "Strong puller" (Baughman).

[92]Dorson, Jonathan Draws the Long Bow, p. 107. Motif X953 (d), "Man grabs bull by the tail to keep it from chasing people, pulls tail out by roots" (Baughman).

CHAPTER 18

OTHER FOLKTALES

Yankee stories frequently center around ludicrous mistakes,[1] and a number of the tales Robinson uses in his fiction deal with absurd misunderstandings. Three of these Danvis yarns have as their protagonist a stock character in American humorous folktales—Paddy, the immigrant Irishman, whose ignorance consistently gets him into disagreeable predicaments.[2] These Irishman stories incorporate the familiar motif of mistaking one animal for another.[3] One of these tales, told by Uncle Lisha, is "baout Joel Bartlett's Irishmun," who mistook a tomcat for a panther. Running from the pasture where he had been chopping, the Irishman cried, "Murther! oh, murther! it's a painter I seen, sure's me name's Pat Murphy!" But Joel Bartlett was able to convince the ignorant Irishman that the panther was actually a yellow tomcat.[4]

In addition, Sam Lovel tells a couple of tales in Irish brogue about Irishmen who mistook skunks for other animals. In what Robinson calls a "time honored tale," an Irishman thinks a skunk is a bird and kills it with his spade. "An' whin I wint to plook the feathers off hur," Sam repeats the tale in Irish brogue, "I was foorced to shkin hur, an' in doun that I shtruck hur ile bag or hur heart I dunno, an' the shmell nearly suffocaytit me, an' I was near shtarvin' afther, for divil a dhrink cud I take, but the shmell of hur was in me noshtrils to kape me awake all night."[5] Another tale that Sam Lovel tells is about Joel Bartlett's Irishman, who mistook a skunk for a cat. The Irishman attempts to capture the "cat" to catch mice in his house, and the consequences are similar to those in Sam's first joke about the Irish. Adopting Irish brogue again, Sam says that "whin I was about to lay me two hands on it, I was shtruck in me face an' the two eyes av me wid a stream av the divil's own wather, an' I was blindit an' shtrangled entirely." When the Irishman went into his house, his wife and children went out, and he had the shanty and the smell all to himself.[6]

In addition to the Irish immigrant, the tenderfoot from the city was also a favorite comic character in nineteenth-century anecdotes,[7] and Robinson uses the stock character of the tenderfoot in another tale involving an absurd misunderstanding. In this story, also told by Sam Lovel, a New Yorker mistakes the noise of a saw-whet owl for the buzz of a sawmill and then misunderstands similar sounding words, both common folklore motifs.[8] According to Sam, the victim of the jokes, appropriately called Mr. Van Brunt, came to the Danvis area from New York to look after his lumbering interests. As he was riding horseback through his woods, he heard a noise like someone filing a sawmill saw. Thinking someone was trespassing on his land, the New Yorker followed the noise, which periodically stopped for two or three minutes and then was heard again farther away. The gentleman decided that the trespasser had the sawmill on wheels, and rode to a tavern and told the barkeep, Hamlin, what he had heard. Then, Hamlin explained:

". . . 'Mist' Van Brunt, 't wa'n't nothin' but a saw-whet 't you hearn.' 'A saw whet!' says th' ol' gentleman, 'I know it, but a two-legged saw-whet, sir.' 'Yes, says Hamlin, 'two-legged, but he wears feathers stiddy clo's,' 'n' 'xplained. Then the ol' gentleman laughed at hisself, an' treated the hull craowd, a dozen on 'em, to ole Jamaiky sperrits 't he brought with him f'm York—twenty ye'r old, they said 't was."[9]

Of course, Antoine, too, has stories to contribute involving motifs of absurd misunderstandings. For example, in the short story "Antoine on the Rail" when Antoine relates the details of his first ride on a train, he embellishes the story with the common folklore motif of the man who fails to recognize his own reflection in a mirror.[10] Antoine tells his Danvis cronies:

"Den Ah'll look in dat leetly winder . . . an' dar was one mans look lak Frenchman, an' he was look so hard at me Ah'll mek bow at him, an' he mek bow at me. Den Ah'll grin at it kan o' pleasant, an' he do jus' de sem. Den Ah'll blow mah nose of mah new hampercher, an', bah gosh, he was pull one jus' lak it for blew his nose! Dat mek me beegin for be mad, have mek fun at me, an' Ah'll look pooty hugly at dat feller Ah'll tol' you, an' he look jus' so hugly to me!

"Ah'll shake mah fis' to him, an' he was shook hees fis' to me, and, bah gosh, Ah'll was be mad for leek it, Ah tol' you. Ah'll t'row mah hat, Ah'll jomp on it, Ah'll pull mah hairs, Ah'll holler grea' deal swore, an' dat feller do jus' sem lak me, an' bose of it faght so hard dat way lak hol' t'under more as fav minute; an', seh, dem folkses ant scare 't all, but dey was laught lak ev'ryt'ing, an' den Ah'll stop for gat mah breeze, an' den, seh, w'at you t'ink Ah'll fan' aout. Wal, seh, dat winder ant not'ing but lookin' glass, an' Ah'll be'n was'e all dat faght on mahself . . .[11]

Another of Antoine's tales of an absurd misunderstanding also incorporates several tall tale motifs. Antoine boasts that although his

Canadian brother-in-law, Jules, was an accomplished fiddler who could play three or four tunes at the same time, Jules was best at fighting.[12] According to Antoine, Jules licked most of the men around, and those he did not lick he nearly scared to death. At last, when there were no more men left to whip or scare, the boisterous Jules scared himself silly when he mistook his echo for the devil coming after him.[13] According to Antoine, one fellow, Jacques Boulanger, decided to undersell the other woodcutters, and the buyers would then give only the lower price to the other Canucks, who chopped wood and sold it for their livelihoods. Everyone was mad at Jacques but afraid to do anything about it, for Jacques was a giant of a man. On one occasion, however, Jules got tight and got into a boasting match with Jacques, although each man was twenty yards from the other, with a hollow between. Relating boasts suggesting the brags of Davy Crockett and other nineteenth-century roarers,[14] Antoine continues the tale:

"Den mah brudder-law holler some more laouder an' Jacques holler back more laouder, too, an' de echo behin' bose of it holler, too, so if dey was ten mans on de hwood. Den mah brudder-law trow hees cap an' jomp on it awful hugly, an' Jacques he paoun' hees breas' of it wid hees fis' an' say he big man' more strong anybody.

"Den mah brudder-law call him dam hol' hog an' jackasses an' bete puante, dat's skonk, an' great many kan o' t'ing an' haow easy he can leek it.

"Den dat Jacques pull off some hees hairs an' say he can heat mah brudder-law, an' den mah brudder-law lif' hese'f by hees traowser an' holler, 'Brooo,' an' echo come back, 'Brooo,' pooty hugly, Ah tol' you, raght behin' Jacques, so de peop' begin for be scare some, an' Jacques, too.

"Den mah brudder-law drink big drink off hees bottle an' gat more drunker at Jacques, an' more madder at it, an' he hopen hees maout for mek de wors' holler he'll make yet. Bah gosh he hopen it so wide de folks behin' see it comin' raoun' hees head of it an' tink it goin' for crack off, an' w'en Jacques see it raght biffore, he t'ink prob'ly mah brudder-law goin' for swaller it, an' he start for run, an' w'en de peop' over dar see dat big Jacques run dey t'ink it 'baout tam for go, too.

"Den mah brudder-law mek so awfly roar you never hear. Oh, it shake all de hwood for mile, an' w'en de echo come back more laouder an' more of it 'Brrooo, brooo, brooo,' mah brudder-law t'ink de dev' an' forty loups gareau comin' aout de hwood at him, so he'll jes' turn hese'f raoun' an' run fas' he can, 'cause he ant come dar for faght all dat hell t'ing, honly jes' man, he gat leek already. . . ."[15]

Another tale of Robinson's concerning an absurd misunderstanding suggests an international tale in which a tree is mistaken for a snake and killed with guns and spears, although it might not be in the Anglo-American tradition as Baughman does not mention it.[16] In Robinson's variant of the tale, Dan'l, a character in "A Vermont Rattlesnake," tells how he mistook a root and the buzzing of a locust for a rattlesnake. Dan'l says,

". . . Well, I hadn't cradled more 'n half way acrost the piece afore I heard a kind o' sharp buzzin' sort of a noise just ahead of me, an' I stood right still an' begin to look, an', by George! there I see a snake kinked along 'mongst the wheat, with his head raised up a little mite, not quiled up rattlesnake fashion; but I knew he was one, for he was all spotted, an' that buzzin' noise kep' a-goin' all the time, the wheat a-wigglin' right where the sound come from.

"You'd better b'lieve I backed off pretty lively, but mighty careful. I hollered to Levi to come there, an' I as'd him if that wa'n't a rattlesnake, for I knew he'd know, 'cause he'd killed 'em.

"He stood off quite respectful, but he looked at it hard. 'Yes,' says he, 'that 'ere's a rattlesnake, sartain.'

"Well, we held a council of war, an' the upshot was, Levi put for the house to git his gun 'at had been loaded for woodchuck all summer, an' I staid an' watched the snake, but the snake didn't stir none to speak of 'fore Levi got back, all out o' breath.

"We made up our minds we hadn't better depend altogether on the gun, seein' we hadn't but one charge, so I got me a good oak stake out o' the fence, an' crep' up, whilst Levi stood ready to give him a shot if I didn't lay him out. Well, I up with my club an' let the snake have it right on the head. Levi stood squintin' along the gun with his finger on the trigger. The' was a locus' riz up an' went off snappin' his wings, but the snake only kind o' flopped up an' lay stiff as a maggit."

"Killed him the first lick, didn't ye, Dan'l?"

"Good land, no! 'T wa'n't nothin' but a butt'nut root—but it was the nighest I ever came to seein' a wil' rattlesnake."[17]

Some of the absurd misunderstanding motifs in the Danvis yarns quite naturally involve the Danvis Yankees. In *Uncle Lisha's Shop*, for instance, Lisha tells Joseph Hill to "tell 'baout ye shootin' the aowl, er I will!" Joseph replies that "I guess you'd make it wus 'n I would, 'n' so I'll tell it." So Joseph tells how he was out to get an owl that had been stealing his wife's chickens. One night he saw the owl sitting on a clothesline post, poked his gun out the window, but shot over the owl. The next Monday, however, when the washing was on the line, Joseph saw the owl sitting on the same post. Determined not to overshoot it again, he aimed a foot below the owl. Again he missed the owl, but he says, "I blowed my harnsome shirt 't hung right below 'im all to flinders."[18] A few nights later in Lisha's shop Uncle Lisha gets the storytelling started by asserting, "Well, . . . le's p'cede to business, 's they say in the leegislatur. We was talkin' 'baout aowls t' other night, wa'n't we? . . . Jozeff he tol' 'baout shootin' one. Hain't ye got nothin' furder concernin' the faowl, Jozeff?" Indeed, Joseph has another tale concernin' "the faowl," and he tells "how Zene Burnham come it on his father." In this trickster story Zene Burnham sets a cabbage on the end of the well sweep and tells his father there is a large hoot owl sitting on top of the sweep. "Git the gun an' shoot 'im," says Zene. "You c'n shoot better 'n I can in the dark." The old man falls for the trick, fires away at the "owl" a couple of times, and cannot understand why the bird does not fall to the ground. Finally he pulls down the sweep and finds only a cabbage, not an owl. By this time, however, Zene has started for home and is in bed when his father gets to the house.[19] Since variants of Joseph's tales cannot be found, it is not certain that these are traditional tales. Nevertheless, the tales share the common traditional motif in which an object is mistaken for an animal,[20] and the last tale utilizes a stock character in nineteenth-century tales, the Yankee trickster.[21]

As Dorson points out, "The Yankee appeared as a scheming knave and fertile prankster who matched his wits against a suspicious world both for business and for pleasure."[22] Accordingly, the Yankee was a trickster as well as a fool. Robinson clearly shows this aspect of Yankee roguery by using in his writings several trickster stories, ranging from international folktale to local legend. A widespread tale of a clever man that Robinson uses is "The Soup Stone."[23] A little tired of the routine meals of roast duck, fried duck, and stewed duck on a camping trip, Antoine longs for oven, pans, utensils, and ingredients to make a duck pie. "Ann Twine's pie," says Uncle Lisha, "is some like the feller's soup 'at I hearn tell on." Then Uncle Lisha tells the following version of an international folktale:

". . . He was a-travelin' an' got short o' money, or mebby he was a reg'lar beggar, I do' know, but ary way, he stopped tu a haouse an' ast for somethin' tu eat, an' they would n't give him nothin'. So he ast 'em if they would n't lend him a kittle a spell an' a spwun, so 's 't he c'ld make hisself a kittle o' stun soup, an' so they did just tu see what he'd du. Wal, he built him a fire side o' the rwud an' sot a kittle o' water a-b'ilin', an' he took an' washed a stun 'baout 's big as his fist an' popped it int' the kittle, an' sot an' watched it b'ile a spell, an' then he dipped up a spoo'f'l an' tasted on 't.

" 'It's proper good,' says he, 'but it's kind er fraish, an' I wish 't I hed a leetle grain o' salt tu put into 't,' an' they went and fetched him a han'f'l an' he put that in.

" 'That's a gre't improvement,' says he, a-tastin' ag'in, 'but it would n't hurt it none if the' was a hunk o' meat in 't; any sort of a scrap 'at you was a-goin' tu heave away. I hain't partic'lar.' An' so they fetched him a good hunk o' meat an' he hove that int' the kittle, an' then says he, 'I s'pose you'd jes' 's live 's I'd pull one o' them 'ere turnips over there? This 'ere soup 's goin' tu be putty strong o' stun if it don't ha' some vegetables in 't.'

"So he went an' got him a turnip, an' whilst he was abaout it he got an onion, an' he cut 'em up an' chucked 'em in. An' when he got it b'iled he eat 'nough tu last him tew days, an' says he, a-rubbin' of his stomerk, 'The' hain't nothin' 'at makes better soup 'n a good stun, wi' a few leetle additions, an' I'm much obleeged tu ye for the use o' your kittle,' says he."[24]

Upon hearing Uncle Lisha's tale about the stone soup, Sam Lovel takes his turn by relating another popular trickster tale, "The Rum and Water Trade," a folktale having Serbo-Croatian analogues as well as a number of American versions.[25] Sam's story has as its protagonist a citizen of Danvis, Wat Palmer, the drunken fiddler in *Danvis Folks*.

According to Sam Lovel, Wat Palmer wanted a drink but had no money. So Wat got two identical pint bottles, one of which he filled with water and hid in his pocket. He carried the empty bottle into Hamner's bar and ordered a pint of the best rum. After Hamner filled the jug, Wat put it in his pocket and told the barkeep he would pay after his next job of fiddling. But Hamner refused credit and demanded the pint of rum. After a great deal of useless begging for credit, Wat gave Hamner the pint of water, and walked away with the pint of rum.[26] In a version of "The Rum and Water Trade" from New York, the trickster hero is "Boney" Quillan, a rafter well known for his talent for singing ballads and for his ability to get free drinks. One evening "Boney" found himself without rum and without cash, so he borrowed a gallon jug, which he half filled with water before walking into a tavern and ordering two quarts of rum. When the barkeep refused credit, Barney poured back two quarts of liquid and made off with a two quart mixture of rum and water.[27] As Dorson notes, "The Rum and Water Trade" was common in nineteenth-century popular literature as well as in the American oral tradition.[28]

Another trickster tale that Robinson uses suggests the motif in which the color of the devil's cows is changed while he sleeps,[29] only Robinson's tale involves a man and his oxen and not the devil and his cows. In *A Danvis Pioneer* Robinson writes that Jerry Morrison took too many pulls on the black liquor bottle that made its rounds at a logging bee. When Jerry was laid behind a log heap to sober, some practical jokers rubbed the smut from charred logs on his white oxen. When Jerry recovered he drove the blackened oxen home, halted them before his own door, and called to his wife, "If this 'ere's me, some b'dy or 'nother 's got my oxen. If it hain't me, where in thunder be I gone tu?"[30]

Variants of another trickster tale involving the motif of a sham death to avoid payment of debt are offered by Uncle Lisha and Gran'-ther Hill.[31] In *Danvis Folks* in his shop Uncle Lisha tells his cronies—Solon Briggs, Joseph Hill, Antoine Bassette, and Pelatiah Gove—about Cephas Worth. According to Danvis legend, Cephas was sugaring about a mile from home and had taken provisions for two or three days. After about a week, however, he failed to return home, so his wife, Beedy, and some neighbors set out to look for him. When they reached the sugar house, they could not find Cephas but found the shanty torn to flinders, a dozen bones gnawed clean, and a piece of a coat. Wolves' tracks were found all around. Beedy had the neighbors gather the bones to take back to Danvis, where a funeral was held for Cephas. Not long after the funeral Beedy said she could not stand to live in a place where she had suffered such a loss, so she left Danvis. About two or three years later a peddler came to the Danvis tavern and told about a man he had met in New York who claimed he once lived in Vermont and who inquired about everybody in Danvis. The peddler could not recall the man's name but said he would never forget the name of the man's wife, Beedy, because it was such an odd name. Thus, concludes Lisha, "Puttin' this an' that together, folks s'mised 't was Cephas Worth, but I d' know."[32] On the other hand, in a shorter version of the same story in another Danvis book, *Sam Lovel's Boy*, Gran'ther Hill, naturally, is more positive about what happened to Cephas. Gran'ther Hill asserts:

> "Wolves! . . . Lord Harry, Lisher! Don't you remember what a hullaballoo the' was over what 's-his-name a-bein' eat up by wolves in his sugar camp? There was his bones—sheep's bones they was,—an' I wonder the critter hed sense enough tu take huffs off, an' the snow all trampled up by the wolves,—every identical track made wi' a right forepaw! An' his woman hed a fun'ral over them bones, an' buried 'em, an' put up a gravestun, 'He is not dead, but sleepeth!" Sure 'nough, so he was, way aout in York State! . . .[33]

In a local history Robinson also reports folklore motifs, of which one is a trickster motif in which stolen property is sold to its rightful owner.[34] In *Along Three Rivers* Robinson writes that several prosperous farmers in his area of Vermont were invited by the proprietor of an old-time store to meet a New York merchant. According to Robinson, Captain Joseph Powers was not introduced to the guest from New York, so the captain presented himself:

> "Mr. _____," said he, marching up to the distinguished visitor, "I am Cap'n Joseff Powers, the greates' hunter in all this Northern kentry. Perhaps you might ha' hearn tell o' me."
> Then Joe Whitlock, who more than once secretly tapped Gen. Amos Barnum's log aqueduct to be paid in whiskey for mending the leak, and sold Captain Bradbury hoop-poles that he stole from the Captain's own woods, arose from his favorite seat nearest the liquor casks and came forward with unsteady steps.
> "Mr. _____, I'm ol' Joe Whitlock, the greates' ol' drunkard in all this Northern kentry. Perhaps you might ha' hearn tell o' me, tew . . ."[35]

Besides the trickster motif of the stolen property that was sold to its owner, this anecdote also suggests boasting motifs common in folklore.[36]

While supernatural tales are less prominent than humorous tales, the few that Robinson uses in his fiction illustrate an important phenomenon of folk culture; that is, in any living tradition along national borders or in other areas where diverse ethnic, occupational, or religious groups have settled, separate folklore repertoires often coexist along beside a common local folklore. For example, speaking of the Upper Peninsula of Michigan, Richard M. Dorson writes, "By 1940 the Peninsula presented a rich population complex . . . A spate of separate folk traditions, both ethnic and occupational, coexisted, while arching over all a new regional folklore had emerged, in the dialect humor common to the whole Peninsula."[37] Dorson proves his point in *Bloodstoppers and Bearwalkers*, where he demonstrates that in the Upper Peninsula of Michigan both Ojibwa Indians and members of various European immigrant groups maintain certain traditions unknown to neighbors outside the respective homogeneous group.[38] As a matter of fact, Dorson has recognized the same coexistence of esoteric folk traditions in Robinson's handling of folktales:

> . . . The French-Canadian wag, Antoine Bissette [sic], speaks in dialect and narrates *contes* about the *loup-garou* strangely at variance with Yankee yarns, but firmly consistent with his own tradition. Indeed, Robinson has caught the mingling of folktale repertoires that flourishes along national borders, a phenomenon rarely observed by folklorists in the field. In northern New England and the Great Lakes states, French-Canadian folk culture, nourished from the province of Quebec, has spilled over into the United States. . . .[39]

Dorson is absolutely right. In *Danvis Folks* when Antoine Bassette relates a supernatural tale of the *loup garou*, learned as a boy from his parents in Canada, Robinson comments that "Antoine's scared face gave evidence of his implicit faith in the story of the *loup garou*." But the Yankees clearly do not share the tradition of the *loup garou*, for Solon Briggs asks, "What specie of predarious animal is these 'ere loose garooses, Antwine? Be they anythin' of the human nater of a or'nary wolf or a loosevee, or a woolyneeg, or what?" In an awestricken voice Antoine explains that the *loup garou* is more like the devil than like anything else. "Dev', dev'," says Antoine. "Some tam day was mans jes lak anybodee, an' den dey was be wolfs, oh, more wusser as wolfs. Dey ketch dead mans in graveyards an' heat it, dey ketch live mans an' heat it." Then Antoine relates a tale about how his grandfather was chased by a *loup garou* as he went to get a priest for his wife, who was about to die. The old man lashed the werewolf with his whip, but the *loup garou* overtook the sleigh anyway and leaped into it. Antoine's grandfather reached for his knife, "cause ef you drew bleed of de *loup garou* he'll turn mans raght off an' go away." The old man could not find his knife, however, and thought he was finished. But as the horse pulled the man and the *loup garou* into the priest's gate, the priest, hearing the man's cries, ran out "an' say some word quick an' laoud an' de *loup garou* be mans raght off so quicker as you mek some wink an' run off in de hwood." Later a man who lived near Antoine's grandfather was seen bearing whip marks on his face for a number of days.[40] Another Canuck in the Danvis stories, Beri Burton, shares the French tradition of the *loup garou*. In *Danvis Folks* when most of the Danvis males join in a wolf hunt and the wolf is finally shot by Gran'ther Hill,

Beri Burton says, "It was some pooty good lucky dat wolf's ant be one *loup garou*. You'll can' keel dat kan o' wolfs 'less you'll shot it wid silver ball."[41]

Tales of the *loup garou*, or werewolf, brought to the New World from France,[42] are quite common among French-Canadians.[43] For instance, in his study of the Canucks in the Upper Peninsula of Michigan, Dorson points out, "For one thing, all Canadians brim over with fearful superstitions, of *loup garou* transformations . . . These are old beliefs, brought over to Canada by Norman peasants from the France of Louis XIV . . ."[44] Harold W. Thompson relates a Canuck tale from New York in which a man in a sleigh is chased by a *loup garou,* as Antoine's grandfather was.[45] Furthermore, Thompson reports a parallel method of freeing the *loup garou* from his wolf form by cutting him and offers a similar method of killing the werewolf by using a special bullet, while he also suggests religious exorcism:

> By all odds the most interesting of the French Canadian tales concern the *loup-garou*, the man-wolf so feared by the Continental French in the seventeenth century. Why a man should be transformed into a beast's shape, or should run about in man's shape acting like a beast, is variously explained; one common theory is that this is a punishment for the neglect of Easter duty during seven consecutive years. Other beast-forms beside that of the wolf are not unknown: the red bull or the white horse occur, even the devil-dog, though that is usually a form chosen only by Charlot (the devil) himself. I have heard also of a *loup-garou* having the head and tail of a wolf but otherwise retaining the form of a man. Frequently the afflicted person may be freed from his wolf-form and nature by being cut, preferably in the forehead with a cross. To kill such a beast you may use bullets with incised crosses and wadding of four-leafed clover; or a score of beads from a rosary will be potent.[46]

Another Canuck tale at odds with Yankee yarns also deals with metamorphosis. At one storytelling session around a campfire in *Uncle Lisha's Outing* Antoine tells a story about a Canadian who liked to fish so much that he was always fishing instead of doing his farm chores or fighting the Indians. His neglect of his duties disturbed the local priest so much that the clergyman changed the man into a kingfisher. All summer the kingfisher had a good time fishing everyday, but when winter came, the bird failed to fly south and kept fishing. When the surface of the river froze, the kingfisher bashed his brains out trying to catch a fish swimming just below the clear ice.[47] Dorson, discussing this tale in *Jonathan Draws the Long Bow*, remarks, "Here magic motives, moral lessons and the power of the priest indicate tales extraneous to American culture."[48]

A third Canuck tradition unfamiliar to the Danvis Yankees is the *feu follet*, the French version of the Will-o'-the-Wisp, which in widespread folk belief is a misleading sprite that generally haunts marshy places.[49] In *Uncle Lisha's Outing* Antoine sees a moving light across the creek from where the Danvis sportsmen are camping, and the Canuck says in a tone showing much alarm, "Dat was de feu follet!" The Yankees' comments, however, show that the *feu follet* is as foreign to them as the *loup garou* is:

"Few follies is better 'n many, Ann Twine," said Uncle Lisha; "but that 'ere hain't nothin' but someb'dy nuther wi' a lantern."

"Oh, no, no, no, Onc' Lasha, dat ant be lamprin' sah; dat was feu follet! Ah do' know haow you call it in Angleesh, but he was very bat t'ing, Ah tol' you."

"What is 't, Antwine?" Joseph inquired; "sort of a one-eyed lew grew critter sech as you was a-tellin' us on oncte?"

The Canadian watched the light till it vanished in fitful gleams among the woods, and then, heaving a sigh of relief, he turned and stooped to the campfire to rekindle his neglected pipe before he answered.

"No, seh, Zhozeff, he'll ant so hugly for keel someboddy lak de loup garou; he more kan o' funny for foolish someboddy. Ah'll had some experiments of it mahse'f, an' Ah'll goin' tol' you of it, me."[50]

Then Antoine tells a tale about how he was led astray by the *feu follet*. According to Antoine, when he was a young man in Canada he was riding his mare to visit his sweetheart when suddenly he saw a light on his father's farm. Thinking someone was stealing hay, Antoine hitched his mare to the fence and walked quietly toward the light. But the farther Antoine walked, the farther the light moved away from him. Chasing the light through a swamp, Antoine got his best clothes so muddy that he could not court his girl that night and consequently lost her to another young man. Antoine swears that he was tricked by the deceitful *feu follet*.[51]

In a supernatural tale told by Uncle Lisha a deceitful man is punished by some mysterious force. In a chapter of *Uncle Lisha's Shop* entitled "The Hard Experience of Mr. Abijah Jarvis," Uncle Lisha tells how a sawyer, Abijah Jarvis, met his death after tricking a boy into eating a hot turnip. Jarvis did not like the boy always hanging around the mill looking at the works and asking questions; so remembering a wild turnip he had ground and had been drying to use in cough medicine, Jarvis gave the boy the turnip on the pretense that it was a ground apple. The old man went into fits laughing at the boy spitting and sputtering, but later old Jarvis paid for his deceit. Things mysteriously started breaking down at the mill, until finally Abijah fell through a frozen pond, unable to get out until the boy he had tricked showed up and pulled him out. After that, however, Abijah was a cripple. The next summer as Jarvis sat on his stoop, the boy appeared with a wild turnip of his own and stuck it under the old man's nose. When Abijah pulled away from the turnip, his tilted chair slipped, and he fell and struck his head. A week or so later Jarvis died. Uncle Lisha moralizes,

" 'N' that's what *he* got for feedin' boys wild turnips."[52]

Supernatural and humorous elements blend in two Danvis stories. In *Danvis Folks* Uncle Lisha tells a tale that involves the familiar theme of a ghost who protects his estate.[53] The story goes that after the death of an old shoemaker, Uncle Ebenezer Hill, Bijer Johns falsely claimed that Uncle Eben owed him for some hides, and Bijer collected the money from the shoemaker's estate. Later Bijer heard the sloshing of a hen that had fallen in a swill barrel he had forgotten to cover when feeding his hogs. He was convinced the noise was Uncle Eben's ghost coming after him, although Bijer's wife assured him that ghosts do not walk in broad daylight. At any rate, Bijer returned the money to the estate and felt relieved until that evening when he discovered the hen in the swill barrel. Realizing his mistake he felt worse than ever.[54] Accordingly, in this story the supernatural motif of the dead returning to regain stolen property is tempered a great deal by the dominance of the absurd misunderstanding motif in which a noise is mistaken for a ghost. Frequently, European supernatural elements are rationalized, changed, or lost in versions collected in the New World.[55]

A final supernatural tale involving the motifs of the unusual features of the Devil's feet and a journey to the lower world is also dominated by a humorous motif in which a shoemaker makes a shoe for the Devil's human-looking foot, but the fit is so miserable that the shoe fits only the Devil's hoofed foot. This tale is told by Antoine, who at one of the gatherings in Lisha's shop maintains that he does not feel like singing or telling a story because he had a bad dream the night before. Using the device of the dreamed visit to the Devil,[56] Antoine says that when he was visiting hell a naked man arrived carrying cobbler's tools and announced that he was not wanted in the other place. The old shoemaker asked to make the Devil a pair of boots, and the Devil revealed his feet, one resembling the foot of a human and the other resembling the foot of a cow. The Devil told the cobbler to make a pair of boots but allowed the shoemaker to measure only one foot. The cobbler decided to measure and make a boot for the human-looking foot, but the finished boot fit only the bovine-looking foot. Consequently, the Devil kicked the old shoemaker out of hell, so the cobbler was admitted to neither place.[57]

Tales in Robinson's writings extraneous to general Yankee tradition, other than French-Canadian supernatural stories, are North American Indian etiological tales. One of these tales appears in the story "McIntosh of Vergennes" when young Donald McIntosh retells a tale that an Indian guest, Wadso, told him explaining how the linn of Otter Creek was created. Donald relates how hundreds of years ago Wadso's people, the Zooquagese, were being pursued by their much stronger enemy, the Iroquois. When the canoes of the Zooquagese were within the range of the arrows of the Iroquois, an old priest of the Zooquagese invoked the "Master of Life" and then plunged into Otter Creek. As the Zooquagese looked back, they saw that the powerful Iroquois canoes were closing in on them. In fact, the Iroquois were just behind the fading ripples marking the spot into which the Zooquagese priest had plunged. At the point where the priest had drowned, behind the Zooquagese, the river suddenly sank and the mighty river rushed over the precipice, engulfing every Iroquois.[58]

The fact that Robinson has a European tell this Indian tale does not agree at all with the observations of folklorists. Dorson points out, for example, that although the American Indian borrowed a number of folktales from European settlers, "the tales of the Indian are never retold by whites." According to Dorson, the "alien style and esoteric ideas" of Indian tales "carried no meaning for white Americans."[59] Nevertheless, although Robinson oddly has a Scotchman retelling an Indian tale, he aptly expresses the white man's attitude toward the explanatory story, for Donald's father calls it a "fule's tale."[60]

In *Sam Lovel's Boy* Robinson reports two other etiological tales, which are appropriately told by an Indian. On one of Sammy Lovel's visits to the Indian camp near Danvis, Sammy boasts he has become so proficient with the bow and arrows that Uncle Lisha bought for him from the Indians that he has hit the ear of a rabbit with an arrow. This leads to Sammy asking one of the Indians, Tocksoose, why rabbits have such long ears and hind legs. Tocksoose explains with the following tale:

"Oh, dat come so, long time 'go," Tucksoose answered, as he punched the bark with an awl and followed it with a thread of root. "Den rabbit have long tail an' short hin' leg an' ear jus' same anybody. Den one day fox be hungry an' chase rabbit, oh, very hard, so rabbit run in hole in rock,—so big hole fox can run in too. Den rabbit go in far end, an' dar lee'l hole go out, jus' mos' big 'nough so rabbit can go t'rough an' fox ketch it by his leg an' pull, an' rabbit pull with fore leg an' cry so hard like baby; squaw near an' come for help it; ketch hol' ear an' pull so fox le' go leg an' pull tail, so tail pull off short, an' squaw pull rabbit out. But he look so he ain't know hes'f,—ear pull out long, hin' leg pull out long, an' tail all pull off mos'; an' when fox see, he ain't know it was rabbit, an' he jump so far wid dat long hin' leg he can't ketch it. Den when winter come an' snow fall, rabbit set still an' let snow come all over him, so fox can't see him close by if he shut up hees eye; an' now he always have ear an' hin' leg long an' tail short, an' he white in winter."[61]

In addition, Sammy asks Tocksoose why minks are black, and the Indian relates another etiological tale:

". . . Wonakake—dat's otter—got mad 'cause mink ketch um so many fish, so he chase mink for kill it, an' mink pooty scare. He all white then jus' same weasel in winter, so otter can see it great way off; an' mink can't hide. So he run in where fire burn tree an' rub hese'f on burnt tree so he all black. Den he turn roun' an' walk back, an' by'm by meet otter run hard. Otter ain't know dat black feller, an' ask it, 'You see mink go dis way?' Mink say no, he an't see it. Otter t'ink funny he can smell mink but can't see it, an' run on fast, but never ketch um mink. Mink like um color so well he always keep it, an' ketch 'em more fish as ever, 'cause fish can't see um so easy, an' so he be black now."[62]

Moreover, in both essay and fiction Robinson uses local legends of person, place, and event. Several of these local legends with familiar themes are found in Robinson's local history, *Along Three Rivers*. In this work, for instance, he mentions a common type of place legend dealing with a cursed piece of land near his home in Ferrisburg. He says that a hollow was "long ago cursed by John Nutting when he lost his holding through a defective title."[63] A second place legend in *Along Three Rivers* concerns an unusual rock not far from the Robinson home:

> Beside the main road fifty rods or so south of the creek, lies a great boulder of light colored stone concerning which a tale was told "that froze our young blood and made each particular hair stand on end," of a traveler murdered for his money, and buried beneath this rock. The only foundation for this story appears to have been in the finding of the remains of a saddle in a hollow stump on the adjacent hill, but we have so few tales of horror to spice the uneventful history of our town, that it would be a pity to let this be a forgotten event, though it is apocryphal.[64]

Another place legend, this one a common type dealing with a lost mine, is found in a Danvis story. On one occasion in his shop Uncle Lisha and his friends speculate on the business of three strangers in Danvis who are staying at Hamner's tavern. Uncle Lisha suggests that the strangers might be "lookin' arter the ol' Injun lead mind 'at folks useter tell on . . . They said the' was a ol' Injin useter come oncte a year an' go up ont' the maountain some'eres an' git all the lead he could lug. They watched him an' followed him, but they could n't never find aout where he got it."[65]

In *Along Three Rivers* Robinson also gives a second local legend dealing with a mine, although this one concerns a deceitful sale of a worthless mine and not with a lost mine:

> There were two more forges upstream, where the Monkton road crosses. One of the forges belonged to the Boston Iron Co. together with four hundred acres of adjacent land, and the Monkton ore bed, whereby hangs a tale of the Yankee smartness. While the Boston Company were negotiating for the purchase of the ore bed some of its members met the then owners at the forge on an appointed day to see the quality of the ore tested. During the process of smelting thirty silver dollars were secretly dropped into the loop, one by one, by a bloomer who was in the confidence of his employer, and the product was of such excellent quality that the Bostonians at once closed the bargain and came into possession of a mine so worthless that it was soon abandoned. The story has its moral, for the instigator of the fraud, after cutting a great figure for a time, died in poverty.[66]

A personal legend that Robinson includes in *Along Three Rivers* tells of Tunis Van Vliet, an early settler in the Ferrisburg area, who was counted out of a lynx hunt because he had neither bullet nor shot for his long smooth bore; nevertheless, Tunis surprised his neighbors by cutting a sinker into slugs and bagging the lynx with his improvised ammunition.[67] This same motif of the remarkable ammunition that is used by a mighty hunter is used by Robinson in one of his stories. In *Danvis Folks* another great hunter, Gran'ther Hill, is counted out of a wolf hunt because he is too old and has neither shot nor ball for his gun. But like Tunis Van Vliet, Gran'ther Hill loads his gun with a sinker and bags the wolf.[68]

Among the most amusing folktales that Rowland Robinson uses in his writings are two catch tales. One of these is a variant of a widespread American tale in which the storyteller gets himself into a dangerous situation with a wild animal, normally a bear, and then does not reveal the denouement. When a curious listener asks what happened, the storyteller reveals that he was killed or eaten. In *Uncle Lisha's Outing* Antoine decides to mend the frayed knees of his trousers, and this task reminds him of a tale. While Antoine's audience listens "with more interest in the manner of his telling than in the matter," the Canuck tells the following story:

"Yas, sah, dey was one man Canada, one tam, an' if you'll ant b'lieved it Ah can tol' you nem de place w'ere he live, nonly Ah 'll fregit now. One tam in de fall his waf was mek it new pair clo's all over, new shirt, new coat, new trouser, every-t'ing. De hwomans he feel putty plump 'cause he 'll weave it all heese'f, an' he lak for look at hees mans w'en he gat all on, for go on de market.

"One day w'en he go, jes' 'fore he 'll ready for start, he 'll hear hees leetly dog bark very hard in de hwood not more as leetly way from de haouse. He was terribly hunter mans, an' t'ink prob'ly de dog was tree up a coon. So he'll took hees hol' fusee an' run off for shot it a minute, an' bah gosh, w'at you t'ink?

"It was pant'er, hol' big feller, hugly lak meat-axe. But de mans he 'll ant scare for run. He p'ant hees gaun an' pull it, an' de flint jes' go 'pluck.' An' de pant'er jomp on de man, 'scroonch,' an' tore off all dat new clo's not more as two ninches wide. Oh, bah gosh, Ah'll tol' you, haow dat hwomans was feel bad w'en she see it all spile up dat clo's she was be so troublesome for mek. Dat was too bad.

. . . .

"Did the man get hurt much, Antwine?" Joseph inquired.
"De man? Oh, he was be keel, Ah b'lieve so. . . ."[69]

In "Just B'ars" Dorson gives a version of a similar story in which the storyteller instead of the protagonist is eaten by a wild animal. The details are different, but the tale ends in about the same way that Antoine's story ends. The catch tale that Dorson reports runs:

Smart finally said he could not then remember but one bear story in which he was the principal contestant with a bear. He said that once when he was out fishing near North Bennington, Vt., in passing through the woods he was clasped in the embrace of a big black bear before he hardly realized his situation. He had a fearful wrestle with the monster, and the breath was fast being hugged out of his body. He thought of a big jackknife in one of his pockets, but had a hard struggle to get at it. Just then Smart started up and was going out the door, when Mr. Chickering said: "Smart, how did the bear finally come out of that fight?" "Oh, the bear," said Smart, "why, the bear killed me."[70]

Robinson uses another catch tale in *Uncle Lisha's Shop*. When Antoine tells how he catches skunks by holding them up by their tails to prevent the animals from ejecting their malodorous secretion, Joseph Hill is reminded of a story, which he relates in his usual irresolute way:

"They raly can't scent when you hol' 'em up by the tail, 'n' that's a fact," said Joseph Hill. "I remember onct when I was a boy ten 'r dozen year ol'—I d'know, mebby I was fourteen—lemme see, 'twas the year 't father had the brindle caow die 't hed twin calves; got choked with an apple—no 't wan'n't, t'was a tater—they was fo' ye'r oles when he sole 'em, the fall 't I was seventeen—no, I wa'n't but thirteen—the' was a skunk got int' the suller, 'n' of course we didn't want to kill 'im there, so my oldest brother, Lije, he took a holt on 'im by the tail an' kerried 'im aout the hatchway with a pair o' tongs, an' then he gin 'im to me, an' I hel' 'im up while he shot 'im. He put the ol' gun clus to his head an' blowed 'im clean aouten the tongs as fur's crost this shop, 'n' by gol, he never scent one mite till then, no more'n a snowball."
"Did he die?" asked the ever-alert seeker after useful knowledge.
"Why, yes," Joseph replied, "he jes' stunk hisself to death, then."[71]

A final tale that Robinson incorporates into his fiction is a form of one of the most popular anecdotes in literature and folklore, "The Obstinate Wife."[72] In one common form of the tale the husband and his obstinate wife argue about whether something has been cut with scissors or with a knife. Finally the husband loses his patience and tosses his wife into a stream. Nevertheless, the obstinate wife gets the last word, for as she goes under the water she makes with her fingers the motion of cutting with scissors.[73] In a French-Canadian variety of the tale, a husband and his wife argue about whether holes in the floor were made by rats or mink.[74] The tale that Robinson gives is told by the Canuck Antoine, and it closely resembles the French-Canadian version, only the animals involved in Antoine's tale are a rat and a mouse and not a rat and a mink. Antoine's story goes:

". . . Wal, seh, Onc' Lasha, der was hol' man an' hol' hwomans in Canada gat marree togedder w'en dey was hol' an' in t'ree day dey was set heat dinny, an' leetly maouse run on de haouse, an' hol' hwomans say, 'See dat maouse,' Hol' mans say, 'It was rats,' an' hol' hwomans say, 'No, it was maouse.' 'Ah tol' you it was rats,' he'll said. 'Maouse,' she'll said, an' dey holler 'Rat,' 'Maouse,' an' get so mad he'll go 'way an' stay t'ree year Den he'll come back, an' she'll was veree glad fer see it. 'It was too bad you'll go 'way so, jes' for leetly maouse.' 'Ant Ah'll tol' you it was rats?' he'll holler, an he'll go, an' never come some more. . . .[75]

Accordingly, Robinson makes extensive use of the main forms of folktales in America. As Richard M. Dorson has pointed out concerning his seminal study of a number of the folktales in the writings of Robinson, "We can document Robinson's tales with extensive parallels from the New England area, lodged in obscure printed sources and recent field collections which he could never have seen. Irresistible evidence demonstrates the presence of valid folklore in the Green Mountain sketches of blind Rowland Robinson."[76]

NOTES

[1] Dorson, *Jonathan Draws the Long Bow*, p. 225.

[2] Motif X621*, "Jokes about the Irish" (Baughman).

[3] Motif J1750, "One animal mistaken for another."

[4] Robinson, *Uncle Lisha's Shop and A Danvis Pioneer*, pp. 141-42.

[5] Robinson, *Uncle Lisha's Shop and A Danvis Pioneer*, p. 148.

[6] Robinson, *Uncle Lisha's Shop and A Danvis Pioneer*, pp. 148-49.

[7] Dorson, *Jonathan Draws the Long Bow*, p. 225.

[8] Motifs J1811, "Animal cries misunderstood"; J1805.1, "Similar sounding words mistaken for each other."

[9] Robinson, *Uncle Lisha's Shop and A Danvis Pioneer*, pp. 152-53.

[10] Motif J1791.7, "Man does not recognize his own reflection in the water." Cf. Motif X1763*, "Absurd disregard of the nature of reflections" (Baughman).

[11] Robinson, *In New England Fields and Woods*, p. 241. Type 1336A, "Man does not Recognize his own Reflection in the Water (Mirror)."

[12] Motif X972, "Lie: remarkable fighter."

[13] Motif X1764*, "Absurd disregard of the nature of echoes" (Baughman).

[14] Dorson, *American Folklore*, pp. 201-214.

[15] Robinson, *In New England Fields and Woods*, pp. 236-37. Cf. Motifs X937, "Lie: loud voice" (Baughman); J2632, "Fools try to frighten one another, but get scared themselves and both flee."

[16] Type 1315, "The Big Tree Taken for a Snake." Motif J1771.1.

[17] Robinson, *Out of Bondage and Other Stories*, pp. 225-26. Cf. Motif J1750, "One animal mistaken for another."

[18] Robinson, *Uncle Lisha's Shop and A Danvis Pioneer*, p. 143.

[19] Robinson, *Uncle Lisha's Shop and A Danvis Pioneer*, pp. 151-52.

[20] Motif J1771, "Object thought to be animal."

[21] Dorson, *Jonathan Draws the Long Bow*, p. 225.

[22] Dorson, *Jonathan Draws the Long Bow*, p. 78.

[23] Type 1548, "The Soup-stone." Motif K112.2.

[24] Robinson, *Uncle Lisha's Outing and Along Three Rivers*, p. 131.

[25] Type 1555B, "The Rum and Water Trade."

[26] Robinson, *Uncle Lisha's Outing and Along Three Rivers*, p. 132. Motif K231.6.2.1, "The trickster returns a bottle of water instead of the bottle of rum he has just purchased" (Baughman).

[27] Harold W. Thompson, pp. 281-82. Motif K231.6.2.2, "Trickster fills his gallon jug half full of water, then has it filled with rum at the store" (Baughman).

[28] Dorson, *Jonathan Draws the Long Bow*, p. 226.

[29] Motif K483, "Color of devil's cows changed while he sleeps so that he does not know them."

[30] Robinson, *Uncle Lisha's Shop and A Danvis Pioneer*, p. 96. Cf. Motif J2010, "Uncertainty about own identity."

[31] Motif K246, "Death feigned to avoid paying debts."

[32] Robinson, *Danvis Folks and A Hero of Ticonderoga*, pp. 99-100.

[33] Robinson, *Sam Lovel's Boy with Forest and Stream Fables*, p. 39.

[34] Motif K258, "Stolen property sold to its owner."

[35] Robinson, *Uncle Lisha's Outing and Along Three Rivers*, p. 256.

[36] Cf. Motifs W117, "Boastfulness"; J2331, "Numskull with unimportant office boasts of it"; X800, "Humor based on drunkenness."

[37] Dorson, *American Folklore*, pp. 136-37.

[38]Richard M. Dorson, *Bloodstoppers and Bearwalkers* (Cambridge, Mass., 1952).

[39]Dorson, "The Identification of Folklore in American Literature," p. 8.

[40]Robinson, *Danvis Folks and A Hero of Ticonderoga*, pp. 123-24. Motif D113.1.1, "Werewolf."

[41]Robinson, *Danvis Folks and A Hero of Ticonderoga*, p. 112. Motif D1385.4, "Silver bullet protects against giants, ghosts, and witches."

[42]See Paul Sebillot, *Le Folk-Lore de France* (Paris, 1904-1907), I, 284-85; II, 205, 206, 373, 437; III, 54-56; IV, 210, 240, 304.

[43]See Paul A. W. Wallace, *Baptiste Laroque: Legends of French Canada* (Toronto, 1923), pp. 42-46.

[44]Dorson, *Bloodstoppers and Bearwalkers*, p. 69.

[45]Harold W. Thompson, p. 116.

[46]Harold W. Thompson, p. 115.

[47]Robinson, *Uncle Lisha's Outing and Along Three Rivers*, pp. 154-55. Motif Q223.6.3*(b), "Man who fishes constantly is turned into a kingfisher" (Baughman).

[48]Dorson, *Jonathan Draws the Long Bow*, p. 224.

[49]Kittredge, *Witchcraft in Old and New England*, p. 215. Motif F491, "Will-o'-the-Wisp." See Wallace, *Baptiste Laroque*, pp. 47-51.

[50]Robinson, *Uncle Lisha's Outing and Along Three Rivers*, p. 67.

[51]Robinson, *Uncle Lisha's Outing and Along Three Rivers*, pp. 68-69. Motif F491.1, "Will-o-the-Wisp leads people astray."

[52]Robinson, *Uncle Lisha's Shop and A Danvis Pioneer*, pp. 210-12. Motifs Q260, "Deceptions punished"; N250, "Persistent bad luck."

[53]See, for example, Dorson, *Jonathan Draws the Long Bow*, pp. 207, 224.

[54]Robinson, *Danvis Folks and A Hero of Ticonderoga*, pp. 125-27. Motifs E236, "Return from dead to demand stolen property"; J1782, "Things thought to be ghosts."

[55]Roger D. Abrahams and George Foss, *Anglo-American Folksong Style* (Englewood Cliffs, New Jersey, 1968), p. 25.

[56]Dorson, *Jonathan Draws the Long Bow*, p. 224.

[57]Robinson, *Uncle Lisha's Shop and A Danvis Pioneer*, pp. 193-94. Motifs F80, "Journey to lower world"; G303.4.5, "The devil's feet and legs"; X240(a), "The shoemaker makes a shoe for devil's foot" (Baughman); Q565, "Man admitted to neither heaven nor hell."

[58]Robinson, *Out of Bondage and Other Stories*, pp. 114-16. Motif A910, "Origin of water features." Cf. Motifs R220, "Flights", D1551, "Waters magically divide and close."

[59]Dorson, *American Folklore*, p. 167.

[60]Robinson, *Out of Bondage and Other Stories*, p. 116.

[61]Robinson, *Sam Lovel's Boy with Forest and Stream Fables*, p. 60. Motifs A2325.1, "Why rabbit has long ears"; A2411.1.4.4, "Color of hare"; A2371, "Origin and nature of animal's legs"; A2378.4.1, "Why hare has short tail"; A2213.4, "Animal characteristics changed by stretching."

[62]Robinson, *Sam Lovel's Boy with Forest and Stream Fables*, p. 61. Motif A2411, "Origin of color of animal." Cf. Motif A2411.1.2.5, "Color of mink."

[63]Robinson, *Uncle Lisha's Outing and Along Three Rivers*, p. 230. Motifs M411.23, "Curse by other wronged man or woman"; M474, "Curse on land."

[64]Robinson, *Uncle Lisha's Outing and Along Three Rivers*, pp. 241-42.

[65]Robinson, *Danvis Folks and A Hero of Ticonderoga*, p. 193. Cf. Motif N596, "Discovery of rich mine."

[66]Robinson, *Uncle Lisha's Outing and Along Three Rivers*, p. 245. Motif K120, "Sale of false treasure."

[67]Robinson, *Uncle Lisha's Outing and Along Three Rivers*, p. 228. Motif X1121.3*, "Lie: remarkable ammunition used by great hunter" (Baughman).

[68]Robinson, *Danvis Folks and A Hero of Ticonderoga*, pp. 107-110.

[69]Robinson, *Uncle Lisha's Outing and Along Three Rivers*, p. 106. Type 2202, "Teller is Killed in his own Story." Motif Z13.2 (Baughman).

[70]Dorson, "Just B'ars," p. 183.

[71]Robinson, *Uncle Lisha's Shop and A Danvis Pioneer*, pp. 147-48. Type 2200, "Catch-tales." Motif Z13.

[72]Stith Thompson, *The Folktale*, p. 209. Type 1355, "The Obstinate Wife."

[73]In *Jonathan Draws the Long Bow*, p. 230, Dorson gives a good version of "The Obstinate Wife" from a popular nineteenth-century American weekly, the *Yankee Blade*, XIII (Dec. 17, 1853).

[74]Type 1365G*, "Rats or Mink."

[75]Robinson, *Danvis Folks and A Hero of Ticonderoga*, p. 191.

[76]Dorson, "The Identification of Folklore in American Literature," p. 8.

CHAPTER 19

THE CONTRIBUTION OF FOLKLORE TO ROBINSON'S FICTION

The Danvis stories of Rowland E. Robinson are especially reward-ing literary forms; for if they are read carefully and intelligently, as indeed they deserve to be, they offer not only enjoyment, but also broaden our knowledge of a segment of American life. The literary value of Robinson's work, however, cannot be estimated without con-sidering the contribution of folklore to his fiction, for his achievement as a writer is his unique ability to present nearly authentic folklore in the faithfully reproduced folk speech of vividly created folk characters who move in an artistically reconstructed folk milieu. As a matter of fact, folklore significantly influences virtually all of the elements of Robinson's fiction: subject matter, setting, language, character, point of view, plot, literalism, atmosphere, tone, and theme.

The subject matter, for example, of almost all of Robinson's fic-tion is Vermont folklife in the early part of the nineteenth century. Of course, like all fictional writers who draw their material from observa-tion of life, Robinson has edited his material. Obviously, it would have been impossible for Robinson, or any other creative writer, to have given in his stories a complete account of every aspect of folklife. Consequently, in his fiction Robinson concentrates on those aspects of the traditional life of Vermont with which he was most familiar. That is, he concentrates on the masculine activities of traditional culture—hunting, fishing, trapping, farming, and "swapping lies"—and the distaff activities, although present, are kept in the background. As a reviewer of *Danvis Folks* has pointed out, "Even when the writer's pen strays from recording the facts of the men with gun and rod,—it sticks to them too closely sometimes for the general interest of the pages,—the women are still kept in the background; for the scene is usually transferred, not to feminine quarters, but to the rustic community's equivalent for the club-house of the city, Uncle 'Lisha's little shop."[1] Nevertheless, although Robinson necessarily has been selective in his subject matter, he drew his material from folklife, and his selection of scenes and events are both plausible and typical of early Vermont village life.

As one would expect to find in regional literature, the scene is a dominant element in Robinson's fiction. As for place, most of Robinson's stories are set in or around Danvis, a fictional mountain village of Vermont. As for time, the Danvis stories take us from the opening of the American Revolution in *A Danvis Pioneer* to the close of the Civil War in *Sam Lovel's Boy*, although most of the stories are set in the early decades of the nineteenth century. It seems that Robinson made no real attempt to identify Danvis with any actual town or village in Vermont. For example, in the "Author's Foreword" to *Uncle Lisha's Shop*, he says:

> The boundaries of the township of Danvis are not more clearly defined than the limits of the county of Charlotte, in which it is situated. Suffice it to say that it is in the State of Vermont, backed at the east by the mountains that gave the State its name, and shut out from the valley of the Champlain by outlying spurs of the same range. Thus fortified against the march of improvement, its inhabitants longer retained the primitive manners, speech, and customs of the earliest settlers of Vermont than did the population of the lake towns, whose intercourse with the great centres of trade and culture was more direct and frequent.[2]

By "Charlotte County" Robinson probably means not the present Charlotte County but the original Charlotte County, which was established in 1772. The original Charlotte County was quite large. It began at the Green Mountains and extended westward along the northern lines of Sunderland and Arlington to the Hudson River. It included both sides of Lake Champlain and extended as far north as Canada.[3] The name "Danvis" no doubt had its origin in an original grant of land located in what is now Addison County and purchased in 1761 by Thomas Robinson; for in *Vermont: A Study of Independence*, Robinson notes:

> In an indenture made 30th December, 1761, Colonel [John Henry] Lydius grants to Thomas Robinson, merchant, of Newport, in the Coloney of Rhode Island, one sixtieth of the township No. 24, called Danvis, for the "sum of one Shilling money one peppercorn each year for seventy years (if demanded) and after twenty years five Shillings sterling annually, forever, on the Feast Day of St. Michael the Archangel, for each hundred acres of arable Land."[4]

Robinson's daughter, Mary, confirms that her father had no particular village in mind as the model for Danvis; however, she maintains that the surroundings that Robinson describes are more like those of Starksboro and Lincoln than those of the towns nearer to Lake Champlain. In fact, Mary Robinson Perkins points out that her father describes the life of these two Green Mountain villages with such fidelity that inhabitants of Starksboro and Lincoln have recognized themselves in Robinson's creations and have felt that they were being ridiculed by Robinson, although that was far from his intent.[5] In any event, in the Danvis stories Robinson uses the actual names of many localities within a fifteen mile radius of his own home, and the internal evidence in his fiction has encouraged most writers on Robinson to identify Danvis with either West Lincoln or Lincoln, Vermont. For instance, in an account based on an essay by Henry Lincoln Bailey and authenticated by Robinson's son, Rowland T. Robinson, who gives West Lincoln as the site of Danvis, Miss Cook says:

> When he was about ten years old, Rowland went to West Lincoln for a day with his father, "by horsepower." While the elder Robinson transacted the business for which he had come, the boy wandered about the village, talking with the farmers who had settled far back there among the hills; absorbing with eager eyes the background of encircling mountains; on the east, the high peak of 'Tater Hill, Hog's Back shutting out the view of the valley to the westward, Beaver Meadow Brook tumbling down from the upland reaches of the hills. He noted the little gray farmhouses set back against the sloping meadows, the cluster of buildings which comprised the center of the village, and farther down the road, the mill. So vividly were the beauty and the seclusion of this mountain hamlet impressed upon him, that forty years later he reproduced in the village of Danvis the setting which he had seen that day. So accurately were the details pictured in his mind that even today those parts of the village which remain unchanged by time may be recognized as the familiar landmarks of Danvis.[6]

Indeed, the internal evidence in Robinson's stories does seem to locate Danvis in the Lincoln Valley. For many of the landmarks of Danvis Valley, such as "Tater Hill," are clearly recognizable as actual landmarks of Lincoln Valley. Moreover, in his foreword to *Uncle Lisha's Shop*, Robinson tells us that Danvis is backed at the east by the Green Mountains and that it is separated from the Champlain Valley by the same mountain's outlying spurs. In fact, Uncle Lisha's farm is so near the Green Mountains that his woodlot is on a westward slope of one of these spurs.[7] Moreover, we learn from internal evidence that Danvis lies in a valley somewhere between Middlebury and Burlington, and that it is at least twenty miles from Lake Champlain.[8] In addition, Vergennes—which in the Danvis stories as well as in reality lies on the First Falls of Otter Creek—is located between Lake Champlain and Danvis; and Danvis is nearly due east of Vergennes.[9] Furthermore, the family names that Robinson uses in his stories were familiar names in the Lincoln Valley in the nineteenth century; surnames on gravestones in a Lincoln cemetery, for instance, include Hill, Purinton, Varney, Gove, and Hamner.

Although Cook and Bailey suggest that Robinson had no contact with the Lincoln Valley after his trip there as a boy, it seems likely that at least some of his many hunting, fishing, and camping trips took him to the Lincoln area. Westbrook, who agrees that Lincoln and Starksboro are the models for the hill village of Danvis, says, "On his camping and hunting trips, Robinson came to know Ferrisburgh and its surrounding townships as well as Thoreau knew Concord. The settings of his stories, for the most part laid in this territory, have the accuracy of a government topographic map."[10] Accordingly, although one can only speculate whether Robinson returned to the Lincoln Valley after his boyhood trip there, it seems reasonable that he did. At any rate, it is certain that Robinson communicated with residents of Lincoln as late as 1878; for in his journal Robinson writes on June 19, 1878, that George Varney of Lincoln gave him some information about hunting the fisher.

Still, although much of the internal evidence in the Danvis stories seems to situate Danvis geographically in the Lincoln Valley, Robinson generally writes of things much closer to his own home in Ferrisburg, Vermont. In *Uncle Lisha's Outing* and *Sam Lovel's Camps*, for instance, the camping trips take the Danvis folk out of their little valley and to the spots where Robinson himself had actually camped, hunted, trapped, and fished. Furthermore, many of the other stories are set after supper in the cobbler shop of Uncle Lisha Peggs, where a group of Danvis males meet to swap tales, and as shown previously, the model for Uncle Lisha Peggs' shop was an actual shoemaker's shop only a short distance from Robinson's home. Nevertheless, Robinson's use of folklore significantly influenced his choice of a mountain village as the setting of his Danvis stories. By geographically isolating his Danvis folk in a valley, Robinson was able to give the citizens of Danvis a kind of homogeneity essential to the preservation of folk traditions. As Westbrook has said of the Danvis books, "Thus for the setting of these books which form the backbone of his work, Robinson quite naturally chose the hills, where change came slowest and the old ways lingered longest."[11]

Robinson's use of folklore in his fiction also influences his plotting. Plot, however, is not a dominant element in his fiction; the plots in most of his stories are of the simplest kind. In fact, many of Robinson's stories may even be called plotless, for as the author himself pointed out, he paid less attention to telling a narrative than to depicting early 19th century Vermont folklife:

"Danvis Folks," with the exception of the first chapter, was originally published in "Forest and Stream." It was written with less purpose of telling any story than of recording the manners, customs, and speech in vogue fifty or sixty years ago in certain parts of New England. Manners have changed, many customs have become obsolete, and though the dialect is yet spoken by some in almost its original quaintness, abounding in odd similes and figures of speech, it is passing away; so that one may look forward to the time when a Yankee may not be known by his speech, unless perhaps he shall speak a little better English than some of his neighbors. In truth he uses no worse now, nor did he ever, though he is accused of it. Such as it was, some may be glad to remember, and chiefly for them these papers have been written.[12]

Nevertheless, although Rowland Robinson's Danvis stories are nearly plotless, they are well-wrought. Each chapter of the Danvis stories is an episode complete in itself that can be read separately with enjoyment. But each story is made a part of a volume and each volume is made a part of the Danvis stories as a whole by the appearance of the same characters and setting. Consequently, although the Danvis stories are nearly plotless, they form a harmonious unit. As a reviewer of *Danvis Folks* says of the first three Danvis books:

> It is so hard not to think of Mr. Rowland E. Robinson's three books, *Uncle Lisha's Shop, Sam Lovel's Camps,* and *Danvis Folks,* as one work that, in referring to them, one feels the same embarrassment that he would feel in referring to some unentitled novel in three entitled parts. Taking a hint from Anthony Trollope, we propose to call them here, collectively, the "Chronicles of Danvis." So to name them has, besides its convenience, the advantage of quite accurately describing their character, and of suggesting, in a word, the reason why it is impossible to think of them apart. . . . owing to their always concerning the same lovely locality, a western county of Vermont bordering Lake Champlain, and the same group of simple, genuine country folk, inhabitants of a tiny village in the hills fifty years ago, they are thoroughly homogeneous. They form, not a novel, but a neighborhood chronicle.[13]

Robinson begins many of his chapters by briefly describing the scene or some aspect of nature, although occasionally he begins a chapter with a few brief introductory remarks relating it chronologically to the previous chapter. The chapters themselves consist mainly of the conversations among the characters, and frequently the chapters serve mainly as frame devices in which Robinson embroiders traditional tales or other items of folklore. Usually the chapters end with an anecdote or with Uncle Lisha closing the storytelling session by announcing that "it's 'baout time 't honest folks was abed an' rogues locked aout." Still, although Robinson's stories are nearly plotless, they are not artless. As a matter of fact, the noted publisher John Farrar has even suggested that instructors in English might teach narrative writing from Robinson's method: "His calculated spinning of an anecdote, his recreation of a dry personality, his pursuit of a subtle climax, the ebb, the flow, the caesura, the real bomb-burst of a country-store raconteur is something very special, very fine and in a real sense, Shakespearian."[14] Similarly, Perry D. Westbrook also aptly acknowledges the influence of oral storytelling on Rowland E. Robinson's technique:

> This technique is a most simple one, based on that prehistoric genre, the

campfire yarn. Robinson will get three or four of his characters together—say Ann Twine, Gran'ther Hill, Uncle Lisha, Sam Lovel—on a camping trip, at a sugaring off party, at a woodcutting or moving bee, at a turkey shooting, or, most often, in Uncle Lisha's cobbling shop. After assembling the characters and describing carefully the activity that is going on—there is here room for much local color and description of old customs—some action, usually humorous, takes place . . . Or, especially if the setting is Uncle Lisha's shop or an evening campfire, one of the characters will spin a yarn, which is usually topped by a taller one by Ann Twine, who revels in his reputation as the greatest liar in Danvis. Thus the books are unencumbered with plot; they are simply a series of sketches involving the same characters and describing various aspects of old-time rural life.[15]

Besides influencing the subject matter, setting, and plot, folklore also contributes significantly to the language of his fiction; for in his stories Robinson uses a literary dialect, defined by linguist Sumner Ives as "an author's attempt to represent in writing a speech that is restricted regionally, socially, or both. His representation may consist merely in the use of an occasional spelling change, like FATHUH rather than *father*, or the use of a word like *servigrous*; or he may attempt to approach scientific accuracy by representing all the grammatical, lexical, and phonetic peculiarities that he has observed."[16] By attempting to approach scientific accuracy, Robinson's literary dialect falls into the latter class. As we have seen above, Robinson points out in the "Author's Note" preceding *Danvis Folks* that he made a conscious attempt to record the folk dialect as well as the other aspects of Vermont folklife. Consequently, although Robinson wrote during a period of American literature when interest in local color fiction was strong, his accurate portrayal of folk speech was for more than just effect.

Most critics have recognized that Rowland Robinson faithfully recorded the folk dialect of his region, but few critics have acknowledged the positive contribution of folk speech to the literary value of Robinson's fiction. As a matter of fact, some critics have even suggested that Robinson's stories would have been more popular if the author were not so concerned with accurately reproducing folk dialect. For instance, in an otherwise enthusiastic review of *Danvis Folks*, one critic says:

. . . Mr. Robinson probably had no deliberate intention of writing for posterity. Still, if given a chance, good work will survive, and there certainly seems no need for burdening it with the hideous phonetic spelling, unpronounceable by any one not acquainted with the dialect represented, which comes from an extreme devotion to scientific accuracy in reporting spoken speech. What will the ignorant make, for example, of "furzino," of "leggo," of "julluk," of "kwut," or of "lhud"? Surely the proper course, in works not avowedly scientific, is to use only as much of local peculiarity of speech as will give proper dramatic value to the talk of a character, as will not confuse the eye with queer spelling, or render any remark unintelligible without special knowledge. Mr. Robinson's subtle accuracy in dialect will make his book unwontedly attractive to Vermonters, who will be helped to recall with pleasurable distinctions the speech of their grandfathers and grandmothers, and it will preserve for the gratification of present and future scientific curiosity a racy and interesting variety of the Yankee speech. On the other hand, it quite needlessly restricts the enjoyment of his human and very appealing work to those people to whom the vanishing dialect he writes offers the fewest difficulties, and cuts it off entirely from popular appreciation by the future but not far-distant generations to whom its gnarled idiom will be utterly unknown.[17]

On the other hand, speaking of Robinson's reputation as simply a reporter of an American dialect, John Farrar maintains, "This aspect of his work is important; but I wonder if it is not misunderstood. It does not seem to me to be a mere matter of reporting. It comes from a belief in the accents of the meeting house on the hillside, of the church in the valley."[18] As Farrar suggests, although the literary value of rustic dialect has been recognized in the works of British writers such as Thomas Hardy, the artistic worth of folk language in the writings of American authors generally has gone unacknowledged. Farrar asserts, "For years the indecent snobbery of young America refused most literature that did not smack of British accents and origins. It was a great waste of time! We could have found in our own midst the very things that, flaming out of a country dialect or a moor with purple shadows over it, produced a Thomas Hardy."[19] In a sense, Farrar is right. Even in the nineteenth century American writers looked to England for stylistic guidance; however, between 1825 and 1925 the language of American prose changed significantly. By the time Robinson was writing towards the end of the nineteenth century, a romantic preference for common language, a nationalistic campaign for an indigenous style, and a pragmatic need to communicate had made a colloquial American style quite acceptable to most readers.[20]

At any rate, Robinson's use of folk language is not simply accurate reporting; folk speech also adds to the literary value of his fiction. His recognition of an inherent beauty in the peculiar similes, succinct proverbs, and jocose sayings of his neighbors figured importantly in the humor in Robinson's Danvis stories. Of course, Robinson sometimes uses expressions that cannot be documented as folk sayings; but even then his apparent inventions sound so natural within the context of folk dialect that it is plausible that Robinson heard these, too, and recorded them. For example, in *Sam Lovel's Boy* when the Danvis patriarch, Captain Hill, argues with the Danvis schoolmaster, Mr. Mumpson, about the value of studying mathematics, grammar, and Latin, the effectiveness of the humor depends not only on Robinson's faithful portrayal of folk dialect and folk psychology but also on the naturalness of Robinson's punning:

"What 's the good o' this 'ere Matthew Mattick's tarnal books?" he demanded. "He hed n't got 'em made when I was goin' tu school, nor yet a-keepin',—do' know as he was borned as he never 'd orter be'n, an' we got along jest ezackly as well-an' this 'ere grammer. What is it for?"

"Why, Captain Hill, grammar teaches us to speak and write correctly."

"Oh, thunder, we spoke an' writ so 't we understood one 'nother, an' what d' ye want? I tell ye, they 're all flummadiddle, your grammer an' your Matthew Mattick an' your square-rhut. Square-rhuts be cussed! Raound rhuts is good 'nough for or'nary folks! In my time we l'arned readin' an' writin' an' 'rithmertic, an' if a feller ciphered as fur as the rule o' three, he was king-pin. More 'n them would n't ha' helped us none 'baout choppin' an' loggin', an' squabblin' wi' Yorkers, an' fightin' Injuns an' Britishers,—no, no, not a soumarkee! But what I should like to know is, what on this livin' airth you, yourself, be everlastin'ly a-studyin' an' a-readin' that 'ere consarned Latin lingo for every identical night. Be you expectin' for tu go a-missionaryin' amongst them Latin critturs? Would n't they eat ye, suppose?" he added, glancing at the master's lean figure.[21]

Although Robinson made no concessions in his use of dialect, he was nevertheless concerned that his reader might not understand his language. Consequently, in footnotes throughout his Danvis stories he explains some of the more unusual expressions, and in his "Author's Explanatory Note" preceding his second volume of Danvis stories, *Sam Lovel's Camps*, he offers the reader some suggestions to help with the dialect:

The Yankee is everywhere, and everywhere is heard his nasal drawl asking a question or answering one. But it is a sign that the manner of his speech is changing that to some readers of "Uncle Lisha's Shop" who are unacquainted with a dialect once common in Vermont, and as yet by no means uncommon in portions of the State, the meaning of some words and phrases used by the old cobbler and his neighbors has not been clear. For the benefit of such readers of this volume it may not be amiss to explain at the outset some forms of speech that are least likely to be understood by them. "Julluk" is a shortening of just like; "god daown," "pud daown," "led daown," and the like, are got down, put down, let down, sat down, with the last letter of the first word changed to d. "Luftu" and "lufted tu" are queer corruptions of love to and loved to. "Callate," and sometimes "carc'late," is to intend or plan, not to compute. When a thing is sold it is "sol'." The "heft" of a thing is its weight and also the greater part of it, and to "heft it" is to try its weight by lifting. The word hold occurs in different forms in one sentence, when you are bidden to "take a holt an' hol' on." "Hayth" means height, the "Hayth o' land," the highest land in a certain section of country; the term was often applied in former times to the Green Mountain range. Creature has slight differences of pronunciation according to its application. A very poor or wretched person is a "poor, mis'able creetur," a wild blade, a "tarnal crittur," a bad man, a "weeked crittur"; and a bull, when not a "toro," is as politely called a "cruttur," the "tt" scarcely sounded. "Mongst 'em," signifies other persons beside the one or more named; as, "John Doe an' mongst 'em." To "shool" is to wander aimlessly; to "flurrup" to move in a lively, erratic manner. A "heater piece" is a triangular piece of land, shaped like a heater or flat-iron. The "square room" is the best room or parlor. A "linter" is a lean-to, a single-roofed building set against a larger one.

When a Yankee "dums" or "darns" persons or things, he is not to be understood as cursing them; church members in good standing do so without scandal as they mildly swear "by gush" and "by gum" and "swan," "swow," "snum," "snore" and "vum."

The Canadian who learns English of the Yankee often outdoes his teacher in that twisting of the vowels which, no doubt brought over in the Mayflower, became so marked a characteristic of New England speech. Some words are very difficult for him to master, but finally he gets the better of most, and no longer says "jimrubbit" for India-rubber, or "nowse" for noise. But stove is his shibboleth. To the day of his death he calls it "stofe," and the generation that follows him can speak it no otherwise.[22]

But Robinson records not only Yankee and Canuck dialects in his stories; he also records a number of other dialects, including Quaker, Indian, Negro, Southern, Scottish, and Irish. As a matter of fact, in *New England Indian Summer*, Van Wyck Brooks notes that there are seventeen dialects recorded in Robinson's books.[23] As a result of his skillful discrimination between characters of different ethnic backgrounds through accurately reproduced folk dialects, the dialogue seems more natural and consequently the characters seem more real than they would have if Robinson had written in standard English. Thus, his use of folk language contributes to the credibility of his stories.

Other than Antoine Bassette, however, most of the main characters in the Danvis stories are Yankees, but Robinson's accurate reporting of folk speech also gives individuality to each of his major Yankee characters. Sumner Ives points out that although the differences in the dialect of individuals in the same social class or geographical area are generally small, "It is a truism of linguistics that no two utterances are ever completely the same, and it follows that the speech pattern of every individual is unique."[24] In his fiction Rowland Robinson notes the several variations of Yankee speech that the linguist observes but that the ordinary local colorist misses; and Robinson differentiates his Yankee characters through their peculiar sayings and accents. For example, in the Danvis stories only Uncle Lisha says, "Good airth and seas!" Only Sam Lovel says, "By the gre't horn spoon!" Only Gran'ther Hill says, "By the Lord Harry!" Similarly, only Solon Briggs' speech is characterized by malapropisms. "I b'lieve I'll take my department an' go hum," says Solon Briggs, as he departs Lisha's shop.[25] And only Joseph Hill's speech is characterized by cautious indecision. "I was kinder meditatin' it over in my mind," Joseph says, "an' I don't seem tu feel r'al'y oneasy 'baout Samwil, ner yet ezackly easy, it don't seem 's 'ough. It 's agittin' consid'able kinder late, an' then ag'in it hain't so late as it might be."[26]

Robinson not only has his characters speak an authentic folk language, but he also based several of his characters on real people. For example, Robinson's daughter reports that the character of Solon Briggs "was the nearest akin to an actual person, being a distant cousin of ours and a Quaker preacher."[27] The Canadian wag Antoine Bassette was based in part on an actual French-Canadian, Joe LeClair, who lived at the Robinson home for a time during a haying season.[28] As we have seen, the Danvis shoemaker, Uncle Lisha Peggs, was also based on a real person, too. The description of Uncle Lisha's shop, the inventory of cobbler's tools, and the references to shoemaking techniques throughout the Danvis stories indicate that Rowland Robinson was more than an occasional visitor to the shop of the village cobbler, Uncle Lisha Green, the prototype of Uncle Lisha Peggs. Accordingly, Robinson's visits to the village cobbler's shop not only gave him material for setting and subject matter, but the visits also gave him the model for a major character in the Danvis stories. No doubt Robinson knew other village craftsmen, too; but other than cordwainer Uncle Lisha Peggs, the other craftsmen in Robinson's Danvis books are minor characters. Nevertheless, these minor characters who are craftsmen have a significant function in Robinson's writings since they help round out his picture of village life and give verisimilitude to his fiction.

Furthermore, there are those who say that Sam Lovel, who would "ruther husk nights an' dig pertaters nippin' cold days" than waste a good hunting day,[29] is a portrait of Robinson himself. For example, Terence Martin says,

> Of all the characters who lounge their way through the Danvis tales, only Sam Lovel possesses qualities of the heroic; only Sam can mark a spot in the woods with a glance and bag the most cunning fox and most savage wolf. Quite probably, he can often be identified with Rowland Robinson; his views on game and the forest and his love of the Danvis locale are on a more idealistic plane than those of his neighbors, and correspond to sentiments voiced by the author. For narrative purposes, Sam Lovel is a peerless hunter; for reasons of propaganda, he seizes every opportunity to cry out against the undue destruction of wild life in Vermont. His answer as to why he spends so much time hunting contains sentiments shared by character and author. . . .[30]

There is no doubt about it; Sam Lovel, indeed, shares Rowland Robinson's love of Vermont's hills and forests. However, Robinson always maintained that Sam Lovel was a creation, not a portrait.[31] Nevertheless, in a historical sketch of his area of Vermont, *Along Three Rivers*, Robinson writes, "The Lovels at Little Otter Creek Falls were also mighty hunters and trappers, whose father used to base his prospective payments on the 'Luck up the East Slang.' "[32] Consequently, it is probably no coincidence that Robinson chose the name "Lovel" for his own mighty hunter and trapper. Although Sam Lovel's sentiments correspond to those of Robinson, their mutual love for the woods, streams, and mountains of Vermont is shared by other Vermonters. For instance, in the *Handbook of the Linguistic Geography of New England* a description of an informant from Robinson's hometown, Ferrisburg, includes, "Loves the woods and mountains around him with almost poetic passion."[33] Moreover, as Martin notes, "Sam Lovel is not alone in feeling a kinship with the portion of nature surrounding Danvis. Admittedly, his perception of that relationship is more fully conscious than are the attitudes of his neighbors; he appears to draw a spiritual sustenance from the woods and streams. But Uncle Lisha, Pelatiah Gove, and Grandfather Hill each sense a superiority in the Danvis locale."[34]

In the Danvis stories all of Robinson's leading characters are men. There are women in his stories, but they are secondary characters, as one would expect in stories of hunting in Vermont fields and forests, fishing in Vermont streams and lakes, and swapping tales in a village cobbler's shop. Robinson's method of characterizing his Danvis males is dramatic rather than narrative. Without describing his characters, he shows them in action, and from their speech and behavior we deduce their personalities and relationships with other characters. Robinson, however, does not probe into the human relationships of his Danvis folk. As Martin has pointed out:

. . . The social intercourse of his characters is incidental; it may serve to illustrate a custom and provide a social backdrop, but it absolutely fails to set anything in the center of the stage. No scenes of emotion exist in Robinson, no seething hatreds or passionate loves, no strife, no undertow of opinion. He presents life as a smooth surface. The group which gathers so often at Uncle Lisha's shop serenely whiles away the time joking and telling stories, although they do profit by Sam Lovel's lectures on hunting and fishing. No real problems indigenous or foreign to the region beset the characters; life is an endless holiday.[35]

Martin is correct in asserting that Robinson fails to include any scenes of strong emotion and that he neglects to explore any complex human relationships in his stories. But the Yankee is not known for wearing his heart on his sleeve; and the culture that Robinson depicts is a traditional one without the turbulence and rapid change of our modern mass culture. Unlike contemporary man in a modern mass culture who must seek his identity, each individual in a traditional society finds his role in life already made for him, and he normally accepts it. Consequently, Robinson writes of man in harmony with society, not alienated from it. Whereas the dominant note in much modern literature is human loneliness in a large industrial state, the dominant theme in Robinson's stories is human cooperation and interdependence. Robinson simply depicts the typical, not the unusual; his characters are staunch friends and loyal sons.

As a matter of fact, Robinson's close observation and intimate knowledge of real village folk enables him to introduce the reader to the Danvis characters as the reader might meet them in real life. As Arthur Wallace Peach has pointed out, Robinson's characters are neither idealized nor simply story types. But as Peach observes, all of Robinson's main characters emerge from the pages to become real individuals, as real as if the reader had really known them in life itself.[36] A reviewer of *Danvis Folks* has said of Robinson's characterization:

. . . Mr. Robinson . . . has lived his life, gone a-fishing or a-hunting, or sat a-gossiping with his neighbors in full brotherly sympathy and understanding. From his lifelong observation and study of them have come the triumphant creations of character in his work. His people are not described, or analyzed, or annotated; we learn to know them as in real life we learn to know our friends, by observing what they do and listening to what they say. As in the drama, character is revealed through action and dialogue. So thorough and so sympathetic is the author's knowledge of his people, and so skillful is he in giving it form, that they seem wholly alive, wholly objective, wholly free from his control. Villagers who have known and gossiped about each other all their lives seem to each other not more concrete and actual than Uncle 'Lisha and his friends seem to us. . . .[37]

Actually, Robinson's choice of dramatic characterization through dialogue and his unconcern for complex human conflict and relationships enable him to work in examples of folklore almost at will. The same can be said for his point of view in the Danvis stories; it was an apt choice for his purpose of depicting folklife. Sometimes Robinson uses a first-person participant point of view in his short stories—in "An Underground Railroad Passenger" and in the first part of "The Gray Pine," for example. But in his stories of Danvis folklife he generally employs an omniscient point of view. In these stories the reader is only rarely conscious of the author's personality. Robinson seldom comments on the action or evaluates the behavior of his characters. Thus, in general, his choice of the objective omniscient point of view for his Danvis stories was a good one, for it allows him great freedom in the telling of his stories and permits him to give a detailed picture of Vermont folklife.

Although Robinson's shoemaker is named "Peggs" and his would-be verbalist is named "Solon," it would be a mistake to try to see his characters as personification, as abstractions disguised as persons. Other than in the folktales included in his frame stories, one looks in vain in Robinson's fiction for the unusual, the impossible, or the improbable. Consequently, the stories of Rowland Robinson can be classified as literal fiction, for they are without allegory or symbolism. Robinson is primarily concerned with presenting an authentic picture of rural Vermont life as people he actually knew or knew about really lived it. Accordingly, he deals with the ordinary and plausible in his realistic stories and has selected his details for their typicality. In fact, the works of Rowland Robinson are significant, especially to the student of American folklore, because of their literal import.

Accordingly, where many authors rely on symbolism to gain universality, Rowland Robinson achieves universal significance through a close study of the folklife of his region and his regard for the typical. Of course, there are many differences between the folk culture areas of the world and even between the folk culture regions of the United States, but there are also many similarities among closely knit rural families everywhere. Many of the folktales that Robinson uses, for instance, are international tales and therefore universal. Indeed, most items of folklore, while having national or regional differences, are everywhere the same and often so familiar that we tend to overlook them. For instance, speaking of the common characteristics of rural families Conrad M. Arensberg says that "we are prone to disregard the familiar; we forget that the familiar stuff of life has often more important implications than the exotic."[38] In a sense, then, the whole past of America is in Robinson's books. By giving a detailed picture of nineteenth-century folklife in his own region, he shows the modern reader what common life was like before industrialization and urbanization. In dealing with the creations of the common man instead of with the unique products of "great men," Robinson has, indeed, more than many urban writers achieved universality in his writings.

The world in which Robinson's characters move is one of rural, virile companionship. The casual, unhurried tempo of his stories; the simplicity and authenticity of his folk language; the details about the town meeting, the militia training, the paring bee, the raising bee, the moving bee; the preoccupation with hunting, fishing, trapping, and farming—all these contribute to the rustic, masculine, and democratic atmosphere of the Danvis stories. Closely related to the atmosphere that Robinson creates is his sympathetic attitude toward his material. As his youngest daughter, Mary, has pointed out, Robinson "loved the old days, and recorded the doings and sayings of that time in all sympathy and kindness."[39] As Westbrook points out, however, "It must not be thought that Robinson was overawed by the quaintness of the old days. The hill-country, then as later, had its meanness and its tragedy."[40] In "Fourth of July at Highland Poorhouse," for example, Robinson depicts the starkness of a New England poorhouse and describes the heartlessness of its severe-faced mistress, Mrs. Warden, who would have the paupers working on the Fourth of July. "What's a lot of porpers got to do with the Fourth of July?" the mistress of the poorhouse asks. "They'll eat jest as much the Fourth as any day, an' they 'e ortu be airnin' the' victuals."[41]

Since Robinson is mainly concerned with preserving oral traditions in his fiction, his Danvis stories are not philosophical. In fact, he does not attempt to complicate his stories with anything more complex or weighty than one would have encountered in ordinary conversation in nineteenth-century rural Vermont. Nevertheless, there is a theme running through Robinson's writings. The few years that Robinson lived in New York City taught him the great difference between the traditional way of life of the early nineteenth-century Vermonters and the modern way of life resulting from industrialization and urbanization. In one of his essays, "The Angler," for example, Robinson shows that the pleasure once found in traditional activities is lost through mass-produced refinements of the means. Thus, he writes:

. . . The youth born to rod and reel and fly is not so enthusiastic in his devotion to the sport as the boy whose birthright is only the pole that craftsmen never fashioned, the kinky lines of the country store, and hooks known by no maker's name. For it is not in the nature of a boy to hold to any nicety in sport of any sort, and this one, being herein unrestrained, enters upon the art called gentle with all the wild freedom of a young savage or a halfgrown mink.

For him it is almost as good as going fishing, to unearth and gather in an old teapot the worms, every one of which is to his sanguine vision the promise of a fish. What completeness of happiness for him to be allowed to go fishing with father or grandfather or the acknowledged great fisherman of the neighborhood, a good-for-nothing ne'er-do-well, but wise in all the ways of fish and their taking and very careful of and kind to little boys.[42]

Similar comments expressing his preference for the traditional way of life can be found throughout Robinson's works. Consequently, in *Danvis Folks* Aunt Jerusha Peggs summarizes the theme of most of Rowland Robinson's fiction when she says, "Old ways is best ways as a gin'ral thing."[43]

Since folklife contributes significantly to the content, form, and theme of Robinson's fiction, the real achievement of Rowland Robinson can be recognized only by looking at the folklore in his writings. Although Robinson was an artist and not a folklore technician, he was a close observer of traditional culture. Taken as a whole, his writings offer a kind of encyclopedia of nineteenth-century Vermont folklife. As we have seen, Robinson had a broad concept of folklore; he was interested in and wrote about nearly all of the traditions, both oral and material, of his fellow Vermonters. Since there have been no systematic collections of folklore from Vermont, save for folksongs, Robinson is worthy of consideration not only as a regional artist but also as a pioneer collector of American folklore. In fact, because he was one of the earliest students of folklife in the United States and because he reported on such a variety of folk traditions, no history of American folklore can overlook Robinson's contribution. The analysis of folklore in his writings, however, is valuable to the folklorist not only because Robinson has been the only person who has collected all kinds of folklore in Vermont, but also because in his stories Robinson demonstrates that in the living folk tradition the various genres of folklore and the several border traditions are not arbitrarily separated in the manner of several published collections. Rowland Robinson gives us a variety of folk traditions which mingle in his native state of Vermont. Consequently, as Richard M. Dorson says, Robinson "should be counted with the most zealous deliberate preservers of native folklore."[44]

NOTES

[1] Anonymous review of Rowland E. Robinson, *Danvis Folks* (Boston and New York, 1894), *Atlantic Monthly*, LXXV (June 1895), 818.

[2] Robinson, *Uncle Lisha's Shop and A Danvis Pioneer*, p. 118.

[3] Zadock Thompson, *History of Vermont, Natural, Civil, and Statistical* (Burlington, 1842), II, 20.

[4] Robinson, *Vermont*, p. 48.

[5] Mary Robinson Perkins, "Rowland Evans Robinson," p. 16.

[6] Cook, pp. 11-12. Cf. Henry Lincoln Bailey, "The Chronicler of 'Danvis Folks,' " p. 434.

[7] Robinson, *Uncle Lisha's Shop and A Danvis Pioneer*, p. 128.

[8] Robinson, *Danvis Folks and A Hero of Ticonderoga*, p. 17; *Uncle Lisha's Outing and Along Three Rivers*, pp. 128-29; *Sam Lovel's Camps and In the Green Wood*, p. 49.

[9] Robinson, *Sam Lovel's Camps and In the Green Wood*, p. 81.

[10] Westbrook, p. 30.

[11] Westbrook, p. 39.

[12] Robinson, "Author's Note," the preface to *Danvis Folks and A Hero of Ticonderoga*, p. 16.

[13] *Atlantic Monthly*, LXXV (June 1895), 817.

[14] John Farrar, Introduction to *Danvis Folks and A Hero of Ticonderoga*, p. 14.

[15] Westbrook, p. 39.

[16] Sumner Ives, "A Theory of Literary Dialect," *Tulane Studies in English*, II (1950), 137.

[17] *Atlantic Monthly*, LXXV (June 1895), 819.

[18] Farrar, p. 11.

[19] Farrar, p. 12.

[20] See Richard Bridgman, *The Colloquial Style in America* (New York, 1966), pp. 12, 41-45.

[21] Robinson, *Sam Lovel's Boy with Forest and Stream Fables*, pp. 130-31.

[22] Robinson, *Sam Lovel's Camps and In the Green Wood*, p. 16.

[23] Van Wyck Brooks, *New England Indian Summer, 1865-1915* (New York, 1940), p. 458.

[24] Ives, "A Theory of Literary Dialect," p. 145.

[25] Robinson, *Uncle Lisha's Shop and A Danvis Pioneer*, p. 195.

[26] Robinson, *Uncle Lisha's Outing and Along Three Rivers*, p. 69.

[27] Mary Robinson Perkins, p. 16.

[28] Cook, p. 54.

[29] Robinson, *Sam Lovel's Camps and In the Green Wood*, p. 137.

[30] Martin, pp. 7-8.

[31] Bailey, p. 435.

[32] Robinson, *Uncle Lisha's Outing and Along Three Rivers*, p. 250.

[33] Hans Kurath, *Handbook of the Linguistic Geography of New England* (Providence, Rhode Island, 1939), pp. 207-208.

[34] Martin, p. 9.

[35] Martin, p. 12.

[36] Peach, p. 14.

[37] *Atlantic Monthly*, LXXV (June 1895), 817.

[38] Arensberg, p. 58.

[39]Mary Robinson Perkins, p. 16.
[40]Westbrook, p. 39.
[41]Robinson, *Out of Bondage and Other Stories*, p. 139.
[42]Robinson, *In New England Fields and Woods*, p. 53.
[43]Robinson, *Danvis Folks and A Hero of Ticonderoga*, p. 116.
[44]Dorson, *Jonathan Draws the Long Bow*, p. 263.

BIBLIOGRAPHY

A. PRIMARY SOURCES: ROBINSON'S WRITINGS

Robinson, Rowland E. *Danvis Folks*. Boston and New York, 1894.

_____. *A Danvis Pioneer*. Boston and New York, 1900.

_____. *Forest and Stream Fables*. New York, 1886.

_____. "Glimpses of New England Farm Life," *Scribner's Monthly*, XVI (August 1878), 510-527.

_____. *A Hero of Ticonderoga*. Burlington, 1898.

_____. *Hunting Without a Gun and Other Papers*. New York, 1905.

_____. *In New England Fields and Woods*. Boston and New York, 1896.

_____. *In the Green Wood*. Burlington, 1899.

_____. "The Life of Ethan Allen." Unpublished manuscript at Rokeby, Ferrisburg, Vermont, n.d.

_____. "Merinos in America," *The Century Magazine*, XXVII (February 1884), 513-522.

_____. "New England Fences," *Scribner's Monthly*, XIX (February 1880), 502-511.

_____. *Out of Bondage and Other Stories*. Boston and New York, 1905.

_____. "Recollections of a Quaker Boy," *Atlantic Monthly*, LXXXVIII (July 1901), 100-105.

_____. "Reminiscences," *Forest and Stream* (October 13, 1900), p. 285.

_____. *Sam Lovel's Boy*. Boston and New York, 1901.

_____. *Sam Lovel's Camps*. New York, 1889.

_____. *Silver Fields and Other Sketches of a Farmer-Sportsman*. Boston and New York, 1921.

_____. "A Sketch of the Early History of Ferrisburgh," *The Vermont Historical Gazetteer*, ed. Abby Maria Hemenway. Burlington, 1868, I, 31-34.

_____. "Some of Grandfather's Stories," *The Vermonter* (April 1934), pp. 123-124.

_____. *Uncle Lisha's Outing*. Boston and New York, 1897.

_____. *Uncle Lisha's Shop*. New York, 1887.

_____. Unpublished notes and journals for the years 1870-1899 at Rokeby, Ferrisburg, Vermont.

_____. *Vermont: A Study of Independence*. Boston and New York, 1892.

_____. *Works of Rowland E. Robinson*, ed. Llewellyn R. Perkins. 7 vols. Rutland, Vermont, 1934-38.

B. SECONDARY SOURCES: WRITINGS ABOUT ROBINSON AND HIS WORKS

Allen, M. F. "In Memoriam: Rowland E. Robinson," *The Vermonter*, VI (December 1900), 67-69. Revised and reprinted in part from *The Vermonter* (August 1898).

Anon. Review of Rowland E. Robinson, *A Danvis Pioneer* (Boston, 1900), *The Nation*, LXX (April 19, 1900), 304.

Anon. Review of Rowland E. Robinson, *A Hero of Ticonderoga* (Burlington, 1898), *The Nation*, LXVII (November 3, 1898), 339.

Anon. Review of Rowland E. Robinson, *In New England Fields and Woods*

(Boston, 1896), *The Dial*, XX (April 16, 1896), 245.

Anon. Review of Rowland E. Robinson, *In New England Fields and Woods* (Boston, 1896), *The Nation*, LXII (March 19, 1896), 241.

Anon. Review of Rowland E. Robinson, *Out of Bondage and Other Stories* (Boston, 1905), *The Nation*, LXXX (April 20, 1905), 312.

Anon. Review of Rowland E. Robinson, *Uncle Lisha's Outing* (Boston, 1897), *The Nation*, LXVI (January 27, 1898), 74-75.

Anon. Review of Rowland E. Robinson, *Vermont: A Study of Independence* (Boston, 1892), *The Nation*, LIV (June 2, 1892), 418-19.

Bailey, Henry Lincoln. "The Chronicler of 'Danvis Folks'," *New England Magazine*, XXIII (December 1900), 430-37.

Baker, Ernest A., and James Packman. *A Guide to the Best Fiction, English and American, Including Translations From Foreign Languages*. New York, 1932.

Betterley, Theresa. "Rokeby," *The Vermonter*, XLVIII (April 1943), 68-71.

"Blind Author Dead," *Burlington Free Press and Times*, October 16, 1900.

Brooks, Van Wyck. *New England Indian Summer, 1865-1915*. New York, 1940.

Burnham, J. B. "A Visit to Rowland Robinson's," *Forest and Stream* (October 10, 1900), p. 302. Reprinted from *Forest and Stream* (December 10, 1898).

Carleton, Hiram. *Genealogical and Famly History of the State of Vermont*. New York, 1903.

Collins, Edward D. Foreword to Rowland E. Robinson, *Uncle Lisha's Outing and Along Three Rivers*, ed. Llewellyn R. Perkins. Rutland, Vermont, 1934. Pp. 5-14.

Cook, Genevra M. "Rowland Evans Robinson (1833-1900): Portrayer of Vermont Background and Character." Unpublished M. A. thesis, University of Vermont, Burlington, 1931.

Damon, S. Foster. Introduction to Rowland E. Robinson, *Sam Lovel's Boy with Forest and Stream Fables*, ed. Llewellyn R. Perkins, Rutland, Vermont, 1936. Pp. 9-14.

Dorr, Julia C. R. "Rowland Robinson," *Atlantic Monthly*, LXXXVII (January 1901), 117-122.

Eaton, Walter Prichard. Foreword to Rowland E. Robinson, *Danvis Folks and A Hero of Ticonderoga*, ed. Llewellyn R. Perkins. Rutland, Vermont, 1934. Pp. 7-10.

Farrar, John. Introduction to Rowland E. Robinson, *Danvis Folks and A Hero of Ticonderoga*, ed. Llewellyn R. Perkins. Rutland, Vermont, 1934. Pp. 11-14.

Fish, Frank L. "Rachael Robinson Elmer," *The Vermonter* XXIV (1919), 87-95.

Fisher, Dorothy Canfield. Introduction to Rowland E. Robinson, *Uncle Lisha's Shop and A Danvis Pioneer*, ed. Llewellyn R. Perkins. Rutland, Vermont, 1937. Pp. 11-16.

Genzmer, George Harvey. "Robinson, Rowland Evans," *Dictionary of American Biography*, ed. Allen Johnson and Dumas Malone. New York, 1928-37

Gilman, M. D. *Bibliography of Vermont*. Burlington, Vt., 1897.

Lanier, Henry Wysham. Introduction to Rowland E. Robinson, *Uncle Lisha's Outing and Along Three Rivers*, ed. Llewellyn R. Perkins. Rutland, Vermont, 1934. Pp. 15-19.

Lewis, Sinclair. Foreword to Rowland E. Robinson, *In New England Fields and Woods*, ed. Llewellyn R. Perkins. Rutland Vermont, 1937. Pp. 3-4.

Martin, Terence. "Rowland Evans Robinson: Realist of the Outdoors," *Vermont History*, XXIII (January 1955), 3-15.

Pattee, Fred Lewis. Foreword to Rowland E. Robinson, *Uncle Lisha's Shop and A Danvis Pioneer*, ed. Llewellyn R. Perkins. Rutland, Vt., 1937. Pp. 7-10.

Peach, Arthur Wallace. Introduction to Rowland E. Robinson, *Sam Lovel's Camps and In the Green Wood*, ed. Llewellyn R. Perkins. Rutland, Vermont, 1934. Pp. 13-15.

Perkins, Mary Robinson. "Rowland Evans Robinson," in Rowland E. Robinson, *Out of Bondage and Other Stories*, ed. Llewellyn R. Perkins. Rutland, Vermont, 1936. Pp. 11-18.

"Recent American Fiction." Anon. rev., *Atlantic Monthly*, LXXV (June 1895), 817-20.

Robinson, Anna Stevens. Unpublished notes dated 1902 at Rokeby, Ferrisburg, Vermont.

Robinson, Duane Leroy. Foreword to Rowland E. Robinson, *Sam Lovel's Camps and In the Green Wood*, ed. Llewellyn R. Perkins. Rutland, Vermont, 1934. Pp. 7-11.

———. "Rowland Evans Robinson," *Vermont Life*, V (Spring 1951), 36-40.

———. "Rowland Evans Robinson—An Appreciation," *The Vermont Review*, II (May-June 1928), 114-118.

"Robinson, Rowland Evans," *American Authors, 1600-1900: A Biographical Dictionary of American Literature*, ed. Stanley J. Kunitz and Howard Haycraft. New York, 1938. Pp. 657-58.

"Robinson, Rowland Evans," *The Oxford Companion to American Literature*, ed. James D. Hart. New York, 1956. P. 646.

"Rowland Evans Robinson," *Forest and Stream*, LV (October 20, 1900), 301.

Rugg, Harold Goddard. "Bibliography," in Rowland E. Robinson, *In New England Fields and Woods*, ed. Llewellyn R. Perkins. Rutland, Vermont, 1937. Pp. 5-11.

Schomburg, Arthur. Foreword to Rowland E. Robinson, *Out of Bondage and Other Stories*, ed. Llewellyn R. Perkins. Rutland, Vermont, 1936. Pp. 5-9.

Spargo, John. Foreword to Rowland E. Robinson, *Sam Lovel's Boy with Forest and Stream Fables*, ed. Llewellyn R. Perkins. Rutland, Vermont, 1936. Pp. 5-8.

Stoyle, Lewis E. "A New England Exponent of Woods and Fields," *The Boston Evening Transcript*, April 22, 1933, Book Section, pp. 1-2.

Temple, Edward Lowe. "Rowland E. Robinson: The Green Mountain Character and Dialect Writer," *The Vermonter*, XXVIII (November 1923), 151-53.

Westbrook, Perry D. *Acres of Flint: Writers of Rural New England, 1870-1900*. Washington, D. C., 1951.

C. SECONDARY SOURCES: FOLKLORE WORKS CITED

Aarne, Antti, and Stith Thompson. *The Types of the Folktale*. Helsinki, 1964.

Abrahams, Roger D. *Deep Down in the Jungle*. Hatboro, Pa., 1964.

———. "Introductory Remarks to a Rhetorical Theory of Folklore," *Journal of American Folklore*, LXXXI (1968), 143-58.

———, and George Foss, *Anglo-American Folksong Style*. Englewood Cliffs, N.J., 1968.

Apperson, George L. *English Proverbs and Proverbial Phrases: A Historical Dictionary*. London, 1929.

Arensberg, Conrad M. *The Irish Countryman: An Anthropological Study*. Gloucester, Mass., 1959.

Barbeau, Marius. *Jongleur Songs of Old Quebec*. New Brunswick, 1962.

Barry, Phillips, Fannie H. Eckstorm, and Mary W. Smyth. *British Ballads From Maine*. New Haven, 1929.

Bascom, William R. "Four Functions of Folklore," *Journal of American Folklore*, LXVIII (1954), 333-349.

Baughman, Ernest W. *Type and Motif Index of the Folktales of England and North America*. The Hague, 1966.

Beals, Ralph. "Acculturation," *Anthropology Today*, ed. A. L. Kroeber. Chicago, 1953. Pp. 621-641.

Beck, Earl C. *Songs of the Michigan Lumberjacks*. Ann Arbor, 1942.

Bolton, Henry Carrington. *The Counting-Out Rhymes of Children, Their Antiquity, Origin, and Wide Distribution*. London, 1888.

Boshears, Frances. "Proverbial Comparisons from an East Tennessee Country," *Bulletin of the Tennessee Folklore Society*, XX (1954), 27-41.

Botkin, B. A. *The American Play-Party Song*. New York, 1963.

————. *A Treasury of New England Folklore*. New York, 1965.

Browne, Ray B. *Popular Beliefs and Practices from Alabama*. Berkeley and Los Angeles, 1958.

Brunvand, Jan Harold. *A Dictionary of Proverbs and Proverbial Phrases from Books Published by Indiana Authors before 1890*. Bloomington, 1961.

————. *The Study of American Folklore*. New York, 1968.

Buckley, Bruce R. " 'Honor Your Ladies': Folk Dance in the United States," *Our Living Traditions*, ed. Tristram Potter Coffin. New York, 1968.

Bulletin of the Folk-Song Society of the Northeast, Nos. 1-12. Cambridge, Mass., 1930-37.

Child, Francis James, ed. *The English and Scottish Popular Ballads*, 5 vols. New York, 1965.

David, Alfred and Mary Elizabeth. "A Literary Approach to the Brothers Grimm," *Journal of the Folklore Institute*, I (December 1964), 180-196.

Davidson, Daniel Sutherland. *Snowshoes*. Memoirs of the American Philosophical Society, Vol. VI. Philadelphia, 1937.

Dorson, Richard M. *American Folklore*. Chicago, 1959.

————. *Bloodstoppers and Bearwalkers*. Cambridge, Mass., 1952.

————. "Folklore in American Literature: A Postscript," *Journal of American Folklore*, LXXI (1958), 157-159.

————. "The Great Team of English Folklorists," *Journal of American Folklore*, LXX (1957), 1-8.

————. "The Identification of Folklore in American Literature," *Journal of American Folklore*, LXX (1957), 1-8.

————. *Jonathan Draws the Long Bow*. Cambridge, Mass., 1946.

————. "Jonathan Draws the Long Bow," *The New England Quarterly*, XVI (June 1943), 244-279.

————. "Just B'ars," *Appalachia*, n.s., VIII (December 1942), 174-187.

————. "Legends and Tall Tales," *Our Living Traditions*, ed. Tristram Potter Coffin. New York, 1968.

————. "Oral Tradition and Written History: the Case for the United States," *Journal of the Folklore Institute*, I (December 1964), 220-234.

Drake, Beverly. "In New England It's Time for Sugar on Snow," *The Christian Science Monitor*, March 14, 1968, p. 5.

Drake, Samuel Adams. *New England Legends and Folk-Lore*. Boston, 1901.

Dundes, Alan. "The American Concept of Folklore," *Journal of the Folklore Institute*, III (December 1966), 266-249.

Earle, Alice Morse. *Customs and Fashions in Old New England.* New York, 1894.

Eaton, Allen H. *Handicrafts of New England.* New York, 1949.

Flanders, Helen Hartness. *Ancient Ballads Traditionally Sung in New England.* 4 vols. Philadelphia, 1960-1965.

————. *A Garland of Green Mountain Song.* Boston, 1934.

————. "Index of Ballads and Folk-Songs in the Archive of Vermont Folk-Songs at Smiley Manse, Springfield, Vermont," *Proceedings of the Vermont Historical Society,* VIII (June 1940), 214-251.

————. "List of Folk-Songs Recorded in Vermont in November, 1939," *Proceedings of the Vermont Historical Society,* VIII (September 1940), 302-311.

————. "The Quest for Vermont Ballads," *Proceedings of the Vermont Historical Society,* VII (June 1939), 53-72.

————, Elizabeth Flanders Ballard, George Brown, and Phillips Barry. *The New Green Mountain Songster.* New Haven, 1939.

————, and George Brown. *Vermont Folk-Songs and Ballads.* Brattleboro, 1931.

————, and Helen Norfleet. *Country Songs of Vermont.* New York, 1937.

————, and Marguerite Olney. *Ballads Migrant in New England.* New York, 1953.

Fife, Austin E. "Jack Fences of the Intermountain West," *Folklore International,* ed. D. K. Wilgus. Hatboro, Pa., 1967. Pp. 51-54.

Finley, Ruth. *Old Patchwork Quilts.* Philadelphia, 1929.

Flanagan, John T., and Arthur Palmer Hudson. *Folklore in American Literature.* Evanston, Ill., 1958.

The Frank C. Brown Collection of North Carolina Folklore, ed. Newman I. White 7 vols. Durham, N. C., 1952-64.

Gomme, Alice B. *The Traditional Games of England, Scotland, and Ireland.* 2 vols. London, 1894-98.

Haliwell-Phillips, J. O. *Popular Rhymes and Nursery Tales.* London, 1849.

Hallowell, A. Irving. "The Impact of the American Indian on American Culture," *Folklore in Action,* ed. Horace P. Beck. Philadelphia, 1962. Pp. 120-138.

Halpert, Herbert. "More Proverbial Comparisons from West Tennessee," *Bulletin of the Tennessee Folklore Society,* XVIII (1952), 15-21.

————. "Proverbial Comparisons from West Tennessee," *Bulletin of the Tennessee Folklore Society,* XVII (1951), 49-61.

Hand, Wayland D. "American Superstitions and Popular Beliefs," *Folklore in Action,* ed. Horace P. Beck. Philadelphia, 1962. Pp. 151-171.

Hardie, Margaret. "Proverbs and Proverbial Expressions Current in the United States East of the Missouri and North of the Ohio River," *American Speech,* IV (1929), 461-472.

Hazard, Thomas Robinson. *The Jonny-Cake Papers of "Shepherd Tom."* Boston, 1915.

Hoffman, Daniel. "Folklore in Literature: Notes Toward a Theory of Interpretation," *Journal of American Folklore,* LXX (1957), 15-21.

————. *Form and Fable in American Fiction.* New York, 1965.

Hughes, Muriel J. "Vermont Exclamations of Early Days," *Vermont History,* XXII (October 1954), 292-95.

————. "Vermont Proverbial Comparisons and Similes," *Vermont History* XXVI (October 1958), 257-93.

————. "Vermont Proverbs and Proverbial Sayings: Part I, A-K," *Vermont History,* XXVIII (April 1960), 113-42.

————. "Vermont Proverbs and Proverbial Sayings: Part II, L-Z," *Vermont History*, XXVIII (July 1960), 200-230.

————. "A Word-List from Vermont," *Vermont History*, XXVII (April 1959), 123-167.

Hyamson, Albert M. *A Dictionary of English Phrases.* London, 1922.

Hyatt, Harry M. *Folklore from Adams County Illinois.* Hannibal, Mo., 1965.

Ives, Sumner. "Dialect Differentiation in the Stories of Joel Chandler Harris," *American Literature*, XXVII (March 1955), 88-96.

————. "A Theory of Literary Dialect," *Tulane Studies in English*, VII (1950), 137-82.

Johnson, Clifton. *What They Say in New England.* Boston, 1896.

Kittredge, George Lyman. *Witchcraft in Old and New England.* New York, 1929.

Kovel, Ralph and Terry. *American Country Furniture 1780-1875.* New York, 1965.

Kurath, Hans. *Handbook of the Linguistic Geography of New England.* Providence, 1939.

————. *Linguistic Atlas of New England.* 3 vols. Providence, 1939.

Landon, Melville D. *Wit and Humor of the Age.* Chicago, c. 1901.

Laws, G. Malcolm. *American Balladry from British Broadsides.* Philadelphia, 1957.

————. *Native American Balladry.* Philadelphia, 1964.

Leach, Mac Edward. *The Ballad Book.* New York, 1955.

————. "Folklore in American Regional Literature," *Journal of the Folklore Institute*, III (December 1966), 376-97.

Linscott, Eloise Hubbard. *Folk Songs of Old New England.* London, 1962.

Lomax, Alan. *The Penguin Book of American Folk Songs.* Baltimore, 1964.

Malinowski, Bronislaw. "Myth in Primitive Psychology," *Magic, Science and Religion and Other Essays.* Garden City, New York, 1948. Pp. 93-148.

Masterson, James R. *Tall Tales of Arkansaw.* Boston, 1942.

————. "Travelers' Tales of Colonial Natural History," *Journal of American Folklore*, LIX (1946), 51-67, 174-88.

Matthiessen, F. O. *American Renaissance.* New York, 1941.

McLennan, William. *Songs of Old Canada.* Montreal, 1886.

Meredith, Mamie. "The Nomenclature of American Pioneer Fences," *Southern Folklore Quarterly*, XV (1951), 109-151.

Munchausen, Baron. *The Adventures of Baron Munchausen.* New York, 1944.

Needham, Walter, and Barrows Mussey. *A Book of Country Things.* Brattleboro, Vermont, 1965.

Newell, William Wells. *Games and Songs of American Children.* New York, 1883.

Opie, Iona and Peter. *The Oxford Dictionary of Nursery Rhymes.* London, 1951.

O'Sullivan, Sean. *A Handbook of Irish Folklore.* Dublin, 1942.

Pearce, Helen. "Folk Sayings in a Pioneer Family of Oregon," *Western Folklore*, V (1946), 229-242.

Person, Henry A. "Proverbs and Proverbial Lore from the State of Washington," *Western Folklore*, XVII (1958), 176-185.

Pound, Louise. "Folklore and Dialect," *Nebraska Folklore.* Lincoln, 1959. Pp. 211-221.

Randolph, Vance. *Ozark Superstitions.* New York, 1964.

————. *We Always Lie to Strangers.* New York, 1951.

————, and George P. Wilson. *Down in the Holler: A Gallery of Ozark Folk Speech.* Norman, Oklahoma, 1953.

Raup, H. F. "The Fence in the Cultural Landscape," *Western Folklore*, VI (1947), 1-7.

Redfield, Robert. "The Folk Society," *American Journal of Sociology*, LII (January 1946), 293-308.

——— . *The Little Community and Peasant Society and Culture*. Chicago, 1965.

Roberts, Warren E. "Folklore in the Novels of Thomas Deloney," *Studies in Folklore*, ed. W. Edson Richmond. Bloomington, 1957. Pp. 119-129.

Rourke, Constance. *American Humor*. New York, 1931.

Sackett, Marjorie. "Recipes," *Kansas Folklore*, ed. S. J. Sackett and William E. Koch. Lincoln, Nebraska, 1961. Pp. 226-238.

Sebillot, Paul. *Le Folk-Lore de France*. 4 vols. Paris, 1904-1907.

Shurtleff, Harold R. *The Log Cabin Myth*. Cambridge, Mass., 1939.

Smith, W. G., and Janet Heseltine. *The Oxford Dictionary of English Proverbs*. Oxford, 1935.

von Sydow, C. W. "On the Spread of Tradition," *Selected Papers on Folklore*, ed. Laurits Bødker. Copenhagen, 1948. Pp. 11-43.

Stevenson, Burton. *The Home Book of Proverbs, Maxims and Familiar Phrases*. New York, 1948.

Taylor, Archer. *English Riddles from Oral Tradition*. Berkeley and Los Angeles, 1951.

——— . *The Proverb and An Index to "The Proverb."* Hatboro, Pa., 1962.

——— . *Proverbial Comparisons and Similes from California*. Berkeley, 1954.

——— . and Bartlett Jere Whiting. *A Dictionary of American Proverbs and Proverbial Phrases, 1820-1880*. Cambridge, Mass., 1958.

Thompson, Harold W. *Body, Boots and Britches*. Philadelphia, 1940.

Thompson, Stith. *The Folktale*. New York, 1946.

——— . *Motif-Index of Folk-Literature*. 6 vols. Bloomington and London, 1966.

Tilley, Morris P. *A Dictionary of the Proverbs in England in the Sixteenth and Seventeenth Centuries*. Ann Arbor, 1950.

Van Wagenen, Jared. *The Golden Age of Homespun*. Ithaca, New York, 1953.

Wallace, Paul A. W. *Baptiste Laroque: Legends of French Canada*. Toronto, 1923.

Waugh, F. W. "Canadian Folklore from Ontario," *Journal of American Folklore*, XXXI (1918), 63-72.

Wilstach, Frank J. *Dictionary of Similes*. New York, 1924.

Wolcott, Imogene. *The Yankee Cook Book*. New York, 1939.

D. SECONDARY SOURCES: OTHER WORKS CITED

Bridgman, Richard. *The Colloquial Style in America*. New York, 1966.

Hemenway, Abby Maria, ed. *The Vermont Historical Gazetteer*. 5 vols. Burlington, Vermont, 1867-90.

Mencken, H. L. *The American Language*. 3 vols. New York, 1962.

Murray, William H. H. *Adventures in the Wilderness; or, Camp-Life in the Adirondacks*. Boston, 1870.

Nathan, Hans. *Dan Emmett and the Rise of Early Negro Minstrelsy*. Norman, Oklahoma, 1962.

Newton, Earle. *The Vermont Story*. Montpelier, 1949.

Onions, C. T., ed. *The Oxford Universal Dictionary on Historical Principles*. London, 1955.

Sears, John H. "Notes on the Forest Trees of Essex, Clinton and Franklin Counties, New York," *Bulletin of the Essex Institute*, XIII (October-December 1881), 174-88.

Simpson, Claude M. *The Local Colorists*. New York, 1960.

Smith, H. P. *History of Addison County, Vermont.* Syracuse, 1886.
Thompson, Zadock. *History of Vermont, Natural, Civil, and Statistical.* Burlington, 1842.
Workers of the Federal Writers' Project of the Works Progress Administration for the State of Vermont. *Vermont: A Guide to the Green Mountain State.* Boston, 1937.